"[Klein] does a vivid and harrowing job of laying out the story of the doomed merger . . . a visceral and chilling portrait of the arrogant cowboy culture that prevailed at AOL in the '90s. . . . The story [Klein] has told in these pages stands on its own as a compelling parable of greed and power and hubris."

—Michiko Kakutani, *The New York Times*

"This story has almost everything: the Internet provider that helped bring America on line, personality clashes worthy of *People* magazine, team rivalries so bitter that readers of *Sports Illustrated* would blush. . . . The one thing the story doesn't have is a happy ending. In *Stealing Time*, Alec Klein details the perfect corporate storm."

—L. Gordon Crovitz, *The Wall Street Journal*

"Klein's book is a page-turner—smooth, insightful."

—Barrington Salmon, *USA Today*

"*Stealing Time* is the first full-length account of who was speeding, who was dozing at the wheel, and who fled the scene amid the sounds of approaching sirens in Wall Street's greatest takeover fiasco since the RJR Nabisco deal nearly fifteen years ago. . . . Alec Klein has told this story deftly."

—Christopher Byron, *The Washington Post*

"Klein has written a corporate saga both investigative and entertaining. . . . This is a business book for the ages."

—Steve Weinberg, *Baltimore Sun*

"Alec Klein is a dogged journalist. His insider story of the union that linked America Online and Time Warner is packed with astonishing anecdotes, data from confidential corporate reports, and blow-by-blow accounts of boardroom back stabbing."

—Kevin Canfield, *The Plain Dealer* (Cleveland)

"It is a great story with larger-than-life characters who alternately bring underlings to tears and hand out Rolex watches at parties."

—Jennifer Files, *San Jose Mercury News*

"An important, solidly reported account of our times."

—Marilyn Geewax, *The Atlanta Journal-Constitution*

"*Stealing Time* succeeds as an exposé of the greed, ego, and desperation that drove both sides to the bargaining table."

—Eric Wieffering, *Star Tribune* (Minneapolis)

"Alec Klein, a dogged reporter for *The Washington Post*, spent two years digging into AOL's business practices. . . . *Stealing Time* is an interesting tale of how two big businesses went awry, mostly through cockiness, a lack of principles, and poor judgment."

—Verna Noel Jones, *Rocky Mountain News* (Denver)

"For employees and shareholders of AOL Time Warner, still smarting over depleted retirement accounts, *Stealing Time* may offer a perverse satisfaction, like picking at a newly healed scab. For historians, it is a worthwhile addition to the burgeoning literature on the follies of history's biggest investment bubble."

—Peter Thal Larsen, *The Financial Times* (London)

"[An] excellent exposé of the deal and its ramifications. . . . An entertaining—and at times frightening—read . . . a cautionary tale that should be read by anyone with an interest in the inner workings of big business."

—Paul O'Kane, *Sunday Tribune* (Ireland)

"[An] engaging account of the ill-fated 2001 merger of AOL and Time Warner. . . . *Stealing Time* is juicy."

—Catherine Yang, *BusinessWeek*

"[A] deft account of the genesis and collapse of the nation's biggest media merger. . . . Klein offers an entertaining window on the times and personalities that turned a grandiose idea into a first-rate mess."

—Jill Goldsmith, *Variety*

"Building his argument with solid facts and juicy anecdotes, Klein shows just why the merger was questionable. . . . A cautionary tale—and one well worth reading."

—Gregory McNamee, *The Hollywood Reporter*

"[A] well-reported Shakespearean tale. . . . In the end, the book is less about business than about human nature."

—Jonathan E. Kaplan, *The Hill*

STEALING TIME

Steve Case, Jerry Levin,
and the Collapse of
AOL Time Warner

Alec Klein

SIMON & SCHUSTER PAPERBACKS

New York London Toronto Sydney

The place where optimism most flourishes is
the lunatic asylum.

HAVELOCK ELLIS, *The Dance of Life*

For Julie-Ann

SIMON & SCHUSTER PAPERBACKS
Rockefeller Center
1230 Avenue of the Americas
New York, NY 10020

First Simon & Schuster paperback edition 2004

SIMON & SCHUSTER PAPERBACKS and colophon are registered
trademarks of Simon & Schuster, Inc.

For information about special discounts for bulk purchases,
please contact Simon & Schuster Special Sales:
1-800-456-6798 or business@simonandschuster.com

Manufactured in the United States of America

1   3   5   7   9   10   8   6   4   2

The Library of Congress has catalogued the hardcover as follows:
Klein, Alec.
Stealing time : Steve Case, Jerry Levin, and the collapse of AOL Time Warner
p. cm.
Includes bibliographical references and index.
1. America Online, Inc.—History. 2. AOL Time Warner—History. 3. Case, Stephen McConnell. 4.
Levin, Gerald M.   I. Title.
HE7583. U6K54 2003
338.7'61004678'0973—dc21   2003050554

ISBN 0-7432-4786-8
0-7432-5984-X (Pbk)

CONTENTS

Foreword: The Phone Call

It all began with an anonymous tip.

I was sitting at my cluttered cubicle in *The Washington Post* newsroom when my phone rang. On the other end of the line was a nervous man who refused to identify himself. What he did reveal, though—in a stealthy baritone—was that an executive had been suspended at America Online. I pressed him for more details, but that was all.

How could I contact him?

I couldn't; he'd contact me.

Click.

It was just a feeling, but the tipster seemed legit; besides, it was a desultory summer day in 2001, and news was slow. So I began the reporting drill, calling my sources that afternoon to see if any had heard about an AOL official getting suspended. Alas, it turned out to be true. That evening, I scrambled to write what I knew for the next day's newspaper—which wasn't much.

Under the headline "AOL Opens Probe," I wrote that Eric Keller, a senior vice-president, had been placed on administrative leave pending an internal investigation of the company's accounting relationship with PurchasePro, a Las Vegas dot-com. The story ran on page E5, deep in the bowels of the *Washington Post*'s business section. Ten column inches—not much longer than a news brief. That was June 19, 2001, and it barely elicited a peep.

Keller?

PurchasePro?

Accounting?

This was before the Enron meltdown, before the whiff of an accounting scandal would resonate with the public. And yet, I was intrigued. It was a chink in AOL's armor, a fortress of a company that guarded its secrets better than the Pentagon just down the road. Indeed, it was said that the Big Brothers at AOL monitored employee e-mail and telephone calls that passed back and forth beyond the security gates of its modern compound in the Northern Virginia suburbs. Little from AOL got out into the public domain—unless it was good news about its millions of new on-line subscribers or the oodles of money that it was making in on-line advertising.

But now this.

I began calling around to find out more. Why had Keller been suspended? What did PurchasePro have to do with it? How was AOL involved? I'd call one source, who'd say he didn't know about it, but why didn't I try so-and-so. I'd call so-and-so, and he didn't know about it either, but he'd pass me on to three other people who might. It was a growing spider web that finally brought me to a memorable phone call.

I began the usual way, identifying myself. "This is Alec Klein, and I'm a reporter at *The Washington Post.*"

Before I could get another word in edgewise, the man said, "How did you find me?"

And just like that, I realized that I had stumbled onto my original tipster.

Suddenly, the information began pouring in as I was introduced to a variety of AOL sources. It wasn't glamorous work. Many of the meetings took place in dingy hotel lobbies and restaurants serving bad food—out-of-the-way places where my sources would never be caught with a *Washington Post* reporter.

These folks were risking a lot. If AOL found out they were talking to me, they might have been fired. Livelihoods were at stake. But they believed there was a duty to expose wrongdoing. And they were trusting that I would take care to protect their identities.

Sometimes, I resorted to unusual precautions, such as camping out in the lobby of one particular hotel. By using its public pay phone, my calls to AOL couldn't be traced back to *The Washington Post*. The hotel became my office away from the office. I got my shoes shined there. I bought the newspaper there. And I visited the gift shop, where I would ask to exchange dollar bills for quarters, so I could make my phone calls.

Invariably, the lady behind the counter would shoot me a quizzical look. She never asked, but I could see the question forming in her arched brows: Why was I asking for change for the public telephone when I had a cell phone latched to my belt? Before long, I became a fixture in the hotel lobby. With all my calls from the pay phone, I think the hotel clerks suspected I was a drug dealer.

Little did they realize I was gathering confidential AOL documents. Within months, a pattern emerged. Through a series of complex transactions, AOL had been inflating its advertising revenue—a key driver of its growth—at a critical time before and after its merger with Time Warner. Had Time Warner known about these unorthodox deals, it could have sought to pull out of the largest merger in U.S. history. Even if Time Warner had to pay several billion dollars in breakup fees, given the rapidly declining stock price of the now-merged company, that would have been a bargain.

This was different from other corporate scandals. No whistleblower had come forward to accuse the company of wrongdoing. The government hadn't discovered anything either. Nor had the company admitted any impropriety.

AOL immediately hired a powerful law firm to kill my stories. The legal team was headed by an affable attorney who was also known in some newspaper circles as a media killer. He had slain the media in several high-profile cases, getting credit for stopping *60 Minutes* from airing an interview with a tobacco whistleblower, which became the subject of a popular movie, *The Insider*. What's more, AOL turned to its outside auditors, Ernst & Young, which reconfirmed the accounting of every deal I had examined.

I was a little worried.

Not my editors, though. One day, Len Downie, the paper's executive editor, called me into his office to chat. We sat there and said little. He asked some questions, but it felt like something more than a conversation, as if Downie were boring into my soul to measure my character. And when AOL and its lawyers arrived at the *Post* to argue against the publication of our stories, I bumped into Steve Coll, the paper's managing editor, in the newsroom. He looked at me in utter shock.

I had shaved.

I was wearing a tie.

My shirt was buttoned all the way to the top.

"You look like a defendant," Coll quipped.

He was right.

Meanwhile, my editors—Jill Dutt, the assistant managing editor for financial news, Larry Roberts, the business editor, and Dan Beyers, the technology editor—were fearless.

In the end, *The Washington Post* published the stories. On the day of the first article, July 18, 2002, Bob Pittman, AOL Time Warner's chief operating officer, resigned under pressure. Within days, AOL confirmed that the Securities and Exchange Commission had launched an investigation into AOL's accounting as a result of the *Post's* stories. The Justice Department followed suit, opening a criminal probe into AOL.

The dominoes began to fall: AOL admitted that it had improperly booked at least $190 million in revenue. And the drama was just beginning to unfold.

—Alec Klein
November 2003
Washington, D.C.

The Confrontation

Steve Case was blabbering on.

Or so thought some of the restless executives assembled in a conference room at 75 Rockefeller Plaza, the lofty Manhattan headquarters of the most powerful media company in the world.

It was the spring of 2002, and AOL Time Warner Inc. was descending into financial disarray. But Case, the company chairman, was still enamored of the unfulfilled promise of the $112 billion marriage of America Online and Time Warner, the largest merger in U.S. history.

The new company, barely a year old, boasted a staggering array of global brands on the newsstands, at the movie theaters, on television. Millions experienced the common denominator of life by reading its magazines, *Time, People,* and *Sports Illustrated* among them. Its movie studios regularly tossed off blockbusters like *Harry Potter.* From CNN to HBO, its cable programming extended across the far reaches of Earth, shaping public opinion and entrancing viewers. It even owned *Mad* magazine.

AOL Time Warner was an inescapable force: The Internet division, operating in seventeen countries in eight languages across Europe, Latin America, and Asia, counted more than thirty-four million on-line subscribers. Combined, AOL and Time Warner products and services reached consumers three billion times a *month.*

With all of this, Case argued, how could the company go awry?

Internet-driven America Online, the Virginia company he helped build two decades ago, would inject new life into seventy-nine-year-old Time Warner, the esteemed New York media and entertainment company he had taken over. The two companies would work together to forge a future when technology merged with media, creating unimagined consumer products, like television, only better. *Convergence,* he called it. One side of the corporate house would fuel the growth of the other. The buzzword: *synergy.* America Online would promote Warner Bros. movies. Time Inc. magazines would sell America Online subscriptions. AOL would tout new albums by Warner Music Group artists, like Madonna and Jewel. The potential for what he believed was the media company of the twenty-first century was limitless.

Except for one thing: Somebody forgot to tell Case the dance was over.

Jeff Bewkes, the HBO chairman and chief executive, could not contain himself any longer.

"I'm tired of this," he erupted, glaring at Case. "This is bullshit. The only division that's not performing is yours. Every one of us is growing, making the numbers. The only problem in this construct is AOL."

Dead silence.

No one knew what to say—not even Case. He sat there, poker-faced. The rest kept mum. It wasn't clear yet which side of the divided house would prevail in a roiling internal power struggle, America Online or Time Warner. AOL, though it had lost some of its luster, was still the over-lord of Time Warner. Bewkes, however, had just uttered what some of his colleagues had been muttering about for months: *The problem was America Online, not Time Warner!* Yes, Case was still chairman of the combined company. But just look at the house he had built: America Online was a bloody mess. Revenue at the on-line division was stagnant in the just-ended first quarter, which was bad enough. But a key part of America Online's revenue, advertising and commerce, had taken a big hit. Meanwhile, the Time Warner businesses were humming along just fine. The cable division had reported a double-digit revenue increase. Even its music business, in the doldrums for months, appeared on the upswing, generating a modest rise in revenue. And though HBO's financial numbers weren't broken out publicly, everybody knew it was doing gangbusters.

That was the company's real crown jewel! Not America Online! Whom did Case think he was talking to? How dare he lecture them!

Until then, executives had refrained from saying as much. This was, after all, polite society. But HBO's Bewkes could get away with challenging the chairman now. Bewkes had long been Time Warner's golden boy. An Ivy League grad who was being groomed for a bigger office in the executive suites, Bewkes had rattled off a string of successes at HBO, including original programming, like *Sex and the City* and *The Sopranos,* that made him virtually untouchable at Time Warner. What's more, Bewkes was holding an ace in the hole: He had been given the green light to read Case the riot act. The okay came from an ostensible Case ally: Dick Parsons, AOL Time Warner's new chief executive officer.

It was a seismic shift, a tangible manifestation of the transfer of power, tinged with a dose of irony. Case had played a key role in ditching Jerry Levin as the company's CEO in December 2001, clearing the path for the elevation of Parsons to the top job. Now, however, Parsons was taking the muzzle off his own people—Time Warner loyalists like Bewkes—who didn't want to take any more guff from America Online, the brash, young interlopers from the suburbs of Virginia. Parsons, ever the polished politician, didn't want to duke it out himself with Case. A proxy fight was more tactful.

"Dick had given him [Bewkes] the tacit nod," said a company official. "Maybe he [Parsons] couldn't do it, but Jeff could."

After the meeting broke, Time Warner executives approached Bewkes tentatively, quietly. There were some whispers: *Atta boy. Way to go. Good for you.*

It was a stunning reversal for Case, the erstwhile dot-com boy wonder who suddenly faced a monumental struggle for his own corporate survival in this, his personal denouement. What had begun as the triumph of the new economy over the old economy at the dawn of the new century had become a merger derided as an epic disaster. Bewkes had finally said it: The emperor had no clothes.

"It was," said a company official, "the dialogue that broke it open."

PART I

The Unlikely Rise
of an Internet Giant

CHAPTER ONE

A FOOTNOTE IN HISTORY

A powder blue Grand Marquis rumbles down a quiet suburban road, approaching faded memories not visited in decades. Hunched behind the wheel is Alan Peyser, a weathered old man, pushing the pedal in white sneakers, searching for the home of a friend long gone.

"I remember where it is now," Peyser grumbles, making a sudden right on Basil Road. "My memory is coming back."

Another quick right on Orris Street, and the Grand Marquis comes to a stop at the end of a cul-de-sac.

There it is: a cavernous, two-story yellow-brick home with big windows and white shutters, a picture of prosperity in McLean, Virginia, a tony suburb of Washington, D.C. "*The Sound of Music* House," Peyser used to call it.

Daisies and shrubs frame the marble entranceway, whose double doors sit shaded under a cool white canopy. Other people live here now. They are not home.

It's a brilliant fall afternoon, and the sky is crystal blue, but Peyser refuses to get out of his car anyway.

Maybe it's his bum right knee, which he's resting with a jostling bag of ice cubes, the aching residue of a tennis match he just played and doesn't want to talk about. Or maybe he doesn't want to remember.

Once upon a time, when he was a man in his prime, Peyser wounded his knee on the tennis court hidden behind this grand house. He stepped on a twig and blew a cartilage during a match against his old tennis foe, who used to live here.

"Is the tennis court still there?" Peyser wants to know.

It is. But the court looks abandoned, cracked down the middle, weeds sprouting from the gaping crevice, like the ghostly grounds of Miss Havisham's, where time is left to rot. The surrounding fence is overgrown with more weeds, and a basketball and volleyball idle by the torn tennis net.

Peyser and his old friend used to play a match here once a week, and after the game (which Peyser usually won), the two men would sit at the kitchen table and, over a glass of juice, dream up wild technology to invent, impossible business ventures to create, a whole wide world to conquer. . . .

That's enough. Peyser doesn't want to think about his old friend anymore. He shifts into drive and pulls off.

"I'm a futurist, so memories—they don't count," he says with a shot of impatience.

But then, Peyser is ensnared by something—a glimpse into the past, maybe—and he stops the car on the side of the road, facing away from the house. He dumps the bag of ice out of the driver's side window.

With faded gray eyes, he squints at the passing traffic in the distance as the past begins to come into focus.

He remembers his good friend, who had the crazy idea that, one day, people would use computers—*computers!*—to communicate, that people would use computers in their homes to entertain themselves and retrieve a wealth of information.

Imagine electronic mail, news, stock quotes—anything. A stream of information would flow from computer to computer through telephone lines, like blood coursing through arteries, giving life to a new digital world. The power and promise of technology would link people together in a global network, sweeping them up in a computer revolution.

Ridiculous. Absurd. Science fiction.

Peyser chuckles. Nothing was impossible to his old friend, who would create a little company that would fundamentally change the world, a little company that would grow up to become AOL Time Warner, the largest media company on the planet.

And his name was not Steve Case.

"I see all these things that say Steve Case was the founder of AOL," Peyser says, "but I know better."

Billy von Meister looked like a normal child: slightly chubby, bespectacled, curious. But once he scampered up to the attic, he suddenly became a mad scientist in a little boy's pair of shorts and striped T-shirt.

Up there, he liked to blow things up.

"It was just for the bang factor," recalled Peter, his younger brother.

Billy conducted chemical experiments on a Ping-Pong table, the perfect surface on which to spread out his bubbling concoctions. At the age of six, he was obsessed with the idea of building a rocket to send Mittie, his beloved German nanny, to the moon.

At Blue Chimneys, a sixty-acre estate in pastoral Mendham, New Jersey, Billy held the title of miracle child, the firstborn to parents who had thought they couldn't conceive.

William von Meister was different from the beginning, which in his case was February 21, 1942. A gifted child, he could read exceptionally fast, boasting phenomenal retention skills that required special test equipment. Even his own siblings were in awe.

Together, the children grew up amid privilege in a grand, whitewashed brick home in the 1950s. There were a cook and a butler and a maid and a sewing room and, outside, a large vegetable garden, towering trees, and a lake, where the children splashed around in the summer, and a steep, long driveway, where they went sledding in the winter. Yet Billy gravitated to the attic.

His experiments always seemed to involve a connection of some kind between two points. Earth to the moon, by way of a rocket. Or two tin cans attached by string. *Can you hear me?* His sister, Nora, would hear a faint echo from one empty tin can, nothing more. *Yes, I can hear you,* she would say, hoping to please her big brother. "I was the guinea pig," she said. "I would hear him clearly, even if I couldn't hear him clearly."

His was a mind in constant motion, wondering how to make things better, absorbing huge quantities of information, comprehending it all, then adapting concepts to his own creative bent. And so it was that Billy graduated from tin-can experiments to building walkie-talkies to wiring intercoms between rooms. Each was a connection. A way to make contact. People talking to each other from distant locations, from point A to point B. Billy learned Morse code. He weaved electronic entrails to build himself a ham radio. Late into the night, up in the attic, the little boy could be heard talking to people all over the world. Paris, Saudi Arabia, Washington . . .

It was as if Billy had an insatiable need to reach out to someone who wasn't there, which often happened to be the case with his parents.

His father, Frederick William von Meister, was a busy man who owned his own offset printing company. His mother, Eleanora, was the scion of a wealthy family and worshiped little Billy but kept a full social calendar, leaving much of the children's upbringing to Mittie and the other servants.

Not that Billy seemed to mind. He found a way to reach out, at least to his father: He built him a gizmo.

A wireless transmitter, it was about the size of a loaf of bread with an orange indicator light and a big antenna. On his way home from work, his father would hold the device outside the car window and push a button, which would send a signal to another antenna attached to a receiver box on the kitchen counter, setting off an alarm.

"That would indicate he was two, three miles away and he had better get his tea," said Peter, the younger brother. Thus warned, the servants would prepare a cup of tea for the master of the house. "It was really a sweet idea," Peter said.

Little Billy was just getting warmed up.

As an adult, Bill von Meister was a big kid. Indefatigable. Optimistic to the point of delusional. He was like a cackling Amadeus, only more irrepressible. Or the ringmaster at the circus. *Come one, come all.* "An idiot savant," recalled Michael Schrage, a former *Washington Post* reporter who chronicled many of von Meister's business forays in the 1980s.

In his home, von Meister shot darts at a board with the kind of blowgun pygmies used to assail wild animals in the jungle. He had a big-screen television, the best stereo money could buy, and a gaggle of video games.

He was a pilot, too, and he raced cars (including a modified BMW M635 with a souped-up engine). Along the way, he earned a clutch of silver cups from amateur competition and costly moving violations on the open highway.

"He loved fast cars and he loved to chase women," Peter said.

It was all part of Bill von Meister's voracious appetite to consume life. He was partial to red wines and good scotch and vodka—to the point that he became an alcoholic and checked into rehab once. He was also a lover of red meat, expensive restaurants, forbidden cigars, and lavish expense accounts, and he smoked three packs of Marlboros a day, claiming no adverse health effects.

But more than anything else, von Meister loved to create.

There was his aborted Spirits of America, a whiskey-shipping business in the early '70s. There was TDX Systems, a telecommunications company founded in 1975 in which von Meister made a bundle with his old tennis partner, Al Peyser. There was The Source, the first embryonic on-line service, which von Meister built in 1978 to give people access to a mainframe computer for some text-based information, including news, weather, and electronic bulletin boards.

"What do people do that is really challenging?" he once told a reporter. "They race cars, climb mountains, go scuba diving, and that's about it. Most really do live lives of quiet desperation. Well, entrepreneurship can be challenging, too. There are rules, but there ain't many."

Especially in his case.

"Bill von Meister was not just a serial entrepreneur, he was a pathological entrepreneur," said Schrage, who went on to become a researcher at the Massachusetts Institute of Technology Media Lab. "Bill von Meister's ideas, on average, when you look back on them, don't seem stupid. But at the time, they seemed outlandish. The big risk was he was such a loon that his looniness would get confused with the idea, because they're so intertwined."

Bill von Meister had a unique way of getting rich people to invest in his loony ideas. Better yet: He had a way of taking their money and not giving it back.

"This was one of the things Bill von Meister was better [at] than any other human I've met, which was taking money from venture capitalists, burning it all up, and then getting more money from the same venture capitalists, and they all felt good about it," said Marc Seriff, a key technological expert on some of his adventures.

Von Meister and his brother, Peter, perfected a technique to extract maximum dollars from the money men. They called it the "Dawn Patrol."

It worked like this: Von Meister would invite a venture capitalist down to Washington, usually a fairly young, well-heeled executive from one of the big brokerage houses in New York. That's when Bill and Peter, who served as his personal lawyer, would do the dog and pony show at the office.

In the early 1980s, the latest loony idea was called the Home Music Store. Von Meister's idea was to beam music—rock, pop, country—up to a satellite from a studio in Utah, which was financially backed by the Osmond family. Yes, *those* singing Osmonds. The satellite would beam the music down to the local cable television system, which would send the digital signal into people's homes, where the music would be tape-recorded on their stereo. The technology *actually* worked, von Meister would gleefully explain to his visitors.

After which, the whole group would head to von Meister's home in McLean, where the liquor flowed freely. This would be followed by dinner at a swank place like The Palm, a celebrity hangout in downtown Washington, where the potential investors would be massaged with more spirits. (Von Meister spent so much time at The Palm that the restaurant eventually framed a caricature of the offbeat entrepreneur.)

Toward one in the morning, von Meister would bid the lubricated visitors adieu and, by the way, *see you at 6 A.M.* for a tennis match at my place. When morning arrived all too soon, he'd trounce them. A quick shower and a power breakfast later, the visitors would begin to droop, their resistance down, whereupon von Meister would move in for the kill, leaning on them about how much money they should invest in his latest scheme.

"These poor guys looked like army recruits at army training," Peter said. "They'd agree to anything, just so they could go home."

. . .

Warner Bros., as it turned out, was less pliable.

High above Manhattan, circa 1981, men in suits sat at a conference table in a tower at Rockefeller Plaza. Von Meister stared across at a polite executive, who wasted no time in delivering the bad news: Warner Bros., the big entertainment company, was backing out of an agreement to license its music for von Meister's proposed venture, the Home Music Store.

In a measured tone devoid of emotion, the Warner Bros. executive explained himself: Delivering music directly into people's homes via satellite and cable would completely shut out music retailers, literally choke off their money supply. In other words, people wouldn't go to the store to buy Warner Bros. music anymore. (Two decades later, record companies would echo the same argument, claiming that Napster, the free on-line music-sharing service, threatened to hurry bricks-and-mortar retailers into extinction.)

The Warner Bros. executive didn't mince words. *Retailers are threatening to throw our records in the street,* he told von Meister. Without the cooperation of retailers, the game was over. *The Home Music Store isn't going to happen,* he said.

You can't do that! von Meister shot back. *We had a deal!*

The executive was unflappable. *Look, you can't pick a fight with us, boys. You don't have the money. But maybe there's something we can do.* He suggested that von Meister consider the video-game market. If von Meister could digitally deliver music into people's homes, why couldn't he digitally deliver video games instead? Warner Bros. owned Atari, the hottest video-game console on the market. *Talk to our people.*

It was a consolation prize. But von Meister, sensing an opportunity and all too willing to turn on a dime, agreed instantly.

And just like that, Bill von Meister entered the video-game business.

George M. Middlemas knew exactly what he was getting himself into from the moment he stepped off the plane in Washington into the unruly world of Bill von Meister. He had been warned.

Keep von Meister out of the first-class lounge at the airport. That's what people told Middlemas, who got the implied message. If you give von Meister money, he'll spend it lavishly on personal predilections, such as expensive wines, not to mention costly business ventures. Which was why Middlemas was in town in late 1981.

A venture-capitalist at Citicorp Bank in New York, Middlemas was down in Washington to decide whether to invest in von Meister's latest foray in the video-game business.

"Skepticism was high, based on Bill's record of good ideas that he had smashed to smithereens," Middlemas said.

The venture capitalist was a natural skeptic, notwithstanding von Meister's reputation. It was part of the job. Middlemas had to be doubtful. The only way to pinpoint the good idea to invest in was to find the fastest path to reject the bad ones. *Think Darwin.* Another Middlemas principle: People weren't the most important thing. That was a myth of venture capitalism. The truth was, he was investing in ideas and markets.

Hence the meeting. Middlemas liked the idea: video games. And there was a potential market: teenage boys.

Von Meister, ever the technical whiz, had developed a cheap and fast modem—basically, a little box with a lot of electronics stuffed in it. The modem, like a video-game cartridge, plugged into an Atari 2600 game console. The modem also connected to a telephone outlet, which allowed video games to be digitally transmitted to the Atari. Von Meister's modem was like a middleman, the bridge between bits and bytes of information traversing through the telephone line into the video-game console, delivering such fare as "Alien: You're caught in a maze littered with alien eggs which you must crush to climb to a higher level. Watch out for roving aliens as you struggle to survive!" Video games—which cost $1 per session—would be ordered by credit card. The modems would cost $59.95 retail.

That was the pitch to Middlemas. From his side of the conference table, von Meister gave off a child's delightful glint, emitting a low, rolling chuckle, laughing to himself, like Willy Wonka on steroids. It was as if he were gleefully saying, *Aren't I clever?*

And then he started ranting about the injustice of the music business, how Warner Bros. had reneged on a music deal, how the corporate world had stabbed him in the back. *But now, things were different! On-line video games! This was a great idea! And there was no corporate muscle to get in his way!*

Across the table, Middlemas was thinking, *I'm talking to a wild man.*

"Sparks almost flew off of his head," he said.

Fortunately, von Meister was smart enough to offset his manic presentation with a sedate sidekick, his numbers man who calmly went over the venture's financial projections. "He was the epitome of probity," Middlemas said, assured by the sidekick's even keel. "It was like Price Waterhouse at the Oscars. I felt okay."

What's more, Middlemas thought this was a great idea. Later, he would scold von Meister for his errant behavior: "You should live in a sealed house, and food and money should come in the door and ideas should come out."

But on that day, the two men simply shook hands. Within weeks, they had a deal: Middlemas forked over $100,000 for his video-game venture, and von Meister raised another $300,000.

For a creative genius, von Meister was strangely at a loss to come up with a jazzy name for his newly funded venture. When nothing else came to mind, he settled on Control Video Corp. by default, the thinking being that the technology lets you, well, control your own video game. It wasn't sexy, but it sounded solid, even reliable, which, given von Meister's haphazard track record, was not an insignificant consideration.

What's in a name anyway?

In his view, the real issue was: *How do we get a child to order an on-line video game with a credit card?*

Bill von Meister promptly spent $5,000 on a hot-air balloon.

Tethered at the Tropicana Hotel on the Strip in Las Vegas in January 1983, the enormous balloon announced in big red letters the arrival of his new video-game service: GAMELINE.

He didn't want to pay for a booth at the Consumer Electronics Show, a big trade confab in sin city, so he did the next best thing: He hired showgirls.

A clutch of buxom ladies in sequined bikinis, high heels, and glittery headdresses escorted potential customers to his lavish suite at the Trop to demo the new product. *See the most exciting game ever invented!* And if that didn't work, von Meister figured he'd lure the crowd with a contest drawing for a one-ounce bar of gold.

"It was a lot of schmaltz," said John Kerr, who served as von Meister's top salesman and best friend.

The girls or the gold were a big hit. Either way, it worked. Orders came pouring in that evening for about 150,000 of the little boxy modems. Control Video was on its way.

People took notice, including one bystander who quietly observed von Meister that night, a preppy introvert with a jutting jaw and boyish flop of hair over his serious brow. His name was Steve Case.

It wasn't love at first sight. It was strictly business.

Steve Case was president of a consulting business called The Marketing Group. In his own corporate literature, he described the firm as a "collection of successful consumer marketing executives who currently have significant responsibilities but enjoy the professional challenge of attacking new and exciting business opportunities."

The Marketing Group was essentially two people—Case and a friend. Case was president of a company that was little more than a name slapped on paper. The firm's letterhead showed a sophisticated San Francisco address—2365 North Point—but that's all it was. Mail sent to San Francisco was forwarded to a miserable little apartment in Wichita, Kansas, where Case lived and hated his day job.

His career rise had been less than spectacular. First, Procter & Gamble, the giant consumer-products company, flatly turned him down for a marketing job. Not taking no for an answer, he flew out for an interview on his own dime and landed a job as an assistant brand manager. Among his forgettable products was Abound, a hair-conditioning towelette that could be massaged onto the scalp. The slogan: "Towelette, you bet!"

Now, he was, in his own written description, "marketing manager of Pepsico Inc. with responsibility for the development and introduction of a $250 million product for the Pizza Hut division."

Translation: Steve Case spent most of his time traveling to small pizza shops, testing pizza flavors. (He scored pizza on five categories: crust, dough, sauce, cheese, and topping.)

Steve Case was in his mid-twenties and quickly disappearing into the morass of middle management.

That is, until he came to see von Meister in the desert. Case was invited to Vegas by his older brother, Daniel Case III, an up-and-coming investment banker at Hambrecht & Quist, who was helping to bankroll von Meister's new video-game venture. Dan, also a member of von Meister's board of directors, made the introductions.

The rest has become the stuff of Steve Case lore, like a Hans Christian Andersen fairy tale about business. It goes like this: Steve Case and von Meister hit it off over dinner. They both agree that the on-line video-game market is just the beginning of something that will change the world. During a bathroom break, von Meister asks Dan whether he can hire his little brother as a consultant.

Wonderful stuff—except it didn't happen that way.

"He was not hired on the spot," said John Kerr, von Meister's right-hand man, who was in Vegas that evening. In fact, von Meister never asked Dan to hire Case. It was the other way around: Dan called von Meister and asked him to hire his little brother. Steve Case got his big break—the job that would set him on a course of fame and fortune—through a simple case of family leverage.

The story was corroborated by Marc Seriff, von Meister's technology guru, when he gave a videotaped brown-bag seminar to AOL employees in April 1996, just as Seriff was preparing to ride off into the sunset of retirement. In the video, he said that Dan called up one day and requested that the company hire his little brother.

"Dan had just given us somewhere in the vicinity of, I think, two and a half million dollars and was the lead investor in giving us five or six million dollars, so disagreeing with Dan was not a viable option," Seriff said.

That Steve Case knew nothing about the video-game business didn't matter. "Steve did have impeccable credentials," Seriff said with a heavy dose of sarcasm. "He'd spent the last two years traveling from Pizza Hut to Pizza Hut, sampling pizza, trying to come up with new flavors for the company, so his credentials were absolutely impeccable."

Von Meister agreed to hire him. In the process, Steve Case earned a nickname that stuck: "Lower Case." Dan, his big brother who had set him up with von Meister, was dubbed, naturally, "Upper Case."

· · ·

The remarkable thing about Stephen McConnell Case was just how unremarkable he was.

His was an upbringing played out across America in the '60s and '70s—the only difference being that he did his growing up in an affluent home with a view of the clear-blue Honolulu skyline.

The third of four children of a lawyer and a retired schoolteacher, Steve Case was born on August 21, 1958, and lived an uneventful childhood marked by the easy rhythms of Cub Scouts, Little League, set mealtimes, required chores, and one hour of television after homework. He was an average student. He liked rock and roll (the Rolling Stones). He wrote music reviews for a small teen publication in Hawaii.

Perhaps, however, there was a hint of Case's future in business: As a child, he and his older brother, Dan, started a limeade stand. Later, they went door-to-door, selling greeting cards and garden seeds. They built a corporate structure of sorts, with a holding company called Case Enterprises. Eventually, the family started calling Case's bedroom his "office." Dan was the front man, the dynamic salesman who did most of the talking. Steve, careful and reserved, preferred the quiet, detached task of handling the back operations.

But more than the childhood ventures, what distinguished Steve Case's youth was his sibling rivalry with Dan—a searing experience that fueled the younger brother.

They were born only thirteen months apart, but Dan was always a giant in Steve's eyes, the fair-haired older brother, the family star, a straight-A student whose constant success overshadowed the younger brother.

Dan understood as much. A few years before he died of a brain cancer, he said, "I defined the market early in our family through achievement. Steve was the third guy up. He had to work to define his own path."

Their paths, however, collided on occasion. Sometimes, it was just a rough game of pickup basketball. Other times, it was a burst of violence between the boys. Ultimately, they learned to negotiate their way through the competition. When it came to college, Steve made an early choice, picking Williams College, their father's alma mater. His B-plus grades were sufficient. That, combined with decent extracurricular activities (he was editor of the high school newspaper) and the legacy factor, was apparently enough to get the Hawaiian resident into the small Massachusetts college in 1976. Dan opted for Princeton University.

While Dan went on to become a Rhodes Scholar and then a rising investment banker, Steve flailed. There was little to suggest greatness looming in his future. He applied to several MBA programs and was rejected by them all. He couldn't get a job at HBO, a division of Time Inc., then being run by a rising young executive named Jerry Levin. He took a job with Pizza Hut that looked like a dead end.

Steve Case had taken Computers 101 in college and hated it. But when Dan opened the door to a consulting gig with von Meister's on-line video venture—a firm steeped in the computer technology of the day—Case seized the opportunity.

It turned out to be one of the smartest moves of his entire career.

The job also paid a princely sum for a young marketing man trying to get out of Kansas: $20 per hour, for a total of $9,000 for his consulting expertise, plus expenses. (Case promised to stay in cheap hotels and fly special coach.)

What von Meister got for his money was a set of detailed reports in which Case gave a good rendering of the Procter & Gamble school of marketing: business objectives, product positioning, corporate identity.

"It was straight out of the P&G booklet," said Kerr, von Meister's sales executive.

But the reports also gave some insight into Case's early thoughts about how to do business. Among them: thwart the competition. For the video-game market, his advice to von Meister was, "Erect barriers to entry (lock up category)." The idea was to make it difficult for other players to get into the same business.

Case also showed a Machiavellian side, telling von Meister, "Concentrate on the perceptions of the product . . . not the realities of the product." Case talked about avoiding "whoring" the product through deep discounting. And he reminded von Meister to be "sensitive to the Orwellian backlash" of an on-line product that could suggest an "invasion of privacy."

But Case grasped the broader implications of von Meister's venture. Video games were just the start. The little modem could also deliver into people's homes a stream of other digital information—electronic mail, stock quotes, sports.

In his reports, Case talked about positioning the video-game service as a "revolutionary, 'breakthrough' product in the home entertainment/information network category." Not right away, though. First, grab the "hardcore gamers." But in year two, Case said, the strategy would be to show that the product "turns your game console into a computer."

Actually, this wasn't Case's insight; it was von Meister's. Indeed, through the GameLine modem, Control Video was preparing to introduce, in stages, such features as e-mail, sports news, and on-line banking. In an all-but-forgotten company pamphlet from the early '80s, von Meister boasted of turning "inexpensive game consoles into sophisticated communications terminals!"

GameLine wasn't just a game. It was a window into the future of the personal computer, the PC. *There would be Mailine! Stockline! Bankline! Newsline! Sportsline!* This is how von Meister pitched the little gizmo to retailers: "Games are only the beginning. When today's joystick jockies turn into tomorrow's information 'junkies'—you'll be there to profit."

"Bill knew where this was going," said Kerr. "Once you got through with the spreadsheet and word processor, what the hell were they going to do with their PC?"

Von Meister, said Middlemas, the investor, understood that the video game was, "a Trojan horse strategy to get into the computer world."

As early as February 1983, industry insiders got a whiff of von Meister's big play. "Control Video, a maker of videogames for the popular Atari videogame unit, is developing an adaptor, which will allow users to access home banking, teleshopping and other teleservices through their videogame consoles," announced *Teleservices Report,* an industry newsletter.

It noted, however, "A number of details are incomplete."

Details weren't von Meister's strength. He was thinking big picture all the way. In a 1983 company publication, von Meister called his modem, "THE CONSUMER ELECTRONICS PRODUCT OF THE DECADE."

That, history would show, would be an understatement.

Bill von Meister was dashing down the hallway of his little company—*did he move any other way?*—when he made a quick pivot and poked his head in the doorway of a colleague: "If a guy named Guido shows up to repo the computers," he quipped, "let me know."

He was joking, of course. But in the jest, there was a kernel of truth. Only a few months after the debut of its GameLine service in July 1983, Control Video was in trouble.

Credit an unfortunate confluence of factors: The company was spending a lot of its precious capital manufacturing the video-game modems, while it was having a tough time convincing video-game makers to license their software. Bottom line: There were lots of boxes but nothing to put in them. Not a good combination.

As if that weren't enough, von Meister was also experiencing firsthand the unpleasant forces of business physics—what goes up must come down—which in this case was the once red-hot video-game market. With Atari suddenly hemorrhaging cash, video games were beginning to look like a short-lived fad, like jumping jelly beans. (Remember those? *Exactly.*)

"It wasn't a business, it was a struggle for survival," said Schrage, the former *Washington Post* reporter, who wasn't sure how long he'd be writing about the company before its expected demise.

Within months, the situation was dire: Control Video had only three thousand customers—about a million fewer than it had hoped for. "GameLine has been slowed by lackluster sales," said a polite report in *Videotex Teletext News*.

"The video-game business is not what it was a year ago," von Meister conceded then.

He was being charitable. The market was kaput. Control Video had shipped forty thousand modems to retailers—who had then shipped back thirty-seven thousand of them.

Back at headquarters, the modems sat around collecting dust. Von Meister thought about stripping the boxes down to their raw material to sell as salvage, but then he discovered a depressing truth. The salvage value of each modem was less than what it cost to ship to the salvager. Behind his small warren of offices was a Dumpster. That's where tens of thousands of unsold modems ultimately ended up.

Creditors were not amused. "There was nothing hilarious about it," said Ed O'Brien, a Control Video board member and executive of LaBarge Inc., a manufacturing firm that lost lots of money when von Meister's company couldn't afford to pay its bills for the modems LaBarge had built.

Von Meister had burned through $20 million in venture capital, and all he had to show for it was $40,000 in revenue. Even that paltry amount did not do justice to how bad things really were: $15,000 of that money came from selling the hot-air balloon he had floated in Vegas. For what it was worth, *that* was a good deal; von Meister got triple what he had paid for the balloon. He may not have known how to sell a modem, but he sure knew a thing or two about selling hot air.

Investors were getting restless to say the least.

In lieu of firing von Meister, they brought in a new guy to help keep the company afloat. The newcomer was to be an informal manufacturing consultant, although he knew not one iota about modems, video games, or manufacturing. He did know something about booze, though. He was a local bar owner. He also happened to be an old U.S. Military Academy buddy of Frank Caufield, an investor in von Meister's company. This old buddy was named Jim Kimsey.

Caufield had first mentioned the idea to Kimsey during a white-water rafting trip down the Colorado River through the Grand Canyon. *You oughta check out this little business,* Caufield had said in passing.

He followed that up with a more desperate phone call. "Here we were, burning through money as fast as we can print it, and Frank Caufield called Jim and said, 'Go over there and figure out what they're doing,'" said Seriff, Control Video's top engineer. "So Jim actually entered the company as a manufacturing consultant. His actual deal was to baby-sit."

The baby in question was von Meister. On arrival in 1983, Kimsey took the office next to the temperamental entrepreneur. The office had belonged to Kerr, the von Meister loyalist. *I'm sorry,* von Meister sheepishly explained to his old friend, *but the investors want to keep an eye on me.*

Kerr, the sales executive, didn't like what was happening. First, Steve Case, the younger brother of a lead investor, becomes a consultant; now Kimsey, the school friend of another investor, shows up.

The biggest mistake you're making is bringing in two of the investors' friends, Kerr cautioned.

Oh, no, no, no, once we get them in, we've got them locked in, von Meister said.

But you're not locked in, Kerr said.

"From day one," Kerr firmly believes, "they were trying to get him out."

. . .

James Verlin Kimsey didn't want to get involved in von Meister's mess, whoever this character von Meister was. But then again, Kimsey didn't intend to become a military hero either, or a billionaire, which happened, too.

"It's the Forrest Gump syndrome," he said, referring to the fictional character who was touched by greatness.

The son of a Washington bureaucrat and a doting mother, Kimsey was a tough street kid born on September 15, 1939, who got kicked out of high school for being a wiseass and couldn't have cared less.

But his indomitable mother cared. "My little Irish Catholic mother was beside herself," Kimsey said.

His mother called on some priests to help with her son. Practically before he knew it, Kimsey was enrolled in a Catholic military school.

Then Kimsey surprised everyone. He became a cadet at West Point, where he learned that there were three answers to every question: (1) Yes, sir; (2) No, sir; and (3), No excuse, sir. Number 3 was the most important. He internalized it. He lived it. He let it guide him throughout his life. He explains it in a quiet, steely voice: "If you are a platoon leader, and one of your men dies, there is no excuse. If you are a CEO, and thousands of your employees are laid off, there is no excuse."

Jim Kimsey was the first member of his family to earn a college degree. Later, he became a chisel-jawed army airborne ranger, serving two tours of duty in Vietnam in the 1960s, avoiding getting killed by the Viet Cong, and—in the midst of incoming mortar and sandbag shelters—building an orphanage in hostile territory.

He cherished those times.

When he returned to civilian life after eight years in the service, Kimsey parlayed $2,000 in cash—everything he had to his name—into a beautiful Horatio Alger story.

It was a simple tale. Kimsey was looking for something to do in 1970, wandering along a downtown block in Washington on a Saturday when he saw a building for sale. The next thing he knew, with no money down, he was a landlord who was in debt to the hilt. What did he have to lose? He rented the top floor to an investment brokerage house. The brokers planned to open a bar downstairs but ran out of money halfway through the job. Kimsey shrugged it off, borrowed some more money, took over the project, and opened his own bar with a novel gimmick that drew immediate attention: a ticker-tape machine. He called it The Exchange.

Starting with one bar, he became a successful businessman, opening a slew of singles watering holes in the 1970s, trendy places with such catchy names as Madhatter and Bullfeathers.

He had become a rich man.

"It just happened," he said of his life. "You can't architect that stuff. But when it happens, you have to be ready."

Jim Kimsey wasn't like Bill von Meister, who rushed headlong into the creation of Control Video. Nor was Kimsey like Steve Case, who rode his older brother's coattails to the opportunity presented by the little on-line video-game company. This wasn't Kimsey's thing.

"The only technology I knew was the engineering course at West Point," he said. "*V* equals *IR*." (Ohm's law: Voltage equals current times resistance.)

The way Kimsey figured it, he was just doing a favor for his old friend. Or, as Schrage recollected it, "He was a skirt-chasing, hell-raising restaurant owner who was put in there to clean up this mess for his West Point buddy Frank."

Kimsey didn't plan to stick around long. He said as much when he asked Brad Johnson, another West Point pal, to join Control Video.

"What do you want me to do?" Johnson asked.

"Replace me," Kimsey answered. "I'm just here temporarily."

Johnson came on board to oversee manufacturing. Like Kimsey, he knew nothing about computers or manufacturing, but also like Kimsey, he was a military man—No excuse, sir.

There was a difference, though. Just as Kimsey was getting involved in Control Video, he was creating a bank-holding company. A Securities and Exchange Commission form he had to fill out asked whether he had ever been involved in a bankruptcy. Suddenly, Control Video took on a whole new light. He felt motivated. There was no way James V. Kimsey was going to be associated with a bankruptcy.

Little did he know what he was getting himself into.

. . .

It wasn't funny, but Jim Kimsey couldn't help smiling. There he was, in a hotel conference room in early 1984, jabbering on about the state of affairs at Control Video before the board of directors, a group of grim investors who didn't like what they were hearing.

It was as if Kimsey were removed from himself, a disembodied spirit watching the proceedings, listening to himself drone on. The place had the feel of a Senate hearing, with board members sitting back in judgment, overseeing the proceedings, which included a bunch of easels and visuals to which Kimsey directed their attention with a pointer. He threw an ironic smile at Frank Caufield, his West Point buddy, who rolled his eyes back at Kimsey. They were like kids back in school. *What were they doing here? They were military guys! They weren't computer wonks!*

And yet, there they were, at Rickey's Hyatt House, a trendy hangout in Palo Alto, California, for Silicon Valley denizens. Christmas 1983 had come and gone, and it wasn't pretty: Control Video had about $10 million in debts and 120 angry creditors banging on the door, wanting to get paid.

Kerr, the sales executive, got up and launched into a presentation about how many modems had been sold at retail. It was a virtuoso performance involving charts and numbers and complicated buzzwords. But it came down to this: Control Video hadn't sold much of anything.

The room fell deathly silent.

"Goddamn," Kimsey finally broke in, "we could've sold more of these things selling them off the back of a pickup truck driving on U.S. 1!"

Caufield chimed in: "You'd have thought kids would've shoplifted more than that!"

Von Meister flushed. People stood up. It was the end of the meeting. It was also the end of the company.

"We realized this turkey isn't going to fly," said Middlemas, a company director.

There was no announcement, nothing to sound the death knell. People just broke off into little impromptu meetings, whispering and scheming. Von Meister, shaken, went up to Kerr, his old friend, and uttered simply, "I'm out." He would stay on board, but only as a figurehead. Kimsey wandered out to the parking lot, thinking, *Now what's going to happen?*

And then it happened: One by one, board members approached him. It was all very informal. Just a little chitchat. At first, Kimsey didn't know what was going on, but then it gradually dawned on him: It was as if board members were kissing his ring. He was being anointed the new godfather of Control Video.

James V. Kimsey was in charge.

"People say you couldn't have done it without Steve Case," Kimsey said, then waved off that idea with a guffaw. "Steve was a twenty-four-year-old marketing *intern.* I couldn't have done it without Marc Seriff."

Seriff, the company's technology man, never seemed interested in taking credit. In 1996, he retired quietly from AOL. But Case? He and his emissaries worked hard to establish his place in the company's history. In an AOL employee handbook, after Kimsey had stepped down as chairman in late 1995, Case introduced himself to new hires as "Founder, chairman and CEO," referring to "when we started back in 1985."

It's true that by the mid-1990s, Case was chairman and CEO. But the company was founded by von Meister, and it was started not in 1985 but in 1983, the year that Case joined as a part-time consultant. Later that year, von Meister and Kimsey together hired Case as a full-time marketing employee. Kimsey remembers the conversation about hiring Case this way:

What do you think about Steve? von Meister asked.

He seems bright, he won't cost you much, and Dan will have to put in more money, Kimsey responded, thinking of the benefits of hiring the little brother of Dan Case, a big company investor. "I was right on all three counts."

Kimsey was the CEO who promoted Case to vice president of marketing in the mid-1980s and to executive vice president in 1987. Case became chief executive officer in 1991.

"When I see this stuff about Steve Case, 'founder of America Online,' it's not quite the case, it's not right," said Brad Johnson, the man Kimsey brought in as head of manufacturing.

Kimsey regards Case—the young Case, before he grew up into media mogul—as a wayward son with an Oedipus complex, a need to slay the father and take the throne for himself. It was a natural evolution. Case rose through the ranks in large part by the process of elimination. As the business was sinking and shrinking to a handful of people, Kimsey was forced to lay off employees—people at higher levels with bigger salaries than Case's. "I fired everybody above him," Kimsey said.

But Case wasn't just cheap labor. Kimsey recognized potential. From the beginning, he marveled at Case's ability to write position papers for the company's investors, even when Kimsey changed course, reversed himself, and decided to go in the opposite direction. "He'd do it with equally compelling logic and passion," Kimsey said. Case, he said, was "very able—like Arnold Schwarzenegger in *Terminator*." As an example, Kimsey cites a scene in which Schwarzenegger, playing a humorless cyborg, scrolls through a menu of potential responses to a meddlesome janitor and emits in a monotone, "Fuck you, asshole." That's how Kimsey thought of Case—"only his response time is quicker," he said.

"He's a cyborg," Kimsey said. "I mean that in a nice way."

They made an odd couple: Kimsey, the brash, blunt, swashbuckling former military man, and Case, introverted, uptight, metronomic. Case, though, looked up to Kimsey as a father figure. "At the time, he seemed awfully old," said Case, who was then in his twenties, while Kimsey was in his forties. "We found ourselves sort of in a foxhole because we both had aligned ourselves more closely with this company that was kind of going nowhere fast," Case said in a videotaped tribute to Kimsey on his sixtieth birthday.

There was another reason Kimsey bonded with Case, selecting him as his heir apparent: "He lived, ate, and breathed this shit," Kimsey said.

Therein lay their difference: Kimsey's idea of fun was biking through the French countryside, which he did one summer in the late 1980s. Case, who was in Paris around the same time, went directly to an industry trade conference, not even making a quick stop at the Louvre Museum.

"He had a maniacal devotion to this," Kimsey said. "It was his life. He is a nerd, an inward-looking person. He likes to communicate by e-mail. He doesn't even like to talk on the phone."

Kimsey needed somebody like this, somebody who wanted to do the work, the nitty-gritty. "Kimsey wanted to get the hell out of there," said Bob Cross, a turnaround specialist who came on board in 1984. Cross didn't think that was a good idea. He suggested that Kimsey get rid of Case. Cross thought Case was preoccupied in marketing the video-game modems like so many pizza boxes, an idea that had failed von Meister. But Kimsey wanted a life. He wanted to go white-water rafting. He always thought he'd return to his old life, keeping his old office on K Street in downtown Washington. Besides, there was nobody else to do the market-ing, and he didn't have time to go out and find someone.

"Cool it," he told Cross. "Case is here, right now."

People warned Kimsey, *Don't put Case out front, don't let him be the face of the company.* But Kimsey began mentoring Case, bringing him to board meetings, presenting him to the media. He tried to teach him corporate pol-itics and, he hoped, "some people skills." It didn't go well at first. In an early interview with *The Washington Post,* Case was so boring—or guarded, de-pending on the point of view—that an incensed Michael Schrage vowed never to speak to Case again, threatening to stop writing about the company unless the colorful Kimsey or von Meister did the talking in the future.

"If you had told me Steve Case was chairman of Time Warner–AOL, you would have had to hospitalize me for internal hemorrhaging," Schrage said. "Silly beyond belief—Steve Case?"

For Bill von Meister, the end of the line arrived one day in early 1985 when he came gleefully skipping out of his office to greet his spanking new BMW 735i.

"How do you like my new car?" von Meister chirped, like a child on Christmas morning.

Kimsey noticed there was the letter *M* emblazoned on the car. "What the fuck does the *M* stand for?" he asked.

"More," said von Meister.

Kimsey, Cross, and Middlemas were all agape. The three men had been standing in the parking lot, nervously waiting for the arrival of an entourage of creditors. Angry creditors. People who hadn't been paid. Companies that were threatening to sue Control Video, or worse—force it into bankruptcy. This was a big day, a defining moment for Control Video. If the creditors refused to accept ten cents on the dollar for what they were owed—and that's all Control Video could afford—then it was all over. Money had gotten so tight that the company had been forced to tape together cardboard boxes to use as office cubicle dividers.

"We have a creditors meeting! Are you crazy bringing in that car?" Kimsey exclaimed. "See that tree? They'll hang you from it and burn your furniture in the parking lot!"

Von Meister looked wounded, his eyes wide like saucers. "What are you getting all upset about?" he asked. "Don't these people understand I have a personal life?"

Cross urged him to get in his new car, go home, and go look after that personal life. Von Meister finally seemed to get the point. Off he drove, down the road and, for all intents and purposes, out of their lives forever.

The company was spared that day. Kimsey never really held it against von Meister. "He was like a puppy you like a lot but you have to house-train," Kimsey said.

Control Video, too, faded quietly into the distance. "It just went into a shoe box," Kimsey said. He gave it a proper burial in the bottom left-hand drawer of his desk.

It never went bankrupt. It just got dressed up with a new name. "The company was not dying but changing," Kimsey said. With the same people, in the same small offices in Vienna, Virginia, he said, "it transmogrified."

On May 24, 1985, Control Video was reborn as Quantum Computer Services Inc., a name that held no special meaning but sounded techie— and official.

"It sounded like it was supposed to be a big company," said Kimsey, Quantum's founding chief executive officer. "It has that ring of credibility."

The media was not fooled. In a published report soon after its rechristening, Schrage of *The Washington Post* put it this way: "But, like a New York cockroach, Control Video simply couldn't be killed off." Of the one hundred employees who had worked at Control Video, about ten were left, including Case and Kimsey.

By 1995, Quantum was a distant memory to von Meister. In his final days, he had other things on his mind. Dying of a fast-spreading melanoma, von Meister had wasted away, losing weight and color. He was broke, and creditors were still beating down his door. As he lay bedridden in a Georgetown hospital, an IV in his arm, Nora, his devoted sister, his shadow, recalled that his mind was racing. All he could say was, "When I get out of here, if I'm alive, I'm going to show how this hospital can do things better."

CHAPTER TWO

A CASE OF AMBITION

Steve Case was dubbed "The Wall." Not to his face. But those inside the company had come to accept this about him: He was a blank expression who was hard to read, who didn't *want* to be read, who would strut down the hallway, his big chin jutting out imperiously, his eyes narrowed in intense concentration, remote, serious, quiet.

Was he aloof or just shy?

Once in late 1987, Cathy Anderson, a company vice president, got a glimpse behind The Wall.

The two were stuck in bumper-to-bumper traffic on a glaring, sultry day, baking on a San Francisco highway. Case, tall and lanky, was scrunched behind the wheel of a clunky little rental. It was a compact, all that Quantum Computer Services's small budget allowed.

Case, then executive vice president, and Anderson, in charge of on-line services, had just finished an introductory meeting with executives of another company. Quantum, still searching for a way to survive beyond the video-game business, wanted to purchase a stock-ticker service. The idea was that customers could access financial information, which would be transmitted over telephone lines, through a modem, into their personal computers—an idea first championed by Bill von Meister years earlier.

Case was about to drop off Anderson at her hotel before he went on to his own tiny furnished apartment in an old building in town. He had been camping out on the West Coast for months, trying to strike a big deal that would make Quantum the on-line service for industry heavyweight Apple Computer, Inc.

For the moment, however, highway traffic was going nowhere, and the conversation turned from business to that place that Case rarely visited: his personal life.

Where are you from? Anderson asked Case.

Hawaii.

Cool! What a beautiful place. Why would you leave Hawaii?

Case looked straight ahead at the highway tapering off in the distance. Then he said matter-of-factly, "Well, you can become the most successful person in Hawaii, and you're still just on an island."

Pregnant pause.

The way Case uttered those unvarnished words, Anderson recalled, "It was just dead straight, like me saying, 'My name is Cathy.'" There was no bravado in it. He didn't mean to make a bold statement. But it left Anderson speechless. It also left her thinking about the incredible insight offered by his off-the-cuff remark. *Well, he's not one of us,* she thought. *He's a different kind of person.*

It suddenly occurred to her: "He had always had his sights set on the world."

Almost from the moment Jim Kimsey took over Control Video in 1984, he went looking for a buyer of the struggling, little firm.

"I wanted out," he said.

When he tried Apple in the mid-1980s, he didn't get the response he was looking for. Apple executives practically rolled on the floor. An effort to sell to Commodore International Ltd., the computer maker, failed as well. But Commodore was at least willing to try a partnership with Kimsey in 1985. So Quantum Computer Services was given a new purpose. It became a software maker. And it ditched the whole idea of making the little modem— the box of electronics—that von Meister had created as an accessory for the Atari video-game console. Instead, Quantum would make software for an emerging consumer market: the personal computer, the PC.

Quantum, however, didn't roam far from its origins. Its software, placed on a disk, would work in tandem with a modem, just as long as someone else made the box. The Quantum software still depended on the same fundamental premise of the old von Meister company: the delivery of digital information over telephone wires. But instead of transmitting video games to an Atari, Quantum's software would allow consumers to receive news, get soap opera updates, make airline reservations, and retrieve other tidbits of information from a Commodore PC. People would also be able to chat with each other through text-based messages on their computer monitors.

It was called an on-line service. And Quantum would run it.

The concept was being tested by a handful of companies in the mid-1980s, including IBM, which were looking for a novel reason for consumers to buy their product. No one was quite sure whether this on-line idea would fly. It required a lot of consumers. Not only would they have to buy a computer, they also would have to pay separately for a modem to gain entry into this self-contained universe. Then they would have to assemble the whole thing, attaching the modem to their computer, plugging it into a telephone outlet. The on-line software, often packed in the computer box, would have to be inserted into the computer's floppy disk drive. On top of that, people would have to order a subscription for the on-line service (a flat fee of $9.95 per month, plus $6 an hour).

Were people willing to do all of that? Even if they wanted to, could they figure it all out?

Commodore hoped so. Sales of its flagship Commodore 64 computer were waning, and the company was looking for something to pep it up. Maybe this on-line communication thing could help.

For its part, Quantum certainly needed the help. Its first stab at developing software left something to be desired. It was clunky and primitive looking. Commodore, though, liked Kimsey and his Quantum management team and introduced them in 1985 to PlayNet, a software firm in upstate New York whose on-line software had a much more colorful look and feel, making it easier for users to navigate their computer screen. PlayNet, which was having an even harder time surviving financially than Quantum, ended up licensing its software to Kimsey's firm, ultimately becoming the backbone of AOL's on-line service. In what might have been the greatest business deal in Kimsey's career, he bought the PlayNet software license for $50,000.

Quantum, shoestring operation that it was, was situated smack-dab in the middle of a suburban wasteland of strip malls, gas stations, and fast-food joints, just off Leesburg Pike in Vienna, Virginia, behind a couple of auto dealerships, down a quiet tree-lined road, past an asphalt parking lot, in a drab, low redbrick building, a warren of cubicles sparsely furnished with rickety old chairs and folding tables likely to be found in a church basement.

Greatness it did not herald.

Bill Pytlovany found out as much when he drove down from upstate New York to join the little company as a software developer in the summer of 1985. Before he could unpack the U-Haul hitched to the back of his car, he was taken in a company van to a furniture store. He came back with an unassembled desk in a box—whereupon Pytlovany was handed a screwdriver and a hammer. He spent much of the rest of the day sitting on the floor hammering his desk together. Welcome to Quantum.

It was, Pytlovany said, "the classic start-up."

There were twenty-five employees at most, and about half worked in customer service. The main event, though, occurred at a flickering computer monitor in a dimly lit room at 6 P.M. on November 1. After a series of test runs, that evening was to be the official debut of Quantum-Link, or Q-Link, the on-line service for the Commodore computer.

Pytlovany and the half dozen other techies weren't the most verbose of sorts, but the tension was palpable as they huddled around the tube, which was wired to a mainframe computer, a white behemoth about the size of a refrigerator, hidden in a cool, sealed, climate-controlled room.

A techie flipped the switch, punching a few keystrokes to perform a computer command. The monitor began to light up. Data streamed in, showing who was getting on-line, at what time, and from what node, or computer address. One after another, the names of on-line users scrolled down the screen, arriving from virtually every point on the map of the United States:

Mikewl from Ohio.

RJ from Pennsylvania.

Even Pytlovany's mother logged on from Scotia, New York.

Amazing! Unbelievable! The system hadn't crashed! Finally, the techies erupted in delight.

"We popped some beers right there," Pytlovany said, "and let out some hoots."

That night, the service peaked with about one hundred simultaneous on-line users—one hundred people, unseen, unheard—who poked around, braving this little virtual world created by Quantum, checking out news feeds, playing backgammon, and chatting with one another.

"No one would've ever imagined what we have now," he said. "I can honestly say that."

They didn't know it then, but a revolution was underway.

By January 1986, Quantum had only ten thousand subscribers. The paltry number prompted investors in the fledgling firm to head for the hills—literally.

Caufield, Kimsey's old West Point buddy, was nowhere to be found. The guy who had gotten Kimsey into this business in the first place had taken a leave of absence from his venture capital firm to go trekking in the Himalayas. Caufield couldn't be reached for anything—and most certainly *not* for more funding for Kimsey's little company.

Fortunately, a New York investor named Alan J. Patricof was willing to take a flyer on Kimsey. In a February 7, 1986, memo to colleagues at his own investment firm, Patricof seemed to look beyond the ragtag operation that was Quantum and see its real potential. Yes, there was a lot of confusion. Yes, the telephones weren't always being answered and, "as a result, a lot of incoming calls are going unanswered, which means that further business is being lost," Patricof wrote then. And yes, the on-line service had run into a "technical bug" that limited it to a maximum of 247 customers who could tap into the system at the same time. Patricof wrote, "they are not only losing revenues but they are probably turning off their subscribers."

But Patricof still liked what he saw in Kimsey. "I must say that I am impressed by Jim and his quiet but firm nature," he wrote in the memo. That was good enough. Patricof invested $750,000 in Quantum—a huge lift for the little firm—a lifesaver, Kimsey said. It also turned out to be a pretty good lift for Patricof, whose return on his investment years later totaled about $20 million.

But in the mid-1980s, it was a big gamble. The feeling was shared by many. Count among them its 120 or so apoplectic, red-faced, vein-popping creditors who continued to scream at Quantum's chief executive officer. This was not Kimsey's idea of helping out an old West Point friend. He could hear Caufield's offer reverberating in memory: *Maybe you could check out this little company.* It was supposed to be a lark. Instead, Kimsey recalled with a crooked smile, "I got sucked in." There he was, a local bar owner, still fielding a barrage of phone calls from creditors, demanding payment on unpaid bills ranging from office supplies to advertising.

Kimsey, the army veteran, wasn't terribly moved. He'd survived Vietnam. "Nothing intimidated me after that," he said. "I was still alive." Besides, he was an expert in kick boxing. What were the creditors going to do—hurt him?

Actually, he reckoned, he could abuse the creditors. In a calm voice, he explained that if they continued to harass him about the unpaid bills, this is what he was going to do to the little company: "I'll bankrupt it, and you'll get zero, absolutely zero."

This usually got the creditors' attention.

Then, Kimsey would explain that, on the other hand, if the creditors gave him a little breathing room, "Maybe there was a 10 percent chance to pull a rabbit out of the hat."

The rabbit, of course, was the ability to keep Quantum alive. Kimsey's own privately held prognosis: "If I was a bookie," he said, "I wouldn't have given us a one-in-a-thousand chance to survive."

By December 1986, the company was barely getting by with fifty-five employees and fewer than fifty thousand subscribers. Things had gotten so bad that he had vacated the upper floors of the building where the company was headquartered, moving the whole company down into the basement, the better to conserve cash. From his perch, with the phone ringing off the hook (more angry creditors), Kimsey would stare out of his office window, barely at ground level and, while he tried to keep his little company alive, watch the rabbits scampering out back in the woods and think of the absurdity of it all.

To escape the madness, Kimsey occasionally walked around the corner to have lunch in a cafeteria in a neighboring building, home of the Greatest Show on Earth: The Ringling Bros. and Barnum & Bailey Circus.

"That irony was pointed out to me," he said, "many times."

In May 1988, Randy Dean was hired as a copywriter at Quantum, although he wasn't quite sure what that meant until his first day on the job, when he was sent home with a Commodore 64 computer. He lugged the machine up to his uncle's loft, where he was sleeping temporarily on a mattress, cleared a card table, and hooked up the terminal to a phone line.

Shazam.

Just like that, he was inside Q-Link, wandering around the on-line service until he found himself in "People Connection," a virtual hangout where people logged on with a user name and chatted, the words streaming down the page as quickly as they could type them. Dean was getting the hang of this. While he was chatting, he launched a video game (the soul of von Meister's machine!). It was called Rabbit Jack's Casino. Dean was playing poker with a bunch of guys he didn't know and had never met from Florida, Texas, and California. It was getting late, around one o'clock in the morning. Somebody said something funny. Dean laughed out loud, then caught himself. He looked around. His uncle's house was completely dark. He had just laughed at his computer—this inanimate object that had drawn him in to another reality, something beyond the zeros and ones in its digital DNA, a virtual realm.

"That's when I got what we were doing," he said. "That was kind of the moment for me."

Therein lay the powerful appeal of this emerging medium. People who used the service could join a fictional world—an on-line realm where they could role-play, where they could pretend to be whoever they wanted to be and meet other strangers in total cyber-intimacy.

"It was a really strange world until I found out what this was all about," said Julia L. Wilkinson, who joined Quantum in September 1988 as a copywriter and quickly got hooked on the service. "For some people, it was their whole social life. That was their reality."

Among Wilkinson's discoveries was a popular on-line nightspot called Bonnie's Bar. It was a virtual saloon, a chat room where people gathered to talk and drink (sort of). A drink was ordered by placing parentheses together to form the shape of a beer mug: {(_)

It wasn't perfect, but people got the idea. If you wanted to send a rose to a lady whom you met at Bonnie's Bar—and what are guys doing in a bar, virtual or otherwise, if not to meet ladies?—you connected an @ to a couple of dashes: —>—>—@

People pretended to get drunk at Bonnie's Bar. Or maybe they really got drunk but kept chatting on-line. Either way, another ritual emerged: Jell-O diving. There was, of course, no Jell-O, nor any diving. But when they were inebriated, it didn't matter. While in Bonnie's Bar, people would declare they were about to dive into a vat of Jell-O, which they performed by placing a series of colons together: :::::::

The more colons, the bigger the Jell-O dive. The origins remain shrouded in mystery, but Jell-O diving began to take on a broader meaning, akin to an on-line christening.

Sometimes, as happens in a saloon, people had too much to drink. And sometimes, things got too real at Bonnie's Bar. Bonnie wasn't just a name on a computer screen—she was a real person, a petite, bubbly subscriber who hosted the on-line saloon and whose first name really was Bonnie. One of her patrons decided to get to know her better. Somehow, he found her postal address and mailed her photographs of himself masturbating.

Maybe it was inevitable. Leave people to their own devices—cloaked in virtual anonymity—and they gravitate toward sex. Blame it on people's inner demon, said Bob Cross, the company's turnaround specialist in the mid '80s. "It happened almost viscerally, almost naturally," he said. The joke was, company managers were scrambling to figure out how to popularize the on-line service when its subscribers were doing it all by themselves.

"The most popular [features of the service] were far and away the sexual chat rooms," Cross said. "The reality of what was happening was, if you just let these folks plug into each other, middle-aged people start talking dirty to each other."

Every night in the late '80s, a subscriber created a chat room called, aptly enough, Sex. It wasn't an official Quantum gathering place, and it didn't always revolve around the topic of sex, but subscribers flooded in anyway. Apparently, the company caught on to the trend. Sex sells on-line services, too.

"Get confidential, expert answers to your questions about human sexuality in the Human Sexuality area in the Learning Center," offered the October 1988 issue of *Q-Link Update*, the company's monthly magazine.

For all the talk about vision, it boiled down to this: Sex didn't fit the company's family-oriented identity, but it was a key driver of the company's growth, even its very existence, throughout the 1980s and early '90s.

"Tacitly, the company understood this was not exactly hurting our business," said Wilkinson, who got a close look at the chat rooms, producing content for its "People Connection" area. "There was a big on-line libido."

So be it, decreed the powers that be at Quantum's tiny corporate headquarters. Give the consumers what they want. Company executives— hardly prudish—chalked it up to harmless naughty talk. It wasn't as if they were trying to evolve the on-line service into a porn site. It was more of a matter of letting freedom reign.

And boy, did it.

Sex chat rooms mushroomed for all manner of proclivities: transsexuals, transvestites. Anything went. For the really salacious stuff, people created private rooms that only they knew about. Thus came into being a thing called cybersex, where people would describe in writing what they imagined they were doing to each other.

"A lot of people learned to type with one hand," quipped Pytlovany, the software engineer.

For Quantum officials, this became not only big business, but tricky business. With sex spreading throughout the on-line service—a *family* on-line service—how could they control it? More to the point, how could they profit from it? A debate arose among some officials in the early '90s. Should they divide the on-line service into two parts—one for G-rated material and the other for R stuff? Surely they could charge extra for the adult version.

Or could they?

The danger was that the company could be tarnished. Officials got nervous about the implications. They imagined a potential headline: "Kiddie

Porn Transmitted!" They got nervous about the financial fallout. In the end, they dropped the idea. Let human nature take its course, went the decree, and move out of the way.

"We recognized chat and individual community was so important to keep people on," Pytlovany said. "I joked about it. You get somebody on-line, we've got them by the balls. Plain and simple, they'll be back tomorrow."

This is the Steve Case you don't know: jittery, nervous, his voice quaking, his hands shaking.

As executive vice president in the late 1980s, he was emerging as the company leader, but he still wasn't comfortable with himself. He would be standing in the auditorium during meetings before a small gathering of the Quantum troops. Even when he knew the material dead cold, when he had gone through the accompanying slides over and over again, when he was delivering a speech he had given countless times before—even then, his insecurities would betray him. People could see it. They could hear it. There would be a lilt in his throat, a slight quaver.

And that was only the beginning of the problem. He wasn't just nervous, he was plain bad. As a speaker, he was monumentally boring. He inspired only a soporific response from a dazed audience.

Steve Case was a painfully shy young man who dreaded the spotlight. Case the child preferred to be ensconced in his "office" upstairs at home; Case the adult still felt more comfortable in the back room. Little had changed—including the boyish mien. Only now, instead of cataloging the sale of seeds and greeting cards, he was an introvert who preferred the silent solace of a computer terminal, cataloging the rise of a tiny on-line business.

Hence, the nicknames: The Wall. The Sponge. The Terminator.

Like a computer, he processed a lot of information, but not a lot came back out. "He would listen very carefully," said Julia Wilkinson. Once she told Case that a publication that posted its articles on Quantum was angry because it had not been allowed to use the word "fuck" in an on-line article, while another publication got away with the word. This wasn't just a matter of foul language. It was an inconsistent policy. Was Quantum going to allow its content providers to say "fuck" or not?

"I was getting a lot of flak," Wilkinson said. "I explained it to Case. He took it all in. He listened. But he didn't offer a verdict. He said, 'Oh, really, that's interesting. Let me think about it.'" (The verdict: The f-word, Wilkinson recalled, could be used in the appropriate context.)

Case always played it close to the vest. One day in 1986, Mark Walsh, an executive with another on-line firm, was looking to do a deal with Quantum. At the end of the meeting, Walsh noticed a picture of a college campus hanging on Case's office wall. He made a stab at small talk.

"Is that UVA?" Walsh asked, referring to the prestigious University of Virginia in Charlottesville.

"No," Case responded.

There was nothing else forthcoming from Quantum's marketing executive. The campus—which happened to be Williams College, Case's alma mater—remained unidentified. "He only said exactly what you needed to know," Walsh said.

A couple of years later, in 1988, their paths crossed again at an industry conference at a Holiday Inn in upstate New York. Down a two-lane country road, a local country fair beckoned. During a break in the action, the two men hopped on an amusement ride. It was one of the contraptions where customers sit in a little pod that spins 360 degrees at an alarmingly high speed at the end of a swinging metal arm. A faint Case stumbled out and wordlessly marched off into the distant woods. When he returned, Walsh remarked, "You look pale." Case, in a perfect monotone, retorted, "Yeah. I just vomited."

"He was the most calm vomiter I had ever seen," said Walsh. (Case was apparently impressed with Walsh as well, recruiting him as an AOL executive in 1995.)

Case never let his hair down, not even during the company's "beer bashes," when employees let loose with a few cold ones in the backyard of the building on Friday afternoons. Case socialized tepidly, but more to demonstrate that he was approachable.

"I think he was aware that he was a figure of responsibility," Wilkinson said. "He was not wild and crazy."

Case's idea of letting his guard down was dressing up in green medical scrubs during a company Halloween party in 1991. He was supposed to look like William Kennedy Smith. The strange thing was *not* that he did look a lot like the member of the Kennedy clan, but that he chose to dress up as a person who at the time was accused of rape.

Usually, however, Case avoided such political faux pas, dressing instead in a Hawaiian shirt and casual slacks, retreating to the comfort and quietude of his computer monitor. There, Steve Case was like an intense pianist madly playing his keyboard late into the night, a study in determination.

"Sparks came off of his Macintosh computer," said Cathy Anderson, the former company vice president. "He just sat there working at the computer all the time, drafting documents, memos, letters."

His giant desk, in an office overlooking an asphalt parking lot, was an antiseptic space devoid of personality. This was work, not home, and it showed on his desk, which was efficiently arrayed with neat stacks upon neat stacks. There were magazines, such as *Forbes* and *Fortune,* and computer periodicals, but most of all there were legal pads. *The legal pads.* These were his personal prioritizing system. It was a necessity. For a couple of years, Case was his own secretary, a job he filled quite ably, filling legal pads with innumerable lists of things to do, things he needed to do, things that other people needed to do.

"If you asked him a question, he could find it in the stack," said Randy Dean, the content programmer, who also worked in the company's business development and advertising departments. "He could pull out a piece of paper without looking for two minutes."

It wasn't just that he was a stickler for detail. Steve Case loved his job. In the wee hours of the night, company engineers would tap into the on-line service by dialing up from their home telephone into the mainframe computer at the office. It was a way to check for problems, like unruly subscribers, whom the engineers could kick off the system if necessary. Special software tools allowed them to identify and monitor who was using the service. It could be one, or even two o'clock in the morning, and among those spotted lurking throughout the service was Steve Case. His handle: Stevec.

Steve Case wasn't just an employee, he was also a customer. Wilkinson learned as much in the late '80s when she was hosting an on-line chat with Timothy Leary, the psychedelic guru from the '60s who had a penchant for technology as well. During his chat, Leary talked about being a "performing philosopher," how he still took drugs, or "aspirin on occasion," and how he was considering the options to forestall death.

"I may have my head frozen or my brain preserved in a laboratory," Leary said during the chat.

All the while, paying attention out of view, was Stevec. "He was just sitting in the audience," said Wilkinson. "I knew because I had the tools to see he was in the audience. You got the sense he was on the service, using the service, that he was not just a figurehead."

Case, the customer, understood the product. Case, the marketing refugee from Procter & Gamble, knew how to package it. Forget about the technology—that was just a backstage rehearsal before the real performance. Everything about the product had to be simple and straightforward, a fact that was often overlooked by the techies, who had a way of getting caught up in the digital widgets and forgetting, in the process, about the customer.

Sometimes, Case's suggestions were so simple it was hard to believe others hadn't thought of them first. Problem: Customers bought disks containing the Quantum on-line software that included local telephone numbers to access the service. But often the numbers were out of use by the time they tried them. Solution: Case suggested that the disk include a toll-free 800 number, which would connect into the system and find the most up-to-date local phone numbers.

"He understood marketing. If you lose them there, you've lost them forever," said Pytlovany, the software developer. "He used to say he wouldn't let anything go out the door unless it was easy enough for his mother to use."

It was common sense. Steve Case wasn't brilliant in the way of Bill von Meister, who could envision whole new industries being born out of thin air (and someone else's money). Steve Case wasn't a swashbuckling entrepreneur like Jim Kimsey. Steve Case was something less glamorous: He was smart, very smart, but most of all, he rose in prominence at the company because, beneath his quiet exterior, he had a plodding, methodical, relentless way about him. He worked hard.

"We followed his sheer brute-force work ethic," said Dean, the co-founder of the *Quirk,* the company's underground newsletter.

There was something else about Steve Case, the way that energy inexplicably flowed in his direction at company meetings. Maybe it was the unintended consequence of his station: He was a young executive on the rise. And yet it was strange that he drew so much attention, with his tendency not to say anything. He would withhold from proffering an opinion until a well-placed moment in a company meeting—and then he would weigh in.

But when that moment came, it came with full force. There was no uncertainty about where Case stood—even when his view was in the minority. Then he spoke with even more conviction, which was the case in the late 1980s during an especially contentious staff meeting.

Executives were debating the strategic direction of the company. Anderson, the vice president, doesn't remember the precise issue at hand, but she remembers that Case kept quiet until the group came up with a consensus: They wanted to take the safe road. Case pounced. He wouldn't hear of it. Over the ensuing days, he argued his case against the group until, finally, he got up from the conference table and, in a rare emotional outburst, threatened to walk out.

You all don't know what you're doing! he barked. *If you want to do it your way, go ahead and do it your way, and I'll go off and do it on my own. I'll start my own company.*

Jaws dropped. There were several moments of silence. It was a starkly uncharacteristic moment, but Steve Case had gotten the attention of his colleagues—and ultimately, he got them to see it his way.

"He was absolutely convinced which way true north was," Anderson said.

The first thing that she thought of was the day in traffic on San Francisco asphalt when Case had made that off-the-cuff remark: *Well, you can become the most successful person in Hawaii, and you're still just on an island.*

Kimsey was a playboy. He was also a businessman with many other interests outside of Quantum, including his string of bars, restaurants, and real estate ventures, and that didn't sit well with his charge.

"Steve would say I was always a part-time executive, and he was not 100 percent wrong," Kimsey said. "I had outside shit. A lot of the time, he resented it."

Case would shoot him a little frown, what Kimsey liked to call an "Elmer Fudd" look, and mumble something under his breath.

"Look," Kimsey would shoot back, "that's the way it is, kid."

Kimsey delegated; Case worked. They made a perfect team. It was clear to everyone that Kimsey was grooming Case to succeed him one day, that Case was already running the show, if not in title, by the late 1980s. Even though he was only executive vice president, Case began to carry himself as if he were already in charge. Maybe it seemed that way because he was reserved, focused. Or maybe it looked that way because Kimsey increasingly trotted him out to speak at company events. Or maybe it was because Kimsey wasn't always around, while Case was there every day, working relentlessly.

"At the end of the day," said Randy Dean, "Steve was the company, and Jim knew that."

Kimsey doesn't remember much of the details, but on a United Airlines flight to San Francisco, he told Case he wanted him to be his successor. "Case would remember the exact date and time," Kimsey said. "He was like a little kid. The next day he was like: 'Is it time yet, Dad? Is it time?'"

Actually, Case's memory is a bit fuzzy, too. But all the same, he remembers the gist. "We were on a plane together, probably '87 or '88, and he turned to me and said, 'Someday you should run this company,' and I really was struck by that, that even though I was still in my twenties, he really believed in me and believed in this medium and thought that in the not-too-distant future I should take this ball and run with it," Case said. "And I've always been grateful for that decision and gratified that he really trusted in my judgment and was willing to bet on me."

Case didn't hide his ambitions for himself or the company. Both, he was convinced, were destined for greatness.

"He kept painting a picture of what was to be, how we were these pioneers, that we were going to win the game and basically show everybody else up," said Anderson, the vice president. "There was a great sense we were out there conquering the world and we were golden."

The rising young executive didn't endear himself to the Quantum board, some of whose members interpreted his aloofness not as shyness but as haughtiness. Steve Case had acquired another nickname. In addition to "Lower Case" and "The Wall" and "The Sponge," he was becoming known, to some board members, as "the arrogant little shit."

Things came to a head in 1988 when a business deal with Apple collapsed. Apple had been difficult to deal with from the beginning, demanding that Quantum adhere strictly to Apple's look and feel in the design of its on-line service, AppleLink. What's more, Apple had restricted the marketing of its on-line service, and then it wasn't happy with the lackluster response from consumers. Now, Apple was threatening to withhold millions of dollars that it owed Quantum.

Somebody had to take the blame. The Quantum board turned to Case, who had made the Apple arrangements in the first place. "The board tried to fire Steve," Kimsey said.

Kimsey, however, wasn't prepared to get rid of his ambitious understudy. Once again, he tried to appeal to logic in his own inimitable way. Just as he had told creditors that they risked getting nothing if they pushed him too hard, now Kimsey told the board it risked losing the investment it had already plowed into the tutelage of Steve Case, executive-in-training.

"We've put $5 million in this guy's education," Kimsey told the board, referring to the amount that the company had poured into the Apple deal. "Now you want to fire him? That's kind of dumb."

Thus, Case's job was saved. In 1989, he put a lasting imprint on the company. With the demise of the AppleLink deal, Case decided it was time to hold a company contest to give a name to Quantum's own on-line service. In the end, he proclaimed himself the winner:

America Online.

There was some debate about the abbreviation: AO or AOL. AO, some feared, might remind people of BO, body odor. Besides, Case aspired to elevate his company to a level comparable to the likes of CBS and AT&T Corp. They went by three letters. So, too, he decreed would Case's on-line service: AOL. (The parent company, for the time being, continued to be called Quantum.)

There was nothing scientific about how he came up with America Online. It did, however, seem to borrow from the concept laid out by California Online, a service he had considered doing for a West Coast telecommunications company. America Online, however, had a broader landscape. And it fit his marketer's sense of what was right and solid: It was simple, and it had mass appeal, the grand sweep of a nation within Steve Case's on-line grasp.

With Case's ascension came an evolving image. The Hawaiian shirts made fewer appearances. For years, colleagues had ribbed Case about looking like a model out of the L. L. Bean catalog, wearing its preppy khaki pants, button-down shirts, belts, and socks. He even carried an L. L. Bean canvas bag with his embroidered initials, SMC. But suddenly he started showing up in suits. People noticed. So did the *Quirk,* which in 1990 offered to buy him a "gift certificate to Zogg's Surf Shop" as a way to bring back the old casual look.

"C'mon Steve," the *Quirk* implored, "your clothing selection is getting downright respectable!"

It didn't take long for Case to get comfortable in his new clothes. Where before he didn't dare challenge Jim Kimsey, now Case felt emboldened to speak his mind about issues of corporate strategy. "There were the normal tensions, with the one knowing who the boss is, but at the same time wanting his point of view listened to," said board member General Alexander M. Haig, the former Nixon chief of staff and Reagan secretary of state.

Haig, seasoned in the ways of power, counseled Kimsey on the young whippersnapper. His advice: Smile. "Here's a guy who's an asset worth having," Haig told Kimsey. "You're the boss and you're going to remain the boss."

Not for long.

In 1991, Case was promoted to president, and then chief executive officer, while Kimsey remained chairman. That October, Quantum finally fell by the wayside, giving in to the growing brand name of its on-line service, which had garnered just under 150,000 subscribers. The company, boasting about $20 million in revenue, was officially rechristened America Online Inc.

With the new name came a new goal: to take the company public. An offering of stock, however, required a different kind of face-lift, one that Case didn't find to his liking. The AOL board decided that Case, baby-faced at the age of thirty-three, lacked the gravitas needed to sell the company to the public. Kimsey, the daring army veteran with the dash of gray, seemed to fit the part of CEO better. Thus, Case lost the title. He grimaced when Kimsey delivered the bad news. But he swallowed it and accepted the apparent slight without a fight. If anything, Case was capable of sublimating. Besides, he was all too aware that there was a lot of money at stake—not just for the company at large but also for executives such as himself and Kimsey, who stood to make millions from shares held in a publicly held company.

The CEO flap turned out to be a hiccup.

When AOL went public on the Nasdaq Stock Market on March 19, 1992, the company raised $66 million. Suddenly, Case was worth more than $2 million on paper. Shortly thereafter, he was given back the title of CEO and appointed to the board of directors.

At the age of thirty-four, Case was a rich man. Even better, perhaps, when he spoke in public, the hand didn't shake anymore, and the quaver in his voice had mysteriously vanished.

By 1993, America Online was still like a little jalopy. The engine, so to speak, didn't have a lot of oomph.

When Matt Korn, the new whiz kid from IBM's famed research lab, arrived at AOL that March, he checked under the proverbial hood and didn't like what he saw. The on-line service tottered along, sputtering at a slow pace.

He noticed that about twenty-three hundred people used the little on-line service one evening. The following night, the same thing: twenty-three hundred people used the service simultaneously. The next day, no change. Korn didn't need to be a computer scientist (which he was) to deduce that there was a problem. The system was maxing out. AOL couldn't sustain any more users at once. "We were bottle-necked," he said.

The jalopy was overheating.

Korn quickly devised a solution: expand the telephone network. Get more computers. Open up some space. Let the data through. The strategy worked. Suddenly, the numbers started crawling up. Like magic, more people started jumping on-line at the same time.

That is, until one late evening in April.

Korn, as he often did, was hanging around the office as the clock neared midnight. He wasn't in a rush to get home. His family hadn't yet moved down to Virginia from New York. Besides, he was still trying to get a feel for the pulse of the place. So he'd walk down the brightly lit hallways, pass by the humming customer call center, and putter at his desk, watching the number of simultaneous users click up and up . . . except that on this one week, the numbers weren't going up.

Curious.

Korn didn't know it then, but it was the sweeps period when the television networks lured viewers with new, tantalizing episodes of gotta-see TV. Korn didn't know people were turning from their computer tube to the boob tube. He thought AOL needed a little goosing, a little good-natured provocation. He picked up his phone, dialed the new marketing executive, Jan Brandt, and left her a message. *Hey, we met a couple of weeks ago,* he said. *I'm the guy who runs operations. The system looks pretty boring tonight. If I wanted boring, I would have stayed at IBM.*

As they say, beware, you may get what you want.

Brandt was no techie, but she knew marketing. Before joining AOL in April 1993, she had been head of advertising at Newfield Publications, where she hit a whopper in direct marketing. She came up with an idea to promote a children's book called *Corduroy* by sending a free copy to prospective customers. If people could see the book—its wonderful photos and illustrations—they'd love it. And she was right. The response to the freebie went through the roof.

Why not try the same thing with AOL?

In some cases, the on-line software was included in the box when people bought computers. But the industry practice was for on-line companies to sell the on-line software separately. But buying the software was just the first step in a long chain of tasks required of consumers to get the service. After they went to the store to buy the disk, they had to insert it in their computer. Then they had to order the monthly subscription. And that's where the real money was—the subscription, not the sale of the little disk. The disk just got customers where AOL wanted them. It was a means to an end. The real game was getting people to pay for the monthly on-line service, the *renewal*. Gillette had perfected the concept: give away the razor but make them pay for the blades, coming back for more. Brandt immediately grasped this. She had the fresh perspective of someone who wasn't steeped in the business. "I was not infatuated with the technology," she said. "I was infatuated with what the stuff did." People didn't know what an on-line service was, let alone who AOL was. "There was no frame of reference," she said. Why not get the product in their hands, then let them try it? Just like the promotional children's book, Brandt thought. *They'll love it.*

Steve Case wasn't convinced. When Brandt called him at home from her car cell phone, he asked how much the direct-marketing test would cost. She didn't know. Maybe $250,000.

You can go ahead and try it, he said, *but it's not going to work.*

For a small company, this was an expensive experiment. During the first mailing, the cost of the disk alone was $1.09, not including postage. A 1 percent response would've been good. But Brandt blew right by that. Nearly 10 percent tried the service.

"The real secret is, it doesn't matter how much the promotion costs," she said. "What matters is how much it costs to get a new subscriber."

Success bred obsession. From direct mail, Brandt moved on to mass-market tests. She put the free AOL disk in what were then considered the unlikeliest places—in magazines, in Blockbuster video stores, even in packaged flash-frozen Omaha Steaks. The disks, like astronauts in training, were treated to all manner of testing to ensure their rigor. For the Omaha Steaks, that meant flash freezing the AOL disks to make sure they still worked after they were defrosted and inserted into a computer. (They did.) Frozen AOL disks were also inserted into PCs to see if they worked. (They did.) And just in case people forgot their free AOL disk in their cars, while they went on the joyrides at Six Flags, site of more free AOL disks, the disks were also heated above 100 degrees Fahrenheit to see if they still worked. (They did.)

The AOL disk was practically indestructible. Brandt used to kid, "These disks have a half-life of like 10,000 years." The free disks were also practically everywhere. Just how many disks did the company give away? "Somewhere between one and seven gazillion," Brandt said.

It was actually closer to the *billions.*

Regardless, the ubiquitous disks did their duty. AOL was becoming a household name. In December 1992, AOL had three hundred thousand subscribers; a year later, it rocketed to half a million.

By May 11, 1993, Bill Gates had taken notice.

AOL's rapid growth was making waves that were reverberating all the way out to Redmond, Washington, the suburban Seattle stronghold of the great Microsoft empire.

The CEO of the software giant had already vanquished much of the computer world, turning Windows, his flagship product, into the dominant operating system—the brains—of the world's personal computers. Now Gates was riveting his gazé on the next emerging technological frontier: the on-line world.

He wanted to get into AOL's business. Or buy it.

A meeting among Gates, Case, and Kimsey was set up that spring afternoon on the Microsoft campus, a sprawling spread with quiet pathways and landscaped foliage, much like a college cloister, the paragon for a new age in technology. Nothing like the humble AOL office.

Beforehand, Russell Siegelman, Gates's point man for on-line services, took his boss aside and warned him to tread lightly with the visitors from the little company in Virginia.

Be cordial, Siegelman suggested. *These guys are going to feel threatened by us.* And yet, Siegelman had his own reservations. He knew it wasn't going to be easy to deal with them. In conversations with AOL officials before the meeting, the message was pretty clear. AOL was willing to do business with Microsoft, but it wasn't looking for a suitor. Gates was hoping to persuade them otherwise. "We wanted to get to know them," Siegelman said, "but our preferred approach would have been to buy the company."

Things started badly almost from the moment Siegelman ushered Case, Kimsey, and their emissaries into a cramped, windowless conference room, near the CEO's suite, in building eight on the Microsoft campus. Gates, the embodiment of the tech age, the Rockefeller of his era, one of the wealthiest individuals in the world, presented himself in his uniquely haphazard way: shaggy-haired, bespectacled, adorned in nothing more formal than a T-shirt and casual slacks.

AOL went the other direction: all suits. The contingent even brought along their investment bankers, which Gates and Siegelman found curious. This was supposed to be an exploratory meeting—or was it?

We're not up for sale, Case blurted out. What's more, if Gates persisted and tried to buy AOL, Case told him he would resist strongly, Siegelman recalled. As a matter of fact, Case went on, AOL had already put in place a poison pill—a corporate measure—to prevent such a hostile takeover. Case had reason to be paranoid. He had just come from a meeting with Paul Allen, Gates's buddy and Microsoft co-founder, who was actively buying up AOL stock with the intention of gobbling it up and making it part of his constellation of companies.

Was Gates in cahoots with Allen?

It was an awkward moment. Siegelman hadn't expected this. Nor had Gates. This was supposed to be a nice get-to-know-you meeting.

Gates brushed it off. Sitting at the head of the wooden table, the Microsoft CEO launched into a philosophical discussion of his options. He talked about buying a percentage of AOL. He talked about getting into the on-line business himself. But never did he threaten to "bury" AOL, as others have suggested about the now-famous meeting of the tech titans.

Siegelman said Gates never uttered a threat. "He was unpretentious, he never threatened," said Kimsey. "He's not like that. He's a nerd, but he's not like that. We talked about an acquisition, we talked about a partnership, but he never threatened."

After the meeting ended and the AOL crew had gone, Gates and Siegelman lingered in the conference room.

We obviously can't buy that company, Siegelman said. *We could follow up with AOL, but it's probably a waste of time.*

Gates instantly agreed: *It's a total waste of time. Don't bother.*

AOL, however, didn't think Microsoft was a waste of time. Kimsey was already doing the calculations of a Microsoft takeover of AOL. "If he makes a tender offer, hmmm," Kimsey said. "As an endgame for me, it was not bad."

Kimsey called his consigliere, Ken Novack, then AOL's outside attorney. *What do we do now?* The path was clear to Novack. Hold a special board meeting in case an offer comes in from Gates.

Much has been made in the media of this meeting, too. Over the years, it has been presented as a classic confrontation between Kimsey, who wanted to do a deal with Gates, versus Case, who stood his ground against the Microsoft monolith. Chairman versus the CEO. Father against son.

Not exactly.

"It was Steve Case who began this approach and presented this possibility [of selling to Microsoft] to the board," said board member Alexander Haig.

When the directors met in June 1993, they recognized that AOL's prospects still were uncertain and it would be in the shareholders' interest to hear what, if anything, Gates had to say. "Steve wasn't against that," Haig said. "I don't know where that came from." Haig also denied issuing a warning that AOL could get "vaporized" by Microsoft, as some have quoted him as saying at that private meeting.

This much was certain: A Microsoft takeover was only theoretical. Gates had never uttered an offer. Siegelman mentioned no number. But AOL brought in its investment bankers to discuss the possibilities. At about $30 a share, AOL was worth about $175 million, its market capitalization. Microsoft might go as high as $40 a share, which would value the deal at about $230 million. The bankers thought that was still too cheap. But if they could stretch Microsoft to about $60 a share, making the deal worth about $350 million, then it might be worth talking turkey.

Don't take an offer under $60, the bankers advised.

Kimsey, who had been looking for a way out of this little company for practically a decade, was game. Besides, he recognized his fiduciary duty to his shareholders, and if his bankers said it was a good deal, then he had an obligation to pursue it.

"If the offer is over $60, should we take it? I would've said yes," he said. "If you don't take it, people [investors] would have sued the shit out of us."

Caufield, his West Point buddy, agreed. So did Kimsey's other military pal, Al Haig. *Get out now, while the going was good.* Paul Allen's unwanted advances had spurred interest in AOL, and the little company was gaining subscribers at an increasing clip, but it was still in third place in the on-line market, behind better-funded CompuServe and Prodigy.

Who knew where AOL would end up, or whether it would even survive?

Case was noncommittal during the board discussion. It seemed that he didn't want to upstage Kimsey. The chairman still ran the show. Kimsey controlled the board with many personal allies. It was clear, however, that the board was not of one mind now. So Kimsey called for a vote, the first ever taken by the company: Should AOL talk to Microsoft, or not?

Although he himself didn't vote, Kimsey's feelings were known: He would vote to open negotiations with Microsoft. Around the table he went, seeking a consensus. But there wasn't one. When the time came to commit himself, Case voted against talks. So did others. The board was deadlocked five to five, assuming Kimsey's vote. There was only one voice remaining to be heard: that of Jim Andress, Kimsey's classmate at West Point and chief executive of Information Resources, Inc., a market research firm.

He was the swing vote. It seemed like a sure bet.

But then Andress voted his conscience: no. He did not want to open talks with Microsoft. Why cave in? AOL was just gaining momentum. Maybe it could make a go of it. Kimsey stared, bewildered. "Okay," he finally uttered, "that's it." This would go no further.

After the meeting, Kimsey instructed Case to call Gates and tell him not to pursue AOL. The little on-line firm would regard a Microsoft bid as hostile. Case left a phone message, but he never heard back from Gates.

Despite the drama attributed to that AOL–Microsoft meeting, it was a moot point. While it's true that Kimsey would have voted to talk to Microsoft, and while it's true that Case voted with the majority against it, Case did not make a grand stand against Kimsey, or against Microsoft.

"That we staved off Gates, that's total bullshit," Kimsey said.

AOL didn't know it yet, but Gates had other things in mind. Instead of buying AOL, he was about to start his own on-line service from scratch.

It is a peaceful moment. Butterflies are fluttering. Bambi is munching on grass in a bucolic setting. Then *thump . . . thump . . . thump . . .* Suddenly the giant foot of Godzilla comes crashing down on Bambi.

The end.

The video stopped. *This,* said the man on stage, *is what will happen to us if we're not prepared.* AOL was Bambi, the little on-line upstart minding its own business; Microsoft was the big, bad Godzilla out to stomp on all the creatures in the meadow.

Now, the man was pacing, sweating, it was hot, the stage lights were glaring in his eyes, it felt like there was no oxygen in the Sheraton Hotel ballroom filled with several hundred AOL employees on that day in November 1994. But no matter. Ted Leonsis, a blazing, corpulent firebrand with jet black hair, was on a roll. "I was a minister," he said. "This was a doomsday scenario: fear, thunder and lightning, fire and brimstone."

Here, Leonsis continued, *is the worst-case scenario. Microsoft shuts AOL out of computer desktops, choking off AOL's distribution. Microsoft blocks AOL from getting deals with content providers. We're hollowed out. I don't know about you, but that's not the road I want to go down.*

Another image flashed on the screen, a quote from *Wired* magazine, which pronounced the demise of AOL: "They are a dinosaur, they are obsolete." Leonsis was in a lather as he barked, "We're not the dinosaur! It's Microsoft that's the real dinosaur!"

And on cue, a rickety cutout of a dinosaur rolled out on stage. ("It was a bad, wooden Home Depot version, painted and made by three or four guys drinking too many beers," Leonsis said.)

But then, it was magic. The lights were flashing, the speakers were blaring U2's "Pride (In the Name of Love)," and people were cheering wildly. *Now's the time,* Leonsis pressed on. *Someday your children will ask you what you did in the war. How we stopped Bill Gates from taking over interactive services.*

Then he urged people to come on stage and sign the dinosaur, to pledge their alliance in this holy war against Bill Gates and his "death star," AOL's nickname for Microsoft. People rushed the stage, crying and hugging and embracing Leonsis.

Mission accomplished.

Ted Leonsis was in his element, a self-described "whirling dervish" who would have made Bill von Meister, the original whirling dervish, proud. Once again, the past circled back to the present. Steve Case owed another debt of gratitude to his big brother, Dan, who had lured Leonsis to run the on-line service, AOL's proprietary service, while Case tackled the emerging World Wide Web, that wilderness open to just about anyone with a phone line and a computer.

Dan had been serving as the investment banker for Leonsis, who was preparing to sell Redgate Communications, his little software and marketing company, in Vero Beach, Florida, to Dow Jones & Co. But Dan counseled Leonsis against the deal. He had a better idea.

Talk to my brother, Steve.

It wasn't just that Redgate Communications had done some neat things, becoming an early industry leader in on-line shopping, a nascent market. Dan knew a bright and energetic leader when he saw one: Leonsis was a live wire. He would be the perfect alter ego to the staid, younger Case.

The AOL chief had his own reasons for hooking up with Leonsis. In late 1994, the company was beginning to feel its oats. That August, it had reached the magical one million subscriber mark. Its stock was humming along, trading at about $80, a price-earnings ratio of 107, making it one of the most expensive tech stocks around. And the company's market value had reached over $500 million. Case, flush with the wampum of a pricey stock, was about to begin a buying binge to make AOL bigger and stronger to take on the big boys at Microsoft. Redgate would be just the beginning.

The next thing Leonsis knew, he was having breakfast with Case at the Le Meridien Hotel in Boston, and before Leonsis had taken a bite out of his fruit salad, Case, never one to dilly-dally with small talk, came out with it: "Why don't we merge our companies?"

Leonsis, feeling like a rushed lover on a first date, quipped, "Can we kiss first? Can I meet your mom and dad?"

Case retorted, "Life's too short to drink bad wine."

"Where Steve is cool, I'm hot and gregarious," Leonsis said.

Where Case was the product of a privileged upbringing, Leonsis was the product of the pull-'em-up-by-your-bootstraps American dream. Raised in Brooklyn, he was the son of a secretary and a waiter who went to work at 4:30 A.M. and came back twelve hours later with his apron packed with small tips. Young Leonsis's job was to stack the nickels and quarters in preparation for his father's bank deposit. Leonsis learned the value of hard work early on, shelving cans in a grocery, operating a forklift, and sweeping the floors and bathrooms of a mill in Lowell, Massachusetts, where his family moved when he was a teenager. As much as he loved his parents, and he did so dearly, Ted Leonsis was determined not to follow in their footsteps.

He didn't. Since 1983, when Leonsis was on a plane with mechanical problems and thought it was all over, he has kept a list of 101 things to do before he dies, called simply, "The List." He's crossed off a bunch of them. He has a way of getting what he wants. That, over the years, has included becoming a media mogul, buying the Washington Capitals, and bringing Michael Jordan to the Washington Wizards, in which he owns a minority stake.

Leonsis turned out to be exactly what AOL needed to get to the next level. Named president of AOL services company, Leonsis immediately grasped the future, introducing new concepts: that AOL was not just an on-line service but also a mass consumer brand. That AOL was a *media* company competing against *Seinfield,* the popular TV program, not against CompuServe. And that strangely enough, AOL needed Bill Gates and Microsoft.

"While people were terrified," he said, "I viewed it as an unbelievable opportunity because now I had a boogeyman."

Not long after his rousing AOL revival meeting, Leonsis bumped into the boogeyman himself in a hallway at a conference for industry heavy-weights in Scottsdale. Leonsis decided to take a different approach: He offered Gates the olive branch.

"Bill, there's all this stuff going on," he said. "You're going to fight us, we're going to fight you. Maybe we can figure out a way to work together."

Gates said he had tried, but AOL didn't want to be acquired. Microsoft was going to get into the on-line business on its own soon. (It was to be called the Microsoft Network, or MSN. D-day: August 1995). Like AOL, Microsoft would design on-line software, which it would offer free to con-sumers on a disk, or preinstalled when they bought a new personal com-puter using Microsoft's Windows operating system. Getting on-line wasn't that complicated anymore. When the on-line software was preinstalled, all the customer had to do was click on an icon from the computer screen, call up the software, and dial up to the service through a telephone line. The alternative, the software disk, was just as easy. Insert it in a computer, download the software, and the computer dialed up the service. Either way, it was really a matter of technology, Gates explained, and if Microsoft knew anything, it knew about the X's and O's of technology.

"If you think this is about X's and O's," Leonsis poked back, "this is going to be your Vietnam."

He was only kidding—or so he thought.

By the time Leonsis returned to AOL headquarters, word had gotten around about his little tête-à-tête with Gates. The building was strewn with signs and T-shirts declaring the battle as "Microsoft's Vietnam."

The gauntlet had been thrown down.

Leonsis groaned inwardly (did he really want to pull the giant's tail?), but it was too late, and he went with it, creating a Microsoft war room at AOL headquarters. Before long, the room was filled with Microsoft ads, computer screen shots, and charts of what Microsoft's on-line service would offer versus AOL's, as well as comments by analysts and the press crowing about how Microsoft was going to kill AOL. Meanwhile, people were assigned to spy on Microsoft, follow its every product release, attend conferences where Microsoft people spoke. They would report back to Leonsis, and an e-mail—subject line: "Microsoft clips"—was distributed regularly.

Everyone got caught up in the fervor, especially Jan Brandt, the marketing guru, who went out, bought a Jaguar, and slapped on the following license plate: FG8S.

Fuck Gates.

Brandt promoted the first person who noticed the license plate in the AOL parking lot.

"For me, it was religious war," she said. "We were this upstart, sort of an alternative kind of company."

There was a shared sense that AOL was changing world culture, that it was bringing people together, connecting them at a time when families live apart, dwelling in big anonymous apartment buildings where there is a dissipating sense of neighborhood, of belonging.

Brandt had come to understand this on a personal level almost immediately. When she took the AOL job, she moved from Connecticut to an apartment, sight unseen, in a complex close to AOL. It was a long drive, especially for her Tibetan terrier, Spenser, who got sick. By the time she arrived in her new place—frazzled, alone, and disoriented—all she had the energy to do was to plunk down her few suitcases, plug in her computer, and go on-line. A familiar voice, that of the AOL service, chirped out, "Welcome." Brandt settled in with a growing sense of calm as she moved into an on-line chat room. There, she began to talk to some of her friends as well as people whom she had never met. It was okay. It was home. "It was," Brandt said, "like carrying a friend in a box."

Or like Alice entering Wonderland, where people logged on and fell down a chute into a comforting world of community. This, Brandt and Leonsis felt, was what AOL was fighting for and why it was fighting against Microsoft.

"It was a seminal moment in the company's history," Leonsis said. "We were of one purpose. We were all running as fast as we could in one direction."

Microsoft was not so nimble.

In 1995, the lumbering behemoth was fighting in a broader theater against Netscape Communications, and Bill Gates considered it a graver threat than AOL. Netscape had developed revolutionary software called a browser that suddenly turned the text-only Internet into a colorful, graphical World Wide Web, where people could surf from place to place with the click of the mouse. Gates immediately recognized the danger: The Netscape browser could become akin to a computer operating system, rivaling his own Windows platform. Something had to be done.

That something turned out to be a key strategic decision: Microsoft devoted most of its vast resources to the browser wars, leaving it understaffed in its fight against AOL in the on-line wars. Siegelman, charged with launching MSN, Microsoft's on-line service, understood the implications. "I thought we should be 100 percent focused on AOL," he said, "but I was in a very small minority because the company was riveted on Netscape."

Siegelman pleaded for more resources as other parts of Microsoft continued to drain his team of software engineers to develop a browser to rival Netscape's. Gates was sympathetic but unmoved by Siegelman. *I agree with you,* he said, *I am hindering you, but we have to do that for a greater cause.*

The cause was so great that Gates gave the green light on a huge deal that he knew would take away the biggest advantage of his own fledgling on-line service: He gave AOL a coveted spot on the Windows computer desktop, putting the AOL icon in front of millions of potential new subscribers. MSN, Microsoft's on-line service, would not stand alone on the computer desktop. It would have to share space and compete for customers. In return, though, Gates got what he wanted. AOL agreed to embed Microsoft's new Internet Explorer browser within AOL's on-line software, making it the default navigational tool for its customers and shutting out Netscape.

It was perhaps a pyrrhic victor for Gates. Thanks in part to AOL's cooperation, Microsoft won the browser wars. But it was a bruising affair that would come back to haunt Microsoft in its long-running antitrust trial against the government. In the process, Bill Gates fell farther behind Steve Case in the race to dominate the on-line world. When Siegelman, drained and discouraged, finally left Microsoft in March 1996, he received a handwritten note from Gates. It was a mea culpa of sorts.

Thanks for all your great contributions, Gates wrote, Siegelman recalled. *MSN is the most puzzling thing I've had to deal with at Microsoft, but we will figure it out. Bill.*

To this day, Microsoft, as the No. 2 player in the on-line market, is still trying to figure it out.

These were the halcyon days of AOL, the King Arthur times, when all was good in the court of Steve.

By February 1995, AOL had two million subscribers and 1,433 employees. That April, its market capitalization reached $1.45 billion, nearly triple its market value of just six months earlier. With its high-flying stock, AOL gobbled up other companies, a string of no names on the scrapheap of technology: BookLink Technologies, Medior, WebCrawler.

Then came The Gap ad campaign. That's when Steve Case really knew he had hit it big. The hip retailer featured the boyish CEO, his deadpan look shot by famed photographer Richard Avedon. The idea was to sell Gap khakis. It also sold an image: that of Steve Case.

AOL was becoming his own stage. In November 1995, as AOL reached a new benchmark with four million subscribers, the company announced that Kimsey was stepping down as chairman, relinquishing the title to Case. Kimsey, finally, was getting loose of the company he had joined as a favor to his old West Point buddy about thirteen years earlier. Not only did AOL *not* go bankrupt, the cockroach with the boxing gloves had helped Kimsey become a billionaire. Now, the old rogue was free to pursue his other interests, which turned out to be a unique blend of escorting beautiful young ladies on dates to posh places, philanthropy, and traveling the world's hotspots, from Colombia to Cuba, to meet with dignitaries as an unofficial ambassador of the United States. Kimsey was later seen on the phone talking to his frequent companion, Her Majesty Queen Noor of Jordan, the Grace Kelly of our times.

Case, meanwhile, found a girlfriend, too: Jean Villanueva.

In March 1996, Case disclosed to his board that he was in a "personal relationship" with Villanueva, AOL's public relations chief. He had separated from his wife of eleven years, Joanne, his college sweetheart. They had three small children. Villanueva was also getting divorced.

Joanne Case always seemed uninterested at AOL functions, a quiet, shy woman who would drift off alone. Villanueva, by contrast, was dynamic, the kind of executive who looked like the life of the party, or who wanted to host one herself. There was something sexy about her, the way she carried herself, the way she dressed, the confidence she exuded.

People began to whisper about Case and Villanueva long before he disclosed the affair to the board. Case had interviewed and hired Villanueva as marketing director in 1988. Since then, they had worked closely. They had traveled on business together. They were passionate about AOL, guardians of an idea that they truly believed in.

And yet, when Case, a careful and guarded man, delivered the news, it landed like an atom bomb. To many, it seemed out of character. It seemed reckless. Why would Case risk sullying his reputation now, just when all the hard work was paying off and AOL was steamrolling? If this was the way he conducted himself in his personal life, wondered one board member, what did it say about the way he conducted business? For some employees who had looked up to Case, the affair was a stunning admission that not all was perfect in the land of AOL.

"Maybe this isn't nirvana, maybe there is something I don't know about," said an employee who has since left. "Everybody I knew felt a little slimed by it."

It was, however, just a blip along his rocket ride to the top.

On April 15, 1996, Steve Case made the cover of *Business Week*. It was one of those clear demarcations, when there was no doubt what had just occurred. *This was it. He had made it.* There he was, lying on top of a pile of those indestructible AOL disks, in a glowing story chronicling his triumphs.

The headline crowed: "The Online World of Steve Case: So far, he has beaten all the odds. Can he keep America Online on top?"

The story talked about how "everybody wants to be on Case's planet" and how "AOL is the most potent force in cyberspace." Deep in the story, near the bottom, there was also a single paragraph that delicately mentioned his affair: "Case notified his directors in early March that he now has a 'personal relationship' with his vice president of corporate communications, Jean Villanueva."

Case's reaction to the article? He was in a fury. So much for the good news. AOL was on top of the world, and Case was the darling of the media, but all he could think about was that mention of his affair.

By the time Case was making headlines, AOL was making up a new nickname for itself in the confines of its frenzied headquarters: GBF.

Get Big Fast.

The hurried nature of things was in evidence everywhere in the mid-1990s. Office blackboards were scrawled with drawings, incomprehensible arrows, and lines. People were late for meetings. Executives were walking and talking in and out of rooms, cell phones attached to their ears, multitasking. The joke around AOL was, it was a "Mad Max machine, wrapped in duct tape, hurtling into its future," said Bill O'Luanaigh, who had joined the company in November 1994 as an on-line producer.

The decor, however, was about to change.

In June 1996, AOL began to move in phases out of its cramped Vienna headquarters, venturing farther out into the suburbs, into the hinterlands of Loudoun County, Virginia. The once-little firm was settling into respectable digs, a sprawling campus to rival the lush spread of its arch-nemesis, Microsoft. Suddenly, AOL was all grown up. Some called it a watershed event. Others called it a disaster.

"The company changed the day it moved out there," said Mark Walsh, the former senior vice president. "The building sucked."

Where the old offices in Vienna had the feel of a kooky little village, the new Dulles campus felt more like a big airport waiting lounge, which wasn't far from the truth. It was the former site of a British Aerospace building, where huge airplane parts had been stored.

The site, said a former AOL executive, "was never designed for human habitation."

True to form, the new facility looked like a cavernous, angular, modern hangar. It was either faux-industrial, or fake chic. Big pillars were spaced throughout, as were dark gray modular pieces of furniture, bright fluorescent lighting, and big ventilation ducts overhead, which made a constant rattling noise. Enhancing the futuristic feel, the new headquarters boasted conference tables with metallic flakes embedded in them—the crushed remains of AOL disks.

Employees were overwhelmed by the sheer size of the place. It was in the middle of suburban nowhere. There weren't many places to eat lunch. It was dark in parts of the building. Office workers were dispersed, creating a sense of disconnection. The hallways were so long and cold and modern that some joked they were really decomtamination chambers that were bombarded with gamma radiation so that when the rank and file walked through them they were cleansed before meeting executives. The loudspeakers, which frequently paged executives, made some feel as if they were working in a bus station. Others thought it felt more like Las Vegas, where casinos pumped in white noise. At the Dulles campus, sounds seemed mysteriously to dampen. Footfalls didn't sound right. This gave the place an otherwordly feeling, where people would walk and wait for an echo that never arrived.

People began to look at themselves and their jobs differently. They weren't scrappy entrepreneurs anymore. The frontier spirit was replaced by a sense that AOL was a big corporation, where adults worked and no longer took naps under their desks in sleeping bags. Some workers came to feel like drones. They called themselves "the pod people." They called the new headquarters "the big house."

Executives preferred a different perception. In the lobby, a silver-lettered plaque served notice to the world of the company's mission: "To build a global medium as central to people's lives as the telephone or television . . . and even more valuable."

It didn't seem like such a stretch.

In November 1995, AOL had made its first foray overseas, establishing an on-line service in Germany. Canada, France, and Great Britain followed the next year. By February 1996, AOL had grown to five million subscribers. It hit the ten million mark in 1997. Early that year, AOL's market capitalization vaulted to $3.45 billion. Within six months, it was up to about $8 billion. In April 1998, AOL's market value exceeded $15 billion. At the end of 1998, its market cap reached $63 billion. Reflecting the rising tide of the Internet, AOL's stock was then placed on the S&P 500 index, replacing Venator Group Inc., the aging retail company once known as the grand old Woolworth.

The crowd was cheering, the band was blaring, and out of nowhere appeared a battered police car, halting in the center of a college basketball court. Steve Case emerged, along with his new sidekick, Bob Pittman, dressed as the movie characters from *The Blues Brothers.* Like the John Belushi–Dan Ackroyd tandem, Case and Pittman were outfitted in dark suits, fedoras, and Ray-Ban sunglasses as they clambered onto the makeshift stage while the band played on, hidden behind a giant screen. Case and Pittman struck a tough-guy pose. Then Pittman, ever the showman, took off his sunglasses and tossed them into the crowd. They loved it. He was a hit. More raucous roars emanated from the audience. There must have been three thousand AOLers in attendance, leaning over in their cantilevered stadium seats. Images of the Steve and Bob show were beamed to more company employees in remote offices across the nation and throughout the globe. No more company meetings in the cafeteria. This was the big, grown-up AOL, full of flash and pizzazz.

"Suddenly, it was a production, it wasn't a family, it was an event, an extravaganza," said a former AOL official who looked on at the well-orchestrated spectacle in bittersweet wonderment.

It was early spring 1997, and for many at AOL, this was their first glimpse of Pittman.

He was the new guy. Steve Case selected him as chief executive of the newly formed America Online Networks division in the fall of 1996 to save the on-line service from its latest crisis—a steep decline in its stock price, questions about how it was accounting for its marketing expenses, the dramatic rise of Internet competitors, and the high costs of recruiting and keeping customers. It was just where Pittman wanted to be: in the middle of a big, noisy swirl.

After Case made the obligatory opening remarks, Pittman took the mike, and there was an immediate intake of breath from the crowd. Unlike Case, a plodding speaker who, by dint of great practice, got by, Pittman was a natural. He was glib. In his intonation, there was the hint of his Southern roots, of the influence of a familial understanding of the pulpit. The pauses came at the appropriate intervals. He stood there, totally at ease, effortlessly communicating to the AOL masses about how the company wanted to own the consumer *eyeballs* on the Internet, how AOL needed to draw on its power as a *distributor* of on-line information, how AOL needed to charge *content providers* a fee to get access to AOL's consumers. In a message from which he would not deviate during his tenure at the company, Pittman preached that AOL, at its core, was not a technology company. *We're a media company.*

People were enthralled. Bob Pittman was among the first of his breed in the corporate world: a rock star.

And Steve Case, by the way, was fast becoming a billionaire.

Case's personal evolution seemed to track that of his company. He started looking hipper. He was better groomed. His hair seemed a touch slicker, the khakis pressed a little crisper. He exuded more confidence, more poise. He wasn't as wooden as before. Many colleagues credited the influence of his new wife, Jean, who had stepped down as the company's publicity chief after their relationship became official but remained an unseen influence. (They married in July 1998.) "She devoted herself to his image and coaching him," said a friend of the couple. Jean Case was quick-minded and insouciant, but more than anything else, she had tremendous public-relations instincts. She understood the importance of perception and positioning, which meant doling out Case to the media and to his own employees in careful increments. Before the move to Dulles, employees used to wander into his office and plop down in a chair without an appointment. But now, Case became less accessible. Employee badges restricted who could open the elevator to his office on the top, fifth floor of the new headquarters. Always surrounded by attendants, Case seemed distant and removed from the ebb and flow of AOL's day-to-day operations. On the rare occasions when he was spotted on campus, employees were reluctant to approach him.

He wasn't just the chief executive of AOL anymore. Steve Case had become an American icon.

PART II

The Deal of the Century

CHAPTER THREE

THE MERGER AND CALIGULA

It was the spring of 1999, and all was not well.

Richard Bressler, Time Warner's chief financial officer, assembled some key company executives one evening at Palio, an elegant northern Italian restaurant a block from 75 Rock, corporate headquarters at Rockefeller Plaza.

Palio, since closed, was a jackets-required place, site of anniversary celebrations and romantic soirées, where the menu boasted such specialties as homemade pasta and mezzalune di zucca con parmigiano e amaretto (pumpkin halfmoons with parmigiano and amaretto cookies). Only on this occasion, Bressler was serving up a different kind of fare: Mary Meeker.

An analyst with Morgan Stanley Dean Witter & Co., Meeker had made her name by picking Internet stocks at the height of the boom. *But what was she doing here?* some in attendance wondered.

Bressler, unofficial consigliere to Jerry Levin, Time Warner's reclusive chief executive, served as host of the evening, introducing Meeker, who then proceeded to do an odd thing: She began selling the Time Warner executives on the merits of the Internet. Meeker explained how Internet companies were valued on revenue, not on profit, as was the case with traditional media companies, like Time Warner.

"Meeker was spinning Richard Bressler to be so bullish about the Net," said one who attended the meeting.

It seemed to some utterly bizarre. *Why were they being pitched? What was Jerry Levin up to?*

Although the prickly CEO was not in attendance, his presence was felt. The Time Warner chieftain was feeling pressure. And it continued to mount. By December 1999, Time Warner's stock, treading water in the $60s, was languishing in the molasses of the old economy, while Internet firms, sometimes fueled by little more than loose cash and outlandish ideas, were flying helium high.

"We all feel a degree of frustration at the failure of the market to value our company in a way that approximates its superior worth," Levin had written in a memo dashed off to his staff.

"Board members felt an enormous amount of pressure," said an official familiar with the directors' thinking. "The feeling was Time Warner was lacking a strategy in the digital world."

Nothing was working.

Despite Time Warner's impressive array of assets, it couldn't generate any excitement. Levin was acutely aware of the problem. Wall Street had fallen in love with those dot-com darlings.

The euphoria was infectious. This was a new day. It required a new business model. *Raise cash! Spend it fast! Who cared about profit?* Certainly not the dot-coms. Time Warner, for all its futile efforts, was no dot-com.

"Jerry was very concerned that Time Warner was not sufficiently part of the computer-y friendly world," said one of his advisers. "Here was this world going in this direction, while Time Warner was laboring in the wrong century. The business was heavily dominated by the bricks-and-mortar world, like the movies and the music. He couldn't get them to focus on making money over the Internet. He wanted to bring Time Warner into the twenty-first century."

After a while, there was a look of desperation in the way that Levin approached the digital divide. It was as if he were throwing spaghetti against the wall and then stepping back to see if any of it would stick. Among the experiments, Warner Music tested downloading and streaming music over the Web. Meanwhile, Warner Bros. and other divisions formed Entertaindom.com, a Web site focused on streaming audio and video, including animated shows specially created for the Internet.

Levin vowed to put "a good part of the Time Warner cash flow into digital construction." He was even contemplating what he called an "internal takeover" of CNN, transforming the company's esteemed twenty-four-hour news channel into the company's digital division. Such a draconian idea caught the attention of Ted Turner, CNN's flamboyant inventor and maverick Time Warner board member. This digital thing, he admitted, was pretty darn hard to figure out.

"We had a big uphill job as a corporation" to catch up with the Internet firms, Turner said later.

Finally, in the latter months of 1999, Levin turned to one of his trusted lieutenants. Bressler, his CFO, was anointed the chief executive of Time Warner Digital Media, a new division created to coordinate the company's Internet strategy. Bressler's unit, Levin explained, would impose a "digital override" for all the company's disparate businesses.

That, as it turned out, was easier said than done within Time Warner's feudal system of warring overlords, where company executives often clashed with each other more than they did with their industry rivals. Frustrated, Bressler and Levin talked about the challenges of moving the company into the digital age. Maybe, they began to feel, it couldn't be done from within. Looking across the landscape, their ruminations turned to which other companies could best help Time Warner make the leap to the Internet. Levin had dinner with the CEO of Yahoo! But the one company he kept coming back to was AOL.

How it could help Time Warner was an unresolved matter. Levin also held some personal reservations about whether he could do business with the Virginia company. "The reputation of AOL was hard-edged deal makers," Levin said. But AOL was also the biggest name in the digital industry, and it reminded Levin of his own early career when he had built HBO, a Time Inc. business founded on new technology, a venture that stretched the boundaries of media but relied on an established way of doing business—customer subscriptions. In AOL, Levin liked what he saw.

"He saw HBO in AOL. He saw himself in Steve Case," said Dave Sickert, a former HBO marketing director and Time Warner vice president of interactive marketing before becoming a director at AOL, running its on-line shopping group. "They were kindred spirits."

Levin said, "No one should've been surprised by the AOL transaction."

· · ·

Among the many myths that have grown up about AOL, here is another: Time Warner could have bought AOL on the cheap and leapfrogged ahead of the rest of the digital competition, if it had moved fast in late 1994.

This much is true: Steve Case and Ted Leonsis, AOL's top executives at the time, did pay a visit to executives at the Time-Life Building to explore options, including a joint partnership and, if ever so fleetingly, an outright sale of the on-line business to Time Warner.

AOL was already paying $500,000 to post *Time* magazine's content on-line. AOL was also paying to use the magazine publisher's mailing list to recruit on-line subscribers, paying *Time* a bounty for each new customer. Now, as Case and Leonsis were being served breakfast in the private second-floor Time executive dining room, they were chewing on other potential business deals with Walter Isaacson, editor of Time Inc. new media—the journalist—and Curt Viebranz, then president of Time Inc. multimedia—the business guy.

But they never talked numbers.

"It may have been broached jokingly," Isaacson said.

"As far as an outright acquisition of AOL by Time Warner, we probably spent thirty seconds on it," Viebranz said. "An institutional will to do a deal was nonexistent. I don't think we knew what we had yet."

Nor did AOL. Case and Leonsis weren't really interested in selling AOL. They had just said as much to Microsoft. *Why would they sell out to Time Warner now?* What they wanted was something entirely different: They wanted the legitimacy of a joint venture with a venerable old media firm. For an upstart still struggling to break into the daylight of corporate respectability, Time Warner represented a potential leg up. AOL had already made inroads by licensing *Time* magazine's content. But that was just an opening. AOL wanted to form a broader joint venture in which it could exclusively control the content of not just *Time* magazine but all of the publisher's stable of publications, stellar titles like *Fortune* and *Sports Illustrated.* The way AOL envisioned it, both companies would hold equity in the new venture. It was a bold proposal, one that made ostensible sense for both sides. Time Warner would get a foothold in the Internet realm before the

72

emergence of the World Wide Web. For AOL, a proprietary on-line service, a universe unto itself, content was king. And Time Warner was the motherlode. The media giant, however, wasn't sold on the idea.

Like many others, Time Warner was trying to figure out how to make money out of this new Internet thing. "Everyone was thinking about it," said Viebranz, the Time Inc. business executive. "How can we make hay in the electronic world? It was the sexy new place to be."

A deal with AOL would have to wait until the new century.

By 1994, Time Warner was knee-deep in its own digital experiment. The grand plan was to build the world's first true interactive cable-television system in, of all places, Orlando, Florida, home of Mickey Mouse.

It was called the Full Service Network. The thinking was that Orlando reflected many of the national demographics—family income among them—so what would work in Orlando, the Magic Kingdom, would work nationwide. The rest of the thinking, however, was pie in the sky.

Here's how it would work: Customers would buy a set-top box, which they would attach by cable to their television. Through the device, they could buy, for example, stamps by using a menu that popped up on their TV screen. The next day, the postman would knock on their door with their order. *Imagine: People would never have to go to the post office again.*

People would never have to visit the auto showroom again either. Press another button, and their TV would show a Chrysler. *Want a test-drive?* No problem. The automaker would bring the car to their home. Customers could freeze-frame their pay-per-view movie and order a pizza on their television screen. McDonald's was thinking of getting into the act, too, offering to deliver Big Macs et al to people's homes.

The Full Service Network was backed by a beehive of company brains, as many as two hundred in all, including a phalanx of engineers and software programmers. The investment community was keen on it. Silicon Valley was agog. In various presentations around the country, the project drew a breathtaking response.

"This was like 'wow!'" said Geoff Holmes, then a Time Warner senior vice president and chairman of its interactive division. "It was like we were rock stars."

Think of the implications. The Full Service Network could change the way people watched television. This was a revolution waiting in the wings. The Orlando project, however, turned out to be a bit of fantasia.

"It was more difficult in complexity than landing a guy on the moon," said a former executive involved in the project.

There was another problem: It was too expensive.

"We were putting $5,000 computers on top of televisions," Holmes said.

That's how much it cost to make the set-top box, the contraption that made the whole thing work. The set-top box, though of little interest to TV viewers, was the brains, the computer that linked the person to the product, transforming it into an interactive experience.

But what consumers in their right minds would spend $5,000?

From the beginning, the project team knew that the device was too expensive. But this was supposed to be a long-term project. Eventually, the strategists figured, the price of the computer would come down. It was a fundamental law of technology: The price of computer chips declines while its processing power rises. Only there was an overriding principle: the impatience of Wall Street.

Holmes described the syndrome this way: "You can't roll it out now, so it's money thrown away." The Full Service Network was not ready for prime time. Besides, it was becoming a drain on cash. By some estimates, the project cost upward of $1 billion.

"Orlando, from a cost perspective, was totally irrational," Holmes said.

Jerry Levin, the Time Warner honcho, loved the Full Service Network. Reared in the HBO culture, he was a cable guy at heart. "It was the promised future of television," said a former executive who worked with Levin on the project. "It was in Jerry's DNA. Jerry, the guy who really put himself on the map and established himself, was the guy who pushed HBO. . . . He was always a guy looking ahead at technology. It's just what he did."

But Levin apparently loved Wall Street more. By 1995, he switched horses and backed another digital project called Pathfinder. It would make the Full Service Network look like a walk in the park.

. . .

It was a beautiful moment. Steve Baldwin sat mesmerized in his new iridescent blue double-breasted suit made in China, the suit he had bought for this very occasion—his first day on the job at Time Warner Inc.

On this May day in 1995, Baldwin was thinking he looked like a million bucks. He was tall. He was thin. He had massive padded shoulders. Not to mention he had been vetted. He had made it through the notoriously rigorous job-application process at the esteemed Time Warner, where candidates' résumés were passed around, committee-like, then the candidates themselves were passed around like so much chattel, and if anyone wanted, he or she alone could veto them.

Maybe it was a holdover from the Henry Luce days. Lore had it that, in the 1950s, would-be journalists at Time Inc. would be ushered into the inner sanctum—Luce's private office—for one final, nerve-racking sitdown interview with the gray eminence himself. After assessing the prospect, Luce, the legendary founder of *Time, Life,* and *Fortune* magazines, would lean in with a penetrating gaze and ask, "What are you worth to me?"

Think carefully. Answer correctly, he'd double your salary, and the job was yours. Answer wrong, and you might not get the job.

It wasn't just a trick question. The patrician Luce wanted to drive home an important point. The recruits should feel as if their very livelihood depended on his largess—or that of Time Inc., the mother ship. This wasn't a company per se. It was a calling. "Getting bigger and more profitable was never the main point about Time Inc., and is not likely to become so," Luce once said. The newcomers should feel that there was no better job than this one, and that they should devote their every energy to this moment, the twentieth century, what Luce called "The American Century." It was Time's manifest destiny, spreading the news to millions across the globe for the betterment of humankind.

In return, Luce would bring to bear the entire Time empire. Once, that meant turning a 707 into an airborne photo lab to make prints of the coronation of Queen Elizabeth II.

Baldwin got the point. The new recruit could hardly miss it. He and another two dozen smartly dressed new employees were assembled around a massive, polished mahogany table inside the beautifully appointed, dark-paneled conference room on the thirty-fourth floor of the Time-Life

Building at 1271 Avenue of the Americas in midtown Manhattan. A framed portrait of Henry Luce stared at the gathering from an easel in a corner of the room. And just in case the surroundings didn't make an impression, Isaacson, the head of Time Inc. new media, made sure he did. Isaacson cut an erudite, regal figure, like Eisenhower briefing the Allied offensive, as he addressed the expectant gathering.

The mission: Conquer the digital world.

Time Warner was the undisputed media and entertainment champion of the modern age, a breathtaking conglomerate born in 1923 with the first publication of *Time,* and which had risen through innovation and corporate marriages through the decades. The far-flung empire reached consumers virtually everywhere, through Warner Bros. movie studios, Atlantic Records, *Sports Illustrated, People* magazine, HBO. Even Bugs Bunny was a company employee.

Now, however, a threat was emerging: the Internet.

A new medium, the Internet was a crazy quilt of personal computers linked to each other, zigzagging information, digital bits and bytes, across a spiderweb network expanding at warp speed. Yet for all the confusion, one thing was clear: The Internet was media. New media, that is. And Time Warner, the old media behemoth, needed to jump into the fray.

Which is where Baldwin came in. He and his new cohorts had been hired to help lead the charge. Their battering ram to the digital future was a Web site called Pathfinder, which had launched five months earlier, in October 1994. It was an Internet clearinghouse, a virtual roof, so to speak, under which all of Time Warner's brands were housed. Point and click on Pathfinder, and from there, computer users could be linked to one of dozens of the company's magazines or other entertainment properties on the Internet.

Isaacson, the general of that May meeting, reminded all of the recruits what was at stake. Baldwin's job, as producer for technology, was to help build Pathfinder, and thus, in turn, build for the greater good of Time Warner. It was a heady moment. Baldwin had grown up with this panoply of brands—*Time* and Warner Bros. and the rest of Time Warner. Now, here he was, sitting in his new suit, one of the few tapped to help build on that tradition, to wage battle in a new theater, the Internet. As he marched out of the conference room, Baldwin was overwhelmed with a burgeoning sense of pride—and dread.

"It was a very important project that directly implicated the future of the company," he said. "I felt, 'My God, I have a crucial role to play in this battle of historic proportions. Am I up to the job?'"

The answer was no. No one was.

Baldwin, however, can be forgiven his optimism. He was new. He didn't know. From the beginning, Pathfinder encountered problems.

Its name, for one.

For all of Time Warner's famous brands known the world over, Isaacson, the Time Inc. new media head, had decided to attack the digital world by creating a brand name from scratch, creating a Web site with a new name. Few would appreciate it, but the name Pathfinder was a literary flourish, an allusion to James Fenimore Cooper's adventure and romance novel of the same name.

"Pathfinder seemed like a really cool name," Isaacson said. "I had liked Cooper as a kid. My friends had nicknamed me 'Pathfinder.'"

The name didn't work. When Pathfinder launched in October 1994, many within Time Warner still had no idea what the Internet was. This was the mid-1990s, the primitive stages of the nascent technology. But once they got the gist of it, a lot of Time Warner people didn't like the Internet. They especially didn't like Pathfinder.

"We quickly learned, the company's attitude toward the Web was ambivalent at best," said Bill Lessard, a Pathfinder producer. "All the people we were supposed to deal with hated us and everything that we represented."

Mainly, what they didn't like was being told what to do. Warner Bros., the West Coast stronghold, had released the first synchronized talking picture, Al Jolson's *The Jazz Singer*, in 1927. *This was history!* Atlantic Records, another powerful Time Warner division, wasn't about to listen to a bunch of computer geeks. The music label simply refused to cooperate. It wouldn't allow Atlantic Records to be included as part of the Pathfinder Web site. *It wasn't going to subjugate itself to these digital nerds!* Atlantic Records had its own site.

The new kids on the Time Warner block took a nonconfrontational approach to Atlantic Records. They went behind the record division's back. "We copied their site," Baldwin said. "We actually replicated it on Pathfinder. But when that happened, the real shit hit the fan."

When Atlantic Records found out that, unbeknownst to it, Pathfinder had basically copied and pasted the music Web site, irate executives gnashed their teeth, urgent meetings were held and, in the end, the music people got back exclusive rights to their own Web site.

Other divisions within the company battled over which one would get displayed on the Pathfinder home page. *People* magazine would scream that it wasn't getting enough exposure. *Money* magazine would yell *it* wasn't getting enough space. The Pathfinder people, caught in the cross fire, would try to explain there were only so many slots. "The situation really did remind me of Italian city-states, a loose confederation warring against each other and against us," Lessard said.

If the divisions weren't complaining about exposure, they were grousing about sundry Pathfinder edicts. Digital file images had to be a certain size. Only specific content could be linked to the Web site. Each division was required to adopt the same navigation bar on its Web page. These weren't arbitrary orders, but requirements of technology, legal liability, and coherent uniform appearance. It was a question of gestalt. Still, Time Warner people bristled. Then they came up with a nickname.

The Pathfinder guys were called the "Nav Bar Nazis."

"In our day-to-day operations," Lessard said, "it was hell. It was hell."

Pathfinder would last until May 1999, when it was given a decent burial—although not entirely. Never one to give up potential customers who might still be looking for the Web site, AOL Time Warner still operates a shorn version of Pathfinder that putters along quietly, a failed and forgotten experiment before Time Warner leapt into the arms of AOL.

"This was really the big initiative by the largest media company in the world, but no one talks about it. It's like it never existed," Lessard said. "No one remembers it because it's such a piece of shit.

"It was their failure with Pathfinder that really led to the AOL merger or acquisition in the first place," he said. "They couldn't wrap their arms around the logic of it. With AOL, you pop in the disk, and in ten minutes, you're talking dirty to someone in a chat room. That's what it's about."

Gerald Manuel Levin, the man, has become one of the most vilified figures in Time Warner history. Jerry Levin, the boy, was spiritually transcendent. Both remain a perplexing study in character.

Gerald M. Levin's ascension to power after pulling off a palace coup against his boss and benefactor is a well-documented tale at Time Warner. Many of his past and present lieutenants—fired, passed over, or surviving—feel betrayed by him. And much of the rank and file, which has lost countless millions of dollars in retirement savings from the company's declining stock after its takeover by AOL, places the blame squarely on Levin's narrow shoulders.

As chief executive officer of the world's largest media company, Levin cut an unprepossessing figure stalking the hallways of the great empire during its most tumultuous, fitful period of growth in the 1990s and into the new century. He was slight of build, dark, and reclusive. By most accounts, he was also churlish, brutal, calculating, and bloodless, reminding some of a ruthless Roman emperor.

"We called him Caligula," said Michael Fuchs, former chairman and chief executive of HBO and also head of Warner Music Group. Fuchs was Levin's closest associate and presumed heir apparent—until Levin fired him, too.

This was the same Levin who was so accomplished in Hebrew that, even before his bar mitzvah at the age of thirteen, he occasionally conducted services at his neighborhood synagogue. "It was a small congregation, and they didn't have many alternatives," he said.

Levin was born on May 6, 1939, into a religious home in suburban Philadelphia. Raised in a middle-class family, he was the son of a successful grocer, who worked long hours and held higher aspirations for his bright son. His mother hoped he would become a rabbi.

Levin aspired to be a baseball player or a teacher. He described himself as a child of the visual age who went to the movies every Saturday morning without fail and, like many children of his era, watched television all the time as it emerged as a new medium in the 1940s. But the visual image did not hold as much sway as the religious. Through his Judaism, he was constantly reminded of how different he was. In his youth, his family was rejected in its attempt to move to a nicer home near Philly's Main Line because they were Jewish. In high school, his classmates went to country clubs forbidden to him because he was Jewish. To this day he hates golf.

For all the angst he went through in his childhood, Levin abandoned the notion of becoming a rabbi when he entered nearby Haverford College, a small school with a Quaker tradition. Instead, he quickly became captivated by Christian philosophy.

"At Haverford, it always bothered me, as a Jew, you weren't supposed to know anything about Jesus," he said. "I studied all religions. I wrote a thesis on the relationship between Judaism and Christianity. . . . I was intrigued by Christian philosophy. You couldn't understand philosophy unless you took Christian theology. I was also interested in Eastern religions. It was clear to me there was no one avenue to salvation."

By the time he left college, he was a changed young man. No longer was he religious. Instead, he chose a decidedly secular path, joining the ranks of the legal profession, then becoming an international consultant, spending a year in Tehran before the fall of the shah of Iran.

All of that, however, was prelude. Levin's career soared after he joined Time Inc. in 1972 as a staff executive of HBO. The pay-cable business was just then emerging when Levin helped persuade Time executives to invest $7.5 million in a satellite service that made HBO available to cable-television systems nationwide. The rest is cable-industry legend: HBO became the dominant pay-cable movie channel and a big moneymaker at Time Warner.

But as with many legends, some quibble with the particulars. Like Case, who took credit as one of AOL's founders, Levin took ownership of the satellite idea, although some executives who worked closely with him said that is an exaggeration. Rather, they said, the idea of putting HBO on a satellite came from other executives and engineers at the pay-cable service. Levin, however, did play a major role. He championed the idea, which made all the difference.

A former executive who believes Levin took too much credit compared him to the kid in the neighborhood who had memorized every statistic on the back of baseball cards: "He's bright, but so are a million people." Levin, he said, possessed an "anal-retentive memory." He also possessed a tremendous vocabulary. "He likes ten- and fourteen-letter words," the former executive said. "He uses them over and over again. The impression you get, when you combine the verbal facility with his anal-retentive facility, is, 'Holy shit, he must know what he's talking about.' But I finally understood, he's not an original thinker. This oracle is not an oracle."

Regardless of credit, the HBO experience left an indelible impression on Levin. Thanks to cable, an emerging technology that represented a new kind of media, a faster-growing alternative to Time's traditional magazine stable, Levin's star rose.

He once confided to a colleague, "Everything I am I owe to HBO."

His passion for the medium was on display in his old Time-Life office, where he kept a quote from George Orwell's *1984* framed on his bookcase: "The voice came from an oblong metal plaque like a dulled mirror which formed part of the surface of the right-hand wall. The instrument (the telescreen, it was called) could be dimmed, but there was no way of shutting it off completely."

An almost messianic zeal overtook Levin. In much the way Case believed in the rise of a new computer medium, Levin firmly believed that cable would eclipse network television.

Levin also learned the power of mergers. When Paramount Communications tried to buy Time Inc. for $200 a share in 1989, Time Inc.'s board fended off the unwanted approach by choosing to instead buy Warner Communications Inc. for $14 billion. Levin, one of the chief architects of the deal, was also one of its principal beneficiaries.

This part isn't in Levin's official bio, as written by AOL Time Warner, but it's a history etched in the minds of those who witnessed it and since recounted in numerous written accounts: After Steven Ross, the co–chief executive of Time Warner fell ill in 1992, Levin plotted to depose the other co-chief, his rival, N. J. Nicholas Jr.

It was like something out of Shakespeare, with Levin playing the jealous Iago to Nicholas's oblivious Othello. Over the years, Levin had been surpassed by Nick Nicholas, a more skilled corporate tactician. And yet Nicholas kept Levin around, ignoring the heeding of advisers who feared that Levin's apparent fidelity and meek bearing were a charade.

While skiing on vacation in Vail with his family, Nicholas was, as they still say at Time Warner, knifed. Backed by the ailing but powerful Ross, Levin corralled the board's support, engineered Nicholas's ouster, and took over as president of Time Warner in 1992.

"He's remorseless," said one who was steamrolled by Levin. "Nothing gets in this guy's way, even though he presents himself as this rabbinical, mousy little guy. He's plotting and scheming; he just doesn't look like he's plotting and scheming."

All that was left was for Levin to consolidate his position, which he did over the next several years. In 1996, he pulled off what he called another "transformational merger." Time Warner bought Turner Broadcasting System from fellow media mogul Ted Turner. The rest was a continuous power play that increasingly isolated Levin. Rarely did he assemble his chief centurions together, said those who held the titles. It was Levin's way of wielding power and maintaining a veil of mystery: Keep them dispersed, fundamentally dependent on him for information, for favor.

Levin evolved into an elusive CEO, offering cryptic remarks. "Jerry became unbelievably stealth-like," said a former Time Warner official. "His standard phrase was, 'Not to worry,'" said one who heard it often. "He always said that to people. He was almost like the Buddhist monk, like the Dalai Lama."

Levin's idea of exerting clout sometimes took a trivial shape: playing the information game. He would call up one of his executives early in the morning and make mention of an obscure news item in that day's papers. *Did you see that?* The bleary-eyed executive, barely awake, would have no idea what Levin was talking about, and would immediately be put back on his heels. "He wanted you to know he was already up at six in the morning," said one who got one of those early A.M. calls. "He wanted to make you feel like you're doing the slothful thing, like sleeping. I'd want to say, 'Shouldn't you be doing something more useful than reading the paper for three hours?' But he loved to do that with everyone. He said to me once, 'The guy with the information has the power.'"

The mantle of power never rested easy with Levin. In one of his first acts as head honcho, Levin in June 1992 defended the incendiary lyrics of "Cop Killer," by Ice-T, a rapper on a Warner music label. In a *Wall Street Journal* op-ed piece, Levin evoked the righteous indignation of a man defending free speech. Yet all Levin did was stir the pot. Some executives viewed it as a move by an uncertain leader trying to look tough. "It was ludicrous, and I think he knew it was ludicrous," said a former Time Warner official. "But at the time, he felt vulnerable. He was viewed as a weak CEO. He was trying to puff his chest out and demonstrate to Hollywood that this suit from Wall Street understood the entertainment business."

Michael Fuchs, the former HBO chief, said he often felt like he had to come to Levin's aid against tough media titans, like Barry Diller, then Fox's chief executive, who could bully the diminutive Time Warner CEO during negotiations. "I used to tell Jerry, 'Tell them, "Fuck you." It's a phrase they're familiar with,'" Fuchs said. "I always felt like I had to defend him, like I had to be an animal to defend him because he was such a wimp."

While other media moguls carried themselves with a distinctive swagger, like Walt Disney Co.'s Michael Eisner, who led by a cult of personality, Levin was no master of the media universe. Instead, he cultivated a different kind of image, less telegenic, less glamorous. He was often described as a quiet man who spent his free time watching movies and TV. And when he wasn't spectating, he was described as an automaton who awoke every day at 5 A.M., ran three miles without fail, worked until past 9 P.M., and voraciously consumed a stack of magazines, legal journals, and books.

But more than anything else, Levin nurtured the idea of himself as philosopher-executive, cerebral, bookish, scholarly, analytical. He was apt to quote Camus's classic work, *The Stranger*. It was an odd choice. By his own description, the book's protagonist, Levin once said, "was basically an observer of things, not really a participant."

Some thought Levin's philosopher image was more fiction than reality. It seemed that way to Fuchs in the early 1990s during a flight on the company jet while he and Levin were heading back to New York after attending a big HBO-sponsored fight in Las Vegas. The two executives settled into their chairs, which faced each other, and began to read their respective books.

Then the real heavyweight bout began.

Fuchs sensed this was developing into a read-off. *Who could read for longer? Who would blink first?* Somewhere over America, Fuchs glanced over and noticed that Levin had fallen asleep. Fuchs was struck by an idea. *Let's test Jerry.* Fuchs closed his eyes enough to fake slumber but still keep an eye on his rival. As daylight broke, Levin rustled awake. As if reminded of the competition, he immediately started to read again. Five minutes later, Fuchs pretended to wake up. Stretching, he asked, "Jerry, did you read all night?" To which, Levin responded casually, "Yeah, I read all night."

"He didn't carry Camus around," Fuchs said, "just in his résumé."

There was another side to Levin, a darker side, which came to full bloom after personal tragedy struck in 1997. Levin's thirty-one-year-old son Jonathan, a popular English teacher at a Bronx high school, was found bound, gagged, and lying dead in a pool of blood in his apartment. Even by the numbingly violent standards of New York, his was a horrifying murder that stunned the city and elicited blaring tabloid headlines. He had been tortured for his ATM bank card pin, then killed with a shotgun blast to the head, the trigger pulled by a former student.

The devastation showed as Levin could barely walk down the aisle of the synagogue at his son's funeral. In one eulogy, a rabbi recounted how Levin, who had four other children, had said his son's teaching was more important than what Levin had done with his own life. One of the first things he did after his son's death was to fly to England and hide away in the library at Oxford University, burying himself in its dusty books, reminding himself of his own youth when he wanted to be an English teacher, like his slain son.

"I just had to get away," he said.

"Many of us thought he would retire then," said one of his former colleagues.

Months later, Levin seemed a changed man. It was in his gait. It was in his face. It was in the drawn lines. He had aged. "He never had the light in his eyes that he had before," said a good friend. And yet, he continued to work—no, he threw himself into his work with abandon—moving from his Long Island home into an apartment in Manhattan so that he could spend even longer hours at the office, which often exceeded 11 P.M. Work was salvation, taking him away from what no one else was ever quite sure: Anger over his son's death? Guilt for not being with him enough? So frequently did he work late that his wife, Barbara, complained about it at dinner parties. His staff took to calling him the "BMW," a reference to the automaker's familiar ad slogan: "The ultimate driving machine."

Through it all, Levin remained as inscrutable as ever, keeping counsel with no one. Those who worked closely with him over the years profess they still do not understand Jerry Levin.

"I always had the feeling, then, as now, that there was something about him that was unknowable," said former Time Warner board member Lawrence Buttenwieser. "He played his cards very close to the vest. It was hard to see what was in his hand. The board accepted his style of management."

Like Steve Case, "The Wall," whom few could read, Levin offered few clues to what he was thinking. Except this: He held a messianic belief in technology, in transformational events, in the next big deal.

Every Monday in the late 1990s, Steve Case assembled his coterie of trusted advisers for sushi lunch in AOL's fifth-floor boardroom.

Where the raw fish came from was something of a mystery. The closest thing to commercial civilization near the AOL campus in Dulles was a Wal-Mart, which ultimately gave way to the inertia of the surrounding suburban diaspora and shut down. And yet, there was the sushi.

And there they were, a men's club of sorts, led by Steve Case, the reticent CEO. Also in attendance was Bob Pittman, AOL's president and Case's number two, who had a tendency to seem like a number one, overshadowing Case if only because Pittman was a marketing whiz and former boy wonder of the music world, a smooth talker and Southern charmer who had helped build MTV out of nothing and made sure everybody knew it. If Pittman didn't outshine Case during those Monday meetings, Ted Leonsis was bound to. The burly leader who had called AOL to arms against the great Microsoft Godzilla was still as voluble as ever.

Sitting more quietly in the boardroom was Ken Novack, the company's resident legal sharpshooter and vice chairman since 1998, a careful man who commuted from his Boston office and believed his first job was to protect his CEO. Then there was Kenneth Lerer, the top PR man, a veteran of office politics; J. Michael Kelly, the excitable chief financial officer; George Vradenburg III, its eminence grise, the company's chief lobbyist; and Miles Gilburne, AOL's head of strategy, who loved to draw diagrams of what he was thinking, which often involved a lot of vectors and circles and lines.

The boardroom where Case & Co. met was nondescript, save for the large oval conference table around which they hunched. The view to the outside world was of the pastoral Loudoun County countryside and, in the distance, the headquarters of another corporation on the move, WorldCom.

But the view didn't matter; what mattered was the free flow of ideas around the table. Case would arrive with an agenda—nothing formal, just topics that he wanted the men to work through, whether it was growing AOL's subscription base, expanding its advertising and commerce business, or making a big, splashy acquisition. The latter became the most prominent topic throughout the late '90s as AOL used its bulging stock price to buy up other companies in what amounted to a landgrab in the digital world. It gobbled up CompuServe, once its biggest rival in the Internet services business, in 1998. A year later, AOL swallowed Netscape, the once-grand software company that had so worried Bill Gates. AOL, however, wasn't simply getting big for the sake of bigness. It was getting big to protect itself from Microsoft.

"If one word describes why AOL evolved in the acquisitions and mergers it did in the 1990s, the word was Microsoft," said Vradenburg, then AOL's chief policy maker.

As AOL had grown into a giant in its own right, the menace from Redmond, Washington, was still front and center in the minds of Case and his lieutenants. Microsoft had considered buying AOL years before. Then it became AOL's rival in the on-line business. Now the two were racing each other for ultimate supremacy on the Internet.

Microsoft, however, wasn't the only concern. AOL wanted to diversify its sources of revenue. "Part of it was strategic, part of it was risk diversification," said one member of the Monday strategy group. Eventually, the men realized, AOL's torrid growth in adding subscribers would peter out. There were only so many people out there. Anticipating a drop-off, it had already begun to build an on-line advertising business, selling space on its vast service, which companies could buy to promote their goods and services.

Then there was the obvious: AOL's stock price. AOL could use its stock to spend billions in search of the perfect acquisition. "The valuation put on our company was so strong, the cost to our shareholders in making a combination was going down," Vradenburg said.

By early 1999, AOL wasn't sated. Another purchase was being contemplated around the conference table in Dulles. The question, as the AOL men consumed slabs of uncooked fish, was this: *What was the next big evolution in the Internet? What, in turn, is the next evolution in AOL's own corporate development?* Which was corporate-speak for saying: *Who can and should we buy next?*

The men chewed on a series of options. As one put it, they could "double-down" their bet on the Internet, expanding in that market. Among the potential takeover targets: Amazon.com Inc., the on-line retailer, or eBay Inc., the on-line auctioneer. Both were what were called "pure play companies," Internet firms strictly speaking. Among the biggest names in the business, both were likely to emerge as survivors from the wilderness of the World Wide Web. Each could be a choice morsel for AOL.

So, the men thought, could AT&T, or Sprint Corp., the giant telecommunications companies. Such a buy could make sense if only because AOL was a huge telephone customer. Its growing on-line service—which exceeded twenty million subscribers by the end of 1999—required an ever-growing telephone network to allow people to dial up to the Web. *Go vertical, go long.* AOL already controlled the content. Why not own the distribution?

Sprint and AT&T, however, weren't terribly sexy. They were, after all, telephone lines. Media companies, on the other hand, were sexy. Columbia Pictures. News Corp. Viacom. Disney. These were glittering companies packed with appealing assets—movies, music, magazines. They had mass appeal. They were global. Now there was some pizzazz. Besides, traditional media companies were all lumbering into the digital age, seeking an Internet foothold. In other words, they were moving into AOL territory.

The AOL men, however, quickly assessed the terrain and understood that the media options were limited. For one, there weren't many big media companies out there. And those that were out there weren't looking to be pursued by an acquisitive suitor like AOL.

"Not all these companies were saying come hither and be our partner," said a member of the Case team.

Columbia Pictures was owned by Japan's Sony. *Out.* Rupert Murdoch wasn't about to give up control of his News Corp. *Scratch that.* Viacom wasn't interested. Disney would have made an appealing prospect, the

AOL men thought. Its movies and ABC television network would nicely complement AOL's Internet presence. But behind the amiable smile of Mickey Mouse was the roar of Disney's chieftain, Michael Eisner. Would the powerful CEO consider himself part of another company unless he were controlling it? AOL put out some feelers. The answer: *Stay away.*

By process of elimination, that left one media company standing: Time Warner.

And what a company it was. It boasted the impressive entertainment assets of Warner Bros., along with publishing, television, and music empires. But it had something else that AOL coveted even more: cable lines.

Time Warner was the nation's second-largest cable television operator, reaching more than twelve million homes. Its cable lines could carry huge amounts of digital data at vastly faster speeds than telephone lines could, not just television programming but also Internet content. Cable, it appeared, would soon make the telephone look like the buggy whip of the tech age. Internet companies hadn't yet figured out how to market and sell the public on the idea of cable access to the Web. It was, among other things, twice as expensive, and who wanted to spend $40 to get to the Web via cable when you could access the Internet for $20 through your telephone line?

But it was clear that cable was the future. And so far, AOL had been selling the buggy whip. Its customers were connecting to the Internet by dialing up through their telephone lines. The technology, however, was slow and bulky. The phone screeched, people got disconnected, and it took time to download images, especially those that were rich in color and graphics. Meanwhile, competitors were driving down the price of on-line services. Internet access was threatening to become a commodity. It was an uncertain future—until Time Warner surfaced at the sushi lunch.

Corporate mergers, like love affairs, usually begin with a courtship. In the case of AOL and Time Warner, the mating ritual began in September 1999 in the most romantic of cities, Paris.

Steve Case and Jerry Levin were in town to attend the Global Business Dialogue, a meeting of media and tech executives, to discuss the state of affairs in the Internet world, writ large. For Case and Levin, it was like a first date—tentative, unfamiliar, grasping. When they bumped into each other at a few meetings, they chatted about business in general, innocent stuff. What was already rolling around in the back of Case's head he never uttered: merger. That would have to wait. Both men were notoriously guarded. At each company, handlers, like nervous parents trying to arrange a marriage, recognized that this was an odd fellowship marked by a twenty-year gap in age between two men who did not inspire warm and fuzzy feelings.

"It was too soon to tell if the personalities would work," said an executive familiar with the initial get-together.

Levin respected Case, but he didn't cozy up to him. "He's not a hugger," Levin said.

Things, though, heated up later in the month, when Case and Levin bumped into each other again, this time in Shanghai at a *Fortune* magazine event, a lavish spread that was a hybrid of journalism and meet-and-greet for the titans of business. Such are the accidents of being a globe-trotting CEO running part of the world. Paris one day, Shanghai another.

But this chance meeting wasn't entirely accidental.

AOL was considering expansion plans in China. That was the story for Case's being there. But he was also stalking his quarry, Jerry Levin. On October 1, Case followed Levin to Beijing to witness China's National Day, a big public spectacle in the wide open space of Tiananmen Square. The Communist leadership paid its respects to Levin, fussing over the diminutive capitalist from New York. Case did the same, standing by the Time Warner chief as the parade marched by, fireworks exploding overhead.

"The objective from Steve's part was to get to know him better," said an official on the trip. "Clearly, it was not just a social interest. If he did a deal, how would the superstructure of the company look? What about senior management? He was beginning to think that something like this would work."

In mid-October, Case put an end to the flirtation. Slow seduction wasn't his style. He phoned Levin and came right out with it: Case proposed merger outright. It would happen the way AOL had done it so many times before, through a stock deal. He called it a merger of equals. Of course, it wouldn't be, but it sounded good at the time. And here was the clincher: He wanted Levin to be CEO of the combined company. Case would be chairman.

"It wasn't, 'Hi, how are you? How are your kids?' It was, 'Let's put our companies together and you can be the CEO,'" Levin said.

This last bit was important. For all the talk about shareholder value and what's right from an economic point of view, mergers often come down to the nitty-gritty of who gets which job. Beneath the numbers, the billions of dollars at stake, mergers are basically about the joining of people. Ego is important, especially to those higher up in the corporate suites. This was no different. Case never really wanted to be CEO. He was never a great day-to-day operator. He had brought in well-seasoned executives to roll up their sleeves and do that for him, people like Ted Leonsis and Bob Pittman. Case preferred the lofty role of big thinker, sitting back in the chairman's wingback chair, cloaked in the stature and respect he felt he never had as a boy overshadowed by a superstar older brother and as a man playing second fiddle to Jim Kimsey at AOL.

"That's the way you did it," he told Kimsey privately. "I'm just doing it the way you did it."

After he hung up the phone, Levin went for a walk through the woods near his getaway home compound in Vermont. Levin, for his part, was never considered a great day-to-day operator either. He had cultivated the image of resident genius at Time Warner, but it was more for his forward thinking about things like beaming HBO up to a satellite. And yet, he had defined himself through his jagged rise to CEO. It was the top job. He would be running the show. Besides, AOL represented a way finally to solve this digital riddle for Time Warner. When he returned from his walk, Levin called Case back and invited him to dinner in Manhattan.

On November 1, the two men met for a clandestine dinner. For privacy, they holed up in a room at the Rihga Royal, a luxury hotel just blocks from Time Warner, in an art deco suite with mirrored French doors and a marble bathroom with brass accents. Style among CEOs was important, even in secrecy—and secrecy was of the essence. At such an early stage, neither man wanted to jeopardize an event as cataclysmic as a merger between AOL and Time Warner. Among the first orders of business was coming up with a code name for the deal. Their choice: Alpha Tango. The *A* stood for AOL, the *T* for Time Warner.

The rest fell into place quickly. AOL retained Salomon Smith Barney as its investment banker, while Time Warner hired Morgan Stanley—the same firm whose analyst Mary Meeker had presented the bullish description of Internet firms to Time Warner executives earlier that year at Palio. Both sides also retained legal counsel—Simpson Thacher & Bartlett for AOL, Cravath, Swaine & Moore for Time Warner. And they began the mad dash to learn about each other's business, a paper-strewn process known as due diligence.

Attorneys on both sides were told to drop everything and jump right into this potential merger. It was the corporate equivalent of a fire drill, with attorneys scrambling over a few days, trying to glean as much insight as possible into the other company through public filings. Some of it was pretty basic: What line of business was the other company in? What kinds of bylaws did it have? Was it involved in any litigation and, if so, how serious was it?

The strange part was that attorneys for the two companies didn't actually talk to each other to learn more about the other side. Instead, as per tradition in such matters, each team operated on its own, using public documents and interviewing employees within its own company who had knowledge about the other company.

Meanwhile, Case and Levin brought in the support team. Case appointed Ken Novack, his trusted legal adviser and company vice chairman, to be AOL's lead negotiator in the talks. It was a wise choice: Novack was viewed as the Henry Kissinger of AOL, a discreet, calming diplomat and a low-profile figure, a fleshy, balding man whose presence at Time Warner would elicit little attention. Novack was not only smart and able, he also didn't lust for power, and so he had the complete confidence of Case. By then fifty-eight years old, Novack had served for a decade as a key executive on virtually every major transaction at AOL, including its acquisitions of CompuServe and Netscape, though he was always quick to give credit elsewhere, to people like Case, the boss. Novack, however, wasn't a yes-man. He was a straightforward, no-nonsense Bostonian who took business colleagues at their word.

On November 16, Case dispatched Novack to New York with senior vice president Miles Gilburne to meet with Levin's personal emissary and trusted adviser, Richard Bressler. Much like Novack, the forty-two-year-old Bressler was a straight shooter. Candid yet careful, he seemed like the ideal point man for Levin: Bressler could bridge the digital divide. As the former chief financial officer, he understood the core fundamentals of Time Warner; in his new role overseeing the company's digital transformation, he was now well versed in the ways of the Internet. What's more, Bressler was not nearly as likely as Levin, the curmudgeon, to pick a fight during negotiations. Bressler was, above all, a pragmatist.

That's why, when Bressler greeted his AOL guests in the executive suites on the twenty-eighth floor of 75 Rock, he sat back and said little. He preferred to take everything in, as was his habit, while Gilburne, the AOL strategist, stood, drawing on an easel.

On large sheets of paper, Gilburne scrawled while the three men hashed out some rudimentary issues: *Did this deal make sense? And if so, how?* They talked about synergy—how to make the combined assets of AOL and Time Warner work so that they were worth more than the sum of their parts. One example: How to cross-pollinate CNN, Time Warner's TV news channel, and *Money,* its personal finance magazine, with AOL's on-line medium for personal finance. There were a lot of broad brushstrokes and grand thoughts and collegial banter as the three men covered Bressler's drab gray walls with sheets of paper. At the end, the men shook hands, but Bressler, lukewarm throughout, reserved judgment.

Then came a hitch. Case and Levin could not agree on some of the most fundamental issues. How would the company be organized? Who would get which senior job? What, for that matter, would the company be called? Everything was considered: TW AOL, Time Warner AOL, American Time Warner. Levin made the final call, which made his own company secondary: AOL Time Warner. "There was never a negotiation," he said. "I'm the one who wanted that name. It had nothing to do with who was acquiring who. . . . Time Warner AOL didn't sound right. AOL Time didn't sound right. But AOL Time Warner sounded felicitous to me."

Levin also abandoned Time Warner's stock symbol—TWX—in favor of AOL, for obvious reasons. "AOL," he said, "was a highly liquid stock." The thinking, he said, was AOL was "the lead on every stock chart, so let's be there."

But even more important than the name, the burning question was: In an all-stock deal like this, where the two sides would each exchange shares in their own company for new shares in the combined company, how much of the new company would each side own?

Who, in short, was buying whom?

AOL, based on its stock price, was worth about twice as much as Time Warner. AOL had a market capitalization of about $160 billion, double Time Warner's. What's more, AOL figured the market would punish its Internet-driven stock if it combined with an old economy media company. AOL, already the tenth largest company in the United States with triple the market capitalization of Disney, said it was practically doing a favor for Time Warner and its anemic stock: "The deal quality was perceived slightly better for them," said one executive on the AOL side.

Thus, AOL wanted a sixty-forty exchange ratio in its favor.

Time Warner, however, did not want to put a price on the deal solely based on the vagaries of the stock market, especially at a time when Internet stocks were climbing up in defiance of all rational business sense. AOL, along with the rest of the Internet sector, was in vogue on Wall Street. Put a dot-com at the end of a company name, and its market value was bound to bounce up.

"Your stock has a lot of fluff," declared one Time Warner official in a meeting with AOL.

Even if the stock market put a lower price tag on Time Warner, the media company was much larger than AOL in almost every other way, including revenue. If the two companies combined, Time Warner would be contributing 80 percent of the revenue. AOL was about the size of one of Time Warner's divisions. Time Warner brought to the table not only the vast majority of assets but also more employees by far and a tradition steeped in seventy-six years of history.

Time Warner wanted a fifty-fifty exchange ratio.

The call finally came: *Abort*. The two sides had reached an impasse. In the latter part of November 1999, AOL and Time Warner decided to nix further talks. The hired guns, a battery of high-priced attorneys and investment bankers, were called off.

"We thought the deal was dead," said one who was involved.

Silence, however, belied a real sense of urgency on both sides. This deal was too delicious to let go of just yet. In a multibillion-dollar negotiation like this, there is some cat and mouse, a lull in the action to get the other side thinking, backtracking, reconsidering. About three weeks later, Case and Levin tried again. On December 10, AOL and Time Warner entered into a confidentiality agreement. Three days later, Novack and his investment bankers met with Bressler and his investment bankers to talk exchange ratio again.

Again, an impasse.

The dialogue revolved around another key financial concern: Would there be a collar? All-stock mergers often come with such a provision, which is essentially a form of insurance against the value of the deal declining. If the shares of one or both of the companies were to swing wildly beyond a certain predetermined range before the merger closed, a collar would automatically readjust the terms of the agreement. Time Warner, not surprisingly, wanted a collar to protect against potential fluctuations in AOL's already exuberant stock price. AOL, just as predictably, wouldn't budge on this point.

"We refused to take a collar," said an AOL executive involved in the talks. "Who knew how long the deal would be pending? We didn't want to take that uncertainty."

Levin finally relented on the collar. He believed in the Internet and the merger. "I'll take responsibility for it," he said, "because I believed it was the right thing at that time."

When Bressler met at Novack's office at Heritage on the Common in Boston on December 23, they still could not see eye to eye on an exchange ratio. AOL was stuck on a sixty-forty split, while Time Warner held to a fifty-fifty deal. All that they could agree on was to talk again, immediately after the holidays.

For such a monumental merger, a landmark deal that would affect nearly one hundred thousand employees, not to mention tens of millions of consumers across the globe, the clincher was an incredibly solitary affair: Levin, like Howard Hughes closeted in his own secure, dark perch, contemplated the deal over the New Year's weekend while, he said, "watching a hundred hours of CNN."

Somehow, it seemed absurdly appropriate. As the world ticktocked into the new millennium, ushering in a new age, the largest merger in U.S. history, the first marriage of new media and old media, depended in large part on one individual pondering while watching his own news channel. Time Warner was a public company, owned by its shareholders and overseen by a dutiful board of directors, but in this transaction, Levin had kept virtually every senior officer in the dark, completely unaware that a merger was in the offing.

"A lot of this deal was about him and his aspirations and his own concepts and his own needs, and it's a fairly stunning example, pretty rare, really, of one man's visions so shaping a business outcome," said a close Time Warner associate.

Levin did not even solicit the opinion of Bressler, then his closest confidant. Bressler just carried out his boss's orders. Levin trusted his own instincts and experience. And why not? He had pulled off a bunch of what he liked to call "transformational" mergers already, buying Ted Turner's media empire in the mid-1990s and overseeing the Time and Warner combination before that at the start of the decade. But AOL, he understood, was different.

"Probably my style, when I really believe in something, is to pretty much barrel ahead, that's certainly true," Levin said. "It wasn't the kind of thing where we had to get buy-in or consensus, because it's kind of dramatic in and of itself."

Time Warner, Levin reckoned, was valuable whether or not it had an Internet partner. But he reasoned that investors would give his company a premium if it joined with AOL. So he played with the numbers. He went for another walk in the Vermont woods. What he came up with was a classic compromise.

Time Warner wanted a fifty-fifty share; AOL wanted a sixty-forty arrangement. Levin split the difference, coming up with an exchange ratio that would give Time Warner 45 percent of the new company and AOL 55 percent.

Levin told Bressler they were going to Washington.

On January 5, Bressler and Novack spoke by phone. A dinner was arranged for the following day at the suburban home of Steve Case in McLean, Virginia. Suddenly, the deal looked like a reality. Levin and

Bressler wouldn't waste time flying on the corporate jet just for a good home-cooked meal, even if it was to meet Internet mavens Steve Case and Ken Novack.

The intimate dinner affair began as most intimate dinner affairs begin: with chitchat, stilted though it was. Said one, "There wasn't that much to talk about." The uncomfortable silence was saved by a tour of the house, which was lovely yet oddly nondescript, certainly not the mansion one would expect from an Internet billionaire with visions of grandeur. It felt like a rich man's comfortable, family place. There were, however, some elegant touches, like the wine cellar, from which Case retrieved a 1990 Château Léoville-Lascase. It was a good ice-breaker, served in the living room, before the four men retired to the dining room, where they sat at a round, linen-covered table, attended by servants.

The food was just a formality. Before chocolate mousse was served for dessert, Case and Levin had wandered from the table for privacy. When they came back, they had a deal. Within five hours, at midnight, they had come to an agreement: AOL would own 55 percent, Time Warner 45. They shook hands.

In a classic sales maneuver, Case made it seem to Levin that Time Warner had gotten the better end of the bargain.

"Steve was worried he'd get killed when we made the announcement," Levin said. "Two reasons: one, it was too high a premium shifting to the Time Warner shareholders, and two, he had all the growth and [Time Warner] was going to pull down AOL, given the slow-growing traditional media businesses."

They also agreed to think about it overnight. As Bressler and Levin flew back to New York in the early hours of the morning, both knew a deal was imminent. "The deal was fifty-five–forty-five, which our investment bankers said was about as low as we could go to be fair to our shareholders," said an AOL executive. By 2 A.M. Friday, lawyers and investment bankers throughout New York were being awakened by telephone calls. At 7 A.M., the Time Warner team was assembled at headquarters. Christopher Bogart, then Time Warner's general counsel, laid out the deal to the company's senior executives. "There was this stunned silence," said one. A moment later, Timothy Boggs, then Time Warner's head of public policy, stammered what others were thinking:

"Wow."

Two hours later, Bressler and Novack spoke and checked with their bosses. "Go forward," Levin told Bressler, who then confirmed with Novack. Within fifteen minutes, at nine-fifteen, the merger was official: AOL would buy Time Warner for $183 billion in an all-stock transaction.

The professionals took over. The thirtieth-floor conference center at Simpson Thacher on Lexington Avenue was packed with a team of high-priced lawyers, investment bankers, and AOL executives, who worked under high security. The kitchen staff prepared meals to keep outsiders, even delivery boys, away. Secretaries were kept oblivious, too. Without knowing the names of the companies involved, they labeled documents by their code names: "Black" for AOL, "Blue" for Time Warner.

By Saturday, when Jean drove her husband to the Dulles airport, Case knew it was nearly a done deal. He hopped on a corporate jet with General Colin Powell, who was then an AOL board member. When Powell joined the company as a director in September, he had become part of a long tradition of military men on AOL's board. But there was more to Powell's appointment than that. A year before he was tapped, AOL had hooked up with Powell, creating a Web site for America's Promise, his national youth campaign. He and Case liked each other. They made a confident pair, talking breezily about post-merger issues, such as leasing a helicopter to make it easier for a quick jaunt to Manhattan, headquarters of the new company. Such talk was a show of bravado because most AOL and Time Warner board members were only then being given the news of the pending merger and asked to attend a Sunday meeting to cast a vote for the largest merger in American history.

And yet, there was no doubt that it would pass.

"By the time the meeting took place, it was a foregone conclusion it would go through," said a principal involved in the transaction. "No one expected there to be an issue."

Then again, Ted Turner was always a wild card.

Over sandwiches, the Time Warner board convened around a big granite table in a postmodern conference room overlooking the Hudson River on the forty-eighth floor of its law firm, Cravath, in midtown Manhattan. All except director Carla Hills, the former U.S. trade representative, had made it, but she wasn't about to miss this historic occasion. She was linked by speakerphone from Beijing. Investment bankers and lawyers rimmed the back rows. The bankers made financial presentations. The lawyers talked about regulatory issues, Delaware laws, and other corporate matters. The Time Warner executives talked about the business issues. Levin addressed the deal itself. The meeting was all standard stuff. A regular, seamless, muted board meeting, except that somebody noticed that Levin had just shaved off his mustache. It seemed symbolic, like he was a new man who had shed one identity for another.

Turner, however, remained very much the maverick. He quipped about Jane Fonda, the movie star with whom he had just separated after eight years of marriage. Alone among the Time Warner directors, Turner also raised some questions about the merits of the deal, whether it made sense for Time Warner to join with an upstart like AOL. But others in the room had already dismissed Turner, who had previously disclosed that he had bipolar disorder and took lithium. Later, Turner confided in a friend, "I couldn't be that smart if I'm the only one with misgivings." At the meeting, his words plunked to the floor, unheeded. *Oh, what the hell.* Turner cast the first vote to approve. The rest of the dominoes fell. The Time Warner board unanimously ratified the deal.

Across town, on the thirtieth floor of Simpson Thacher, the AOL board was still meeting. There was a similar tableau: All but one board member, who was connected by speakerphone, was in attendance, circled by bankers, lawyers, and uneaten catered food. And just as in the Time Warner meeting, a single voice of dissent was raised by a maverick: General Al Haig.

Haig didn't like the way this was playing out. It bothered him that Case had sprung this deal on him and other board members just the night before. He also was irked that some board members, though not him, seemed to have been briefed on the deal well before their arrival at the board meeting. He wasn't happy that the room was stacked with "lawyers from gunwale to gunwale." He didn't like the hurried nature of the board meeting, with directors like himself having to fly in at the last minute. "It was too fast from my point of view and I thought so at the time," he said.

Haig also was concerned about how the two companies would mesh, especially since they were so different, Time Warner being a loose confederation of fiefdoms, AOL being a well-honed, centralized operation. And what was all this talk about *synergy?* He was dubious about this notion of cross promoting properties between AOL and Time Warner. Where did that idea come from? And how would the combined company achieve such high revenue targets as the executives laid out at the meeting? But most of all, Al Haig didn't like the price AOL was paying for Time Warner. AOL was doing just fine by itself. Its prospects looked strong. Time Warner, he pointed out, wasn't a "barn burner" of growth.

"It seems to me, we're paying a hell of a price, and that raises a lot of questions that haven't been answered," Haig told his colleagues.

Silence.

"I was a skunk in the garden party," he said. He chalked it up to being "psychopathically blunt." His comments weren't appreciated. "It was like throwing a cold mackerel on an otherwise euphoric session," he said.

That night, Haig said, "I was tempted to resign." But he didn't. Instead, other directors broke the silence, touting the deal, and the meeting moved on without further ado to the minutiae of taxes, accounting, and whether to maintain dual headquarters in New York and Virginia.

Case, sitting in the CEO's chair at the middle of the table, seemed at peace, or impassive. One could never tell. There was certainly no way of gleaning from his expression that he was about to consummate the biggest deal in American history.

By about 9 P.M., it was done. AOL's directors, including Haig, who had given in to the inevitable, unanimously approved the deal. ("It was a done deal," he said, "I'm not a fool.")

After Time Warner's marathon session, which extended beyond eight hours, Levin placed a conference call to Case. There was applause. Case let glimpse a smile. The celebration, however, was brief. Some of the negotiators lingered behind and, as they had done the night before, stayed up throughout the night to work out the final details. Others, sleep-deprived, just crashed at home.

The champagne stood by, unopened.

. . .

On the morning of January 10, 2000, the telephone rang in the bedroom of Michael Bromley, then a business development director for AOL devices, in the leafy suburbs of northern Virginia.

His boss broke the breathtaking news: AOL had just announced a takeover of Time Warner. Bromley, half awake, still in his bathrobe, croaked a simple response: "Why?"

Bromley registered an unsettling thought. "Why did we need this old, slow-growth company?" he wondered. "If everything we'd been told prior to that was about our growth, what was the value we were gaining here? Were we saying we weren't enough and we needed other businesses to make it real?"

After hanging up the phone, he wondered out loud, "Is this the beginning of the end?"

For Bromley, it was. In just over a year, he would be laid off. Looking back now, he said, "The Internet bubble ended the day we announced the AOL–Time Warner deal. That was the day we realized the Internet would not stand on its own."

At the time, however, AOL was on top of the world, and Steve Case was its king, hugging and high-fiving people in an unusual display of exuberance for "The Wall" on the most public of stages, a press conference in New York.

"Steve looked like a kid at a rock concert," said Bill Burrington, then a senior vice president of AOL Europe. "That was the defining moment."

At forty-one years old, Case, obscure P&G marketer, pizza-flavor tester, low-level functionary at an unknown Virginia video-game firm, was suddenly the master of the greatest media company on the planet.

Even better, perhaps, the underestimated younger brother was finally more successful than his older brother, Dan, who by then was quite a success himself as head of Hambrecht & Quist, the San Francisco investment house.

Steve Case had made it.

With a price tag of $183 billion, this was, at the time, the biggest merger in history, surpassing the then proposed $115 billion acquisition of Sprint by MCI WorldCom. The AOL–Time Warner merger, since reduced to $112 billion in value, was eclipsed in Europe by the telecom Vodafone PLC's hostile takeover of Mannesmann AG in a $182 billion deal in 2000. But the AOL–Time Warner deal remains the benchmark in the United States.

The worldwide reaction was swift. NBC anointed Case a "boy wonder," and its network anchor, Tom Brokaw, declared "a whole new universe created overnight." ABC called Case a "revolutionary." *USA Today* said it was "one of those rare events that seems to change the world overnight."

AOL Time Warner presented itself as a prototype for a new kind of conglomerate. The potential was staggering. In early 2000, AOL had about twenty-two million subscribers, more than six times that of Earth-Link Inc., then the No. 2 player. AOL's merger partner, Time Warner, controlled huge swaths of the entertainment business. It could funnel its content through AOL's Internet lines. AOL could use Time Warner's huge cable system to reach millions of new subscribers. Time Inc. could promote its magazines to AOL's millions of users. And yet it almost seemed unimaginable. *Time Warner?* The seventy-seven-year-old media giant, founded in 1923 by Henry Luce—*Henry Luce*—had been scooped up by AOL, an upstart still in its teens. How could it be? On the day of the announcement, AOL had only a fraction of the revenue Time Warner had—23 percent, $5.2 billion to $23 billion. AOL hadn't even made the Fortune 500 list the previous year. This was the signature moment of the new economy, the ultimate triumph of the Internet over the stodgy firms of the twentieth century.

Somewhere, no doubt, the spirit of Bill von Meister was toasting the deal over a stiff drink.

Von Meister had approached Warner years ago about investing in his little digital music scheme. And though it had squelched that venture, the media company had turned him on to Atari, Warner's video-game unit. That, in turn, had paved the way for the formation of Control Video, which morphed into Quantum Computer, the predecessor to AOL. Now, AOL was back in business with Warner, which had since merged with Time. Things had come full circle.

Few seemed to appreciate the irony of history on that day. But at the announcement of the merger Case, who had built his image around the casual khaki look, seemed to understand the import of the moment. He wore a tie. Levin, who at sixty years old had been reared on the Time button-down look, wore an open collar. Much was made of the tie–no tie symbolism. New media guy in charge of old media guy. But the truth was, Levin hadn't been wearing a tie for some time.

"I've been saying that this will be the Internet century," Case said that day. "We are going to be the global company for the Internet age."

Case, in a nod to the other goliaths on stage with him—Levin, Bob Pittman, Dick Parsons, and Ted Turner—offered a wry remark at the news conference that held more meaning than he realized. "There are a lot of cooks on stage," he said, "but there is a big meal to serve."

Levin chimed in, "We've become a company of high-fives and hugs."

Turner, not surprisingly, uttered the most memorable line of the day. It was a little disingenuous given his earlier reservations about the deal, but he said he had no problem voting for the merger.

"I did it," he said, "as enthusiastically as when I first made love some forty-two years ago."

Some in the audience tittered. It was an unscripted remark, which, for him, was in character.

But this wasn't the AOL way. Within minutes, a Time Warner executive got a taste of the new style. After he got off a telephone interview, a low-level PR functionary from AOL who had been hovering nearby recounted what he had just said and explained how to say it better next time.

"I realized this is a spy, like a Moscow maid," the executive said. "It was so offensive."

Led by Kenny Lerer, AOL's wily PR man who carefully managed the dissemination of information, AOL had put together a "black book" for the occasion. It was, in essence, a script for executives to follow in talking to the press, to Wall Street, to employees, to business partners. Little, other than Ted Turner himself, had been left to chance. Lerer's people wrestled with the language, such as the provision of the deal that required three-quarters of the board to oust the CEO or chairman.

"People thought that might be thorny," said one involved in the deliberations. The concern was that it would be viewed as a measure put in place to protect Case and Levin—or worse, that it would suggest that some didn't think this merger would actually work.

Few, however, were that prescient.

· · ·

Days after the deal was announced in early January 2000, four rich and powerful men convened on a Wednesday evening over Chinese takeout to talk about how to organize the new company.

Meeting for the first time as the transition team were Bressler, the Time Warner digital guru, Parsons, Time Warner's president, and their AOL counterparts, Novack, the legal counselor to Case, and Pittman, AOL's president and marketing point man.

It started out politely. The men deferred the odious task of actually talking about who would get which plum job. "It would've been awkward to come down to names," said one. But they talked about the assets of the company, how to "maximize value for shareholders" (corporate-speak for goosing the stock price), compensation schemes in both companies, and how to coordinate their different PR operations. They hoped to meet at least once a week.

Alas, it didn't work out that way.

In fact, Bressler was left out in the cold when it came to appointing executive slots. It was a bit of a stunner since he had been one of the select few actually involved in clinching the merger for Time Warner. But Bressler had been lukewarm to the merger from the beginning. And he was expendable. Bressler was Time Warner's digital guy, its Internet chieftain. After AOL, packed with Internet chieftains, took over the shop, he became, as they say, redundant.

Many other senior Time Warner executives lost out in the personnel shuffle to their new AOL brethren. There was a widespread feeling that Levin had ditched his own folks and thrown in his lot with the newcomers from Dulles, just as many felt he had done when he abandoned his Time Inc. people to curry favor with the powerful forces within Warner Communications a decade earlier.

"It was fairly stunning," said one who ended up with the short of the stick. "This is a guy who is very, very close to himself. It's hard for anyone to have a genuine relationship with him. On the other hand, Case cared adamantly about his own guys."

It wasn't supposed to work this way. The two companies had hired a management-consulting firm to analyze the organizational chart and recommend who should report where. But Case and Levin grew impatient as the process drew out, so they dropped the consultant, met over a weekend, and hammered out the details themselves. When executives were called, it was already a fait accompli. Parsons, Levin's president, served as messenger. "Here's how it's going to be," he told one of the Time Warner executives who lost out to his AOL counterpart. Parsons told the crestfallen executive to stand by the fax machine and read the press release it was about to spew out.

It was a new day indeed.

Case, meanwhile, was making the rounds. That included taking Levin, his new partner, on a tour of AOL's Dulles campus shortly after the merger announcement. It was the five-cent tour, which included a brief inspection of the NOC, AOL's Network Operating Center, which looked like a NASA command center before rocket takeoff, only less glamorous. But it was the best show on the otherwise muted campus. Case, for his part, played gracious host, pointing things out, making unfunny jokes. But from the get-go, it was clear that Case and Levin actually had very little in common. The chitchat felt forced. It would have been a dull day but for the visit they made to the little convenience store on campus. Case, strangely playful, put an America Online headband on Levin's graying pate. Not only did Levin look ridiculous, he looked like he wanted to kill Steve Case.

By the time the klieg lights had faded, after the media had moved on to the next big story, Case soberly addressed about two hundred AOL lieutenants in a private meeting at Dulles headquarters in the first weeks of 2000.

Case had reverted back to casual wear, an open collar and khakis (when in Rome . . .). Standing at the podium on the raised platform of the Seriff Auditorium, Case was finally getting around to taking his own senior people through the merger, answering questions.

There were a lot of them. AOL's stock was still flying pretty high. Time Warner's wasn't. *Would AOL still issue stock options? Would the combination bring down our growth rate? Would it have a mitigating effect on our stock?*

(It already did: In the days that followed the merger announcement, AOL's stock dropped precipitately.)

While the rest of the world was marveling at the meaning of this mega-merger—ushering in the Internet era—Case found himself in the curious position of defending the deal to his *own* people. Why did AOL need to pull off the largest merger in U.S. history? Why did AOL need to merge with a stodgy old firm like Time Warner to become the world's largest media company?

"Senior management wasn't quite sure why we did it," said one. "We worried about our culture. Time Warner was a pretty big, ugly beast."

This was the feverish time of the tech boom, when a simple idea, like selling groceries on-line, could bring billions in an IPO, Silicon Valley was minting millionaire secretaries by the day, and AOL was king of the digital heap—a swaggering company pumped up on a steroid-like stock price.

What did AOL need Time Warner for?

Case's answer: "Capital preservation."

During the meeting, the AOL chief explained that the company's wild ride couldn't last, that for all the buzz about the Internet and AOL's place at the vanguard, it would ultimately come to an abrupt conclusion. AOL's stock price would eventually fall.

"Irrational exuberance," he would later call it, borrowing the phrase from Alan Greenspan, chairman of the Federal Reserve Board.

His calculation was that the Internet sector was already overvalued. There was too much hype. Other Internet firms, he told the group, were little more than smoke and mirrors, few were even profitable, and when the public made that discovery, it would collapse on AOL, buckling its own stock.

"He thought AOL would potentially be hurt," said one in attendance.

But before it all came tumbling down, Case told his minions that AOL needed to make a move—to preserve its capital, its lofty stock price. Thus, AOL's all-stock acquisition of Time Warner.

People who attended the meeting in Dulles didn't understand. The takeover of Time Warner was supposed to be the crowning achievement of AOL, the convergence of the world's largest on-line service with an array of powerful entertainment assets that stretched from the CNN television network to the *Time* magazine empire to the esteemed Warner Bros. movie studio.

And yet Case understood that there was another truth.

The Internet was real, and AOL had a legitimate product that millions across America used as an on-ramp to the Internet. But in the end, Case knew that the hype could not be sustained, not even at AOL.

What he didn't tell the gathering that day was that before the merger, signs of financial weakness were beginning to blip on AOL spreadsheets. Internal AOL documents show that as early as the fall of 1999, just as Case made his initial approach to Levin, AOL's pipeline of future, big advertising deals was projected to slow in volume and revenue. That, combined with AOL's greatest asset, its stock price, gave Case all the incentive he needed to pull off the Time Warner deal.

"It was," said a company executive, "Steve's masterstroke."

CHAPTER FOUR

AOL VERSUS THE WORLD

The lights were dim, the long, polished conference table packed with power brokers. In another era, this dark-paneled room would have been smoke-filled, the kind where prosperous men in expensive suits waved fat cigars and plotted and schemed to dominate the world. Only this was the afternoon of June 5, 2000, in downtown Washington, D.C., at the plush offices of Howrey Simon Arnold & White, an international law firm of considerable heft on Pennsylvania Avenue, a short power walk from the White House. And the subject at hand was merely the domination of the media world, as threatened by the proposed merger of AOL and Time Warner.

Cokes and cookies were served at the secret gathering. Seated in a plush leather chair at the head of the table was the avatar of Washington insider politics: Preston Padden. Charming, dynamic, flamboyant, and described by some as slicker than a used-car salesman, Padden gleamed with a well-modulated tan and the breezy confidence of a street fighter who relishes a good corporate brawl. It was in his blood. Padden, then fifty-one years old, was born in Washington and raised in the hallways of political power, working for the likes of tough-guy media kingpin Rupert Murdoch of media powerhouse News Corp.

Padden, akin to those who had risen from the mail room, had started as a switchboard operator at Washington TV station WTTG and made his way through the ranks with his rapier mind and wit. When the Fox network was just getting off the ground, he was known as "Preston the Enforcer" for his bruising dealings with the network's affiliates. Later, he went on to become president of ABC television. Now, his official title was executive vice president for government relations at ABC's parent, Disney. But it might have been more accurate to call him Michael Eisner's point man.

Padden had a direct line to the Disney chieftain, who, like many others, took a shine to Padden's glib charm, and Padden did Eisner's bidding in the nation's capital, which often included high-decibel, public scrums with Mickey Mouse's avowed enemies. The world-famous rodent may have had an amiable smile that captivated the hearts of children in the Magic Kingdom, but when it came to business, Disney was no pushover. Mickey Mouse was known in Washington circles for eating its enemy's heart for lunch.

On Disney's plate, at that moment, was the matter of the AOL–Time Warner merger. Although the deal had been announced a few months earlier, in January 2000, it was far from a done deal, if Padden and his Disney crew had any say in it. And they would. Before AOL and Time Warner could wed, they would need to get the equivalent of a marriage license. They needed approval from two U.S. regulatory agencies—the Federal Trade Commission and the Federal Communications Commission, not to mention their regulatory counterpart in Brussels, the European Commission.

Padden, eyeing an opportunity to make some noise here and abroad, assembled a standing-room-only crowd of interested parties—about thirty in all—that included others who worked in the shadows of the Capitol for major corporate interests, including Microsoft, NBC, Barry Diller's man at USA Networks, the Bell telephone companies, and a host of AOL Internet rivals, including EarthLink. But in addition to the standard-bearers of corporate America, Padden had invited those whose mission in life was to slay the beast of imperial capitalism—the nonprofit, public-interest folks who never saw a merger they liked.

"It had the makings of an unholy alliance," said Jeff Chester, then head of the Center for Media Education, a nonprofit that was basically a one-man wrecking ball—Jeff Chester himself, a quixotic, fast-talking, five-foot-five-inch fire hydrant of a consumer advocate, by way of Brooklyn, New York.

For Chester, who had made a living chomping on the leg of big business, it was a surreal moment. This was the kind of room where mergers are struck, not struck *down,* he thought. "Reversed gravity," he called it. There he was, in a dark suit, sitting two chairs away from Padden, also in a dark suit. "I always feel weird in those type of settings because they're the type of people I like to turn in to the Justice Department," Chester said.

But he was able to resolve his own internal conflict by applying simple logic: "I needed them." Disney not only had the financial war chest to take on AOL and Time Warner, it also walked into meetings with federal regulators with the mantle of corporate officialdom. Chester would work behind the scenes, supplying Disney with, as he put it, "all this dirt" that he would dig up on AOL and Time Warner's business plans and strategies.

Padden, for whom all is fair in love and corporate war, had no such compunctions. This wasn't personal; this was business.

Padden, the don of this gathering, thanked everyone for coming. *I can speak only for Disney,* he said, *but we see the AOL–Time Warner merger as a competitive threat, and we're concerned.* Padden talked about AOL as the "gatekeeper" of the Internet, erecting a "walled garden" around its proprietary on-line service, a comfortable place where consumers were shut in, unaware of the World Wide Web beyond its virtual walls. *We want to see how people feel about this merger and whether we can do something together,* he told the gathering.

That, for Padden, was being delicate. But everyone grasped the message: Who would join Disney in this fight?

Around the room they went, introducing themselves and their cause. When it was Chester's turn, he said, "I represent digital democracy and I'm interested in the free flow of information and the digital world." The response from the suits? "They looked at me like I was from another planet," he said. And yet, for all of Chester's throwback, 1960s hippie, utopian strivings, he did have something in common with his Wall Street opposites. There was no resolution at that June meeting, but there was a consensus: For its sheer size, its broad scope and potential power, the merger of AOL and Time Warner struck fear.

"Everyone was concerned about the impact of the merger on the emerging [Internet] marketplace, and the only question was whether anyone would commit to anything," Chester said. "This was the biggest merger in American history, and it posed grave threats to competition."

In the days immediately following the January announcement of AOL's merger with Time Warner, company officials on both sides quickly moved to secure support on Capitol Hill, including two powerful Senate committee chairmen running for president, Orrin G. Hatch (R-Utah) and John McCain (R-Ariz.), who showed a keen interest in the big business deal.

Steve Case, the AOL chief, and Jerry Levin, his Time Warner counterpart, as well as Dick Parsons, Time Warner's president, made more than fifty courtesy calls to key senators and representatives. Case, deploying his celebrity status, made the rounds, visiting with different offices. The Internet was still a financial juggernaut then, and his presence alone would make an impression, cultivating some goodwill. Though not a gregarious executive, Case had been prepped by his people. This wouldn't be small talk; that wasn't Case's strength. It was too late for a "personality remake," said one AOLer, but there were other ways Case could be persuasive: *Such-and-such issue is what the senator cares about. Here's his pet project. These are the likely subjects to be raised.*

It is all a part of Washington tradition: genuflecting. It has its place. Ego stroking does work, even among would-be presidents striding along the corridors of power. Neither the Senate nor the House had any direct say in approving the merger—they were mostly bystanders to an unfolding drama—but seasoned politicos understood from the beginning the importance of paying their respects. For one, the Commerce, Justice and State Subcommittee of the Senate Appropriations Committee controlled the purse strings of both the FTC and FCC. Run afoul of a key member of Congress, and the agencies could suddenly find themselves with curtailed budgets. Incurring the wrath of the wrong politician also could lead to dire consequences for companies like AOL and Time Warner. "Members can mess them up in other ways," said a Hill veteran. Using its indirect influence, Congress could introduce a bill, say, that put a halt to

Internet spam, or junk e-mail, which, despite the protestations of AOL, could put a crimp in its on-line marketing exploits.

"In any situation like this, what one might do is go to the Hill if you want to give a regulatory agency a push," said one who did as much on the AOL–Time Warner merger. "It's much more the power of persuasion."

It's a subtle thing, but effective all the same. A powerful senator can nudge an independent agency, like the FCC or FTC, to look into particular matters, including whether the merger violated antitrust laws. Forces on Capitol Hill can also give political cover to the federal agencies to take action, to make their jobs easier. It is almost like a wink: *Go ahead, impose regulatory restrictions.*

For AOL and Time Warner, it was a simple calculation: Solidify support among those in Congress who were already in their camp. Shore up support among those who were on the fence. And they went to see their opponents. Even if they couldn't convince them to see the errors of their way, it was protocol.

No doubt, Capitol Hill intended to keep a close eye on the merger proceedings; it was, after all, the biggest deal ever. Whether members of Congress would weigh in remained unclear. The companies, however, left little to chance, hiring a battalion of lobbyists to minimize political damage, even though few, if any, expected a regulatory challenge to the AOL–Time Warner merger. The two companies were in different businesses. One was Internet; the other, movies, music, and other entertainment. There was little overlap to suggest that a combination of the two companies would create a monopoly.

It was supposed to be routine. It was supposed to be a breeze. It was supposed to be a slam dunk. But no one counted on Stephen Heins. Hell hath no fury like a tiny Internet service provider scorned.

Halfway across the country, in the remote, small downtown of Oshkosh, Wisconsin, inside a nearly vacant, rundown mall, in a seven hundred-square-foot office, at a little cubbyhole of a desk sat Heins, then a fifty-six-year-old aging flower child, a tall, angular, affable fellow who also happened to be a sleeping giant.

While Steve Case and Jerry Levin were masters of the media world,

Heins held sway over his own small universe: about twenty-eight hundred customers in a fifty-mile radius who subscribed to NorthNet LLC, a small Internet provider. Heins, NorthNet's marketing director, was one of four employees. There was no secretary. But when Case and Levin announced their merger, they also pledged to open Time Warner's cable-television network, the nation's second largest behind AT&T, to AOL rivals who wanted to offer Internet service to Time Warner's more than twelve million cable subscribers. Heins thought they were talking to him and his ilk.

Heins, like many other Internet providers, wanted to get access to Time Warner's cable lines. They were faster than telephone lines. Cable represented the future of the Internet, offering a more robust delivery system than copper telephone wires to transmit digital information. Speed was becoming increasingly important as the Web moved to more colorful graphics and audio and video content. It seemed simple enough to Heins. Case and Levin had made an "open access" pledge. Heins wanted to take them up on the offer.

So, on a wintry March afternoon in 2000, he hopped in his 1988 Mazda 626 and, adding about 20 miles to the 140,000 miles on the odometer, drove to Time Warner's regional office in nearby Appleton. By NorthNet standards, it was as grand as the Taj Mahal, a newly built, state-of-the-art cavernous brick building—no, *facility.* "Plush, in a cable company sort of way," he said. Not that he got to see much of it. He made it as far as the receptionist. When he asked to talk to someone about getting access to Time Warner's cable lines, the secretary not only didn't make anyone available, she refused to tell him the last name of anyone who worked there. Heins, not easily ruffled, left his business card and asked that someone get back to him.

Nobody called. Heins paid other visits. The same scenario played out. No one was available. No last names. It became a ritual. "I kept going back every month from that time on," he said, "but I never got past the receptionist."

March turned to April, which turned to May, and while the bleak, snowy tundra of Wisconsin held firm, so did Heins's resolve. "I was getting madder by the minute," he said.

It wasn't just that he was being stonewalled. It was also that Case and Levin had made a pledge, and now it seemed like empty words. "They were going to say one thing in public and act entirely differently in the real world," Heins said. And for the former flower child, there was an important principle at stake. "I viewed it as a First Amendment issue," he said. "I saw it as a monopoly who controlled the [cable] pipes and potentially controlled all the information that traveled over them."

Steve Heins had a cause.

The man on a mission also was developing a plan. With each spurned visit to the regional Time Warner office, he was building a case, although he wasn't quite sure for what purpose. Meanwhile, he had made contact with some public-interest advocates in Washington who had given him the telephone number of Time Warner's cable headquarters in Connecticut. When he got through, he asked for an application for NorthNet to apply for access to Time Warner's cable lines. Things were beginning to gel. Before long, the application arrived in the mail. It asked detailed questions about NorthNet's business and required a signature to ensure confidentiality. Heins didn't like that last part. He didn't want to sign something that he couldn't disclose to others. What happened if he found a smoking gun? He didn't want to tie his hands.

An idea: Get another Internet service provider in northern Wisconsin to make the application. He did, it did, and Time Warner sent back a "term sheet," its proposal under which it would give an Internet firm access to its cable lines. Heins arranged a meeting with the other firm, which had made the application. They picked a coffee shop located halfway between them, in Green Bay. The men met, exchanged documents. Right away, Heins could see there was a problem with what Time Warner was asking. If an Internet firm wanted access to its cable lines, it had to pay up—big time.

Time Warner demanded 75 percent of an Internet provider's revenue from all subscriber fees, the lifeblood of its business. Time Warner also wanted 25 percent of the Internet firm's revenue from other sources, such as advertising and other electronic commerce fees, even though they were not transactions directly related to Time Warner's cable business. There was more: Time Warner wanted approval control over the Internet firm's home page, the first screen that customers saw. Time Warner's terms were so onerous, Heins thought, that they effectively undermined AOL and Time Warner's open access pledge.

"This was so anticompetitive that Joseph Stalin could barely have improved it," Heins said.

But he had the evidence he wanted, the smoking gun. Open access? Heins was going to show them. He faxed a copy of the Time Warner term sheet to his consumer-advocate contacts in Washington, who showed it to their attorneys, who went bug-eyed. *Did Heins realize just how explosive this was?* He did. "My only concern was, how do we get this into the public record?" he said.

He booked a flight to Washington and, again with the help of the D.C. consumer advocates, arranged a meeting with a gaggle of staff attorneys at the Federal Trade Commission, which was reviewing the merger. For nearly four hours, Heins held court in a big conference room at FTC headquarters with nine highly trained government attorneys and an economist or two, reviewing the Time Warner term sheet, building a potential court case to block the largest merger in U.S. history.

AOL and Time Warner had just messed with the wrong guy.

In the first few months after the merger announcement, other opponents began to mobilize, quietly dispatching emissaries to Capitol Hill to raise concerns about the deal. Disney, not surprisingly, was at the forefront, led by that pied piper, Preston Padden.

For weeks, Disney, along with several major music concerns and about a dozen Internet firms, buttonholed congressional aides and senators and representatives. Capitol Hill was ablaze with e-mail messages and letters raising questions about the merger. Padden, who had flown out to Los Angeles to get the okay from his higher-ups for his public campaign, said Disney simply wanted an assurance, preferably in writing, that AOL and Time Warner would treat their rivals' content the same as their own on the Internet and over cable lines.

While Disney and other corporate interests ratcheted up their campaign, so, too, did the consumer groups, creating a pincer-like approach to the politicians and regulatory agencies reviewing the merger. Jeff Chester, head of the Center for Media Education, viewed his contributions and those of the other public-interest advocates a bit less romantically.

"We're the subminiature Chihuahuas," he said, "but we bark really loud."

Even the Chihuahuas of the public realm have a system, though.

Chester, almost manic in the way the words could not catch up with the speed of his brain, played the role of "propagandist and organizer," said Andrew Jay Schwartzman, president of the Media Access Project, a public-interest law firm. Schwartzman, for his part, served in the role of lawyer, preparing legal filings for submission to the regulatory agencies. Mark Cooper, research director of the Consumer Federation of America, was the numbers cruncher, the economist. And Gene Kimmelman, co-director of the advocacy group Consumers Union, was the big-picture strategist who was knowledgeable in the ways of antitrust law and legislation.

The quartet was a bit like the Marx Brothers of consumer advocates. For one, they were lovable underdogs representing the public. They were seen as almost inseparable in their uphill battles waging war against the windmills of corporate America. Which is not to say they didn't have an effect. Together they had played a key role in helping the government craft tough regulatory requirements on a number of big deals, including the Time Warner–Turner Broadcasting merger in 1996. The AOL–Time Warner merger, they felt, represented a potentially graver threat to competition.

Early on, Kimmelman and his colleagues let their concerns be known at all the regulatory agencies. So, too, did a series of other interests, including not just Microsoft and Disney, but also the American Civil Liberties Union, AT&T, NBC's General Electric Co., BellSouth Corp., Verizon Communications Inc., SBC Communications Inc., RCN Corp., and scores of small Internet service providers. Even those who had no direct dealings with AOL or Time Warner carefully observed the proceedings from the sidelines, if only to ensure that the merger wouldn't eventually tread on their turf.

"I don't believe in my seven years [at the FTC] there has ever been a transaction in which more third parties filed more white papers, challenging the validity and antitrust laws," said Robert Pitofsky, then the FTC's chairman. "There was practically a queue around the block of lawyers and CEOs."

The queue reached all the way across the Atlantic, where European fears quickly materialized.

What would a combination of AOL and Time Warner mean on the Continent? AOL was already among the biggest Internet players in Great Britain,

France, and elsewhere, and Time Warner's vast array of entertainment and media assets, ranging from Bugs Bunny to *Time* magazine, were plastered throughout Europe. Many already feared the invasion of the Big Mac.

Now what?

An answer—in jest—arrived in an e-mail that made its way across Europe, from London to Hamburg, Germany, until it reached the third-floor corner office of Michael Haentjes, chairman and chief executive of Edel Music AG, a major European concern. When he opened the e-mail, he chuckled at the notice:

"In a surprise announcement, AOL Time Warner announced Friday that it had acquired France. This marks the first time that a multimedia company had purchased an entire nation."

Steve Case was quoted as saying, "We had considered other countries, but we were just blown away by France's great visuals and incredible depth of content." Levin added, "It's all about the cheese. They've got some really stinky cheese."

The implied message was clear: *Watch out for those acquisitive Americans.*

From the very beginning, AOL and Time Warner executives knew that the issue of open access would be tricky business. The weekend before the January merger announcement, George Vradenburg, the AOL policy chief, paid a visit to the Washington office of his Time Warner counterpart, Timothy Boggs. The two men faced a major problem: How do they find a new policy to resolve an inherent contradiction in the two companies' positions on the matter of open access?

Before the merger, AOL had been front and center, lobbying the federal government and city officials throughout the country to get them to require cable operators, such as AT&T and Time Warner, to guarantee that Internet service providers, like AOL, would get access to customers served by their cable systems. Time Warner had stood on the opposite side of the argument, along with AT&T, insisting that, first, their cable systems were not a public works project but a private enterprise in which they had invested heavily, and, second, the government shouldn't meddle in what was essentially a private business matter.

But now, AOL had worked out a deal to buy Time Warner. Suddenly, all of AOL's lobbying for open access didn't seem that important. And could Time Warner continue to argue against open access when AOL, its acquirer, had so adamantly fought for it?

"How do we rationalize this?" wondered one participant in the talks between the two companies. "It ended up being our huge bugaboo."

Part of the solution was for AOL to perform a classic Washington maneuver. "They essentially did a flip-flop," said William E. Kennard, then chairman of the FCC, which was reviewing the merger.

AOL was not only a pioneer in the open-access movement, it was also a big financial backer and member of the OpenNet Coalition, a group of more than nine hundred Internet service providers that, according to its mission statement, was "dedicated to promoting the rights of all consumers to obtain affordable, high-speed access to the Internet from the provider of their choice." Shortly after the merger announcement, AOL dramatically scaled back its involvement. At the same time, AOL ordered its paid guns to stop actively pushing another open-access initiative, Nogatekeepers, a Web site the company had created to corral the support of public-interest advocates.

Publicly, AOL spun its story this way: It said it never liked the idea of forcing AT&T and other cable operators to do anything by dint of government action; rather, AOL said it would voluntarily open Time Warner's cable lines to competitors. Time Warner came around to the view that it was in accord with AOL's idea to open its cable lines to one and all. Case and Levin sought to defuse the simmering controversy by announcing in late February 2000 that they had signed what they called a "memorandum of understanding," pledging to allow rival Internet service providers to connect to their cable lines.

Congress wasn't convinced.

"Given that this document lacks both enforceability and specificity, this committee remains to be convinced of its value beyond the boardroom and public relations office of AOL Time Warner," said Orrin Hatch, chairman of the Senate Judiciary Committee, during the first public hearing on the merger in late February.

The debate, though lively, was largely abstract. About 45 percent of U.S. households then had Internet access, and about 90 percent of them reached the Web through traditional dial-up telephone wires, which were open to all of the more than seven thousand Internet service providers competing for subscribers. Only 10 percent, or about four million, got on-line through cable and other high-speed, or so-called broadband, networks. That number, however, was expected to double annually by some estimates. Already, AOL had twenty-one million subscribers, six times more than its nearest competitor, EarthLink, and rivals feared the gap would widen if the others couldn't get access to those fast cable lines.

"This proposed merger reminds me of 'a tale of two cities,' with portents of either the best of times or the worst of times," said Senator Patrick J. Leahy (D-Vt.)

Case tried to assuage the senators at the hearing. "We certainly hope to lead a whole new era of innovation in our industry, but we won't be the only company out there," he said.

His words didn't temper the concerns of committee members. Senator Mike DeWine (R-Ohio), chairman of the Antitrust Subcommittee, seemed to echo the prevailing sentiment when he said, "The more I examine this deal, the more I am convinced that it does raise very significant competition and public policy issues that must be thoroughly explored."

As far as Microsoft was concerned, the seeds of unrest were planted well before AOL announced its betrothal to Time Warner. Back in the summer of 1999, AOL and Microsoft, the two inveterate rivals, squared off in an unusual cyberwar, trading blows over an emerging technology that would test the resolve of federal regulators: instant messaging.

It was a decidedly high-tech skirmish: AOL and Microsoft computer programmers, sitting at their keyboards on opposite sides of the country, fired off digital salvos, silent and invisible but all too effective, in a mounting brouhaha that involved software clones, computer hacking, the exploitation of a software bug, and a bizarre case of cloak-and-dagger, courtesy of a Microsoft employee masquerading as an independent computer consultant seeking to discredit AOL.

Perhaps this is the way wars of the next millennium will be fought.

This twentieth-century war, though, was about what most wars are about: territory. AOL, in this case, had most of it, controlling about 90 percent of the instant-messaging worldwide market, led by its flagship service, AOL Instant Messenger. Microsoft's MSN Messenger, lagging far behind, desperately wanted to play catch-up—and for good reason. Instant messaging was a phenomenon. It hadn't reached the radar screens of many adults, but millions of teenagers were going gaga. Instant messaging allowed computer users to send text-based messages to each other even faster than a traditional e-mail. Jot a message inside a little pop-up window, push the Send button, and *pow,* it immediately popped up on the receiver's computer.

Instant messaging was based on another hugely attractive technology to business interests. They called it "presence detection." It was jargon for a simple concept: Instant messaging allowed computer users to see—to *detect*—who else was on-line at that very moment. The instant-messaging software came with what AOL dubbed a "buddy list," which instantaneously showed who were logging on and off their computers, so that users knew when to ping their buddies with an instant message. Imagine the business implications of knowing when people—consumers with credit cards—were actually on-line, potentially ready to spend money.

And here was the pièce de résistance: Instant messaging was free. Computer users only had to download it from the Web onto their hard drives, and they were ready to go.

As they said in industry-speak, it was a *sticky* application. The more people used it, the more they came back to it. Kids loved the immediacy of it, the anonymity of it. For them, it was a safe, secure way to interact, to socialize behind the blushless, acneless face of their unflappable personal computer. For AOL and Microsoft, the emerging technology represented something even more tantalizing: another potential source of big business. That's where the dispute arose.

AOL, as the market leader, refused to open its instant-messaging program to rivals. AOL users could talk to other AOL users but not to those of other instant-messaging services, such as Microsoft's MSN Messenger. AOL claimed it was simply a matter of wanting to secure the safety and privacy of its own instant-messaging customers. Besides, AOL said it was looking into how to make its software interoperable—compatible—with others. That argument, however, convinced few. AOL had a more compelling reason to maintain a closed loop: When you're in the lead, why give an opening to a competitor?

Microsoft, for its part, said that it wanted to make its instant-messaging software interoperable with AOL's so that users of both programs could talk to each other. Microsoft compared it to the telephone. What happened if customers of one carrier, say, AT&T, could talk only to those who also used AT&T? It would be like the Tower of Babel. A whole lot of talking, but not a lot of communicating. Instead, the telephone was an open system. There were different carriers, but everyone was allowed to talk to everyone else. That, Microsoft asserted, is the way it ought to be with instant messaging. It was a matter of freedom. Microsoft's public assertions, like AOL's, sounded benign, if not downright patriotic. But like AOL, Microsoft had its own business motives: By linking the two instant-messaging programs, Microsoft could grab more customers.

Enter the clone.

AOL wouldn't play ball, so Microsoft turned to its own strength—developing software—and created a clone of the AOL Instant Messenger program. The clone allowed Microsoft users to send instant messages to AOL users—until AOL figured out what was going on and electronically blocked Microsoft users from its network. Microsoft, unbowed, tinkered with its software and found a new back door to AOL's software. Not to be outdone, AOL again identified the Microsoft intruder and erected another digital wall.

Back and forth it went—at least thirteen times in all. Then somebody got a little carried away. In August 1999, months before the AOL–Time Warner merger announcement, a man identifying himself as Phil Bucking of Bucking Consulting, sent an e-mail to Richard Smith, a leading computer-security expert. Bucking said he was writing to Smith because Smith had "significant credibility with the press." Bucking was developing his own instant-messaging service and was looking into how AOL was using a security flaw to block Microsoft customers.

"I think you would agree that this is a heinous and risky action," Bucking wrote in his e-mail. "I am perfectly fine with AOL and MS [Microsoft] fighting it out with standard software practices, but putting user security at risk is unacceptable. It is inconceivable that a company would even consider doing this."

It was an impassioned missive. It also came from a Microsoft employee. When Smith made the discovery, Microsoft looked into the matter and concluded that the e-mail came from one of their own—but the company wasn't sure who. It was an unauthorized plant.

Moments after AOL announced its Time Warner takeover, a flurry of e-mails and phone calls began zipping back and forth between Redmond, Washington, and Washington, D.C. Microsoft executives were alarmed, especially those who were already waging war with AOL over rival on-line services and instant-messaging systems. AOL, its arch-nemesis, was now making a bold move by gobbling up Time Warner. *Can we do anything about this?* Redmond wanted to know. *We can try,* said its people in Washington, *but it won't be easy.* It was time to activate Microsoft's small but effective lobbying machine in the nation's capital.

After the summer showdown over instant messaging, the merger presented another chance for Microsoft to make headway in its attempt to force AOL to open up its instant-messaging service to rivals.

"It was an opportunity to politicize this issue a little bit," said a Microsoft official.

The first order of business was to alter public perception. The summer feud over instant messaging had been framed in the press as a battle of the behemoths, big, bad Microsoft taking on big, bad AOL. Sympathies were short in coming. "We thought having Microsoft take the lead was not a smart thing to do," said Ross Bagully, then chief executive of Tribal Voice, a unit of CMGI Inc., one of the instant-messaging firms that joined forces with Microsoft against AOL. "We didn't want it to look like a battle of the giants. It was important that smaller companies like myself kept a front position, because we thought we would get more traction. It's not an accident that we didn't talk about CMGI [the parent company]. We talked about Tribal Voice."

Thus, the solution: Find proxies. Introduce the public to small firms, the Davids of the instant messaging world, like Tribal Voice, fighting AOL, the Goliath. Create an instant-messaging coalition. Then give it the look and feel of a grassroots campaign.

The contours of such a plan began to take shape in early 2000 on a cold, cloudy day in an industrial office park on the outskirts of Boston. A crew of seasoned publicists from the big Edelman public relations agency in New York was ushered into a bright green conference room. There, they met with executives of CMGI. Like Microsoft, CMGI was a tech titan, though of lesser notoriety. It owned two small instant-messaging firms, not just Tribal Voice but iCast. On the table beckoned breakfast and a question: How to leverage the AOL–Time Warner merger to pry open AOL's instant-messaging service to rivals?

The discussion turned into a free association in search of a message, with the PR people trying to pull a story out of the rambling ideas presented by the instant-messaging executives. It was a complicated story involving technology that most people hadn't heard of. How do they frame the issue? How do they explain that AOL was blocking users of rival instant-messaging systems from communicating with users of AOL's service? What is the tag line? What's the one sentence that can crystallize the basic message?

Margaret Heffernan, the iCast chief executive, locked into the debate. "Tear down that wall," she blurted out.

Instantly, her pronouncement resonated with everyone in the room. Reagan. The popular president had uttered that famous phrase at the height of the Cold War: *Tear down that wall.* The association was a positive one: The instant-messaging forces, by echoing the Reagan phrase, were the good guys. Then, there was another association: the Berlin Wall. It was fraught with negative connotations, which is what they wanted, because it was associated with AOL, builder of a virtual wall around its instant-messaging system. "It made immediate sense," said one. Somebody scribbled the phrase on a pad. And a PR campaign was born. Before long, the tag line appeared in glaring red letters in ads in the political press: "TEAR DOWN THAT WALL!"

The message was signed by "FREE IM," the "IM" being instant messaging. But while Free IM sounded like a populist movement, the ads didn't explain who was behind it: Tribal Voice and iCast, the subsidiaries of a big corporation, CMGI. It was, though, an effective message. "You're putting both political pressure on and public pressure on," said Blair Levin, then a consultant hired by CMGI to advise it on the regulatory part of the AOL merger. "No CEO, whether fair or not, likes to be put in a corner with the defenders of the Berlin Wall."

Edelman, CMGI's hired public relations gun, was just getting warmed up. Other effective propaganda material included small FREE IM stickers that showed the AOL icon, a little yellow man, locked behind bars, a tear running down his cheek. There were also FREE IM buttons. Bright orange, they stood out on the lapel of a dark suit, the armor of choice in Washington jousts, especially in committee hearings where those buttons might make an impression from the gallery.

Edelman's efforts, later recognized as one of the "100 Best PR Programs of 2000" by an industry trade firm, were far-ranging. "Activities included pre-briefing media, leaking testimony, providing comment before and after events and distributing supporting documents," the company stated in a written description of its plans.

Edelman also came up with IMUnified, the name of a broader coalition that included various instant-messaging interests. The coalition made some headway, too. In March 2000, at the second Senate hearing on the merger, the Commerce Committee quizzed Case and Levin about a variety of topics but honed in on AOL's instant-messaging service and why it wasn't open to rivals. Case argued that AOL had done "a number of things" to create an "inclusive community," citing licensing agreements with several competing Internet service providers. But it was a hollow point. These other firms were simply licensing to use AOL's software. This was not the same as making the service compatible with those of its rivals, a fact not lost on Senator Conrad Burns (R-Mont.), chairman of the Commerce Subcommittee on Communications.

"The spectacular growth of the Internet itself was made possible by the development of open networks, not closed systems," he reminded the AOL chief. "Unfortunately, in the instant-messaging area, I fear we are headed in the other direction."

At precisely 12:01 A.M. on May 1, 2000, the world changed.

Somebody at Time Warner cable pulled the proverbial plug, and television screens went blue, zapping Disney's ABC programming in more than three million homes across the nation, from New York City to Houston to Raleigh-Durham to Los Angeles to Fresno to Philadelphia to Toledo.

This was serious business: More than one million New York homes alone were about to be deprived of the hit TV game show *Who Wants to Be a Millionaire*. Instead, Time Warner began telecasting a message, a long scrawl at the bottom of the blank screen, explaining in cryptic terms that it would not let Disney "force our customers to walk the plank one more time," adding that Disney had agreed to long-term contract extensions with other cable companies but not with Time Warner.

Huh?

The picture quickly came into focus: Time Warner had thrown Disney's ABC stations off several of its cable television systems over that simplest of American business institutions: a contract dispute.

Time Warner, in an unusually public attempt to punish a rival, had thrown down the gauntlet. It was an unvarnished display of power, a bloodless battle that was the television equivalent of the shelling of Fort Sumter in Charleston harbor, announcing the Civil War. Simmering antagonisms had finally bubbled up to the surface.

The fight centered in part on how much money Time Warner was willing to pay Disney, which owned ABC, to let Time Warner carry Disney-controlled cable networks on its systems. The fight also involved demands by Disney that AOL and Time Warner, when they merged, guarantee equal access on their cable systems for Disney cable channels. Looking to the wave of the future, Disney also pushed for equal access for its Internet content and interactive-television offerings under development. The real kicker, though, was this: Disney whispered that if AOL and Time Warner didn't play ball, Disney would make their lives miserable during the merger review before the various regulatory bodies.

The Time Warner "boys in Stamford," site of the cable operations, were "tired of being jerked around by Disney," said one involved in the talks. Levin reviewed the situation. So did other high-level Time Warner executives. Tossing Disney off of a cable system was a draconian measure, but maybe it wouldn't come to that. Maybe, Time Warner surmised, Disney was bluffing, and it would pull back its demands once Time Warner threatened to cut it off its cable network.

"There was this strange idea that Disney would blink," said an official involved in the talks. "But whenever did they blink?"

Disney not only did *not* blink, it immediately went on the offensive. The same day Time Warner pulled the plug, ABC requested an emergency ruling from the FCC to force Time Warner to restore transmission of its programming.

Time Warner responded quickly as well, stating that it was only react-ing to a stalemate in negotiations, accusing ABC of refusing to extend talks by eight months rather than setting a May 24 deadline, when the sweeps period ended.

Then they took off the gloves. A brawl, naturally, brought out Eisner's enforcer, Preston Padden, a veritable quote machine, who did not disap-point, telling the press, "Some deranged individual has deprived all of these people of ABC."

Not to be outdone, Time Warner Cable came out with its own spin. "When the AOL merger was announced, they thought they could use that to extract more money from us," said spokesman Michael Luftman, "because they felt we would be so sensitive to any controversy that we would agree to virtually any deal to keep things quiet."

Time Warner alleged that Disney tried to up its programming fee by $300 million. ABC said the figure was a lie. Tom Kane, president of WABC-TV in New York City, entered the fray, saying in a press release, "This blackout is a frightening foreshadowing of the implications of the Time Warner–AOL merger." The Disney war machine was in full deploy-ment: Other executives of ABC stations parroted the remarks in similar press releases.

Even feisty New York City Mayor Rudolph Giuliani couldn't resist a jab, slamming the cable industry. "This is an example of what happens when you allow monopolies to get too big and they become too predatory and then the consumer is hurt."

A day later, Time Warner and Disney temporarily called a truce. By midday, Time Warner resumed airing signals from ABC stations. But it was too late: The cat was out of the bag. What had started as a quiet, back-channel campaign to slow the AOL–Time Warner juggernaut was now an all-too-public jihad. For the first time, Disney publicly called on federal regulators to block Time Warner's merger with AOL.

"This is broader than television," Padden said then. "This is about whether there should be a policy prohibiting AOL–Time Warner and cable companies in general from owning the content seeking to travel over its monopoly pipeline."

Padden had used the word that AOL and Time Warner most dreaded hearing on Capitol Hill: *monopoly.*

From then on, Padden was launched like a ballistic missile, crisscrossing the airwaves, stating his case against the merger on Time Warner's own CNN and CNNfn as well as CNBC, ABC, CBS, and NBC, not to mention virtually every major newspaper in the land. Meanwhile, Disney produced a splashy video, featuring a grave narrator, decrying the potential evils of an AOL–Time Warner combination. Titled *Consumer Choice in the Broadband Marketplace of Tomorrow,* the video was distributed far and wide across the capital and the media.

What was basically an issue of money had quickly devolved into a holy war for Disney and a monumental public relations blunder for Time Warner and its merger partner, AOL.

It "greatly complicated our lives," said an official involved in the merger talks with the government. The problem "was more cosmetic than real, but as often happens in Washington, the cosmetic becomes real."

The result, said Vradenburg, AOL's chief policy maker, was, "It changed the complexion of the merger and the way the government was looking at this."

Difficulties emerged from the very start, beginning with an arm-wrestling match over which antitrust agency would review the merger: The FTC or the Justice Department. Both wanted it. Or rather, both Bob Pitofsky, the FTC chairman, and Joel Klein, the top antitrust enforcer at Justice, wanted it. In the labyrinth of government, there is usually a formal process to make such decisions, a code, a regulation, a flowchart, something. Not here. In such cases, it was up to the two antitrust agencies themselves to reach a gentleman's agreement. Usually, the question of jurisdiction is handled at the staff level. But the staffs couldn't agree, so it was kicked up to the bureau directors at each agency. They couldn't decide either. So, said Pitofsky, "This one went all the way to Joel and me."

There were all manner of reasons on both sides. At Justice, Klein argued it had handled various Internet-related cases. At the FTC, Pitofsky had done cable deals and television programming. Justice had already gotten the big fish before this case—the Microsoft antitrust trial—but that had originated at the FTC. Phone calls went back and forth across Pennsylvania Avenue between Pitofsky's office and Klein's office. They met, they exchanged memos. The two old friends cajoled. But for all of their legal arguments, there was another reason both sides wanted the AOL–Time Warner deal: It was important.

"Why do you go to work if you're an antitrust attorney?" queried Art Amolsch, a former Nixon political appointee who publishes *FTC Watch*, the bible of the agency's goings-on. "It's because you want to play in the big game. These guys wanted to play in the big game."

For Pitofsky, there was perhaps another motive. A former law professor, Pitofsky had worked hard to revitalize an agency once known as the "little old lady of Pennsylvania Avenue" that worked in the shadow of its big brother up the street, the Justice Department. The FTC still seemed like an anachronism, a secretive, independent law enforcement agency better known for a pair of hulking sculptures standing sentry outside its squat, utilitarian stone building. Titled "Man Controlling Trade," the statues showed a pair of men of exaggerated musculature using their bare arms to restrain braying horses back on their heels.

The FTC's mission, however, wasn't outdated. The FTC was still there to protect consumers from big business, from big bad monopolies, from the malfunctions, if you will, of a capitalist society. Pitofsky understood this at a core level. Hugely influential as FTC chairman, he was nonetheless a modest man, a rare combination in Washington.

Pitofsky was an erudite, measured, avuncular government official who was also a member of a book club and played in a father-son-daughter softball game on Sundays. A product of Paterson, New Jersey, he was the only son of a silk-factory worker and a mother who worked in a dress shop. A classic achiever, he was the first in his family to go to college, attending New York University, then Columbia School of Law. But his path to a career in antitrust law was an accident of timing. When he joined a New York law firm early in his career, he was assigned an antitrust case that lasted for about two years. Had circumstances been different, he said, he could have become an environmental lawyer just as easily.

But now, if there was anybody who knew about antitrust law, it was the FTC chairman. Pitofsky had been a professor at NYU's School of Law and a visiting professor at Harvard Law School, and was now on his third tour of duty at the FTC. Even more, he was an expert versed enough in the law to have written a textbook that former President Bill Clinton had used when he taught antitrust law in Arkansas.

The AOL–Time Warner merger, however, presented perhaps the greatest challenge to the seventy-year-old Pitofsky.

It was not so much a matter of personal pride. Pitofsky had long held the notion that media mergers—involving the marketplace of ideas—should be held to a higher standard. "What is antitrust about? Is it only about prices and output?" Pitofsky said in his professorial way. "Should we treat the merger of two newspapers the same as two bread companies? I don't think that's what Congress had in mind. It just seems to me, not that there are different standards, but you can apply stricter scrutiny."

This was about the First Amendment, freedom of speech, the free flow of ideas in a democracy. This was no time for his agency to take a backseat.

"In the end," Pitofsky said, "we agreed by an eyelash that the FTC had a better claim."

For Steve Case, business with the FTC got off on the wrong foot—literally.

The AOL chief executive, in a gesture of utter disdain, kicked his feet up on the table as he was being deposed after the merger announcement by government attorneys in the confines of the threadbare, drafty old Federal Trade Commission.

He might as well have been at the dentist. The grimace on his face was apparent to all as he was being quizzed by a bunch of low-level, salaried government attorneys. Add to that, Case's proclivity to disaffect people with his blank expressions. It didn't make a good combination.

But this FTC deposition was part of the process. Even billionaire CEOs who straddle the world like so many jolly green giants have to bend to the will of those persnickety government lawyers, answering their questions about the potential antitrust issues raised by a merger. But Case never saw an antitrust problem. AOL was an Internet firm. Time Warner was a bricks-and-mortar entertainment firm. They were in *different* businesses. They didn't overlap. All of his high-powered attorneys had told him so. It was not a traditional so-called horizontal merger of two companies in overlapping businesses. Rather, AOL and Time Warner were in complementary businesses, which made it a vertical merger, in antitrust parlance, which, in most cases, meant there was no fear of monopoly. Steve Case couldn't fathom why he was being grilled in the first place. This was a no-brainer. *Right?*

Just as soon as the FTC staffers concluded their questions—actually, a nanosecond before they finished—Case was up on his feet and, without even a feeble attempt at small talk, without shaking hands, he was walking out the door.

"This meeting is over," he announced.

Suffice it to say, Steve Case didn't make any new friends at the FTC that day. His behavior, said one familiar with the meeting, "was taken with sufficient forcefulness. It was taken as recalcitrance. But from the CEO's point of view, they were frustrated with the increasing second-guessing of the business, almost the second-guessing of their decision making. The [FTC] staff was taking that kind of attitude. There wasn't a warm and fuzzy relationship."

Frosty was more like it, as the FTC staffers pushed ahead in the ensuing months, taking dozens of depositions, questioning Jerry Levin and other senior executives as well as their rivals. The companies were compelled to produce confidential documents to the feds, which yielded some information that raised even more questions about the merger. Among them was a document that suggested the companies should consider favoring a business model in which AOL's high-speed Internet service traveled over Time Warner cable lines instead of riding over juiced-up telephone lines, a technology called digital subscriber line, or DSL. What was alarming to investigators about such a strategy was that DSL was the main alternative to cable for high-speed Internet service. If AOL essentially allowed DSL service to wither away in markets where Time Warner cable prevailed, it would practically force customers to opt for Time Warner's cable service, creating a de facto monopoly.

But that scenario was speculative. Who actually knew what AOL and Time Warner would do? Better yet, who could predict how the Internet market would unfold? The future is an elusive thing, especially for government attorneys grounded in what happened before, in the guiding light of precedent. How do you put restraints on a business when you're not even sure where it is going?

The here and now wasn't that easy to figure out, either. Many within the FTC held the same view that Case did—that this was a vertical merger, which antitrust enforcers have traditionally been leery of regulating.

"We were all freaked out," said one FTC official. "What was going to happen to the case?"

Indecision lingered for weeks, culminating on a summer day in 2000 when about twenty FTC staffers assembled in a corner conference room to discuss the merger. The stormy skies overhead reflected the dark and gloomy mood within. There was no agenda and, as it soon became clear, they had few ideas about which legal theories to pursue. The group talked about instant messaging but got nowhere. AOL dominated the field, but did its merger with Time Warner change the circumstance? Did the merger add to AOL's dominance? It didn't appear so. The issue dropped with a thud. For the moment, there were some who weren't sure whether there was a coherent "antitrust injury," said one of the participants. "Some people were dumbfounded. I'm not sure how much people believed there was a case."

Pitofsky, however, had a supple mind, and the FTC chairman's thinking evolved as he pored over the deluge of data coming in from all sides. Never before had the chairman so rolled up his sleeves. Usually, he deferred to the FTC staff and the antitrust bureau director, allowing himself to be guided by their research, their theories. But this was different. "I was more active in this case than in any other," Pitofsky said. "It was the biggest case in the history of this country."

As such, Pitofsky made a point of holding staff meetings in his office once or twice a week, at the end of the workday, around five or six in the evening. On his office couch, a set of lawyers armed with pens and legal pads briefed the chairman. He took these opportunities to listen, to find out what the staff was learning, to hear their line of evidence.

By the summer, the FTC began working closely with the Federal Communications Commission, the other federal agency reviewing the AOL–Time Warner merger. The FTC, after its initial hesitation, had concluded that AOL's dominance in the instant-messaging market wouldn't be altered by the merger, which meant that it was off-limits to the antitrust agency. The FCC, however, had a different mandate—a broader charge to look after "the public interest." As a result, the FTC handed off instant messaging to the FCC for further review.

Meanwhile, the FTC began to sharpen its legal attack, focusing on the issue of open access. A theory was emerging: Point one, if Time Warner failed to open its cable lines to competitors, AOL could dominate Internet services in cities served by Time Warner cable. Point two, if AOL dominated Internet service over those cable lines, while it also took the lion's share of business among customers who got Internet access through DSL lines or traditional dial-up telephone lines, then the combined entity, AOL Time Warner, would have so much market power that it would crush the competition. That brought the FTC to point three: The combined company must be forced to open up Time Warner's cable lines to rival Internet services providers, or face a court challenge.

That this matter would have to be resolved became a certainty in late June 2000 after shareholders of AOL and Time Warner, meeting separately in Virginia and New York, voted overwhelmingly in favor of the merger. About 81 percent of the Time Warner shares were in favor of the deal. But the margin was closer among AOL stockholders.

Despite the company's concerted effort to get out the vote, including mass mailings of glossy brochures and thousands of calls directly to stockholders, proxies representing 43 percent of the shares were not returned. Most likely, these were people who didn't open their mail, or figured their vote wasn't really going to make a difference. Either way, those were counted as no votes.

As a result, although a mere 2 percent of all outstanding AOL shares voted against the deal, only about 55 percent were in favor, which was not exactly a landslide, as company officials tried to portray it.

Things hadn't gone quite according to script at the AOL shareholder meeting at a Tysons Corner hotel in the Virginia suburbs. With more than three hundred shareholders in attendance, the meeting ran about thirty minutes over the scheduled one hour allotted, and executives faced a litany of questions from more than thirty dubious shareholders, many of whom zeroed in on AOL's stock price, which had declined about 25 percent since the merger announcement.

Steve Case tried to calm the agitated crowd, saying, "As we get closer to the merger date and people get more confident about it, we will get more momentum in the stock."

Around the same time, restive regulators in Brussels were beginning to ask questions about the deal as well. In June, the European Union announced it would launch a detailed probe of the AOL–Time Warner merger. The Europeans were concerned about the company's ability to unfairly dominate the Internet, but they focused on the emerging world of music distributed on-line. AOL Time Warner could "dictate the technical standards for delivering music over the Internet and monopolize the music player software," the EU warned.

It was an ominous smoke signal from across the Atlantic. The EU decree came a few days after its regulators said it planned to extend its inquiry into a separate bid by Time Warner to create a joint venture with EMI Music Group PLC, a combined recording powerhouse that would control about 20 percent of the world market.

The regulators were coming out of the woodwork. Suddenly, the AOL–Time Warner merger didn't seem like such a sure thing anymore.

On August 5, 2000, Richard G. Parker stepped out onto the veranda of the Silverado Resort, and for a brief moment, all seemed good with the world.

Parker, the FTC's top antitrust attorney, was back in his old stomping grounds in the Napa Valley on a glorious day, crystal clear and eighty degrees. His boyhood home, though, was a small northern California town, not this newfangled chic scene. Parker, a gruff cowboy at heart, wasn't part of the wine-and-cheese crowd. He was a Westerner. He wore cowboy boots with his thousand-dollar Italian designer suits. But he could appreciate the atmosphere. The stylish Silverado hotel looked out over a spectacular golf course, mountains, and a vineyard, all in one breathtaking sweep of the eye.

Parker, however, wasn't on vacation. This was the site of an antitrust conference, a confab involving members of the private bar as well as public legal officials like himself. That, for the time being, seemed beside the point, too. Breaking off from the conference, Parker had brought another participant in tow with him for a quiet moment on the scenic veranda: Joe Sims, AOL's lead outside attorney on the merger. They had things to discuss.

If Parker was gruff, Sims was downright combative. Maybe a prize-fighter in a previous life, Parker surmised. "A rough dude," Parker called him, reminded of Jack Tatum, the frightening Oakland Raiders football player, only not as dirty. Parker, at the age of fifty-two, still sported a baby face. Sims, by contrast, was at fifty-six years old a scruffy sort, with hair buzzed short, and a beard, and certainly no tie, unless, of course, he was paying his respects to the FTC chairman. Otherwise, the two attorneys were cut from the same legal cloth: aggressive, smart, effective.

But on this morning, neither was in combat mode. Over iced tea, the two began a desultory conversation about the pennant race. Parker was a San Francisco Giants baseball fan; Sims rooted for the rival Los Angeles Dodgers. The banter seemed to hint at the true competition between the two men, AOL versus the government, and it wasn't long before talk of baseball gave way to the real issue at hand.

AOL and Time Warner had produced reams of documents for the government, and the FTC staff in turn had identified potential issues to explore. But there had been no real negotiation between the two sides. Now, it was time for Parker to weigh in.

He casually mentioned the FTC's concerns about the anticompetitive threats posed by the merger. "Let's try to get the right people in a room and see if there are areas to fix," he suggested. Parker had no illusions about where Sims stood. He knew the AOL attorney would argue that there was no antitrust issue, but Parker reckoned he could start a dialogue.

"Let me know if you want to try to solve these problems or slug it out in court," he offered.

"Of course, I'll talk to you," Sims countered.

For a moment, it looked as if the two sides could reach a settlement without a protracted fight. Parker, however, was disabused of that notion soon enough. As it turned out, that August day was the Napa Valley calm before the Washington storm, which began to swirl two weeks later.

Room 385 at the Federal Trade Commission, site of the first big negotiating powwow in August 2000, did no justice to the enormity of the moment. It was a drab, government conference room. At times, the quartz clock on the wall would stop working, which seemed appropriate. The room seemed frozen in time, suspended by a tight federal budget. Which explained the fake ficus tree and the haphazard assemblage of three tables that together made up a big conference table.

Ringing the table were heavyweights on both sides, government and company, including some hired guns whose hourly rate far exceeded $500. On AOL's side was Paul T. Cappuccio, its general counsel, a gregarious quick thinker and facile speaker. By his side was Sims, the aggressive outside counsel for AOL, and his counterpart, Robert D. Joffe, the well-mannered outside attorney representing Time Warner. Christopher Bogart, Time Warner's youthful general counsel, also joined the group.

At the other end of the table were the FTC's chief negotiators—Parker and Michael E. Antalics, the FTC's head attorney reviewing the merger, recently recovered from a heart attack.

Parker opened the meeting by laying out some of the FTC's concerns. He explained how the merger could threaten competition on the Internet. AOL's dominant on-line service, combined with Time Warner's massive cable-television network, could claim an overwhelming advantage in the emerging market of high-speed Internet access. If AOL's on-line service rode over Time Warner cable lines into people's homes, how would another Internet company, which didn't own a cable network, compete?

Attorneys for the companies immediately dismissed the point, arguing that they had already pledged in their memorandum of understanding to make Time Warner cable lines open to AOL's Internet rivals. That should be sufficient, the attorneys asserted. But Parker and Antalics thought differently. The memorandum of understanding was a pledge, not a promise. It wasn't a guarantee. And while the government was sure that the companies planned to play nice, the FTC attorneys wanted to *make* sure, by getting open-access terms in writing, as part of a consent decree, a legal settlement.

What's more, they wanted a firm timetable, a schedule by which the companies would allow rival Internet services on Time Warner's cable network. And one other thing: The FTC wanted specific provisions to ensure that Time Warner's cable network did not subtly discriminate against other Internet service providers, or rivals, such as Disney, which wanted to offer interactive-television content over Time Warner's cable lines.

The government had gone too far, the companies felt.

"That's crazy!" Sims pounced. "That doesn't make sense!"

Interactive television didn't even exist yet, not in any way that could be described as anything but rudimentary and nascent. The companies said they would never submit to a settlement in which their hands were tied in how they negotiated commercial agreements with other companies, be it Disney or other Internet service providers. There was no way they would commit to anything but general language promising open access and nondiscrimination.

Sims, leaning over the table by this point, said the companies would go no farther, and besides, the government had no case.

Parker, also leaning over the table, dug in, insisting he had a good case.

"This is a war-zone issue!" Parker shouted. "This is a problem! This is antitrust problem one-A. This is a winner! Why can't you see that?"

Even Joffe, the unflappable Time Warner attorney, got into it. An elegant man of fifty-seven, Joffe was an antitrust authority for whom anything but a measured tone was out of character. But in this case, there was a lot at stake. His law firm, Cravath, Swaine & Moore, stood to gain a reported $35 million in fees if the companies prevailed in their run through the regulatory agencies. It was believed to be among the largest fees ever for a corporate transaction, but Joffe's firm also was taking a gamble. Cravath would get very little if the merger collapsed. That may have explained why he so uncharacteristically raised his voice, arguing that the government's theories didn't make good antitrust sense. "This is all about your power as gatekeeper," he said.

An FTC staffer, mindful of Joffe's reputation, interjected, "You're supposed to be courtly."

By now, Parker was gesticulating and Sims was giving it right back, arguing their points in overlapping words heard by neither. "They started coming at us, ripping and snorting," Parker said.

Just as the tension was reaching a crescendo, a broad smile broke out on the animated face of Cappuccio, the AOL general counsel. He reached into his leather briefcase and pulled out a doll with a shrunken head and wild, fiery hair, much like a cartoon character called the Tasmanian Devil. What the child's toy was doing in his briefcase wasn't clear, but from across the table, Cappuccio began waving it at Parker, who immediately lost his train of thought, as well as the steam in his venom, and burst into laughter.

"It totally threw me off," Parker said. "That really stopped me."

The tension broke, as the rest of the group laughed along. Later, Parker's staffers quipped that the Tasmanian Devil doll was so effective in shutting him up that they ought to get one just in case he acted up with them. Parker's wife, who later heard about the incident, apparently also thought it was a good idea. She bought a doll, which now sits on his dresser at home.

The jocularity, though, masked a more sober reality at that meeting: Nothing had been resolved. By that time, in late August 2000, both sides were entrenched. The companies were convinced that there was no case, that the government was bluffing. The FTC attorneys were equally persuaded that they not only had a case but might have to go to litigation.

"At that point," Antalics said, "we were thinking we were going to court. We were preparing for that."

In the byzantine world of the FTC, the actual decision makers, the five presidentially appointed members who sit behind closed doors and vote yea or nay on the great and mighty mergers of the land, don't have anything to do with the companies under review until the final throes of the deliberation. By tradition, companies first deal with the FTC staff, which makes a recommendation to the commissioners on whether to block or approve a deal. It's custom—nay, it's good manners—for negotiators to deal with the FTC staff before getting perhaps one shot at approaching the individual commissioners.

Or so thought the strategists at AOL and Time Warner.

"The parties seeking to clear a merger need the staff," said Vradenburg, AOL's former chief policy maker. "If they recommend against approval, you're a loser."

For all of the bluster of the attorneys representing AOL and Time Warner, they didn't want to go over the heads of the FTC staffers. They didn't want to annoy them. But by waiting, AOL and Time Warner had ceded significant ground to their opponents, including Disney and Microsoft, which had been relentlessly lobbying the commissioners. "By the time the commissioners got to see the companies [AOL and Time Warner], they'd been inundated by our adversaries," said an official involved in the talks. "They made our life more difficult."

For the merging companies, it was a tactical mistake. The question was whether it was a fatal mistake.

Among those who had often wondered about the companies' long absence was commissioner Mozelle W. Thompson, a bear of a man with a warm manner, who first suggested that the agency take on the big media case. Thompson was not the kind of commissioner who appreciated the indignity of being ignored. But when Case and Levin finally arrived at the FTC for meetings with commissioners in late September 2000, Thompson thought he would forgive them their trespasses and show them just how open he was to their approach.

By way of introduction, he seated Case and Levin at his round conference table and explained that he, Mozelle Thompson, was an AOL subscriber. Case seemed to appreciate the business. Thompson gave equal time to Levin, adding that he, Mozelle Thompson, also was a Time Warner subscriber. And what's more, he, Mozelle Thompson, happened to be watching ABC in New York when his television screen went blue because Time Warner had blocked Disney's programming over a contract dispute in May.

Case punched Levin in the arm and quipped, "Way to go, Jerry." Levin was not amused. He turned ashen.

Thompson wasn't simply teasing the two CEOs. He was sending a message: He was aware of the companies' market power, and the Disney dispute had shown how Time Warner could wield it. "Their lawyers realized my statement was serious," Thompson said.

The commissioner, however, wasn't so sure whether Case and Levin were taking him seriously. When he asked about the case, they insisted there was no antitrust issue. At one point, Levin said, "The problem with you, Mr. Commissioner, is that you don't understand the Internet and how it works."

Thompson, a proud man, didn't appreciate the slight. Though he didn't say it then, he had been a featured speaker at meetings on the subject of the Internet. Obviously Levin and Case didn't know that he had lectured on the subject at Princeton University, where he had earned an MPA degree from the Woodrow Wilson School of Public and International Affairs.

Never mind that. Thompson forged ahead, asking about their plans to develop interactive television. Again, they brushed him off. It was an emerging market, they said. It was just being born. There was nothing to regulate.

At that moment, what came to Thompson's mind was a magazine buried under a pile of papers on the conference table, where Levin and Case sat. The cover of the magazine, *eCompany Now,* had a headline that announced, "Interactive TV: It Lives!" Thompson had read the story.

The magazine, incidentally, was a Time Warner publication. Thompson let it pass. But he harbored deep reservations, given the CEOs' attitudes at that meeting. More than ever, that convinced him he would approve an FTC settlement only if it included safeguards to ensure that the companies lived up to their commitments. "I had to have hard terms about what they were going to do," he said. "And I had little faith in their trust-me perspective."

The companies' position was that Thompson was all but a lost cause. They were convinced he would vote against the deal, regardless of what they told him. "He took the position that we were the devil incarnate," said one person involved in discussions with the commissioner. "He was personally offended that he wasn't more personally catered to. If we had been smarter, we would have slobbered over him. But no one had the stomach for it. Disney was better at slobbering."

Case and Levin fared little better in slobbering over the FTC commissioner who, because of his powers of persuasion over his colleagues, counted the most in the process: Bob Pitofsky, the chairman.

That fall, when the two CEOs and Dick Parsons, the Time Warner president, entered Pitofsky's chambers in Room 440 of the FTC, they were greeted by the usual trappings of government power. On the wall hung a photo of Pitofsky with President Clinton. Another with Jimmy Carter. What Pitofsky really prized, though, was a photograph of graceful power: Babe Ruth, the Sultan of Swat, swinging for the fences. But nothing about Pitofsky himself projected the arrogance of power. In his low-key way, the FTC chairman deferred to Rich Parker, the agency's top antitrust lawyer, to set out the government's case, as they sat at Pitofsky's conference table.

But when Parker began to speak, laying out the FTC's concerns about interactive television, Levin snapped, "You don't know what interactive

TV is. It's a new market. How can you seek relief where there isn't a product area?"

Parker, suppressing his ire, resumed where he left off—and then it happened again: Levin cut him off, arguing over the existence of interactive television. Parker couldn't believe the audacity. "Do you want to discuss this?" Parker screeched. "Because if you want to interrupt me, we can't have a discussion."

At that moment, the meeting could very well have gone up in flames.

"I guess I am arrogant at times," Levin said. "But here's somebody, a bureaucrat, telling me about interactive television and how it should operate and trying to say it's an antitrust issue when [it] isn't. There's no business, and besides, we're probably better able to make that a business at some point. So, yes, I was offended by that."

But Parsons, a diplomatic executive who years earlier had served as a political aide to Nelson Rockefeller, took the initiative. Where Levin was slight of build and prickly, Parsons was broad and cuddly. Levin had often leaned on the dynamism of Parsons to smooth things over, to make nice when Levin had scowled. Many thought Levin was grooming Parsons as his successor. A former banker, Parsons knew how Washington worked. He had served in the Ford White House on domestic policy. Parsons, by all accounts an affable fellow, a big teddy bear, knew how to submerge his own ego, deferring personal satisfaction for the right moment. And *this* wasn't the right moment. He didn't say a word. Instead, ever so lightly, Parsons tapped Levin on the shoulder, and the confrontation was immediately defused.

It didn't last long.

Picking up where Levin left off, Case defended the merger by explaining that he had gotten so rich that, with this deal, he could focus on doing good deeds. The part about his good deeds got lost. What stuck in the minds of some of those in attendance was how Case had boasted of becoming so rich.

Levin, however, trumped his merger partner's faux pas. On his way out, Levin bragged that he was himself an attorney well versed in antitrust law, and he had been through other big mergers before. Levin was confident about the outcome if the case ended up in litigation. "I'd like to do the case myself," he quipped.

Levin wasn't entirely kidding. Within the mock bravado was a kernel of truth, if not an apparent threat to the FTC chairman. Levin was displaying his fangs. To those who had worked with the Time Warner chief over the years, it wasn't a surprise.

"He deals in a context where brinksmanship often works," said one of his associates, who added that Levin, in the rarefied air of chiefdom, had gotten used to dealing with people without much deference. "Jerry doesn't suffer fools gladly."

In retrospect, Levin said, "Steve and I were not the best team."

Pitofsky didn't seem to mind. He laughed at Levin's boast. He even empathized. Levin and Case didn't get to be CEOs for nothing, he thought. The two men really believed that the FTC was bluffing, that it had no right to subject them to delays and cross-examinations. Their lawyers had been telling them this all along. And yet, Pitofsky thought, they hadn't seen all of the information the FTC had amassed, evidence it could bring to bear to prove an antitrust violation.

Though he laughed it off, Pitofsky was of the belief that the case was veering inexorably toward a courtroom showdown. "I thought they were dug in, I thought they would not adjust and give us what we wanted in the order," he said. "I thought there was an exceptionally good chance that [there] would be litigation. It would be a monstrous case to litigate, but then, we had taken on other monstrous cases to litigate."

Preparing for the worst, Pitofsky asked a big favor of Parker, who had been planning to step down shortly and move back into private practice. Would Parker stay on at the FTC to lead the case? Pitofsky saw no other way. Parker was a terrific litigator, he had already taken some of the depositions in this case, and he knew the issues cold. Parker didn't hesitate. He welcomed the chance.

Levin and Case had miscalculated the government's resolve, and the two executives had shown little respect in the process. "The proper stance for coming in to talk to the commission is really on bended knee, strategy-wise, and they didn't do that," said a former FTC official involved in the process. "It was real cockiness. They were sort of trying to negotiate from a position of strength. That was not a positive step in the process. There's always this heel digging in that takes place, and that's the first time I sensed the FTC side dug in."

What's more, this former official said, the CEOs were apparently unappreciative of one important thing about Pitofsky: "He doesn't like to lose."

His record bore this out. Since he had become chairman in 1995, the agency had brought suit to block eleven mergers, and in nine of the cases the parties either abandoned the deals, reached agreement with the FTC, or lost. Only twice did the FTC lose. The agency didn't have the glamour of the other government alphabets, like the CIA or the FBI, but all the same, the FTC was a force to be reckoned with. "In reality," this former FTC official said, "it has the power to destroy, and this is the most blatant power for the government to interfere with private commerce and to say, no."

The other side, naturally, viewed the problem differently. To AOL and Time Warner, it wasn't so much a question of how to deal with the FTC as how to deal with Pitofsky, whom they quickly began to perceive as the focal point of resistance.

"Pitofsky made it horrendously more complicated because he was so worried about what the effect of the merger would be," said an official involved in the negotiations. Even if there wasn't an antitrust issue, there was another issue, which the companies believed gripped the FTC chairman with fear: the sheer *bigness* of the merger. "If he couldn't figure it out, he felt he should prevent it [the merger] or at the least slow it down," the official said.

The companies were all too aware of another Pitofsky problem: This was his last hurrah before his term expired and he stepped down as chairman. "He viewed this as the most important merger that the FTC was ever involved in," the official said. "This was his swan song. He didn't want a blistering attack that he had sold out to the capitalist pigs."

Time, however, was on Pitofsky's side. As September moved into October, AOL's stock was still dropping, continuing the trend that had begun when the companies had announced their merger more than nine months earlier. Since then, AOL and Time Warner had been trying to reassure increasingly jittery shareholders that they would be done with federal regulators and close the merger by the fall. Suddenly, that timetable was in doubt. Case and Levin looked as if they were back on their heels as opponents of the merger pressed their case. At the first House hearing on the deal that fall, members of Congress grilled the two CEOs about a range of merger issues, taking special interest in instant messaging, which was gaining traction, thanks to the media campaign being waged by Microsoft et al.

Meanwhile, Dave Baker, the top public policy official at EarthLink, turned up the heat, complaining about the companies' lack of progress in making Time Warner cable lines available to Internet rivals. Around the same time, Disney-AOL documents came to light, showing how AOL's Internet service could favor its own content over that of its rivals, effectively shutting customers inside AOL's "walled garden," a point hammered home by Disney's Preston Padden.

Even in victory, AOL and Time Warner found defeat. In October 2000, the European Union approved the AOL–Time Warner deal, but only after Time Warner was forced to call off its separate music merger with EMI. With that matter behind them, the companies discovered back home that the FTC was preparing court documents to block the merger, if it came to that. In an illustration of just how serious they were, agency lawyers had asked some of the companies' competitors to sign affidavits indicating they would testify in a lawsuit if the government sought to block the merger.

On October 17, AOL's stock price hit a fifty-two-week low, falling 17 percent. Time Warner's shares, whose fate was intertwined with that of AOL, dropped 16 percent.

Such stock gyrations were worrisome to company executives, especially Cappuccio, AOL's general counsel, and Bogart, his Time Warner counterpart. Both urged their negotiators to move quickly to reach a settlement with the government. Part of the fear was that investors were losing confidence in the companies' ability to close their deal and realize all the benefits of their merger. But more was at play: AOL did not want to be lumped with the rest of the dot-com sector, which was now struggling. The Nasdaq, declining steeply since March, was showing no signs of a recovery. And for employees and executives alike at AOL and Time Warner, millions of dollars in their personal wealth were at stake, through shares owned in the company and stock options. For the first time, it was dawning on company executives that the FTC was gravely serious. The government might actually take them to court.

"Litigating with the government is a very difficult task," said Joffe, Time Warner's outside counsel. "The government comes in cloaked with the mantle of righteousness. Between litigation and appeals, we're talking about six months, and every time the FTC hiccupped and it was reported in the press, the stock prices jiggled."

The FTC attorneys, aware of the pressure, continued to push the companies on concessions in October. At first, AOL and Time Warner agreed to offer rival Internet providers the same terms they gave to AOL, or to Road Runner, Time Warner's own high-speed service. But that wasn't good enough. The FTC argued that AOL and Time Warner could charge themselves higher prices to justify higher prices for competitors. So the companies offered more, agreeing to give rivals the same terms AOL received for carriage on other cable networks. But that wasn't good enough either. The FTC asserted that AOL could make a deal so specific to itself that no one else could take advantage of it.

In late October, with patience wearing thin, an AOL executive noted, "It's an odd negotiation when there's only one side, us, and you don't move at all." Antalics, the FTC attorney, retorted, "Well, it's really not that unusual. We just adopted the Time Warner method of negotiation."

By early November 2000, it had come to this: Before the FTC would approve the merger, AOL and Time Warner had to sign a contract with a major rival Internet service provider, giving it access to Time Warner's cable network. And the FTC wanted the right to review the contract, just to make sure AOL and Time Warner didn't pull any funny stuff.

Parker, the FTC attorney, delivered the stern condition to the companies. The idea, however, had originated with Pitofsky, the chairman, who had crafted a similar solution in a previous, related case: the merger of Time Warner and Turner Broadcasting Systems in 1996. Then, one of the central concerns was how rivals would compete with the combined companies' all-powerful, twenty-four-hour news network, CNN. Pitofsky's solution was to require the companies to open their cable network to a future rival twenty-four-hour news channel.

Regardless of whose idea it was now, AOL and Time Warner didn't respond well to the same principle being applied to this merger. They were appalled at the notion of signing a contract with what they viewed as a government gun practically aimed at their head, forcing a competing Internet service provider on the Time Warner cable network. The howling could be heard emanating from Room 374, Parker's office at the FTC.

"It's not going to happen!" erupted Sims, AOL's lead outside attorney. "That's the stupidest fucking thing I've ever heard!"

"This was a high-decibel meeting," Parker recalled.

At the end of it, the two combatants were back to chatting about sports, this time pro football. It was the season. Parker was a San Francisco 49ers fan. Sims was a die-hard fan of the Washington Redskins. They carried on in a breezy fashion, but neither attorney let on that he was not feeling particularly good about how the meeting had just concluded. The FTC attorneys were convinced that AOL and Time Warner were fed up, ready to fight the government in court. The companies were no less encouraged about the FTC's warlike stance.

The situation looked even grimmer a few days later, on November 9, in Room 432, the cavernous hearing chamber at the FTC. The curtains were drawn. There was no food or water on the long, narrow table. Along one side were the five commissioners, with Pitofsky, the chairman, in the middle. Along the other side, facing them, were Parker, Antalics, and a battery of other staffers.

Parker rose to give what essentially would be his opening argument in the United States versus AOL and Time Warner. He was even armed with a diagram propped on an easel, illustrating the antitrust problem: how a combination of AOL and Time Warner created a monopoly in high-speed-cable Internet access. It was a difficult theory to press, a "vertical" case where two complementary businesses stifled competition. Parker also laid out a secondary case, a more traditional "horizontal" theory in which AOL and Road Runner, Time Warner's high-speed Internet service, over-lapped in the same business and could also create a monopoly in markets where both services were available.

To settle with the government, Parker explained to the commissioners, AOL and Time Warner had finally agreed to sign a contract with a rival Internet service provider, giving it access to Time Warner's cable network for high-speed service—but only after the merger was approved.

The question on the table: Vote on the deal, as is, or give the parties more time to come up with a better proposal.

Parker gave the commission his recommendation: Let's push the companies to sign a deal with an Internet firm now. "I'm thinking like a lawyer," Parker said, "I'm thinking I can improve on this. Let's keep pushing."

The commissioners asked a slew of questions. But it was clear that the merger did not have the necessary three votes to be approved. "Different commissioners had different parts of the deal they were concerned about," Pitofsky said. "At least three, four, and up to five were not ready to let this go through. It was an accumulation of unwillingness to let the deal go through."

Mozelle Thompson was persistent in his general dislike for the entire transaction. Even Commissioner Orson Swindle, a staunch supporter of the deal, wanted to ensure that there was a strong set of conditions. Commissioner Sheila F. Anthony was concerned about what would happen if the deal ended up in court. Pitofsky wanted the companies to strike a contract with an Internet firm, giving it access to Time Warner cable lines. And Commissioner Thomas B. Leary, echoing his colleagues, feared how the companies could leverage their market power in content—movies and music—to gain an unfair advantage over their competitors.

"People definitely were getting to the end of their rope," said one participant in the room.

When the commission emerged more than two hours later, it issued a statement saying it had voted five to zero to give the companies more time—but only three more weeks.

There wasn't much fight left in the companies. Only eleven days later, they had a contract: Time Warner struck a deal opening its cable network to EarthLink. One official chalked it up to "deal fatigue."

"We wanted to get the process going as fast as possible," said another.

The FTC attorneys weren't taking any chances. Even with a contract in hand, the companies had yet to sign a consent agreement, a formal settlement with the government. And the commission hadn't voted yet. Until the consent agreement, the FTC crew assumed nothing.

Over the Thanksgiving weekend, Antalics, the FTC attorney, worked on a legal brief. Parker, for his part, had prepared thick accordion folders stuffed with documents for each possible eventuality—one labeled "W" for "war," or litigation, the other marked "P" for "peace," or settlement.

The FTC war machine included documents in more than one thousand boxes and a team of about ten staff lawyers and half as many paralegals. The agency had enlisted economists and technical experts; it had taken dozens of depositions and sworn statements. Parker, as he had promised Pitofsky, was prepared to work full-time as the lead attorney on the lawsuit.

"We had a damn good case," he said.

"If they hadn't adjusted their order, they would've been sued," Pitofsky said.

But Joffe, the Time Warner outside counsel, wasn't sweating it. He had devised a novel legal strategy. It went like this: The government was better off with a consent decree than if it took the companies to court. Joffe's argument was simple, if not sublime. First, the government could very well lose in court. But with the consent decree, the FTC would have what it had fought so hard to obtain, a contract signed by the companies guaranteeing open access to a rival Internet service provider offering high-speed service over Time Warner cable. Nobody in the cable industry had struck such a far-reaching contract.

If, on the other hand, the government sought to block the deal, there would not only be no merger, there also would be no open access. Without a deal, Time Warner would be free to strike a deal with AOL, giving it unfettered access to Time Warner's cable lines. How would the FTC explain *that* to the public? The commissioners would look ridiculous, the companies argued.

"The FTC found itself in a situation where it could win the battle but lose the war," said an official involved in the talks.

Pitofsky, a terrific poker player, didn't show his hand when presented with the predicament. But he knew the government was better off with a consent decree than a courtroom confrontation.

"It had the advantage of being absolutely true," Pitofsky said.

On December 13, 2000, one day before the scheduled FTC vote on the merger, AOL and Time Warner were still scrambling for votes. By their count, it was three-two, their favor, good enough for passage. But the companies didn't want a squeaker. If it was possible, a unanimous vote sounded a whole lot better in the court of public opinion.

The problem was content. More to the point, the problem was Mozelle Thompson—still. The outspoken commissioner had serious reservations about whether AOL and Time Warner would use their cable lines to discriminate against the content of rivals, such as Disney. His concerns were shared by commissioner Leary. AOL and Time Warner groused that this was all Disney's dastardly doings (read: Preston Padden). But it was there, all the same. And the merging partners figured they needed to do something. The only problem was that Levin, the Time Warner chieftain, had drawn the line on this issue of content. "Levin had said most of the issues are compromisable issues, but this content issue is a religious issue," said an official familiar with his thinking. "He said, 'We're not going to let the government regulate content.'"

It was always in the back of his mind. "If we get stuck at the FTC," Levin said, "we walk away."

The AOL–Time Warner team figured it could thread the needle this way: It would submit to the agency a notice of complaints from rivals if it failed to provide content on a nondiscriminatory basis over cable lines or on interactive television. Levin went for it. His negotiators quickly dispatched the offer in a two-page fax to Antalics, the FTC attorney.

It was close, but not quite what Antalics & Co. had in mind. He tinkered. Late in the afternoon, he rang Joffe and Sims, the companies' lead outside attorneys. The FTC attorney asked for more. Antalics wanted to broaden the content provision so that it covered not only rival Internet service providers but television programmers as well. Joffe and Sims weren't pleased.

"They went crazy on the phone," Antalics said. "They just said, 'That's it! Sue us! The answer is no!'"

There was a pause on the line.

Antalics, in his dogged, low-key manner, let it linger. He had a unique way of using dead silence to speak for itself, to employ a pause to extract another concession in a negotiation. Then he said calmly, "If you want me to tell the commission no, I'll tell them that. I don't know if it'll be the last thing, but if you want me to tell them no, I will."

Sims and Joffe considered the options briefly, then came up with this: *We'll call you back in half an hour.*

Meanwhile, the rest of the staff continued to work on two tracks: Sue or settle. Parker was talking to potential witnesses. Eric London, the agency's spokesman, prepared two news releases, one titled in bold, "FTC APPROVES AOL/TIME WARNER MERGER WITH CONDITIONS," the other declaring, "FTC TO CHALLENGE AOL/TIME WARNER MERGER," with a smaller headline: "Agency Charges Deal

Would Substantially Eliminate Competition in Broadband Internet Service."

The latter would not be needed a day later. The companies' attorneys had called Antalics back and relented.

Back in Room 432, where just a month earlier the commissioners had struggled to find daylight, approval was all but a foregone conclusion. The chairman called for the vote: "Aye," began Leary. Then Swindle. Then Thompson. Then Anthony. And, last, Pitofsky himself. The deal was approved five to zero.

After nearly a year of Herculean negotiations, the companies were restrained in their public response. They didn't want to crow too loudly for fear of incurring the wrath of the FCC, the *other* agency—the last government agency—winding down its review of the merger. But in a carefully worded internal e-mail to employees, Case wrote, "This represents a major milestone towards bringing AOL and Time Warner together. Pending approval by the FCC, which we're confident will be granted in the next few weeks, we expect to begin operating as one company by the end of the year or the early days of 2001. As we near that historic moment, we're more certain than ever of the strategic vision embodied in our merger."

The reaction elsewhere in the AOL empire was bittersweet. For most of 2000, the company had bent over backward to try to ensure that nothing controversial emerged from within its walls. The idea was for the two merging companies to quietly go about their business, without putting any undue attention on their market power. They didn't even want to trot out any gee-whiz products. No need for that. Besides, there were various other distractions plaguing company officials, like job security.

"A lot of stuff got put on hold," said one. "In truth, during the merger review, a lot of AOL senior executives were trying to get their jobs at [the new company] AOL Time Warner, then positioning themselves with Jerry [Levin] and the new team. There was a lot of wasted energy. Looking back, it was like, 'Jesus, what the fuck were we doing for a year?'"

But it wasn't quite over. The FCC, eager to cast off its reputation as a backwater agency that would rubber-stamp the AOL–Time Warner merger, was determined to have its say.

PART III

———

The Wild Days

William von Meister, an irrepressible entrepreneur who loved wine, women, and creating the Next Big Thing. Although von Meister remains an obscure figure in history, he is credited as the father of America Online. (Undated photo, courtesy of Nora Macdonald)

James V. Kimsey, the founding chief executive of America Online. A maverick, a bar owner, and a military hero, he never intended to get involved in AOL, but he steered the company through its early struggles and groomed a young Steve Case to succeed him. (Courtesy of Frank Johnston, *The Washington Post*)

Steve Case, former chairman of AOL Time Warner. Also a former pizza-flavor tester for Pizza Hut, Case orchestrated the largest merger in U.S. history. Nicknamed "The Wall" by colleagues at AOL, here he looks on stoically at a congressional hearing where he defended the merger of AOL and Time Warner.

(Courtesy of Robert A. Reeder, *The Washington Post*)

Jan Brandt, the former marketing whiz. She wasn't enamored with AOL's technology, but she loved what it could do: bring people closer together in a virtual community. In the early 1990s, she came up with the daring idea of blanketing America with free AOL software disks to get people to try the service.

(Undated photo, courtesy of AOL)

The final issue (September 1990) of *Q-Link Update,* a clunky company newsletter begun when the on-line revolution was just starting in the late 1980s. AOL was then called Quantum Computer Services, and the on-line service was known as Q-Link. Publication was discontinued when the company began sending out information to its subscribers on-line.

Ted Leonsis, the firebrand executive whom Case hired in the mid-1990s to rouse the AOL troops in a holy on-line war against the big, bad behemoth, Microsoft. (Courtesy of Tracy A. Woodward, *The Washington Post*)

David M. Colburn, the former president of AOL's business affairs. As the company's top dealmaker, he personified the brash dot-com era. Favoring cowboy boots and a five o'clock shadow, Colburn became such a powerful figure that, within AOL, many simply called him "God." (AOL file photo)

Robert W. Pittman, a Mississippi preacher's son and one of the founders of MTV. He went on to join AOL in the mid-1990s and rescue it from a host of financial and technical crises. But his rave reviews created tension with his boss, Steve Case, who suspected that Pittman was trying to grab the spotlight. (Courtesy of Frank Johnston, *The Washington Post*)

At AOL headquarters, Case puts a headband on then Time Warner CEO Jerry Levin's head and seems to enjoy the prank more than Levin. In the end, neither man got the last laugh as they were both forced out of the company they created. (Courtesy of Frank Johnston, *The Washington Post*)

A reflection of ambition. Visitors to the AOL campus are immediately greeted by this lobby plaque, a reminder of the company's lofty ambition to create a medium as powerful as television. (Courtesy of Robert A. Reeder, *The Washington Post*)

At the January 10, 2000, announcement of AOL's takeover of Time Warner, the principals take the stage to celebrate the largest merger in U.S. history. Case, Levin, and Pittman have since been forced to resign. Ted Turner, the company's largest single shareholder, has resigned. J. Michael Kelly, then the parent company's chief financial officer, was effectively demoted when he was later transferred to the on-line division. Only Richard D. Parsons has survived unscathed—so far. (AP/Wide World Photos)

Robert Pitofsky, the mild-mannered former chairman of the Federal Trade Commission. He was prepared to take AOL and Time Warner to court to block their merger if they did not agree to his conditions to ensure competition in the marketplace. In the background are Pitofsky's two top FTC attorneys then handling the merger: Richard G. Parker, *center,* and Michael E. Antalics, *right.*

(Courtesy of Robert A. Reeder, *The Washington Post*)

William E. Kennard, the former chairman of the Federal Communications Commission. AOL and Time Warner officials expected little resistance from the FCC during its merger review, but Kennard was determined to play a role, even when the companies applied political pressure. (Courtesy of Dudley M. Brooks, *The Washington Post*)

Steve Case whispers to Jerry Levin during a Senate Judiciary Committee hearing on the merger. Neither man expected the government to fight, but federal regulators were put off by the disdain shown by Case and Levin, and opponents of the deal mobilized effectively to raise questions about it. (Courtesy of Ray Lustig, *The Washington Post*)

Ted Turner, otherwise known as Captain Outrageous. A media visionary, Turner quickly grew disenchanted with the merger. Levin had squeezed Turner out of a major role; in turn, Turner worked behind the scenes to get rid of Levin. When revelations emerged about irregular accounting at AOL, Turner lost faith in Steve Case, helping to engineer his ouster as well. (Courtesy of Michael Williamson, *The Washington Post*)

Dick Parsons, the forgotten man who emerged in charge. While Steve Case, Jerry Levin, and Bob Pittman were getting all the attention as the brains of the merger, Parsons, ever the politician, took a backseat with grace. The move proved smart when the merger soured, and the board of directors turned to Parsons to heal the wounds of a company rife with infighting. (Courtesy of Frank Johnston, *The Washington Post*)

CHAPTER FIVE

SKIN GAME

A high-pitched whine emanated from the man at the microphone. Heads turned instantly. The screeching voice, like fingernails running down a chalkboard, was a rude harkening back to the main event. Sooner or later, David M. Colburn, he of the slow nasal drawl, was bound to take center stage. As president of AOL's business affairs division, Colburn commanded attention wherever he went, which was especially true at his own holiday party that December day in 1999. Besides, he had paid for the festivities out of his own pocket, as he usually did. He had earned the right to grab the mike. Decked out in jeans and cowboy boots, Colburn straddled the low platform stage in his airy backyard in suburban Potomac, Maryland, and addressed his fellow business associates, some eighty people who had gathered to celebrate not only the holiday season but also the growing triumph of AOL, the undisputed Internet giant of the land.

Colburn kibitzed. He lauded his people—the deal makers under his charge—for doing a great job in bringing greater glory to the AOL empire. And then he introduced three men dear to his heart. They were middle-aged, short, and dressed casually. Little distinguished them, except this: They were rabbis.

Colburn, who considered himself a devout Jew, asked the three men to join him on stage.

151

I brought you here not just because I want to see you, Colburn said. *You're here to help us, to pray for us.*

The rabbis seemed happy to oblige. There was a catch, though. With Colburn, associates said, there was always a catch. Sometimes, the catch was a minor clause to his advantage buried deep in a revised contract, a provision Colburn had inserted to alter a multimillion-dollar business deal.

But in the matter at hand, the catch was put out there for everyone at the party to witness: The rabbis weren't there just to pray for AOL souls. Colburn wanted them to pray for AOL stock. He offered a deal: If each rabbi agreed to pray for AOL's shares to rise to a certain level, and they hit that level, Colburn promised to donate $1 million to a Jewish cause.

"So you have skin in the game," he explained, cackling.

But Colburn wasn't joking, not about *skin in the game.* It was a term he favored in his bare-knuckle negotiations when he was extracting millions from companies that wanted to advertise their goods and services on the AOL on-line service. Colburn, the company's top deal maker, always wanted AOL's business partners to have skin in the game, to have a vested interest, which usually came in the form of millions of dollars in cash paid to AOL. That, Colburn believed, would make his business partners work harder to make the relationship with AOL work. If they have something at stake, like their financial survival, they will perform. Same with the men of faith. If the rabbis had something on the line—to the tune of $1 million—they wouldn't just be praying for Colburn's soul.

He would have skin in the game, too. If the rabbis' prayers were answered and AOL's stock did rise, Colburn would be out a cool $1 million. Not that he would miss it. He was already a multimillionaire—some put his net worth at more than $250 million—which he had earned mostly through stock options. It was the way legions at AOL minted money back then: Stock options gave Colburn, as they did other employees, the right to buy AOL stock at a certain price at a specific time. The idea was to wait until the stock rose above that price, buy the stock at a discount, then turn around and sell it at the going market rate and reap a huge profit.

Lord willing, AOL stock would rise high enough that Colburn would make enough to donate $1 million to the rabbis, with plenty to spare. The stock was a pretty sure bet. The way AOL's stock was ticking up, up, and away, reaching beyond $90 a share that December, he didn't exactly need God's help.

Then again, why take chances?

One rabbi, however, wasn't completely sold on the deal. Sensing that Colburn was open to further negotiations, the rabbi offered a counterproposal. He said he would pray for AOL's stock to rise only if Colburn started showing up at religious services at the synagogue. Colburn acceded, and the three Jewish leaders agreed to pray for AOL's stock to rise.

Colburn, as usual, won the negotiation.

Together, the rabbis offered their blessings and thanks, while Colburn stood by, pious and grave, his eyes shut, wishing for a big payday, spiritual or otherwise.

It was a stunning moment, a surreal confluence—if not an unholy alliance—of religion, greed, and the intoxicating whiff of power that lay in AOL's grasp at the height of the Internet boom of the 1990s. Some were appalled by the prayer. And yet no one uttered a word in protest. It wasn't the place, not before dozens of Colburn's closest associates. Besides, who wanted to incur the notorious wrath of David Colburn?

"How do you pray for the stock to go up?" wondered an AOL official in attendance. "It's ridiculous."

A man of his word, Colburn was soon thereafter found in a Jewish temple, cleaning a rabbi's office. He told a friend he was volunteering. Apparently, the deed did not go unheeded. AOL's stock, continuing to soar in those days of the Internet star, hit the mark.

There was so much to David Colburn, all of it so outrageous and comical and scary and brilliant and successful and charitable, that he almost defied human description. And yet there he was, an open book, a raging, exploding caricature of a personality, a combustible force of nature. It was who Colburn was, or wanted to be, or couldn't help being.

At AOL, his stature grew to such epic proportions that he earned a nickname: God.

This was not your typical deity. To begin with, there were his black cowboy boots, emblazoned with the AOL logo. Colburn's sense of fashion leaned toward jeans and tank-top undershirts in an I-don't-care-what-the-hell-you-think manner of dress that he displayed at important company meetings. There was a bit of *Miami Vice* in his look, grizzled, rumpled, clad in a T-shirt boasting a cartoon character under a green glen-plaid suit jacket. Some tossed it off by saying he was just an eclectic dresser. Others said he was simply a bad dresser. Eventually, friends persuaded him to get rid of the so-called wife-beater undershirt look. It didn't play well, not even in the hyper-casual milieu that was AOL.

"He's like the older guy in a boy band," said a former AOLer who worked for Colburn. "He wants to be hip and cool, but it's not cool anymore because you're in your forties."

Colburn also favored the five o'clock shadow look, as if to remind others that he was too busy for such minutiae as personal grooming. But he did care. Otherwise, why would he brag to his friends about the dark hair plugs he got from South America to cover up his balding head? He combed his hair forward, and yet he would make cracks about other AOL executives who were losing *their* hair. Some thought there was an implied strategy in that: Attack first, strike first.

The man was a walking contradiction, somehow athletic but paunchy, charismatic yet rough-hewn, crude yet religious, aggressive but kind, tall and imposing except for that squeaky squeal of a voice, which some believed he exaggerated for effect and at which even Colburn himself poked fun.

"There's a lot of disparities to David Colburn," said a former AOL official who worked with him. "He's like Tony Montana from *Scarface* meets Andy Warhol."

So there it was—the ruthless gangster with the effete, artistic sensibilities. Who knew this was the man of the moment? The king at AOL was supposed to be Steve Case, or so the public was led to believe throughout the 1990s. Case was the public persona of AOL, that boyish, clean-cut executive from the Gap ads in crisp khakis and denim button-downs. Case did steer the prodigious AOL ship, but he didn't actually operate the levers and switches. He served another purpose—that of the public face of AOL, marketing the service as clean family fun. It was all geared to that wholesome purpose, including the cheerful voice that greeted consumers when they signed into their AOL accounts: "You've got mail!" Or the cartoonish icons that populated the AOL service, like the little stuffed mailbox, the edges rounded, the colors bright and harmless. It was designed to be innocuous, simple—so simple, in fact, that critics came to call it, derisively, "the Internet on training wheels."

But behind the unthreatening image, another dominated at AOL's Dulles headquarters: the menacing visage of David Colburn.

The cowboy executive came to personify the aggressive company as it hurtled into the wild, throbbing heyday of the late 1990s and the turn of the twenty-first century. Even more, Colburn came to embody the brash dot-com culture that pervaded the entire industry.

Colburn was a stand-up comic, or an obnoxious bore, depending on your point of view. Either way, he was unfiltered. On one occasion, when a new company official entered Colburn's office, Colburn greeted him with, "Who the fuck are you?" At a big company meeting, Colburn handed a microphone to another AOL official and told him to "stick it up your ass, it's safe sex, but you'll probably like it." At one of his parties, he asked a personal question of one of his underlings, "When was the last time you fucked your wife up the ass?" The underling's wife stood by silently in utter shock.

"You tolerated him because he had power," said a former AOL official who was subjected to some of Colburn's rants. This former AOLer chalked up Colburn's outrageous behavior to the power and wealth that rained on him and his peers. "They ran their own little empires," he said. "They were like kings. Money kind of corrupts your sense of power."

Officially, Colburn's title was president of business affairs, overseeing a group of about one hundred deal makers who were in the middle of many of the company's biggest and most complicated transactions. Usually the deals involved selling on-line advertising space, those rectangular "banner" ads that appear on people's computer screens when they log on to their AOL accounts.

Unofficially, though, Colburn was known as Steve Case and Bob Pittman's muscle. While Case ruled AOL as chairman and chief executive, thinking big thoughts about future technology, Pittman ran the day-to-day show as company president, pushing aggressive financial targets for AOL. Colburn was their go-to guy. He pushed the buttons. On big deals, when AOL was negotiating multimillion-dollar contracts, it was left to Colburn to extract the last dollar, to bend the other side to his will.

Colburn was an unlikely enforcer. The son of a well-to-do toy manufacturer in the Milwaukee suburbs, he came from a Conservative Jewish family, where their annual tradition included buying a new Cadillac. As a boy growing up in the 1960s, he liked to play basketball, a game he played with ferocity, much as Steve Case did in his own youth. When Colburn didn't like a call, he'd get into an opponent's face. Or he'd just foul him. A lot. And hard. That brazen style carried over when he became a West Coast corporate lawyer, although little about Colburn's professional life pointed to a dazzling future. For more than a dozen years, Colburn remained an associate in a law firm without getting elevated to partner. But when he joined AOL in 1995, he quickly established his credentials as an effective deal maker.

Less than a year on the job, he negotiated a seminal deal to get the AOL icon on Microsoft's Windows start page, valuable real estate on the computer desktop because it suddenly gave AOL access to untold millions of Microsoft customers who might sign up for the on-line service. With the deal, AOL wouldn't have to send free disks to get people to sign up. The software would be preinstalled in the computer.

Colburn employed an effective technique to broker the deal. Some called it a club. He threatened to use the Netscape software browser if Microsoft didn't agree to put the AOL icon on the Windows start page. Microsoft, fearful that Netscape's browser could topple the Windows operating system hegemony in the personal computer world, agreed. For Colburn, it was a beautiful thing. AOL didn't have to pay a dime to its arch-rival for the prime placement. Instead, AOL agreed it would adopt the Internet Explorer browser, Microsoft's software program.

With that deal, Colburn was a made man at AOL. He commanded respect as a brilliant corporate strategist, who, like a chess master, was always thinking ten steps ahead in a negotiation. Colburn knew the specific details of a contract negotiation better than anyone else. He took the time to rehearse. He read prodigiously and remembered effectively. He was devoted, e-mailing people at midnight to review specific details. Colburn was disarmingly frank as well, knowing when to ask for exactly what he wanted out of the other party. He also knew when to go for the jugular.

His was often a bone-jarring negotiating technique that was filled with swearing and threatening. During one phone call in his office, he was heard yelling at someone, belittling him, tearing him down, screaming, "Don't be a fucking idiot!"

Someone, who happened to be passing by, asked another bystander whom Colburn was talking to.

"A client," came back the answer.

The threat of David Colburn became so powerful that it inspired fear well beyond Dulles, all the way to Silicon Valley among would-be partners of AOL. Few wanted to get in the ring with him.

"David had such a reputation that you could always use his presence as a threat," said Neil Davis, a former senior vice president. "It was like, 'If we can't get over this issue, we have to get David on the phone.' I could always invoke David as the court of appeals."

It was no exaggeration. Just the tread of his cowboy boots was enough. "His presence caused a ripple of fear," said an AOL official who worked for him. "You could always hear him coming."

Colburn had a habit of entering an AOL conference room late, as if to underscore that, as the most powerful person at the table, he could arrive whenever he wanted. But he didn't necessarily sit at the head of the table. That, too, seemed to send a message to all of those present. "He didn't give a shit where he sat," said an AOL official who worked with Colburn. "He was so powerful, it didn't matter."

Colburn, for all his power, could also be a big teddy bear. "Yes, he swears, screams, and yells, but he also gives millions to religious Jewish charities," said a close Colburn associate who has known him for years. "Though he's gruff and though he's pushy and he's got one of the worst personalities for this, he cares more about people than I do even. That's the truth."

Another friend said Colburn quietly gave his company driver, who refused to borrow money on religious principles, a considerable sum of cash to buy a house and a car, no strings attached. "His persona was a kicker and a screamer and an asshole, but there was another side," said another close colleague. "David was capable of being an incredible softy."

A former AOLer put it this way: "There are times when you almost think he's human."

Colburn thought so, too. He professed to be mystified by his overbearing reputation. Once, while sitting in plush leather seats in the spacious company jet, his fellow AOL executives seemed comfortable enough finally to confront Colburn with an uncomfortable question: *How could he be such a mean bastard?*

"I'm a nice guy," he insisted in his high-pitched tone. "I don't get it."

Colburn was a softy when it came to children. In June 2000, he celebrated his daughter Rachel's bat mitzvah by hiring one of the hottest boy bands on the planet: 'N Sync. The party favor reportedly cost $1 million.

Nearly two years later, in March 2002, Colburn pulled out all the stops for his other daughter, Jessica, at her bat mitzvah party, paying $35,000 to rent much of the ground floor at Washington's Union Station. The featured attraction was rock star Dave Matthews. How much this cost isn't known. Jessica's shindig also featured boxing promoter Don King and a Las Vegas theme, including a casino with fake $100 bills bearing Jessica's picture.

Colburn and his prodigious parties became industry lore. They even made it into an episode of HBO's popular sitcom *Sex and the City*, when Samantha, one of the main characters, was hired as the publicist for a wealthy girl's bat mitzvah. After Colburn learned of this apparent reference to his own familial indulgences, he screamed, he cursed, and then he called up a bigwig at his sister cable network and ordered fifty copies of the episode.

When Myer Berlow started playing with a hunting knife, Neil Davis knew there was a problem.

Davis, an AOL advertising executive, was in the middle of giving a business presentation in mid-1998 in a small Seattle conference room when he noticed Berlow, his boss, fidgeting. Berlow, the head of AOL's advertising division, was bored. Not a good thing. It was a hazard to Davis's health, judging by the length of the knife that Berlow was tapping impatiently on the surface of the conference table.

"The blade was six to eight inches long," Davis reckoned, from a glance out of the corner of his eye.

"It wasn't a hunting knife," Berlow later insisted. "It was a pocket knife."

Colburn, who was also in the room, didn't seem bothered by the glint of the knife. But the other person there, Jeff Bezos, the chief executive officer of Amazon.com, appeared alarmed.

"Bezos's eyes became the size of saucers," Davis said.

Things were not going as planned. AOL was trying to pitch Amazon, the emerging on-line retailer, on the benefits of advertising its goods on AOL's Internet service. But Davis, a compulsive contrarian, had other ideas. He had always wanted AOL to buy Amazon. He had even crunched the numbers, massaged the idea, and thought of selling off Amazon's warehouses to save money. He knew that the retailer, a growing force in electronic commerce, would be one of the on-line survivors. He wanted it to be a part of the AOL universe. Which is why Davis included the slide that Berlow and Colburn had explicitly warned him *not* to use, the one about how Amazon should be integrated within the AOL service. Amazon, Davis explained to Bezos, should have its own "tab," marking it clearly for consumers within the AOL shopping section of the Web site.

"That's moronic," Colburn sputtered, then turned to Berlow. "What the hell is Neil doing?"

Berlow glared at Davis, pointing the knife at him. "If you don't take that slide out," he said, "I'm going to stab you."

Berlow appeared serious. He was not only pointing the knife at Davis, he started approaching him with the weapon. "Bezos thought I was going to get stabbed," Davis said.

He didn't. But he did shut up, and AOL went on to strike an ad deal with Amazon.

It was never clear why Berlow was carrying a knife that day, but then again, there was much about Myer Berlow that was mystifying, if not a bit zany.

Maybe it was something in the water. Berlow, as it happened, was raised in the same neighborhood as Colburn, a Jewish suburb of Milwaukee. Berlow not only knew Colburn, who was about ten years his junior, but was also best friends with Colburn's older brother.

The oldest of six children, Berlow was born on April 25, 1950, in Cambridge, Massachusetts, and grew up on a farmhouse across the highway from Colburn's home. Berlow was the precocious son of a physician, a voracious reader who became politically active in the 1960s and 1970s, studied

Russian at the Leningrad Polytechnic Institute in the summer of his junior year of high school, and then went off to Kenyon College to major in religion. All of which apparently prepared him for a career in advertising.

When Berlow joined AOL in 1995 as vice president of national accounts, he already had twenty years of experience working at ad agencies in New York, L.A., and Miami. Few in northern Virginia, where fashions tended to lag behind the big cities, were prepared for the razzle-dazzle of Berlow: the black Armani suits, the indigo button-downs, the black and silver ties, the dark hair drawn back in a ponytail, the frenetic pace.

He was constantly on the go, beginning at 6:30 A.M., when he could be found sweating on a StairMaster in the company's basement gym, while reading a book. A colleague, perspiring at an adjoining StairMaster, once asked him what book he had chosen. He said he was reading about ADD, attention deficit disorder.

"Oh, yeah, my brother has that," the colleague said.

"Oh, I had that, too," Berlow responded. "But I'm better now."

It seemed an odd confession, though not to Berlow. And not to the colleague after she got to know him better. "That makes sense now," she said. "What you see is what you get."

Berlow didn't try to pretend. In the thick of negotiations with top executives of another company, he once played video games on a handheld device. In a meeting with Sony executives in Tokyo, he tossed aside polite convention and requested that they give him two PlayStation video consoles because they were impossible to get in the States. While Colburn bragged about his hair plugs, Berlow boasted about his own personal makeover: plastic surgery to remove wrinkles under his eyes, and caps over his teeth. His favorite movie was *The Godfather.* His philosopher-hero was Machiavelli, whom he liked to paraphrase: "Whether it is better to be loved than feared or vice versa. My view is that it is desirable to be both loved and feared; but it is difficult to achieve both and, if one of them has to be lacking, it is much safer to be feared than loved." To which, Berlow said, "Machiavelli has been given a bad name."

Berlow read science and history, owned his own plane, had a gun license in Idaho, and couldn't resist the lure of eBay, on which he successfully bid for a 1969 Mercedes. His buying spree got so out of hand that the boxes shipped from eBay piled up in his office, many unopened. He couldn't bring them home; his wife would kill him. So in the middle of meetings, he would start pulling out jackets and other clothing he had won through auctions, handing them out to his staffers to try on for size and take home. During the holidays, his secretary would toss an expensive catalog to numerous colleagues and tell them to pick out whatever they wanted. It was on Berlow.

Among the rich at AOL, Berlow was one of the richest, so rich in fact that he seemed almost numb to money. On a trip to Las Vegas in 2000, he barely noticed when he was down $60,000 while playing blackjack by himself against the dealer at the high-roller table at the Mandalay Bay Resort and Casino.

"He says it's a Zen activity for him," said a colleague.

Playing quickly, he reversed his losses and walked away with about $130,000. As he was heading back to his suite, he tried to hide his winnings by shoving wads of cash down his pants.

He was generous. He was brilliant. Many AOL women thought he was the best-looking man on campus. "He's so charming that even if you know he's not telling the truth, you smile and accept it anyway," said Randy Dean, who worked as Berlow's right-hand man in building AOL's advertising business in the mid-1990s.

Berlow also rubbed people the wrong way. Mark Walsh, a former senior vice president, called Berlow "an acquired taste." Part of the problem was the company culture. When he arrived in 1995, Berlow was trying to turn AOL from a subscription-based business into an advertising medium, and some of the AOL computer programmers turned their noses up at the idea. *Advertising on the Internet? What a crass idea.* In those days, AOL fostered independence, and some programmers took that for gospel, refusing to post the ads that Berlow had sold on the on-line service. A livid Berlow left a voice mail for another company official. "Who," he once asked, "do I have to fuck to get you people to do your jobs?"

The answer was, Steve Case.

Like the programmers, Case hated the idea of sullying AOL with a bunch of on-line ads. It wasn't consumer-friendly. In a staff meeting during the mid-1990s, Case said as much after Berlow had convinced Sprint to buy $5 million—then a considerable sum—in banner ads that would run across the bottom of the Web page.

"I don't like it," Case said.

Berlow reminded the CEO that Sprint, the big telephone company, was going to pay $5 *million.*

Case was unimpressed. *What really bothers me,* he said, *is the ads are in a place where members will see them.*

You don't really mean that, Berlow said.

Case did.

Berlow exploded: "Are you out of your fucking mind? You used to work for Procter & Gamble! How much would they pay for ads that nobody would see?"

Offended, Case stormed out of the room and asked Ted Leonis, then running the on-line service, to fire Berlow. Leonsis, who understood Berlow's value, declined. Case let it go.

After a while, Case accepted Berlow, just as he tolerated Colburn. Case left it largely to Leonsis, then his successor, Pittman, who became AOL's president in 1996, to deal with the two colorful executives. Sometimes, though, it was hard to distinguish Berlow from Colburn. Some called them "the terrible twins." Not only had they grown up together, they were fast friends as adults when they weren't screaming at each other. Colburn, the attorney, helped review Berlow's divorce papers. Neither wanted the other promoted sooner; they were simultaneously promoted from senior vice presidents to presidents of their respective divisions in 1999. "He [Colburn] and Myer are like Frick and Frack. What one gets the other wants," said one who worked with both men. "Myer and David are alike. Myer's just a better dresser."

Berlow played good cop to Colburn's bad cop when negotiating with other companies. As AOL's top salesman, Berlow's job was to woo clients. As AOL's top deal maker, Colburn's job was to get the best possible terms. The joke around the company was that Berlow strapped clients into a chair, and then Colburn beat the stuffing out of them.

Before the strangling and the death threat, the meeting in Dulles began innocently enough.

Colburn sat back while Berlow reviewed a proposed deal with executives of Music Boulevard in 1997. It was supposed to be a slam-dunk. Colburn and Berlow had already gone through the numbers. They had done the calculations. Music Boulevard, an on-line music service, was going to pay $8 million over three years to run ads on AOL.

Except that Berlow was suddenly hit by an epiphany: It occurred to him that, at $8 million, Music Boulevard was getting a good deal. No, not good. Great. He and Colburn had based the price of the deal on assumptions about how much in sales and profits Music Boulevard would derive from the ads it bought from AOL. And yet, right in the middle of this meeting, even as they were dotting their *i*'s and crossing their *t*'s, it dawned on Berlow that there was an entirely different metric by which this deal should be measured: If Music Boulevard launched an initial public offering of stock—and its parent company, N2K Inc., had already filed a registration statement with the SEC to do just that—then an ad deal with AOL, already emerging as the industry leader, would be worth much more than $8 million. Call it *gilt* by association. AOL was golden; thus, Music Boulevard would be golden, too. Racing through Berlow's mind was an appalling notion: *Backed by an AOL ad deal, these Music Boulevard executives stood to personally gain millions from an IPO!*

Berlow quietly tore out the pricing page from the proposed contract: That $8 million figure soon vanished in a crumpled piece of paper in his fist. Then dashing off a quick calculation in his head, he threw out a number on the fly. "The price is supposed to be $16 million," he said.

The Music Boulevard executives were perplexed. This was a final review of the contract, to which they had already agreed. And the price tag was $8 million. Colburn threw a scathing look at Berlow, then tried to salvage the situation, turning to the Music Boulevard executives. "Myer is saying it's worth $16 million, even though we're asking for only $8 million," Colburn explained.

Berlow, unmoved, corrected Colburn, insisting that he did mean $16 million, not $8 million.

Berlow could see Colburn's staffers fidgeting. Rising from the table, Berlow said he needed to go to the bathroom, and he asked a seething Colburn to join him. A new Colburn hire, on his first day at AOL, tagged along. As they moved out into the hallway, the new hire broke the silence by beginning to say, "I think—," before Colburn snapped back, "What did you say?"

Glaring at the new hire in his Brooks Brothers suit, Colburn barked, "How long have you been here? I don't give a fuck what you think! Shut the fuck up!"

Then, he turned his death glare onto Berlow. *The deal,* Colburn snarled, *was supposed to be $8 million, not $16 million.* Berlow hissed that he knew that. Berlow proceeded to explain why he had doubled the price, then yelled at Colburn for being a complete idiot for not picking up on his implied cues. "Since you fucked up the sale, David," he said, "every dime under $16 million you should pay out of your own pocket!"

Colburn snapped. Grabbing Berlow by the throat, Colburn rammed him against the wall, screaming, "I'm going to kill you!"

Berlow was instantly overcome by tears—of laughter. Colburn, befuddled, loosened his grip on Berlow's neck. *Why are you laughing?* he asked. *You're not even scared.*

"Well, David, I knew you couldn't do anything," Berlow retorted. "I could beat the crap out of you."

The only thing Berlow was afraid of was that Colburn would hit him in the face, and the mark would show when they went back into the room to finish the deal with Music Boulevard.

The chastened new AOL hire said, "Oh my God."

He gazed at Colburn and Berlow as if he were wondering how he had so utterly ruined his career by taking this job. Colburn and Berlow, no worse for the wear, reentered the room. In the end, they didn't get $16 million.

They got $18 million.

AOL also got a cut of Music Boulevard's sales.

It was just the beginning. Almost from the start of Berlow and Colburn's tenure in 1995, AOL faced a threat to its very existence—stiff price competition from other Internet service providers. In late 1996, AOL responded by abandoning the hourly fee that it had been charging customers, replacing it with a flat-rate monthly charge. Users, however, began to spend more time on-line, taxing AOL's network and eating into its profit margin. That's where Colburn and Berlow came in. AOL set its sights on getting companies to buy ads to promote themselves on its vast on-line network.

Ad revenue was intended to keep the company growing at a fast clip after the growth of its basic business—monthly subscriber fees—began to ebb. "Advertising was supposed to be the big thing to defray concerns about AOL plateauing," said Michael Bromley, a business development director for AOL consumer devices until he was laid off in 2001. "On Wall Street, it's not what you make, it's what you're perceived as."

Nobody understood this better than Berlow and Colburn. The Music Boulevard deal had driven home an important lesson—companies would be willing to pay a premium to advertise their goods and services to AOL's millions of subscribers. And as the company grew into an increasingly dominant industry leader, rarely would it be as difficult for Berlow and Colburn to jack up the price.

To many, the deal that broke the dam wide open involved Tel-Save Holdings Inc. It approached AOL in 1997, saying it had up to $50 million to spend marketing its long-distance service through banner ads and other promotions on-line. To Colburn, $50 million was a lot of money—but if a company said it had $50 million to burn, there must be more. Using the chutzpah that characterized his dealings, Colburn doubled the price, demanding $100 million even though on-line advertising was still an unproven medium and he wasn't even sure Tel-Save had the money. It did. And then Colburn asked for more, negotiating an equity stake in the upstart.

Other deals fell into place. In spectacular fashion, advertising and commerce revenue at AOL rocketed from virtually nothing from the time Berlow and Colburn arrived in 1995 to more than $2 billion in 2000—about a third of the company's overall revenue—largely because of their handiwork. Through brute force and key strategic decisions, Colburn and Berlow helped reshape AOL from a one-dimensional on-line service dependent on subscriptions to a major advertising force in the mass media.

When AOL announced its blockbuster takeover of Time Warner in January 2000, the mania was in full swing. Start-ups were lining up to strike a deal with AOL, perceived as a blue-chip Internet firm in a sea of untested wanna-bes. Two factors were at play: Dot-coms were rich with venture capital and clamoring to promote themselves. Second, a big advertising deal with AOL was considered the ticket to respectability for dot-coms taking their stock public. And for good reason: In 2000, 45 percent of all U.S. households using a telephone dial-up connection subscribed to AOL or its subsidiary, CompuServe. What's more, four out of five Americans surfing the Web inevitably reached an AOL site, whether it was MapQuest, the popular tool for driving directions, or Moviefone, the on-line ticketing service.

The company, as Steve Case had envisioned in what he called his "AOL Everywhere" strategy, was indeed becoming ubiquitous. It was also becoming all-powerful. Dot-coms weren't just hoping to give AOL their money, they were *pleading*. In one case, Neil Davis, the AOL advertising executive, came up with the idea of promoting energy on-line after reading a news article about how Congress was deregulating the industry. Looking for the biggest player in the field, Davis came across Enron Corp. But as he was negotiating with the big Houston concern, other energy firms got wind of the deal and sought to woo AOL. Green Mountain Energy Co., an environmentally friendly concern, even rented a hot-air balloon, flying it over the Dulles campus to catch the eye of AOL executives—until it was ordered down. It represented a hazard to the nearby airport. Davis, for one, wasn't convinced by Green Mountain's gesture. "We were looking for *green*," he said, but not the kind Green Mountain was proffering. "And Enron had more money."

Long before it went down in the flames of a massive corporate scandal, Enron spent about $60 million to promote itself on AOL for about seven years, Davis said. The hot-air balloon, though, left an impression. If companies were that desperate to do a deal, then AOL deal makers figured there was an opportunity to exploit the situation. They would raise the stakes by selecting only one company in each market sector. A winner-take-all scenario. AOL deal makers came to understand that they could make or break a dot-com just by picking which one to do business with. "I would basically pick the winner of [an industry], their stock would go up, and they'd be instantly rich, and they'd do anything for me," said an AOL business official who marveled at his own power.

In early 2000, for example, AOL pitted Homegrocer.com against Webvan.com, two on-line supermarkets, in a contest to see who would pay AOL more to promote its service. One would win; the other would be left to find a way to promote itself on the Web. Homegrocer apparently wanted AOL more. Even though the dot-com was actively marketing its on-line grocery service in only two cities at the time, it agreed to pay AOL $60 million over five years, a staggering sum. AOL, in turn, agreed to give Homegrocer exclusivity on its on-line service, shutting out Webvan. Homegrocer wasn't just banking on beating out Webvan; it figured its massive promotions reaching AOL's millions of subscribers would make its IPO that much more attractive. Only Homegrocer didn't factor this in: By paying AOL so much up front, it couldn't survive. Instead, Webvan ended up buying Homegrocer. Then it, too, went kaput in July 2001.

AOL officials weren't particularly sympathetic.

"Playing companies against each other was morally questionable," said an AOL executive. "But you know something? If you are in this thing for survival—remember, we had Microsoft breathing down our necks with all the money in the world—we had to do this. You do the best you can." A pause, then, "Should we have played people against each other? I don't know. A certain amount of me says, 'I'm sorry,' but it was about survival. We didn't have a choice."

As in the Homegrocer deal, AOL recognized that dot-coms, whether they had a real business plan or just a garage-store dream, were looking to use AOL for the big kill, the air of Internet credibility to pull off a gargantuan IPO that would make the founders rich. Besides, there was little chance that AOL could talk dot-coms out of these deals, even if it wanted to—not at the height of the frenzy.

"We have all these people walking through the door with cash. The question is, where do we put them?" said Dave Sickert, former director of AOL's on-line shopping service. "You had so many people walking through the door with wads of cash. It was life or death to them if they couldn't cut a deal with AOL. It was ludicrous."

The ludicrous graduated to the sublime in early 2000 when a top AOL marketing official began having her own personal stair-climber machine shipped to whichever hotel she stayed in while on business. Until one time, when for some unexplained reason, someone forgot to send along her exercise contraption. The hotel, as it turned out, didn't have a stair-climber either. For the marketing executive, this was a full-fledged emergency that required drastic action. Solution: Out of her own pocket, she bought a new machine for a couple of grand, and upon checkout, left the gleaming machine in her hotel room for the next guest.

Call it the privilege of wealth, AOL style.

The dot-com feeding frenzy was creating obscene riches at virtually every level of the company. It was a simple calculus: Dot-coms paid whopping fees to promote their wares on AOL. AOL, in turn, reported whopping revenue growth, which spurred investors to buy up its stock, which continued to rise, which prompted employees to cash in their ever-building stock options. It was the beauty of AOL. Everyone got stock options. The higher up you were, the more options you got. But there was enough to go around, and everyone, it seemed, was becoming an instant millionaire at Dulles headquarters. An increasingly common status symbol at AOL was whether you had your own airplane.

"There were a lot of pilots at AOL," said a former official who knew plenty of them.

Twentysomethings and secretaries retired with seven-figure bank accounts after a few years on the job, thanks to the incredible windfall from stock options. It got to the point where employees practically worshiped at the altar of AOL's stock. During the height of the Internet boom, in 1999 and the early part of 2000, the first act of the morning for many AOL employees was to log on to their computers, check their on-line portfolio, and stare in amazement at their growing AOL assets.

"It was like, 'Wow, I just made a few thousand dollars just by sleeping,'" said an official.

The almighty stock option became a fetish object, a love thing, a glimpse into a not-so-distance future for AOLers where freedom reigned—or least early retirement on a secluded beach. When AOLers were hired, they were typically given a major grant of stock options that took four years to vest before they could cash out. A new term became popular: "FYIV."

"Fuck you, I'm vested."

That's what you could tell your boss after four short years on the job. It was a lure few could resist. Options made people work hard, and the harder people worked, the better the company would do, the higher the stock price would rise, and the more money they would make from their options. Employees came to call themselves "options whores."

Wealth made people do things they might not otherwise. Some built 8,000-square-foot homes, or took yearlong honeymoons to see the world. Neil Davis, the AOL advertising executive, admitted that he, too, got caught up in the wealth game. His own extravagance was to spend about $60,000 to rent a private island off the coast of Tortola in the British Virgin Islands, a favorite hangout of Rolling Stones guitarist Keith Richards, to celebrate his fortieth birthday with a bunch of friends in December 1999. Davis spared no expense, serving lobster dinners in private huts and flying in a reggae band from another island.

"It got a little crazy," he said of the money.

"I was a victim of it, too," said Bill O'Luanaigh, a senior project manager of the AOL on-line service.

He was one of the early beneficiaries of AOL's success, buying a 911 Porsche Carrera with a snazzy whale tail in late 1995. His wife didn't approve of the expensive toy, especially the time she tried to drive it when she was pregnant. The alarm went off, automatically disabling the ignition system and locking her inside. She barely squeezed through the sun roof.

"My wife actually called the Porsche the other woman," he said.

He got rid of it after his daughter was born, but not before he purchased an A4 Audi, which he liked to use for recreational racing on a deserted road behind the AOL campus. That Audi was good enough to beat a performance-enhanced Ferrari—bought by another suddenly rich AOLer—in a half-mile blur past the company guard booth. Through his rearview mirror, O'Luanaigh watched his competitor fall behind, cackling in delight.

"I had him by a good half-car length," he said.

When O'Luanaigh wasn't drag racing in expensive cars, he was struck by the profundity of all this new-found wealth at AOL. "The experience of it is very weird," said the former English major at the University of Maryland. "I'm walking around there, and people are starting to become millionaires. You suddenly wake up and on paper, you're wealthier than you ever expected to be. I have more money than I expected to have in my entire life. It wasn't a goal of mine. It flipped things on [their] head."

. . .

It was the logic chain of too much money: Wealth begot parties. Parties begot good times. And good times, on occasion, begot trouble.

That was the case in early 2000 when a handful of AOL business officials took a spontaneous excursion from Dulles to San Francisco on the corporate jet. They called it a "team-building trip."

The destination: The Gold Club topless bar on Howard Street.

"It was like, 'Fuck it, let's party, let's go to San Francisco,'" said an AOL official. "So we go to a strip bar, and you're like, 'Fuck, this is a family company, and we're expensing a strip show!'"

Both men and women from AOL attended.

Said another AOL official, "The lavish parties, the crazy antics—it really socialized you. You had to toe the line."

If a few carousing AOL officials went to a strip bar, it was overlooked. But it didn't end there. On the night before Super Bowl XXXV in Tampa Bay in January 2001, when the Baltimore Ravens beat the New York Giants, cars were inching along in bumper-to-bumper traffic while pedestrians streamed by. Tossing caution to the wind, some AOL executives walked around the side of a building, barely veiled from the revelry, and proceeded to snort "coke on the hood of a car," said one who witnessed it. "You have to not give a shit about anything."

Alarming thoughts raced through this person's head, including an imaginary headline if they were spotted: *Top AOL Execs Caught Doing Coke at Super Bowl.*

There were other dalliances that never made it into the papers: Parties held by AOL officials with, in one case, a girl lying panty-less on a pool table. Rarely, though, did the partying emerge publicly in the workplace.

Most reckless behavior took place beyond the confines of Dulles, in a more evolved adult playground: Las Vegas. When company executives traveled to Sin City, they were sometimes greeted by a limo and a wealthy AOL business partner who put them up at the Mansion at the MGM Grand, the exclusive province of the high roller.

Built on the side of the gigantic casino, the mansion is a Tuscan-inspired architectural spread hidden from the masses, composed of enormous suites, with fireplaces in most every room, ranging from three thousand to fourteen thousand square feet.

The businessman, however, didn't limit his largess to grand suites. One of his close associates said he also "set them up on his own credit line" so that the AOL execs could gamble freely, to a point, without fear of losing their own shirts. The businessman had his own reasons for being so generous: "He wanted to build their loyalty to him," the associate said.

If the credit line didn't work, he offered the AOLers another inducement: high-priced call girls. "I guess it was his way of doing business, of closing deals, of making them happy," said another colleague of the businessman.

When asked about inappropriate behavior at the company, including sex and drugs, AOL said it was unaware of such activities and did not condone them. Some of its employees thought otherwise, saying the untoward behavior had a socializing effect, a way of bonding AOLers, like the little mischievous boys of *The Lord of the Flies*. "Everyone has dirt on everyone else," explained a company official who tried to distance himself from the wild activities. "It's mutually assured destruction, so you don't fuck each other."

A former official said the powerful glue that kept people bound together at AOL was the stock option. You didn't tattle on the indiscretions of another lest you threaten your own net worth. "It created very high stakes, a sense of loyalty," he said. "It was like, you shouldn't mess around with these people. You accepted the way they were. It was like, 'Wait a minute, I never dreamt of anything like this. I'm lucky.' Guys like Bob [Pittman] and possibly Steve [Case] were trying to get wealthy their whole lives, but for the rest of us, we took a flier on a job at a small company, and gosh darn it, it went crazy. So rocking the boat, you didn't want to do that."

Somewhere along the way, sexual chatter became almost commonplace in the company lexicon. On the AOL plane, men sometimes felt emboldened enough to talk breezily about which AOL women they wanted to have sex with, discussing in detail the various pros and cons about each one. Blatant ogling of AOL women was not uncommon. Sometimes behavior seeped into more dangerous territory. Women at the company described having to fend off the unwanted advances of their bosses. At least two of them said they never reported the problem, because they considered it an unpleasant reality of the workplace.

"You're talking about men who thought they had a right to anything," said a woman who said she was harassed but accepted it as part of the terrain.

It worked both ways. Some AOL men groused that some of their female counterparts got ahead by using sex to their advantage. One former official called it "on-the-desk performance reviews." Others called the politics of sex part of the job: People got drunk, they hooked up in a hotel room, affairs raged on, marriages broke up, and AOL moved on.

It was, many said, part of the wild ride that was the Internet. Dot-coms played it fast and loose, and AOL was at the heart of this rollicking revolution, creating an entire new medium. In effect, people drank the Kool-Aid. The feeling was, "There were new rules and we're creating them," said an AOL official.

So many AOLers were rich and powerful that some came to believe they could do whatever they wished. "There was a sense of invincibility," said a former official. "We were exempt from the normal curbs on behavior."

Another departed AOLer looks back ruefully on her experience, calling it "the cowboy culture." "It was out of control and we knew it," she said. "It reminded me of all the excesses of the eighties."

Blood flowed on Sundays at 9 A.M. on a regulation basketball court outside David Colburn's large clapboard and stone country-style house. There, he gathered his loyalists—a group of business affairs deal makers who wanted to move up the corporate ladder. Attendance was de rigueur. What he taught his disciples was his way of playing sports—and doing business: roughly.

As he did as a youth, Colburn played a ferocious game, breaking down his opponents with rough elbows, blatant fouls, and name-calling.

"It's the way he gets people to love him and fear him," an AOL official said. "You don't go to play, you go there to be abused."

Colburn ruled the basketball court, but business affairs was his real domain. It was a hard-charging unit of one hundred or so deal makers, including many lawyers, who toiled in an obscure building—Creative Center 4, or CC4—across the street from Dulles headquarters. And yet, for all its distance from the focal point of corporate power, the hand of business affairs was felt far and wide. Within the company, the prevailing belief was that business affairs—known simply as BA—held considerable sway over other departments, if only because it negotiated and finalized most of AOL's largest transactions.

"We were the best, we were BA, we were untouchable," said a former AOL official.

Word got around, even among new initiates to AOL. At a one-day orientation welcoming new employees to AOL in 2001, officials took pains to address the aggressive unit, saying it was trying to tone down its act. "You may have heard about BA," a vice president said. "We're trying to clean that up."

At least one new employee in attendance didn't understand what the fuss was all about. She learned soon enough, after working with some members of Colburn's unit. "Where there's a will, there's BA," she said. "I try not to pay attention or find out about them."

It was almost unavoidable, though. BA was the heavy artillery brought in to close a transaction. Colburn's deal makers usually got involved in advertising deals after the sales force had reached a general agreement with clients. Business affairs officials would draw up a list of proposed terms, extracting as much as they could and then reviewing the fine points of the deal structure with the company's accountants. The unit's work was also blessed by executives at the highest levels, including Pittman, the AOL president, to whom Colburn reported. But there was no mistake about who was calling the shots. Business affairs deal makers answered to one person only: David Colburn.

Few in business affairs dared stand up to him. He didn't tolerate it. While Colburn was chewing out somebody on his team, the others often felt not empathy for the victim but relief that they had been spared. "You're sort of embarrassed, sitting in a room with another business manager who's getting his ass chewed out, and it's like, 'Where am I sort of supposed to look?'" said a former AOL official who saw this scenario play out on more than one occasion. "It's one of those uncomfortable moments. I'm not sure whether I should make eye contact with anybody. I'm thinking, 'Gosh, I'm glad he's not bitching at me.'"

Deal makers who worked for Colburn dreaded his weekly staff meetings. These were supposed to be times to brief him on the status of business deals, to walk him through the terms of a complicated transaction. Instead, though, they often turned into times for Colburn to second-guess his troops, to puncture holes in their thinking. Rarely did they walk him through an entire deal. It usually didn't get that far. While they were talking, he would flip through the pages, not listening, then stop and suddenly ask about a specific detail—oftentimes a detail from an earlier version of a contract from a week before. "An inane detail," said one of his deal makers. "He could always find something you don't know the answer to."

Colburn didn't hesitate to go after anyone on his team, not even a former NFL linebacker. Ted Rogers, a former Washington Redskin, thought he had faced terror on the gridiron. But that was before Colburn beckoned Rogers, then a new member of his deal team, outside AOL's fifth-floor boardroom in early 1999. Colburn had just emerged from a meeting of "Op Com," the operating committee of senior executives, chaired by Pittman, which was still underway. With other top executives within earshot, Colburn relentlessly screamed at Rogers for a paperwork mistake—getting the wrong AOL executive's signature on a particular deal. The berating became water-cooler legend: If Colburn could decimate Rogers, a 250-pound, six-foot-two-and-a-half-inch former linebacker, what about the rest of his crew?

"Maybe I deserved it," Rogers said. "I don't know. I felt completely demoralized because it was my first deal."

Rogers, a gentle man despite his football aggressions, couldn't stomach the Colburn way. After only fourteen months, he quit his AOL job in May 2000.

Every couple of weeks, Colburn set his sights on another member of his team whom he could make an example out of, someone to poke fun and yell at, before building him back in his own relentless image.

"He'd put an arm around you, and say, 'Things are going to be all right, I really love you,'" said an AOL official. "He'd say a kind word, and it'd make your day. It's like an abusive father."

He could be generous as well, bestowing financial rewards on those who performed well in his units. Colburn played a key role in deciding which of his people got stock options. And he sent favored underlings and their spouses on weekend getaways to places like New York, all expenses paid, including limousine service, Broadway shows, and lavish dinners.

To win his favor, many young deal makers not only sought Colburn's approval, they *became* him. At one of his parties, some of his underlings dressed up as Colburn, wearing cowboy boots and a T-shirt. That, however, was just a lark. It wasn't so funny when the mimicking spilled over into the office, as a cadre of Colburn storm troopers emerged in similar garb, needing a shave, swearing and cursing at colleagues, rudely interrupting people from other divisions during company meetings. Some even adopted his high-pitched honk of a voice. Or they just screamed like he did.

"That's what we did, we screamed," said a former executive. "We said stuff like, 'Don't fucking do this!' 'How many fucking times do I have to tell you that?' It was a screaming culture. 'Goddamn, I don't have time for that!' It was the lingo, it was the currency."

Colburn set the tone at AOL, but some feel the sense of urgency would have been there anyway, albeit at a lower decibel level, even if he hadn't been there. In the 1990s and into 2000, AOL was leading the way in the evolution of a new medium, trailblazing an Internet vision against the pressing realities of Wall Street, which always demanded immediate financial results from the on-line firm.

"We didn't have the niceties of time," this former executive said. "Tensions were high. It was really hard and the pressure was intense and the pressure was continual. You knew we had goals for the company, we had a mission for the company. Time was short. Deals were getting done quickly, and they were hugely important to the company. Wall Street was getting impatient with the company, and that is no lie, so the pressure was there."

Colburn, though, ratcheted up the pressure, encouraging a hyperaggressive atmosphere, and many of his charges took his cues, fighting even among themselves over the pettiest of issues, such as who had the bigger office. In one instance, two vice presidents were promoted to senior vice presidents at around the same time in the late 1990s. But when they got new offices, one executive suspected an inequity. He pulled out blueprints and measured the square footage of each office. His suspicions were confirmed when it turned out that the other guy's office was bigger than his by a few feet.

"He blew a gasket," said a former employee who worked with him.

Walls were moved, and his office was reconfigured to make it as large as his counterpart's.

It became the BA way. Yield nothing, no matter how small. There was no shortage of testosterone within Colburn's unit. Many women said the Colburn culture was infused with the feeling of a boys' club. Women who wanted to have children, or had children, were at a distinct disadvantage in getting plum assignments or promotions, some said. "If you wanted to get ahead, you needed to be available pretty much 24-7 for the company," said a former female executive. "But even the women who were giving the 24-7 didn't seem to get promoted as much as the guys were."

Another woman who worked at AOL called the company, "Boys' Town." "AOL," she said, "was nothing but the Boys Club of America."

Colburn's unit could have been called the Wild West just as easily. When AOL was negotiating with another company, deal makers said that some of their colleagues who knew of the transactions but were not directly involved would use that information to buy stock in the other company before its deal with AOL was announced publicly. The outcome was predictable: When the AOL deal was disclosed, the stock in the other company would invariably shoot up, and the AOL deal makers who had been given a heads-up about the transaction in advance would sell and make a handsome profit.

"We knew it was wrong, but people did it," said an AOL official.

Flattery, perks, and obscene wealth created a potent combination in Colburn's charges. Suddenly, deal makers weren't negotiating; they were demanding, as in the case when Neil Davis, the advertising executive, dictated terms in a deal with four brokerage firms. Each, he told them, would pay AOL $25 million for a two-year promotional deal, and that was it.

"It's nonnegotiable," he told them.

Others quickly picked up on the same approach. "I would joke I'm a mafia enforcer," said a former deal maker. He would approach prospective clients, tell them what to do, and then say, "Do we have an understanding? *Capisce?*"

Usually, they did.

"It was very real, the cowboy arrogance," said a former AOL executive. "It was very much inherent in the culture. 'We're AOL, we can screw people. We will squeeze every last dime out of you because of who we are.'"

Sometimes the arrogance went so far that even Colburn put on the brakes. Such was case in the late '90s when a new deal maker tried to make a good impression on the boss. During a weekly staff meeting, the new guy explained that he had negotiated a $5 million ad deal with a dot-com, but he was convinced he could get more. As a matter of fact, he told Colburn, he had already been working to squeeze twice as much out of the dot-com.

Colburn, however, was already aware of this. The dot-com had called Berlow, the top AOL sales executive, to complain about how much pressure was being applied by this new deal maker. Berlow, who was also sitting in on the meeting with Colburn, told the young deal maker to settle for $5 million. But the newcomer wouldn't hear of it. He had done his homework, the dot-com was a public company, he knew how much money it had in the bank, and he was convinced its board of directors would approve a $10 million deal.

"Look, they can afford $10 million," he insisted.

Berlow countered, "I can afford a Rolls, but I'm not going to buy one."

"I can too," the deal maker shot back.

Colburn, enjoying the scene, chuckled. Then he weighed in: The deal was $5 million, end of discussion. Colburn, however, couldn't resist smiling approvingly at his new charge.

"He was like the proud father looking at the lion cub who has his first kill and is all excited about it," said the deal maker.

The aggression, however, didn't sit well with others. Randy Dean, for one, was disturbed when he witnessed brash deal makers at work, verbally beating up on business partners. "I definitely saw that at meetings," he said, "They weren't always nice about it." But afterward, Dean, then an AOL advertising executive, would catch up with the deal makers and try to explain to them why "strong-arm tactics" weren't always a good idea. He tried to appeal to logic. AOL, he stressed, would have to work with these companies after striking a deal with them. It was only the beginning of what AOL hoped was a long-term relationship. Why start off on the wrong foot? Not to mention that such arrogance didn't put AOL in the best possible light with other prospective business partners.

Sometimes, Colburn's deal makers listened. Sometimes, they didn't. "Who cares?" said one. "We're making money."

To many, that's all that seemed to matter. *Do whatever is necessary.*

"He created these foot soldiers," said an AOL official "who went to war for him."

By late 1999, many companies seeking to do business with AOL were no longer viewed as potential partners. They were a target, to be used. The first order of business was for AOL deal makers to find out how much money the dot-coms had raised in venture-capital funding, then try to extract as much as possible from them in on-line ad deals. Informally, AOL's goal was to get a minimum of 50 percent of a dot-com's venture-capital funding.

" 'Fuck 'em,' that was our mantra," said an AOL official. "We'd say that all the time. We took it to heart. 'Destroy them. Fuck 'em.' You lived by that."

In negotiating deals with companies, another AOL official said the aim finally reached this basic level: annihilation. "When we walked away," he said, "they wouldn't remember their own names. It was crazy. It was the high of the deal. It was the high of the battlefield."

It was part of the full-throttle approach of BA, which spawned a whole series of effective but ethically questionable techniques normally reserved for unwitting dot-coms. There was little mercy, even though AOL was often dealing with naive newcomers in their twenties and thirties who had never negotiated a business deal in their lives.

"We took them to school," an AOL official said.

The first gambit many deal makers learned was this: "You make a mistake" on purpose, said one versed in the art. To wit: When trying to pitch the virtues of advertising on AOL, a deal maker would offer a PowerPoint presentation to a prospective client. One of the slides, however, would include the logo of the client's rival, as if AOL had accidentally mixed up some of the slides from another presentation. The deal maker, pretending to be embarrassed, would apologize profusely. It was a sham, of course, but it achieved the intended effect. It would seem that AOL was negotiating a similar deal with the client's rival, which would spur the client to strike first.

"Another thing we'd do is create an insane deadline," said an AOL official. "We called it 'the crunch time.'" It would start out as a slow waltz between AOL and a prospective client, involving lots of wooing and pretty words about how great the client's business was, how neat it would be if the two sides hooked up, how wonderful it would be if the client bought ads on AOL.

Naturally, AOL wouldn't mention that it was having precisely the same slow dance with multiple partners. Weeks would go by—then AOL would suddenly demand immediate action. Abruptly, deal makers would draw up a contract, slam it on the table, and order the prospective client to sign it within twenty-four hours or, worse, by the end of the day, or else AOL would take the offer to another party, which happened to be standing by—"even if it's all bullshit," said an AOL official.

What had begun as a delicate courtship would end up with an ultimatum that would leave the client reeling—and usually agreeing.

Another effective technique was called "the escalation." At the beginning of a negotiation, a low-level AOL deal maker would insist on dealing directly with the top decision maker of the other company, even if it went as high as the CEO. That was an important part of the strategy. AOL didn't want the other side to be able to say that it needed to go back and check with the boss on a concession. It was a matter of controlling the environment. All the while, AOL knew that it would pull the rug out. Just when it seemed a deal was done, and the other side had signed the contract and sent it back for AOL's signature, the deal maker would suddenly declare that someone at a higher level at AOL had thrown a roadblock in the deal. "Then, at the end, we'd take back our concessions," said one who did as much. Sometimes this happened even after the two companies had celebrated the deal with what they called a "launch party." The other company, reluctant to back out of the deal at such a late date, often conceded to AOL's wishes.

One company called dealing with AOL "trench warfare." Deal makers produced mammoth contracts the size of telephone books and even harder to get through—and then waged hand-to-hand combat over the specific language contained in them. AOL executives also made officials of other companies sit around for hours, in a so-called waiting game, just to let them know they were not important.

When all else failed, AOL deal makers sometimes concocted a fiction to drum up business. That happened in early 1999 when AOL was mired in a long-term deal with Preview Travel, an on-line travel agency that showed little promise. Preview Travel had little financial backing, its on-line content was sparse, and AOL, which owned a small equity stake in the firm, wasn't getting much in the way of ad revenue—$18 million over seven years, tops, said Neil Davis.

So he devised a plan to get out of the deal: Get somebody to buy Preview Travel. "I came up with the idea," he said. First, he massaged the idea with Eric Keller, a business affairs executive, to make sure "it didn't sound like some sort of drug-induced hysteria," before he ran it by the higher-ups. There was only one hitch: Nobody was interested in buying Preview Travel. With the help of Colburn, Berlow, and Keller, Davis said he created the illusion that someone was courting the small travel firm. "I made it up," he said. "I basically created a situation where people thought that Preview Travel was on the block and that AOL was going to be supportive of a long-term deal with the new partner."

What Davis didn't account for was this: Microsoft, AOL's nemesis, arrived on the scene, kicking the tires to see about buying the little on-line travel business. Davis, an inveterate AOLer who couldn't countenance the idea of having *anything* sold to Microsoft, quickly scrambled to see if the parent company of Travelocity, another on-line travel service, was interested in making the purchase. It was, and before long a deal was done. AOL got out of its deal with Preview Travel, and in the process, Davis pulled off a gargantuan ad deal, getting the new owner, Travelocity's parent company, to agree to a $200 million, five-year deal.

"It was," he said, "the perfect scenario."

Or so he thought. He didn't know it then, but playing it fast and loose would ultimately catch up with AOL. Through aggressive deal making, AOL grew to great proportions, reaching the pinnacle of its power when it acquired Time Warner. But the bruising techniques and negotiations left a string of financially hobbled dot-coms that eventually couldn't pay their bills. Many would die soon. For the time being, though, AOL was living by Colburn's credo, extracting skin in the game.

CHAPTER SIX

WHO LET THE DOGS OUT?

On September 27, 2000, in Room 2322 of the Rayburn House Office Building, Steve Case didn't look so boyish anymore.

The familiar mop of hair, hanging low over his inscrutable brow, looked gray, as if he had forgotten to dye it dark for this cameo appearance in public. Then again, maybe gray was the look he wanted—somber, stately, like the gray suit he had chosen for the occasion. No more Gap khaki for Mr. Case. Or maybe time, compressed in a whirlwind of wealth, fame, and power, was finally taking its toll on the forty-two-year-old master of the universe. The golden boy of the Internet had lost some of his magic dust in the nine-plus months since he had gleefully pranced across a New York stage, high-fiving the announcement of the biggest merger in U.S. history.

Case hadn't counted on this: The deal had yet to give birth. It remained an unresolved matter before federal regulators. And here he was, again hunkered down before a dubious gallery of Congress, being riddled by persistent questions from politicians who were fearful of the looming media juggernaut that would be Case's province.

"This merger has been the most scrutinized merger in history," he pronounced, clench-jawed, before members of the Subcommittee on Telecommunications, Trade and Consumer Protection.

Some things, however, never came to light.

At about the same time Case was giving testimony on Capitol Hill, little more than thirty miles away, a young, hard-charging AOL official in Dulles was busy pulling off a remarkable business transaction that would test the limits of accounting and ultimately draw Case into a massive firestorm, threatening the mega-merger he had orchestrated.

"It was the most wacked situation in the history of international business," said a former official familiar with the deal.

BA was at it again.

AOL's aggressive business affairs unit had launched one of its rising young stars on a rush job. AOL was short of its targeted advertising revenue for the quarter ending September 30, just days away. The company needed to make a deal fast to close the gap, or face the wrath of investors.

It was a crisis of its own making: In recent years, AOL had been increasingly emphasizing the importance of advertising revenue—its fastest-growing business—and it set ever-larger targets for itself every quarter. Wall Street analysts, taking the cue, based their stock recommendations in large measure on the company's ability to reach its own aggressive goals.

AOL could not afford to falter—not now, not as its stock was eroding, not as it was pushing to finalize its takeover of Time Warner.

Time was running out as the young official headed into the office early one day that fall to call London before the business day ended there several hours ahead of Dulles. He needed to reach Wembley PLC, a major British entertainment company.

"I was instructed to contact Wembley and cut an ad deal," said the young official. "We needed to get the deal done before September 30 because the company had to book it" as revenue for the quarter. "It was clear to me that AOL management was under enormous pressure to close the Time Warner transaction."

Wembley, a gambling operator with greyhound racetracks in the United Kingdom as well as Rhode Island and Colorado, was far afield of AOL's Internet-based business. But by an accident of past business deals, Wembley suddenly represented an opportunity to help pull AOL out of the fire.

Wembley owed AOL money from an obscure legal dispute.

The origins of the legal case reached back to 1992, when Moviefone Inc., an on-line ticketing firm, and a former Wembley subsidiary set up a joint venture to develop hardware and services for automated movie-ticketing sales. The parties had a falling out, the matter went to arbitration, and three years later Moviefone won an award against the former Wembley subsidiary. None of which had anything to do with AOL until AOL purchased Moviefone in 1999 and inherited the $22.8 million arbitration award, plus interest, which had not yet been paid.

AOL could have taken Wembley back to court. But officials huddled and concluded it would have been costly to litigate with an overseas company, and the outcome was uncertain. Instead, that September, AOL offered Wembley an alternative: Buy $23.8 million in on-line ads. That would also save the British firm money, requiring Wembley to spend $3 million less than the arbitration award including interest.

Wembley, sensing AOL's urgency, played hardball. "The Brits knew we needed this bad," said the young official. When he made the pitch, he was first met by silence on the other end of the long-distance call. Then they put a question to him, point-blank: *What do we need the ads for?* Why would Wembley advertise on AOL? It was in the gambling business, not the Internet industry, and only some of its operations were based in the United States.

The young AOL official groped for an answer, consulted with other business affairs officials and, after considerable research, came up with this: dogs.

Wembley, as it turned out, was preparing to launch 24dogs.com, an on-line greyhound-racing Web site. Still under construction, the site would allow gamblers to check the odds and place a bet on a dog—a potentially lucrative business for the British to tap into as the market for betting on-line expanded into audio and video format.

When he got back to Wembley, the young official suggested that AOL could run the ads promoting the Web site. The British mulled the offer. Still, they didn't seem quite sold. Nor did they seem to be in a rush. AOL was. The quarter was closing fast, and the young official couldn't afford to wait. To book the revenue in the quarter, AOL needed to run the ads before September 30 to conform with accounting rules. BA decided there was no other choice: Without Wembley's knowledge, business affairs officials ordered AOL employees to lift artwork—a picture of a racing greyhound—off the British company's 24dogs.com Web site. The techies then created banner and button-sized ads out of the image and, unbeknownst to the Brits, started running them on AOL's on-line service.

Dogs popped up everywhere.

The greyhound ads appeared on various AOL sites, reaching out into cyberspace as far as Spinner.com, its on-line radio service. To maximize the amount of revenue it could generate, AOL ran as many as three or four Wembley ads on a single Web page. The number of greyhound ads, however, got to be a little too much, even for some at AOL. It got so bad, in fact, that a Spinner official on the West Coast felt compelled to call an AOL official.

"Dude," the Spinner man complained, "my home page looks like a dog site."

Not for long. Within about an hour of posting the greyhound ads, Wembley's unfinished Web site crashed from an overload of customer traffic from AOL. But before the British discovered the problem, AOL got its deal. Wembley agreed to buy $23.8 million in AOL ads.

Thanks to BA's aggressive negotiating, the terms of the deal also favored AOL. At its own "discretion," AOL would dictate when and where the Wembley ads ran throughout AOL's vast network. Such a provision meant that Wembley's ads could appear at any time or place—not necessarily targeting its core audience. But, said an executive familiar with the deal, the British were never really interested in the ads; they wanted to wipe out the legal case, which they got to do at a considerable savings.

According to a copy of the confidential settlement between the two companies, AOL and Wembley released each other from all claims. It stipulated that "AOL will promote various Wembley USA websites with 1 billion [ad] impressions to run at AOL's discretion. Such promotion is: a) a good faith gesture by AOL to expeditiously and amicably settle the arbitration matter, and b) a way to demonstrate the potential of AOL's interactive properties to drive traffic to Wembley USA websites."

For the British, the settlement came with a beneficial side effect: a U.S. tax break. Wembley did not mention AOL by name, but in its 2000 annual report, it stated that the "$23.8m [million] has now crystallized as an allowable deduction for federal tax purposes against U.S. income."

AOL officials tried to stop Wembley from issuing a press release to the public about the matter, but it did so anyway. Wembley did, however, make a small allowance. On October 5, without mentioning AOL, it announced "the settlement of the longstanding U.S. arbitration award between Wembley Inc. (its 100 percent subsidiary) with Moviefone Inc." Wembley also noted its $3 million savings. AOL officials, fearing that their stealth deal might have gotten out, cringed when they saw the announcement on the other side of the Atlantic.

Their secret was safe for the moment. What's more, AOL ran enough Wembley ads to book $16.4 million in that quarter. In the same three-month period, AOL converted another unresolved legal action into ad revenue, a $13 million deal with Ticketmaster, a majority-owned unit of USA Interactive Inc. Several AOL officials privately expressed qualms about the legitimacy of the deal. "It stinks to high heaven," said one company official familiar with the matter. And yet, in each case, David Colburn, head of business affairs, signed off. So, too, did AOL's internal accountants.

"It got us through the third quarter," said a former official. Neither deal was publicly announced by AOL, but the company had another way to mark the occasion. A handful of business affairs officials gathered in a vice president's office and whooped it up by blaring a popular hip-hop song on a personal computer: "Who Let the Dogs Out."

Back in the spring of 1999, Colburn was flipping through pages and pages of numbers at one of his weekly staff meetings. Big numbers. Astronomical numbers. AOL's advertising backlog had reached $1 billion. It was hard to believe, but his deal makers had sold $1 *billion* in advertisements that hadn't *even* run yet on the burgeoning on-line service.

"How," he finally uttered, "do we improve on a $1 billion backlog?"

There was no answer from the dozen or so people sitting at the conference table in Dulles.

"This is incredible," Colburn persisted. "What do we have to do to increase the numbers?"

More silence.

It was as if the group were giving Colburn room to ruminate, to marvel at what was largely his own creation, this moneymaking deal machine, which had helped lift AOL's stock price to dizzying heights. AOL's market cap—the company's value based on its stock price multiplied by the number of shares outstanding—had reached an astounding $140 billion.

AOL was worth more than Disney, Viacom, and CBS *combined.*

"Are we ever going to be a trillion-dollar company?" he wondered out loud, a look of utter disbelief on his face.

No one responded.

"Everyone thought it was kind of crazy," said one who attended the meeting. "But at the time, we thought it was doable."

Steve Case didn't, not by November 1999. Six months after Colburn mused about the notion of AOL becoming a trillion-dollar company, the dream was turning into a nightmare. Case began receiving internal company reports pointing to a stark reversal of fortune on the horizon. Investors didn't know it, but suddenly AOL's backlog—its pipeline of ad deals—was showing a disturbing downward trajectory.

A confidential report dated November 4, 1999, showed just how bad the situation was: The company had signed forty-seven deals valued at $694 million from July to September 1999, but in the next three-month period, from October to December, so far only fourteen deals had been signed, valued at $457 million. Less than a week later, on November 10, another internal report showed the same weakness. And by January 14, 2000, four days after the AOL–Time Warner merger was announced, a further report indicated there was still no pickup.

Case began to feel pressure from all sides. In the first two days after the deal was announced, AOL's stock plunged about 17 percent, and Time Warner's declined 12 percent. Then the tech-laden Nasdaq Stock Market went into free fall in March as dot-coms, running out of cash, began to implode. This didn't bode well for AOL, which reportedly got as much as 60 percent of its ad revenue from dot-coms. How would it replace the failing business?

Pressure, meanwhile, kept building from federal regulators who were reviewing the merger. What Case had assumed would be a walk in the park had turned into a test of wills with the government. Things got so bad that associates of Jerry Levin, the Time Warner chief, began to whisper that he should get out of the merger. *Just pay the $4.4 billion breakup fee.* Hefty as it was, some told him they thought it would end up being a pittance compared to the disaster that lurked in an AOL marriage.

The admonition came from bankers, from consultants, even from Levin's own people. Levin, however, had staked his reputation on the deal, and he wasn't backing off. Neither were Case and other AOL executives. They were, however, acutely aware of the threat of the deal collapsing. And they were convinced there was only one thing to do: project confidence.

With the merger still pending, there could be no hiccups—or so came the directive from David Colburn to his deal makers in business affairs and across the company. AOL's quarterly earnings reports should show—*must* show—that the on-line giant was maintaining its financial momentum. Had AOL failed to do so, officials feared a terrible chain reaction: Wall Street would begin to lose confidence in the company, investors would clamor for drastic action, AOL's stock would suffer even more than it was, and Time Warner would have to pull out of the proposed merger.

"There was always pressure," said an AOL official. The feeling was, "We have to hit the quarter, there's no other way but to hit the quarter, or we're screwed," he said. "The company, our stock will tank. It's like breathing air." As a result, executives concluded that they could not lower their financial targets, lest they alarm Wall Street and their dance partner, Time Warner.

"We had to maintain this facade, to show the Street that AOL was not backing away from its numbers," the AOL official said. "At this point, we understood we couldn't tell the Time Warner side how much trouble we were in."

Throughout the yearlong merger review, from January 2000 to January 2001, the same scenario played out quarter after quarter: As a fiscal period was coming to a close, AOL officials would find they were in jeopardy of falling short of the company's revenue projections. Deal makers would be pressured to construct unconventional deals to inflate AOL's advertising revenue. The greyhound ad deal with Wembley wasn't the only one.

"They're called 'BA specials,'" said an AOL official, referring to business affairs. He said that some who refused to cooperate in these schemes were "cleared out of the department, paid off, marginalized, or destroyed in the company."

That included James Patti, a senior manager in business affairs while the merger was under review. When he told senior executives he was uncomfortable with some of the transactions pushed by his unit, he found an unresponsive audience. Executives, he discovered, were preoccupied with another pressing problem: getting the merger approved as market conditions deteriorated.

"The bubble had clearly burst, but senior management was under enormous pressure to hit the [financial] numbers and close the Time Warner transaction, which would diversify the revenue base and lower the risk profile of the company," Patti concluded.

Patti, who had just received a merit promotion for his work on major business deals, was promptly laid off in 2001. He believes his removal was directly related to his refusal to participate in the BA specials.

"I had been asked to paper many of these questionable deals and was unwilling to cooperate, making my concerns known to management," Patti said. "The layoff came exactly one week later. Ultimately, I was happy to leave the company with my integrity and professional ethics intact."

Patti represented a small yet real threat to AOL's attempt to clinch its Time Warner deal. But the company wasn't concerned only about the merger. Officials were concerned about their own financial well-being. The wealth of numerous AOL executives was tied directly to the company's stock price. Through options, Case and others had already achieved phenomenal riches. The merger only raised the stakes—and cranked up the pressure. Under the deal terms, most of the stock options of AOL employees vested one year after the deal closed. If they wanted to cash in, they could not afford a misstep.

"It's emblematic of the big stock-options grant," said a former AOL official. "The fact that everyone has options creates an almost perverse incentive to prop up the stock at almost any cost."

On a June afternoon in 2000, an anxious AOL executive rushed up to the cubicle of a manager in business affairs, instructing him to draw up documents for a new advertising deal with Sun Microsystems, the giant computer and networking company. It seemed like a perfectly forgettable moment, just another workaday deal. Except for this: The Sun deal heralded the onset of a rash of BA specials through the rest of the year.

The timing of the deal couldn't have been better. With the Time

Warner merger pending, the whiteboard in the manager's cubicle was beginning to show fewer new ad deals in the works and more old deals falling apart because financially strapped dot-coms couldn't afford to pay AOL anymore. "It was already clear the deal pipeline had fallen off a cliff," the manager said.

That AOL turned to Sun wasn't surprising. The two companies had a tight relationship. AOL had just spent $300 million buying Sun hardware, which AOL used to expand its vast on-line network to connect computer users to the Web. Under the new agreement, AOL promised to buy an additional $250 million in Sun hardware over two years. But there was a twist. AOL, short of its revenue targets, needed to sell some ads. Thus, AOL offered Sun a deal: If you buy our AOL ads, we will buy your Sun hardware.

"As an incentive for us to make the above [$250 million] purchase commitment, Sun agreed to purchase $37.5M [million] of ads over the next 3 quarters," a deal maker wrote in an internal memo.

In AOL's parlance, it was called a barter deal. AOL was exchanging goods, computer equipment for ads. But the barter deal was partly cosmetic: The company wanted to make its financial books look more attractive in the eyes of Wall Street when AOL announced its quarterly revenue results.

There was another feature that made the deal even more notable: Sun didn't actually have to pay a dime for those $37.5 million in ads. Instead, Sun would give AOL a credit for $37.5 million worth of computer equipment, and the two companies would call it even.

"They will pay by providing AOL with an equivalent credit for future hardware purchase," the memo stated.

AOL had just found a way to book $37.5 million in ad revenue by essentially agreeing to front the money for the Sun ads. Said an AOL official familiar with the arrangement, "It was fake money." AOL put it a different way in its deal memo. Under the heading "Metrics of Success," the company stated, "Recognize ad revenue in exchange for the additional purchase commitment (achieved)."

The deal was signed off by the company's accounting policy unit. But some within the company were convinced that the transaction hid part of its true intent.

"The bottom line is, it wasn't about the advertising," said a former

AOL executive involved in the deal. "AOL didn't care about the value of the equipment. What AOL did was leverage a current relationship and turn it into ad revenue."

Other barter deals followed as the Time Warner merger inched closer to fruition. The company, however, was careful to keep such transactions quiet. "They wanted to keep it under the radar," said an AOL official. As long as barter deals in a single fiscal period didn't exceed 10 percent of AOL's overall revenue, internal accountants reckoned they didn't have to report them in public filings. In what became known as the 10 percent rule, deal makers, aware of the threshold, were constantly calling over to AOL's internal accountants to see if they had gone too far. Not that there were any irreparable mistakes. If the revenue from barter deals did happen to spill over the line, deal makers were simply instructed to shift the deal to the next quarter. As it was, they made certain they came as close as possible to reaching that 10 percent ceiling.

No opportunity was overlooked. Deal makers even bartered keywords, terms that AOL users could use to search any number of subjects. When, for example, a movie studio agreed to use an AOL keyword for consumers to find out more about an upcoming film release, the mere mention of AOL was worth a certain amount of money to the on-line company. Officials tracked so-called in-kind barter deals. The company also hired an independent media firm to estimate the worth of such keyword mentions. And then AOL's deal makers went out and traded them for on-line ads. The list of companies with which AOL bartered keywords was staggering. According to a company e-mail from one AOL official to another in September 2000, the list included CBS, CNN, E!, Food TV, HBO, MTV, VH1, the NBA, NPR, Oprah, PBS, Rosie O'Donnell, TVKO, and the Weather Channel. The result: AOL generated tens of millions of dollars in ad revenue from arcane deals about which investors and Wall Street had no knowledge.

"Every quarter, we were trying to max the barter revenue we could recognize," said a former deal maker. "BA was hyperaggressive about it."

Late on a Tuesday evening in the summer of 2000, David Colburn erupted—again. Only this time there was something different. The self-assuredness seemed missing. Colburn was slightly off his game. There was a hint of uncertain urgency in his screeching voice, a desperate plaintive-ness underneath his impatience.

One of his young deal makers had struck a deal in principle with another company—a price had even been set—but talks were bogging down in the details. Colburn, displeased, burrowed in, demanding an explanation, spewing venomous expletives.

Why isn't this getting done?

Are you capable of doing this job?

Is it too much for you?

The young deal maker tried to stammer out an answer, but all that came out were tears.

"Excuses are like assholes," Colburn snarled. "Everyone's got one."

These were the grim times.

By August 2000, the Nasdaq was hemorrhaging and dot-coms were disappearing faster than you could say Yahoo! For public consumption, AOL officials insisted that all was still well in Dulles. But behind closed doors, senior deal makers convened weekly emergency meetings around a long conference table in the boardroom, sandwiched between the offices of Case and Pittman, both of whom were conspicuously absent.

Before the deal makers was a growing list of struggling companies—many of them dot-coms on life support—who were pleading to restruc-ture their ad deals. They simply could not afford to pay the exorbitant fees that AOL had so deftly extracted from them as part of long-term con-tracts. Through its aggressive deal making, AOL had literally negotiated its way into big trouble.

"Those were the days when people would leave meetings in tears, liter-ally," said Neil Davis, the former senior vice president. "It got to the point where you couldn't be stupid, you couldn't dwell on the minutiae, you couldn't waste anyone's time."

While Colburn ran the meetings, Myer Berlow, his counterpart in charge of advertising, joined in, even if that meant tapping in by speaker-phone from the company jet. The situation was serious. To underscore the gravity, the two men frequently took turns drilling their deal makers about the need to get AOL's business partners to pay up.

The conversation, like a predictable three-step dance, usually went something like this:

Why can't you get this deal closed? Colburn would shout.

Why can't you do this? Berlow would scream.

Then the deal makers would throw up their arms in futility.

"Colburn was always reminding everybody what pressure we were in because of the merger," said an AOL official. "He'd say, 'Are you guys crazy? Are you forgetting what we have to accomplish?'"

The merger "was definitely part of everyday life," said Jonathan Salkoff, a manager in business affairs who was laid off in January 2001, after the merger was final. "It was definitely out there."

The pressure tightened like a vise: AOL's stock was continuing to erode, the advertising market was showing no signs of reviving, and the company was getting nowhere in its negotiations with federal regulators reviewing the merger. The last thing AOL needed was to show in its quarterly earnings reports that it was buckling under the weight of failing dot-coms that couldn't pay their AOL bills anymore.

So AOL uttered nothing publicly about the problem.

And yet, by that August, it was getting harder to keep a lid on it. In confidential reports, AOL closely monitored the status of these threatened ad deals, giving a detailed snapshot, week by week, of the health of the dot-coms, whether large or small, how much they owed AOL, what AOL was doing to get its money, how the dot-coms were responding, and how much money AOL reckoned it could lose if the dot-coms didn't pay their bills.

It wasn't a pretty picture.

Snapshot: Living.com, an on-line furniture business, owed AOL $1.2 million. In an August 18 memo, AOL stated, "They are out of $, wanted to look at new deal but then backed out completely."

AOL's conclusion: "Not solvable."

The company was right: Living.com shut down that month.

Snapshot: BigEdge.com, an on-line sporting goods retailer, "Demanded restructuring conversation with 3 options (including terminating deal outright)," AOL stated in another internal document.

AOL figured its "upcoming payment of $500[,000] may be in jeopardy."

Again, AOL was correct: BigEdge.com was a part of MVP.com, a struggling firm backed by such luminaries as Michael Jordan and Wayne Gretzky, whose domain name, trademark, and other assets were sold off to SportsLine.com in January 2001.

Snapshot: Owners.com, an on-line real estate broker, was more than 120 days late on a $139,000 payment and more than 30 days late on an equal amount. AOL tried to work something out, but its internal documents said the dot-com "had been unresponsive to Biz Affairs and Account Services. . . . Legal is drafting a termination letter."

Owners.com didn't last either. In October 2000, it was acquired by Homebytes.com.

Dozens of other deals threatened to collapse. In the September 30 fiscal quarter alone, the company estimated it risked losing $23.2 million in revenue, according to another August confidential report. It was a significant sum, especially since officials hoped this would be AOL's last quarter as a stand-alone company before U.S. regulators approved its merger with Time Warner.

Still, AOL kept investors in the dark.

By September, another internal company document described a bigger problem: AOL was "at risk" of losing more than $108 million in ad revenue in fiscal 2001, from July 2000 to June 2001, with most of the jeopardized revenue owed by dot-coms.

Again, the company didn't disclose the problem.

In early October, the situation appeared bleak. Berlow, the head of ad sales, tried to break the news delicately during a presentation in AOL's fifth-floor boardroom before a group of senior executives, including Pittman. As a way to ease into it, Berlow presented a series of slides, a heaping pile of numbers and bar charts that explained where AOL sales had been in previous quarters, how they compared to prior years, and what the assumptions, risks, and opportunities were expected to be in calendar 2001. Somewhere in there, Berlow also briefly mentioned, by the way, that he expected the growth in ad revenue to slow a touch.

Pittman didn't miss the reference.

"Look, I know things are tough," Pittman said.

Growing restless, the AOL president told Berlow to skip the rambling preamble. Pittman just wanted to know whether Berlow expected AOL to hit its advertising revenue target for calendar 2001—about $2.7 billion. Berlow tried to pick up where he left off, shuffling the slides fast and furiously—until Pittman told him to cut to the chase: *Are we going to hit our number?*

Chastened, Berlow finally owned up: no.

AOL would not hit $2.7 billion next year; $2.4 billion was more like it, and that number, he cautioned, would be difficult. While he was at it, Berlow broke some more bad news: The company risked losing more than $140 million in ad revenue in calendar 2001, in large part because of ad deals lost in the wake of the dot-com meltdown.

Wall Street had no idea.

Instead, AOL officials privately considered their options to shore up the faltering ad business.

"All these multiyear deals were proving to be a joke," said a former deal maker. "We didn't know whether to take them to court, throw more [advertising] impressions at them, or get them to send more money."

AOL did consider taking the struggling firms to court to get them to pay for the ads that they had agreed to buy. AOL, however, determined that such a strategy wouldn't be prudent because the public court filings would reveal some weakness in *its* core business.

"It wasn't the kind of publicity AOL wanted," said a former deal maker involved in some of the dot-com ad deals.

So AOL officials went to work. In an attempt to salvage what it could from failing ad deals, AOL came up with some creative solutions. In some instances, AOL would continue running ads for dot-coms that were behind in their payments, fully aware that they had already begun to show financial weakness but had yet to cancel their contracts. AOL would then negotiate a final termination payment, treating the fee as ad revenue earned for ads AOL already had run.

In other cases, when a dot-com terminated its ad deal early, AOL would keep the advance payment it had already received and book it right away in the quarter as ad revenue rather than spreading out the payments over several quarters, as specified in the original agreement.

A third strategy was to renegotiate a struggling dot-com's ad deal to shorten the term of the contract. The dot-com would pay AOL a fee for breaking the deal early, and that fee would be incorporated into the new, shorter-term ad deal, effectively creating a balloon payment. AOL would count all of the revenue, including the fee for renegotiating a shorter-term deal, as ad revenue.

"It was totally deceiving," said an AOL official familiar with the practice. "It was recognized as revenue. There should have been an asterisk" indicating it was a gain from restructuring.

AOL officials, however, reached a different conclusion. In the three-month period that ended September 30, terminated or restructured dot-com deals amounted to about $14 million in revenue, or about 2.4 percent of AOL's total advertising and commerce revenue. In the following quarter, ended December 31, such agreements totaled about $10 million, which represented about 1.5 percent of total advertising and commerce revenue. Figuring that the dollar amounts involved in restructurings were relatively small, they decided there was no obligation to tell the public about them.

Besides, such a disclosure would have defeated the purpose. With each restructuring, the operating principle was to put off the day when the dot-com advertising swoon would emerge in the company's own financial statements. "People were very worried about it," said an AOL official. "They didn't tell anybody, but the [financial] exposure kept getting bigger and bigger."

Ultimately, AOL executives were forced to confront the matter head-on.

By mid-October 2000, investors were getting jittery. Shares of Yahoo!, a key AOL competitor, plunged 21 percent after the company reported strong ad growth but acknowledged that the pace could not be sustained. On October 17, AOL's stock plunged 17 percent on similar concerns. The following day, AOL went to extraordinary lengths to downplay the effects of the industrywide slowdown in advertising. During a conference call with Wall Street analysts and the national media, Steve Case tried to put all worries to rest.

"AOL's advertising growth is right on target," he said, as part of the company's final quarterly earnings report before its merger with Time Warner was completed.

Then he went even further. In an allusion to the litany of dot-coms going under, he suggested that AOL would not only survive the industry shakeup, but it would also capitalize on the shrinking playing field, capturing even more ad business. "The current advertising environment benefits us because it will drive a flight to quality," he said.

Just in case anyone missed the point, Pittman, AOL's president, also dismissed the impact of the weakening ad market. "I don't see it," he remarked, "and I don't buy it." And J. Michael Kelly, then chief financial officer, added an exclamation point, calling AOL's ad revenue growth "very healthy, and I can't say that strongly enough."

Backing up their claim, the executives trotted out an impressive figure—an 80 percent increase in ad revenue in the September 30 quarter, over the comparable period a year earlier, a huge leap that blew past the estimates of numerous Wall Street analysts.

The message apparently got through. AOL was prevailing in the rough waters of the new economy—or so concluded several Wall Street analysts who took AOL's optimistic reports as a sign of the company's strength in the teeth of a slowing ad market. For AOL, it was like getting rave reviews at opening night. Analysts, liking what they saw, encouraged investors to buy AOL shares as the merger neared.

"Solid advertising revenues attest to AOL's hybrid subscription/advertising model, which so far has provided the company with more protection from the dot-com meltdown than other large new media companies," wrote analyst Youssef H. Squali, then of ING Barings LLC, in a research note a day after AOL's conference call. Reiterating his "strong buy" rating on AOL's stock, he added, "The AOL Time Warner merger continues to progress well and is on track to close in the fall."

Reaction at Dulles was less enthusiastic. The mood was better characterized as confused among those who had been privy to AOL's scramble to shore up its ad revenue. *A flight to quality? AOL not impacted by the ad slump? What in the world were Case, Pittman, and Kelly talking about?* So went the buzz among a handful of AOL officials who had listened in on the analyst conference call. Gathered around the water cooler a day after Case and Pittman's Pollyannaish pronouncements, they wondered what it all meant.

"When the statement[s] came out that we weren't being impacted, we were surprised," said one puzzled official. "Well, we didn't know what was going on."

The group, however, decided to give Case and Pittman the benefit of the doubt. Perhaps the ad market wasn't as bad as they feared. "We didn't want to be alarmists," the official said. Besides, Case and Pittman were in charge. Maybe, the group concluded, the two executives knew something the rest of them didn't.

. . .

When Robert W. Pittman was born in 1953, he was cast in the role of the original outsider. The younger of two sons of a Methodist minister, his was a nomadic life, with his peripatetic father moving from church to church in the Deep South before settling the family in Brookhaven, Mississippi. Pittman, the perennial new kid on the block, was also the runt of the lot, which seemed to serve its purpose, attuning him to the needs of others.

"I learned to read people's attitudes so I never got beaten up," he once said.

At the age of six, he lost his right eye when a horse threw him during a Thanksgiving holiday at his grandparents' farm, and that, too, seemed to serve its purpose. Doctors fitted him with a glass eye. But Pittman seemed determined to prove his worth. As a child, so lore has it, he learned to overcome his lack of depth perception by practicing fly-fishing, casting the rod repeatedly into a bucket. Tom, his older brother, reckoned that Pittman didn't just want to prove his worth. He wanted to make it big time. "Bob always wanted to be rich and famous," Tom once said. "That was clear."

He also yearned to fly airplanes. But his father refused to pay for flying lessons. Undeterred, the young Pittman went looking for a job. The local supermarket turned him down for a grocery-bagging job. Instead, walking in off the street, Pittman got a part-time job as a deejay at WCHJ, a local station. Just like that, he had found a way to pay for flying lessons, and a spectacular career was born.

He was fifteen years old.

Suddenly, Pittman was on his way, blazing through a series of gigs as radio programmer in Pittsburgh and Chicago, paying close attention to market research, heeding the wants of the consumer. He never finished college, but in 1977 at the age of twenty-three, he became program manager of New York's WNBC. Working at 30 Rockefeller Plaza, Pittman cut an odd figure: shoulder-length hair, a beard, thick jewelry, and white linen outfits. They called him "the hippie from Mississippi." But that wasn't quite right. Underneath the counterculture garb of the 1970s was a sharp-edged corporate barracuda. In short order, he fired much of the station's staff, brought in his own people, and WNBC became the nation's No. 1 station.

Everything about Bob Pittman seemed to happen fast and decisively. In his late twenties, according to legend, he met a woman named Sandy on a commercial flight. That evening, she invited him to spend the night at her parents' home. By the next day, they were engaged.

Around the same time, in 1979, Pittman moved quickly again, becoming vice president at cable giant Warner Amex Satellite Entertainment, a joint venture between Warner Communications and American Express Co. This is where he blasted into orbit. He helped create a little thing called MTV.

Pittman has been accused of taking too much credit for the creation of Music Television, the twenty-four-hour rock-and-roll music video channel on cable television, and he did once call it "a pet idea of mine." But he has since admitted it was more of a collaborative effort among a handful of Warner executives. Regardless, most are in agreement on this point: Pittman, who started off in charge of programming for MTV when it went on the air in 1981, was quickly made chief operating officer and built the channel into the wild cultural phenomenon that it soon became. In 1981, Pittman was named *Performance* magazine's Innovator of the Year. Three years later, he barely missed out to Peter Ueberroth for *Time* magazine's Man of the Year. His consolation prize: *Life* magazine called him one of five contemporary "original thinkers" of his time. By the mid-1980s, MTV's executive vice president and chief operating officer was pulling down $200,000 a year, part of which he spent on a wardrobe overhaul, including conservative gray suits, red ties, black wing tips, and a gold Rolex watch. He didn't just look the part of corporate raider, he played it, too. In 1985, he and other MTV executives sought to take the company private in a leveraged buyout, the vogue of the times. Although Viacom ended up with the successful bid for MTV, Pittman managed to make out fairly well for himself. He eked out about $2.3 million through the sale of stock options.

Money, though, wasn't everything.

Declaring that he didn't want to be known only as "Mr. MTV," he left as chief executive officer in 1986 and a year later became Mr. Quantum Media Inc., a joint venture with MCA Inc., which he formed to produce records, television programming, movies, and videos. Among his big hits: the introduction of talk show as shrill theater with the abrasive *Morton Downey Jr. Show*. Before long, though, Pittman was back in the Warner fold, returning as an executive adviser to CEO Steven Ross in his merger with Time Inc. By 1990, Pittman was named president and chief executive of Time Warner Enterprises, heading up new ventures, which included turning around the struggling Six Flags Entertainment theme parks. Even then, he was thinking synergy. Under his tenure, he introduced a Batman amusement ride, capitalizing on Warner's entertainment properties. His favorite story, however, was the time he roamed the amusement park grounds disguised as a janitor to better understand what was wrong with customer service.

It was an unlikely image. Pittman was one of the beautiful people, a regular name dropped in gossip columns. Along with his socialite wife, Sandy, the Pittmans were dubbed "The Couple of the Minute" on the cover of *New York* magazine in 1990. From Mississippi hippie to corporate raider, he was now a member of New York's A-list. He had all the right cultural credentials, including a board seat on the New York Shakespeare Festival, of which he eventually became chairman.

When he wasn't in Manhattan, he could be found in Aspen, or St. Barts, or perchance, on his Harley-Davidson motorcycle, cruising the roads with *Rolling Stone* publisher Jan Wenner. Pittman counted among his other friends news anchor Tom Brokaw, lifestyle maven Martha Stewart, and musician Quincy Jones, who became godfather to Pittman's son, Bo.

"He was enamored with celebrity," said a close associate. "He dropped names all the time. You'd wonder, was it to be a name-dropper, or if this was just his world. Maybe it was a bit of both. But it was clear, he didn't take to people just because they were people. He took to people for who they were. It's about power and status. Money helps you get there, but after that, you need something else."

In a way, Pittman seemed a prisoner of his own mystery. He was always on. He rarely let his guard down. "Brand Bob," people called him. There was always a circle of privacy around him. He arrived at parties late and left early. "He knew when the party was over, and it was over before the party was over," said a colleague. "He just lived and breathed the career of Bob Pittman."

For Pittman, work life and life outside of work became one and the same thing. His social calendar was always booked three or four months ahead. He and his wife were always heading somewhere for the weekend. To Telluride. To Great Falls, Virginia. To northern Connecticut. (His first wife, Sandy, climbed Mount Everest, an ordeal chronicled in the best-seller *Into Thin Air.* They divorced in 1997. Then Pittman married Veronique Choa, an elegant graphic designer for Hachette Filipacchi magazines.) Meanwhile, there was always a rock star to hang out with in the Caribbean. He liked the Marshall Tucker Band. But Pittman never seemed to sit down for a minute. He professed to have no patience for fiction. What was the point? "It's not beautiful writing," he told a friend, "if it's not real."

In 1995, Pittman's career came to a brief standstill when he left Time Warner following an acrimonious falling out over the sale of Six Flags. He had wanted an equity stake in the amusement park operation, but he didn't want to invest much in it. Time Warner squeezed him out instead. Once again, he managed to make the best of it. His walking papers came with a reported payout of about $20 million. Within months, Pittman was chief executive of Century 21 Real Estate Corp. It seemed far afield for the media master, but it quickly turned into another smart move. Not only did he purge Century 21's all too familiar yellow jackets from the corporate attire, Pittman soon encountered the next company that would vault him to a higher level of stardom: AOL.

With the Internet beginning to make headway in the mid-1990s, Pittman envisioned what it could do for him: Century 21 could list properties on-line, saving agents' time. The workforce could be wired for e-mail, creating a more efficient sales force. And then there was the matter of advertising its real estate service on-line. The question was: How much did Pittman want to spend promoting Century 21 on AOL?

During a meeting in 1996, Myer Berlow, then heading AOL's nascent ad business, suggested $2 million.

"I'll give you a million," Pittman responded.

Ted Leonsis, Berlow's boss, immediately agreed. Berlow, always looking for the last buck, nudged Leonsis later, telling him he could have extracted $1.2 million from Pittman. Either way, it was a lot of money to AOL then. Pittman found out as much during a meeting later in 1996 with Berlow. Pittman asked whether AOL had many $1 million ad deals.

"Just one," Berlow said. "You."

Pittman retorted, "I hope I won't be the only asshole."

He wouldn't be. Besides, it wasn't a sucker move. Being the company's first million-dollar advertiser brought not only honor but also goodwill. Leonsis was impressed with Pittman, and he wanted Case to meet him, too. So he set up a lunch at a café on Route 7 near the AOL office. Pittman was nothing like they expected. All his ink about being a wild and creative entrepreneur belied the crisp executive who presented himself in a suit, white shirt, and tie. In his breezy fashion, Pittman reminisced about his earlier days at MTV. Immediately, Pittman and Case hit it off. "He had this spark in his eye about the Internet," Case said at the time. "He recognized that this would be the next big thing."

While Pittman took a bathroom break at lunch, Case and Leonsis turned to one another and instantly agreed: The next thing for Pittman was to join the AOL board, which he promptly did. But Leonsis wasn't finished. In the summer of 1996, he enticed Pittman and Veronique, his wife-to-be, on a cruise in the Mediterranean along with another couple. The chartered yacht was appropriately dubbed *The Midway,* as in the halfway point in Leonsis's gregarious life, which he was celebrating on this, his fortieth birthday. As part of the celebration, the AOL executive banned cell phones and e-mail, not because he didn't want to talk shop; but because he had other business to take care of. He was trying to convince Pittman that it made sense to abandon the Century 21 ship and join AOL as a top executive, even while the company was struggling through its growing pains.

Pittman never had a chance.

In October 1996, Steve Case announced Bob Pittman as the new member of his executive team, the man who would lead AOL to the next stage.

"Steve did the work, I did the close," said Leonsis, who remained an executive but took on a less prominent role after Pittman's arrival.

For all the wooing, it turned out to be a difficult transition for Pittman. AOLers, ensconced in the quiet suburbs of Virginia, hadn't seen anything as exotic and glamorous as Pittman, a denizen of the New York cool and hip society. No chinos and denims for him, Case notwithstanding. For Pittman, there was usually a sports coat and a collared shirt involved.

Where Case always seemed to have a little bit of a grimace about him, Pittman was smooth, sleek, Hollywood. Hardly anyone noticed the glass eye—except one official who reported to Pittman. This official would tell others about how Pittman removed the fake eye and cleaned it during meetings. He would also tease his boss, saying he'd present a pie chart showing poor financial results in front of his blind eye, so he couldn't see just how bad things were.

Pittman didn't blend in. He adorned his fifth-floor AOL office with recording-industry memorabilia, bright green chairs, and Japanese screens. "He must've spent thirty grand on a feather boa and a tiger skin couch," said a former colleague. "There were weird vases, big and expensive, and strange lighting, and highlighted art." Not the typical Office Depot staples seen elsewhere in the bland building. But there was no camouflaging where he really was. Just beyond his office stood the flagship of suburban America: Wal-Mart. Which might have explained Pittman's aversion to the northern Virginia landscape. He was filled with wanderlust, piloting his twin-engine Piper Cheyenne on weekends—and even midweek—to homes in Manhattan, Telluride, and Roundhill, Jamaica.

Or maybe it was just the toll of the job. From the beginning, AOL engulfed him in one crisis after another. When he joined, AOL took a huge financial charge to address persistent questions about how it accounted for its marketing expenses. At the same time, the company was undergoing an upheaval in its basic business model. To compete with low-cost rivals, AOL was switching from a metered service, whereby it charged subscribers for on-line usage by the hour, to unlimited access, which brought an avalanche of new customers, tying up the telephone network and creating what became known as the great busy-signal debacle. Pittman was in his element. More than a creative force, he was a turn-around specialist. He had done it at radio stations, at MTV, and at Century 21. One of his great strengths was getting down into the detail, pushing people for results, making things happen. Pittman held regular meetings, immediately identified technical problems, and attacked. It was all rock and roll from there.

At noon on December 21, 2000, David Colburn swaggered to the stage in his black cowboy boots, sporting his trademark five o'clock shadow—and a confident sneer.

From the podium, Colburn beamed at his audience, packed with about one hundred members of his team, who had settled in for the monthly all-hands meeting of BA in the windowless, basement-level Seriff Auditorium at AOL headquarters. Others were patched in by teleconferencing from Ohio and California.

Colburn enjoyed these moments. He liked the attention. Sometimes he used the opportunity to initiate new recruits to his deal-making machine, forcing them to sing their college fight song in front of the whole restless horde. But not today. On this day, he let his people wait for him as they quietly munched on their catered lunch of sandwiches, salad, fruit, soda, and bottled water featuring the blue AOL triangle logo.

It was time to hand out the Bammy Awards.

BA's version of television's Emmy Awards, the Bammys were given to the best performers in Colburn's division.

This month, Colburn bestowed the Bammy's gold-star plaque on Kent Wakeford and Jason Witt, who had put together a complex transaction with PurchasePro.com Inc., a Las Vegas software maker. Colburn praised the two men for the aggressive way they had constructed the transaction to generate revenue for AOL, calling the deal "science fiction" according to several people at the meeting. (Colburn does not recall using those words.)

Wakeford and Witt joined Colburn on stage and graciously accepted the plaque. In his acceptance speech, Wakeford said the award couldn't have been possible without AOL's internal accountants, who he said came up with the deal's clever structure.

The crowd roared with laughter over the tongue-in-cheek remarks. But not everyone was amused.

"It was one of those moments you realize how screwed up these people are—for rewarding people for making up revenue, for making up numbers," said one in attendance.

"The sheer arrogance, the feeling of being untouchable, was amazing," said another attendee. "It was just incredible that he would say that, that he would flout revenue-recognition rules."

Wakeford, caught up in the moment, also thanked someone who was not in attendance but went along with AOL's complex transaction: Charles E. Johnson Jr., PurchasePro's flamboyant founder and chief executive officer.

They called him "Junior."

Johnson was an unlikely AOL business partner, a former gym and video store operator, with a tuft of platinum blond hair, a mischievous grin, and a country-boy twang, by way of Lexington, Kentucky. Before he launched his Vegas software business in 1996, Johnson liked to brag that he didn't know the first thing about technology. He didn't even know how to use e-mail. The world of high finance wasn't his thing either. What he was was a basketball jock.

Johnson couldn't dunk the ball, but he sure had a mean jump shot—and a maniacal work ethic, an unrelenting belief in his ability to overcome, which is why he had made it as a six-foot-tall point guard on the University of Cincinnati basketball team. More than twenty years later, Johnson was still a jock who liked to challenge visitors to a game of "horse" at the regulation-size basketball court behind his Greco-Roman palace of a home, rock music blasting from the outdoor speakers into the arid landscape on the suburban outskirts of Las Vegas, the Strip gleaming in the distance like a desert mirage.

By then, he had lost something on his long-range three-point shot, but no matter. His home was his personal playground, which he was proud to put on display for old friends from Kentucky who knew him from way back when. The cavernous place had the trappings of the newly rich. One associate called it "nouveau riche bordello." It didn't look lived in. Rather, it seemed like a big heaping slab of house made for effect. There were big white classical statues. Spouting water fountains. A personal movie theater with surround sound. A walk-in closet with countless suits, scores of which looked exactly alike. A steam room big enough, Johnson said, to make him comfortable sweating next to another guy. And his own fully stocked basement gym with gleaming weights and a refrigerator packed with dietary juice to quench his workout thirst.

Johnson liked to live healthy, favoring tossed salads with a spare piece of chicken and a side of bottled dressing. He also liked to live large. At a moment's notice, he would offer to take friends and some people who were practically strangers as well on his personal airplane for a quick week-end getaway to a lush tropical locale. During a lavish party he threw during one Super Bowl weekend, he carried around a shopping bag, handing out Rolex watches to his favorite friends, while the hired band, Earth, Wind & Fire, strummed tunes. The party, said a colleague, cost Johnson $750,000. "This was just beyond the pale," said the colleague. Another time, Johnson bought a custom-made suit for every man who worked at PurchasePro, some one hundred suits in all. Other times, he sent employees on all-expense-paid trips to Hawaii or the Caribbean.

"He was," said a former associate, "like the high school kid who wanted to be liked."

"If I had to describe him in a single word, it would have to be cunning, but cunning with no hubris," said Chris Benyo, who worked with Johnson as PurchasePro's senior vice president.

For Johnson, every situation represented a potential opportunity. He was at his best, however, in the gym. There, he got his big break in basketball. It was also in the gym where he got his big break in business. Or so he tells the story. Before he made his millions in PurchasePro, he was working out at a Las Vegas gym in the mid-1990s when he met Steve Wynn, the casino impresario, and the two entrepreneurs got to talking.

Wynn's Mirage Hotel and Casino, a huge operation, bid out for a lot of goods and services, everything from bedsheets to poker chips. Johnson reckoned the casino could set up a way to do its shopping on the Internet—and save money. Wynn just needed a guy to figure out how to slap together the software to make it happen. Wynn liked the idea enough to hand Johnson $50,000. A former PurchasePro official said it wasn't quite that romantic. "To Wynn," he said, "it was get-off-my-back money."

Regardless, PurchasePro was on its way. The company was soon developing and marketing software for electronic-commerce transactions. Hotels, for example, could use the company's software to create a Web site to buy and sell bed linens and other goods and services. Hilton Hotels Corp., among others, became a customer.

It wasn't long before such on-line business-to-business transactions—known as B-to-B—became the hot thing, which put Johnson in the middle of another opportunity. He seized the occasion, approaching the biggest industry player about striking a partnership: AOL.

It seemed like a good match. For PurchasePro, a dot-com on the rise, an AOL deal could give it greater respectability, not to mention another potential source of revenue and an expanded base of customers. AOL, for its part, was always on the lookout for new opportunities, and it wanted to get in on the B-to-B action. So the Internet giant struck a deal with Johnson's start-up in March 2000.

But as with many AOL relationships, this one was complex, featuring many tentacles created in large part by the notorious BA deal-making unit. AOL agreed to use PurchasePro's software as the technology back-bone of AOL's Netscape small business portal, which customers could use by paying a monthly subscription fee. AOL also agreed to sell Purchase-Pro's software to other companies, earning up to a 50 percent commission for each sale. But the most exotic feature of the deal was this: AOL earned $3 in performance warrants for each dollar of revenue it generated for PurchasePro under their marketing partnership. A performance warrant, like a stock option, gave AOL the right to buy shares in PurchasePro at an agreed-upon exercise price. Under their deal, the warrants gave AOL the right to buy shares in PurchasePro for $63 each. But in December 2000, with the dot-com's shares in decline, the two companies agreed to revise the deal, according to a confidential AOL deal memo circulated to executives for their signatures.

As part of the revised arrangement, PurchasePro agreed to reduce the exercise price for each share of PurchasePro stock an AOL warrant could buy from $63 to 1¢. The change required a simple fix on a piece of paper. But it did the trick: With that reduction, AOL estimated it would earn $30 million in the quarter ended December 2000 by exercising the warrants, internal company documents show. It worked like magic. AOL would buy PurchasePro stock for 1¢ per share and resell them at their market price.

The deal did magic to AOL's financial books, too. Although AOL was to generate $30 million through the sale of PurchasePro stock, AOL treated the windfall as ad and commerce revenue.

"$30MM [million] of revenue from performance warrants vesting in calendar Q4 [the December quarter] will be treated as advertising revenue," AOL stated in its confidential executive summary of the deal.

Johnson, the PurchasePro CEO, was not aware that AOL had converted the performance warrants into ad revenue. "The warrants had nothing to do with ad revenue," he said. "They were directly related to selling our marketplace software to our customers, suppliers, and partners."

Officials of PurchasePro worried about their own company's role in the deals. "There was always consternation about the AOL deals," said a former executive of the Las Vegas outfit. PurchasePro, however, had some tangible reasons for making the deal. In return for reducing the warrants' exercise price to 1¢, AOL agreed to generate $10 million in revenue for PurchasePro, according to AOL's internal memos.

PurchasePro got its $10 million this way: AOL paid it $4.9 million to cover the cost of giving one hundred thousand AOL customers a free month's subscription—at $49 per user—to PurchasePro's marketplace service, which was co-branded with AOL's Netscape portal. AOL also agreed to buy $4.6 million worth of PurchasePro's software, which AOL would distribute to some of its business partners. AOL would come up with another $500,000 by selling ad space on PurchasePro's on-line marketplace.

The bottom line: AOL essentially paid $9.5 million for $30 million in warrants, netting $20.5 million.

PurchasePro understood "it had a vehicle that could get them [AOL] immediate revenue recognition," said a former official of the dot-com.

The deal got the okay from a host of AOL departments, including business affairs investments, interactive marketing/business development, ad strategy, legal, accounting policy, and netbusiness, its small business unit. Eventually, however, the partnership between AOL and PurchasePro collapsed. In May 2001, Johnson stepped down as PurchasePro's CEO after the company badly missed its financial targets.

With Johnson gone, the rest of the dominoes fell quickly. AOL stopped reselling PurchasePro software in the first half of 2001. And by November 2001, Arthur Andersen LLP resigned as PurchasePro's independent auditor after noting what it considered deficiencies in the design and operation of PurchasePro's internal controls.

For a couple of heady years, PurchasePro had been the archetypal dotcom, a money-losing software venture led by a swashbuckling executive who took his firm public during the Internet euphoria of 1999, struck a big deal with AOL a year later, and hit it rich through his stock holdings. But it couldn't last.

"Some weird shit happened, but [an AOL deal] was a valid business approach," said Benyo, the former PurchasePro senior vice president. "The strategy was valid, the partner was valid. The question is whether the execution was what we would have hoped it would've been."

An AOL official said execution had nothing to do with it. The PurchasePro deal, she said, was a creature of business affairs—the BA special. "PurchasePro," the official said, "is probably the hairiest one of them all."

AOL vice president Robert O'Connor was working at home in his study on Monday, January 1, 2001, when he noticed a strange thing while checking his e-mail: a banner ad for Telefónica S.A., the giant Spanish telecommunications company.

It didn't make sense. O'Connor, head of finance for AOL's advertising division, knew that the Telefónica ads should have stopped running at the end of December. But a day into the new year, there they were, blinking all over the AOL service. The ads were even running on prime AOL real estate—including the inbox where millions of customers checked their e-mail. He figured someone in AOL operations must have just forgotten to take them down. And yet, O'Connor noticed another troubling sign: There was a link from the AOL welcome page—the best real estate of all, the first Web page people saw when they logged on to the service—to a Telefónica Web site, which was in *Spanish*. Why would the English-language welcome page be linked to a Spanish-language site? It must be a mistake, he thought.

The first thing the next day, O'Connor went on a fact-finding mission. When he went down to the cubicle of the AOL account service rep who had handled the deal, O'Connor asked her why the Telefónica ads hadn't been pulled down. The account rep explained there was an oral agreement between Telefónica and business affairs.

BA? An oral agreement?

"You can't do that," O'Connor blurted out.

Well, this is between BA and Telefónica, she said.

"How do you know?" O'Connor persisted.

Telefónica called up and said we owed them ads, she said.

O'Connor held his tongue. He suddenly realized that, with all of his questions, he was making the account rep nervous. He didn't want to upset her. He was upset enough for both of them. O'Connor, a certified public accountant by training, was the kind of guy who didn't countenance monkey business. To O'Connor, the entire operation had been compromised. This was a serious problem. AOL wasn't supposed to be running ads based on an oral agreement. If the written contract called for the ad deal to end in December, then it was supposed to end in December, and not a day later, no matter what anyone said in an oral side agreement. *And what was BA up to? Why was BA meddling in this?* That alarmed O'Connor. It occurred to him that he should report this up the chain of command, to his own boss, Myer Berlow, the head of the ad division. *But what if Berlow told him to leave it alone?* O'Connor marched across the street, from his office in Creative Center 3 on the AOL campus, to headquarters and plunked himself down in the office of the company's internal accountant.

"I think," O'Connor began, "we have a problem."

When he explained it, the accountant let out an exasperated, "Aw, shit." Then he picked up the phone and dialed a senior vice president in business affairs and demanded to know what was going on.

As it turned out, it was another BA special.

In the final days of December, AOL had found itself in a familiar predicament. The Time Warner merger was ensnared in a regulatory mess in Washington, AOL's stock was still eroding, and not even the dot-com restructurings were going to save AOL from coming up short in its targeted ad revenue. That is, unless BA could broker a deal to sell $15 million in on-line ads to Telefónica—and run all the ads before the end of the quarter.

Telefónica agreed, but there was a catch. The Spanish telecom would spend $15 million on ads that would run in December *only* if AOL would make a side agreement to continue running hundreds of millions of ads for months beyond December, as a bonus. Without the bonus, Telefónica would have insisted on running the $15 million in ads over several quarters, which would have forced AOL to book a smaller amount of revenue in the December period. The BA deal makers couldn't let that happen.

That's why the Telefónica link from AOL's English-language welcome screen took users to a Spanish-language site. It didn't matter—so long as AOL could get credit for running the promotion. Nor did it matter that Telefónica's computer servers couldn't handle all of the customer traffic from AOL. What mattered was AOL succeeded in getting its $15 million deal before December 31, as accounting rules required.

In the end, AOL's internal accountant determined that the $15 million December ad deal was really part of a longer-term commitment, which included the ads that had run as part of the bonus deal. As a result, AOL fixed the books, moving about $5 million of the Telefónica revenue from AOL's December quarter to the next period. With a sense of relief, the accountant thanked O'Connor for catching the problem and asked him how they could stop it from happening again.

The funny thing was, O'Connor told him, AOL already had all the proper controls in place. There was actually a baroque method to the Internet-driven madness. So intricate was the process that it usually took up to six months for AOL to bring a major advertising deal to fruition.

The big dance began when AOL's interactive marketing division—the sales unit—made the initial contact to sell on-line ads to other companies. This was the wooing period when the two sides would talk in general terms about the so-called carriage plan—the number of on-line ad impressions, the placement of the ads, and the estimated cost. But once the two sides reached a general agreement, that's when the romance ended and business affairs, the muscle, entered the picture. BA, working to clinch the deal, would go over the economics of the deal and draw up a "term sheet," a basic ad agreement. AOL's legal team would then review the term sheet and transform it into a formal contract. After that, the two companies would enter the home stretch, tinkering with the fine points of the contract, which often required BA to consult with its internal accountants to structure the deal properly.

Even then, O'Connor marveled, many other people within AOL had a hand in any given ad deal. Even Ernst & Young LLC, AOL's outside auditor, was called in periodically to review deals. And when the two companies finally came to an agreement on the contract, business affairs distributed it for formal sign-offs by several other affected AOL divisions, not just accounting and legal, but also ad strategy, ad operations, revenue

and inventory management, communications, account services, Web promotions, technologies, investments, business planning and operations,
and AOL strategy and operations. Usually, the sign-offs were done by
e-mail. But the bigger the deal, the more likely the sign-offs would be
done in person, followed up by e-mail. As a final measure, the official who
had shepherded the deal from the beginning would bring the contract to
David Colburn's office and walk the top executive through the various
terms and conditions. Colburn, the final arbiter in the process, would give
his verbal okay and sign the contract.

How, then, could Telefónica happen?

"At the end of the day, the question is, 'Are the contracts going to be
legally correct?'" said an AOL official familiar with the deal-approval
process. "That's always the conversation—the contract, the term sheet.
But that doesn't get to the spirit of the deals."

The SEC had raised questions about how AOL structured deals before.
Concerns about AOL's accounting had emerged in 1996 when critics
started to scrutinize the way AOL booked its marketing expenses. Under
Steve Case's leadership, AOL spread its marketing costs over several years
instead of deducting it when the money was spent, adopting the model of a
manufacturing company accounting for the cost of *factory* equipment.
When Case finally abandoned the controversial practice that November,
AOL was required to take a $385 million charge, wiping out years of paper
profits—years when a profit was critical to keeping the company afloat.

Less than a year later, in 1997, Case proclaimed that AOL had adopted
"new gold-standard accounting policies." But that same year, the SEC
rejected another paper profit that AOL had booked. Then in 1998, the
reverse problem arose: The SEC said AOL posted a loss when it should
have shown a profit. The company was allegedly trying to post as much of
a loss upfront so that it could avoid spreading out the cost over subsequent
quarters, which would reduce future earnings. In May 2000, the SEC
intervened again, alleging that AOL had violated federal securities laws by
issuing inaccurate financial reports in the mid-1990s when it spread out
the cost of its marketing expenses. AOL denied any wrongdoing but paid
a $3.5 million fine—then the biggest amount in history—and restated
three years of earnings as part of an SEC settlement.

How AOL managed to wrangle through a series of accounting confrontations without ruining the company amazed even those who worked there. "I could not believe how Teflon-like AOL was," said Mark Walsh, a senior vice president until he resigned in August 1997. "If people only knew how close to the edge that company was."

O'Connor, the AOL vice president of finance, was all too familiar with AOL's past. When the company's internal accountant asked him what they could do to prevent future problems, O'Connor turned to him and said, "You can have the greatest controls in the world, but unless the people doing the deals have integrity, it doesn't matter what the hell you do."

Berlow, O'Connor's boss, had some questions of his own. During a staff meeting about a week after the Telefónica incident, when Berlow noticed that his division was going to come up a little short of its revenue target, he asked a senior vice president what had happened.

You better ask your man O'Connor, the senior vice president said.

When he did, O'Connor explained what had happened with the Telefónica deal, how BA had made an oral side deal, how he had taken the matter to accounting, and how the problem had been fixed in time. Berlow, stunned, had only one thing to say: *What the hell are you doing talking to accounting? You work for me. I don't want you talking to accounting anymore.*

"The question I had was, why are you working on accounting on this?" Berlow recalled. "Interactive market should not be involved in revenue-recognition questions."

O'Connor, not dissuaded, looked at Berlow as if he were nuts and said, "You know me better than that."

If Berlow had, he would have known O'Connor wasn't done talking to accounting.

At the same December 21, 2000, meeting when David Colburn handed out the Bammy Awards, AOL's top deal maker also crowed about what a great year was nearing an end at the company.

Had the dot-com bubble burst? *Nah.* Was AOL feeling the effects of a lingering advertising slump? *Pshaw.* And what about the Time Warner merger? With certitude, Colburn assured the gathering that the deal would close soon. The company had already wended its way through the European Commission, and then the Federal Trade Commission. That was the tough part. Now AOL was down to its last hurdle: the Federal Communications Commission. *That* federal agency, he assured the audience, wouldn't get in AOL's way. The Internet giant always found a way to win.

"We're still on top," he declared lustily.

As a measure of just how good things were, Colburn closed the meeting by offering a small token of his appreciation to everyone present: a boxed bottle of champagne.

Colburn was right about one thing. The merger was indeed winding down.

Nobody expected stiff resistance from the FCC. Led by Bill Kennard, a cerebral, cautious, low-key chairman, the five-member body was known to be shy about imposing its regulatory will on the merger, notwithstanding its activist leanings. The Democrats held a three-to-two majority over their laissez-faire Republican colleagues. But through months of negotiating, AOL had achieved a primary goal within the regulatory agency, instilling its mantra about an emerging industry with developing technologies: *Don't regulate the Internet.*

And yet, as an FCC vote neared, all sides in the debate began to mobilize for one last push in the fitful final weeks of December 2000 and into the first days of January 2001. That push was directed in a single direction: at the chairman. By virtue of his office, Kennard set the tone for the agency. Although he could not control the votes of his four colleagues on the commission, he directed the work of the FCC chief of staff, who, in turn, relayed Kennard's wishes to the cable division. And it was there, among the cable staffers, that the heavy lifting was done on the merger.

Kennard was wrestling on his own with questions raised by the merger. How, for one, do you deal with a merger of the nation's No. 1 Internet service provider (AOL), with the nation's No. 2 cable company (Time Warner)? Instant messaging, in particular, had become a nettlesome issue. The real-time communications service was an evolving technology, and no one was quite sure which way it would mature. "We didn't have a crystal ball into where that marketplace was going," he said.

AOL and Time Warner resolved to help guide his thinking. They targeted Kennard with a last-ditch squeeze play involving presidential politics.

After the Florida recount, when it became clear that George W. Bush was going to squeak into the Oval Office, Kennard got wind from his sources that AOL and Time Warner were threatening to wait him out. The two companies could see to it that Bush replaced Democrat Kennard with a Republican as FCC chairman. The new chairman, in turn, could decide to put a halt to the FCC's merger inquiry, allowing the merger to proceed.

"I was running out of time as chairman," Kennard said.

But he wasn't about to cave. Instead, the FCC chairman sent word through Dick Parsons, Time Warner's president, who was spearheading the company's talks with the government, that he was committed to finishing what he had started. Kennard wasn't going anywhere until June, when his term expired. Bush could tap another FCC chairman, but the president would have to choose from the existing panel. Kennard would lose the title, but he would remain on the commission. The FCC would still be controlled by the Democrats, three to two, for six more months. Kennard knew that AOL and Time Warner didn't want to wait to get the merger approved, not after already holding out for a year. Shareholders would erupt in open revolt. Already, the stock of both companies was reflecting investor jitters.

"I knew they couldn't wait," Kennard said. "I knew it was a bluff. Their stock was trending down."

Outnumbered though they were, the Republicans on the commission weren't backing down either. Michael K. Powell, one of the two GOP members, was a powerful voice of dissent against imposing any regulatory conditions on the merger. He was the son of General Colin Powell, an AOL board member and Bush's choice for secretary of state. Kennard had approached Powell about this apparent conflict of interest. But there were few absolute bars under the FCC ethics rules. The standard was whether a reasonable person in the community would consider that Powell's position created the appearance of impropriety. Though the elder Powell stood to gain personally from the FCC's vote to approve AOL's takeover of Time Warner, the younger Powell apparently didn't think there was any ethical problem for him. He was going to participate.

So, it turned out, was Bill Gates.

In the final weeks of deliberation at the FCC, the Microsoft chieftain decided to weigh in. Lobbyists for the AOL rival figured they had done all they could to restrict the merger. Now it was time for Gates, the big kahuna, to make a personal appeal. The biggest name in the tech industry called some of the commissioners, expressing his concerns about what the merger would do to consolidate AOL's market dominance over instant messaging. AOL, taken aback by Gates's personal appeal, was appalled. Microsoft was neck-deep in its own fight over an antitrust trial brought by the U.S. government. Microsoft was battling against government intervention in the software marketplace, which Microsoft happened to rule. But with instant messaging, where Microsoft was playing catch-up to AOL, it was arguing the opposite, demanding that the government intervene.

"It is such a deep hypocrisy to use the government to manage how IM [instant messaging] developed," said George Vradenburg, then AOL's top policy maker.

All's fair in love and mergers, though, or so it seemed. Microsoft was equally incensed by a final maneuver pulled off by AOL. With an FCC vote imminent, Microsoft lobbyists heard through the grapevine that AOL officials had met in secret with FCC officials about a potential regulatory solution that AOL could abide by, thus paving the way for an affirmative vote.

All meetings between the agency and interested parties were supposed to be publicly documented in what were known as ex parte filings. And yet, Microsoft couldn't find a filing for this meeting. When a Microsoft lobbyist pressed the FCC staff about the not-so-secret meeting, they finally produced a belated ex parte filing from AOL. It was a game lobbyists were all too familiar with. When a party doesn't want the other side knowing what it is up to, it can delay disclosure by filing an ex parte on paper rather than digitally. A paper filing requires more work. A secretary has to scan the document before it is posted on the FCC Web site.

Another technique was to say as little as possible in the ex parte filing, which is precisely what AOL did. In its belated filing, dated December 14, 2000, lobbyists for AOL simply said that the company met with the FCC "regarding instant messaging." What was actually said about the topic remained a mystery—until Microsoft officials pressed agency officials for more information. What they found out led Microsoft to dub the belated AOL filing the "nonsmoking gun."

AOL understood that the FCC couldn't simply approve the merger without imposing *some* conditions, or it would look like a rubber stamp. So AOL suggested a compromise: Impose a condition requiring AOL to open its instant-messaging system to rivals, but only if AOL offered "advanced" instant-messaging services, such as video conferencing over the Time Warner cable network. The beauty of the compromise was that it would look like the FCC was taking a relatively tough stance on instant messaging, but it would actually do nothing about the current state of the emerging market. AOL would still dominate instant messaging, Microsoft would still be far behind, and who knew when AOL would start introducing "advanced" features? Publicly, AOL would howl about the injustices of the regulatory process; in private, it would celebrate.

Microsoft, alarmed by such a compromise, scrambled to undo it. But it was too late. "Despite all our prodding and cajoling and lobbying, they weren't going to move," said a Microsoft official.

On January 11, 2001, it was finally over.

The FCC voted five to zero. Microsoft saw this coming: The chief condition required AOL and Time Warner to open their instant-messaging system to three rivals if the merged company added advanced services in the future.

A year and a day after their betrothal was announced, AOL and Time Warner officially tied the knot.

Supporters and opponents of the merger both claimed victory. That evening, Stephen Heins, the former flower child from Wisconsin, went out and downed a couple of beers in a local tavern. The marketing director of NorthNet, the small Internet service provider, had stirred up huge trouble for AOL and Time Warner within the federal agencies. No one else in the Oshkosh bar seemed to appreciate the moment, as Heins watched himself on a CNN interview, taped earlier in the day, talking about the progress that was made during the arduous merger process. At first, Heins may have been ignored by the receptionist at Time Warner, but when all was said and done, his quotes in the press haranguing the big bad behemoths had been included in more than 150 news articles and translated into nine languages, including Japanese, German, Portuguese, Chinese, French, and Spanish.

Take *that*.

Officials of AOL Time Warner toasted, too. Except they didn't seem particularly ebullient given the long, hard wait. The same evening Heins bought himself a couple of beers, several key AOL officials in the Washington office, in the shadow of the White House, celebrated the consummation of the largest merger in U.S. history. Someone ran out to a corner grocery, came back with a bottle of cheap champagne, popped it in a third-floor conference room, and passed around paper cups. The imbibing didn't last long. Exhausted, people went home to sleep. They had a new company to run.

Within nine hours after the FCC approved the merger, workers had taken down the gold-block "Time Warner" lettering from the facade of 75 Rockefeller Plaza in midtown Manhattan. In its place, a new sign had been erected, heralding a sea change in the media world:

AOL Time Warner.

Some things didn't change.

In the spring of 2001, just months after the AOL–Time Warner merger was approved, Bob O'Connor and his two young boys were riding an Amtrak train, rumbling back to Virginia after a quick weekend jaunt up to New York, when his cell phone rang. On the other end of the line was an upset AOL employee who worked for him. She told O'Connor that a junior financial analyst had manipulated an internal company report inflating the amount of revenue AOL owed Homestore Inc., an on-line home and real estate service.

What?

O'Connor already knew that Homestore shared revenue with AOL from advertising sold on Homestore's house and garden areas within the AOL on-line network. Homestore also received a revenue share from certain house and home ads that appeared in other areas of the AOL service. Every month, AOL financial analysts received a report from operations, showing the level of ad revenue and an estimate of Homestore's share.

But what was inexplicable to O'Connor was that someone had instructed the junior financial analyst to change an internal AOL report, inflating Homestore's ad revenue by an additional $2 million. Who ordered the change?

Business affairs.

O'Connor had two reactions. First, he was livid. Second, did someone in BA think he was an idiot? This maneuver was so overt, so plainly wrong. Maybe BA hadn't counted on the junior financial analyst having a sudden pang of conscience. But he told his manager, who called O'Connor. And all O'Connor could think of was, *Telefónica, all over again.*

It was another BA special. As soon as he got off the phone, O'Connor called AOL's internal accountant. The official was speechless, until he finally uttered, "I'm so mad."

"How do you think I feel?" O'Connor responded. "BA went down three levels in my organization to manipulate a report."

Fortunately, AOL hadn't cut a check to Homestore yet. The BA maneuver was short-circuited, and the internal AOL report was fixed. O'Connor didn't find out why BA had wanted to inflate Homestore's revenue share by $2 million. But it left a queasy feeling. BA, it seemed, would stop at nothing to get what it wanted.

O'Connor was concerned enough that he started warning other AOL officials that the company was treading on dangerous ground. He tried to appeal not to their sense of morals, but to practical considerations. He painted an alarming—but realistic—picture: As the ad market continued to weaken and the value of on-line ads dropped, AOL would be forced to sell more ads to reach its revenue targets. Eventually, he told them, AOL would run out of on-line space—"inventory"—to run ads where consumers would actually view them, the criteria by which ad impressions are based.

As it was, AOL was racing to run all the ads it was selling. In some cases, AOL resorted to what was known internally as "jackpotting." The term referred to gambling slot machines, where, for example, three cherries in a row wins. In AOL's case, jackpotting meant it would run the same ad three times on a single Web page, often at the bottom of the screen, where it was less visible. It was a jackpot for AOL because the company would credit itself for running three ads, even though the viewer saw only one promotion. The advertiser, who paid for three ads, was the big loser.

AOL also took advantage of its "ad rotation" to run more ads. When viewers looked at a screen, the Web page automatically refreshed itself at a specific interval, sometimes eight to ten seconds. But at the end of the quarter, when AOL was trying to meet its financial targets, it would increase the speed of the ad rotation to get credit for running more ads.

In the final days of a quarter, AOL employed an even simpler technique: It ran ads before it had signed a deal with a company that was negotiating to buy the ads. It was a variation on the Wembley dog ads.

Things were getting out of control, and O'Connor wanted to make sure top management was aware of it. He took the "inventory" issue all the way up the chain of command—to Robert Friedman, then head of AOL's interactive marketing division; Joseph A. Ripp, AOL's chief financial officer; J. Michael Kelly, the division's chief operating officer and former chief financial officer of the parent company; and Mayo Stuntz Jr., executive vice president of AOL Time Warner's cross-divisional initiatives. O'Connor thought he was doing the right thing.

But in late February 2002, AOL executives sent O'Connor a different message: He was not a team player and didn't have a bright future at the company anymore. O'Connor, stunned, immediately agreed to resign. But Myer Berlow, his former boss, who by then had been promoted to president of global marketing solutions for AOL Time Warner, tried to persuade officials in Dulles to stop O'Connor from leaving.

In a March 8, 2002, e-mail to Barry Schuler, then chairman and chief executive of the Internet division, Berlow defended O'Connor.

"The only reason you know that there is an inventory problem is that Bob [O'Connor] continued up the ladder with the inventory problem (Bobby-Ripp-Kelly-Mayo) and shot his career out the window," Berlow wrote to Schuler.

Berlow's missive went nowhere. O'Connor left the company on March 29, 2002, without negotiating a severance package. He was disillusioned. "Clearly, a lot of what they were living on was revenue that was not of the highest quality," O'Connor said. "I don't know if they're still in denial, but there were some pretty big business issues they were not willing to face. For nine months, I tried to get these guys out of denial. I tried to take the perfume off the pig."

PART IV

The Culture Clash

CHAPTER SEVEN

THE SHORT-LIVED HONEYMOON

Neil Davis had been warned. *Be understated. Don't make a scene. Let the Time Warner people run the meeting.* But late in 2000, Davis couldn't help himself. He was an AOL advertising executive, reared in the brash Dulles milieu, and to hell with the Time Warner folks!

Besides, it wasn't his style to hold back. Myer Berlow, his boss, should have known better when he cautioned Davis to keep a lid on it. Had Berlow forgotten what had happened when he bought Davis a traditional handmade suit one Christmas? Davis, in his inimitable style, had it retooled into a flashy avant-garde statement by rearranging the lapels and the buttons on the jacket. And *that* was tame compared to the time Davis, an AOL senior vice president, had showed up decked out in a purple windowpane suit, black shirt, and pink tie for an important meeting with the chief executive of another company. Berlow had screamed over his loud fashion statement in front of the startled CEO, but all for naught.

Davis wasn't about to reform his ways. Not on this evening, not as he was carving into a medium-rare slab of New York strip, while pitching a potential deal with Hasbro Inc., the giant toymaker. Davis, a master salesman, could eat and talk with the best of them. Never mind that he was supposed to keep his mouth shut and defer to the three Time Warner executives dining with him that evening at Morton's, the clubby steakhouse in New York. No way was Neil Davis going to let himself be upstaged. This was one of the first meetings—if not the very first—in which AOL and Time Warner were working together in earnest as a single company, selling their combined media assets to a potential client. The U.S. government hadn't okayed the AOL–Time Warner merger yet, but the two companies, confident that the approval would come any day, were beginning to function as one. Davis wanted the honor of closing one of the first deals. And the three Time Warner executives, reserved and low-key as their corporate culture dictated, decided to let him have it, remaining mute, wearing polite smiles all around.

With his boyish charm, Davis tried to wow Alan Hassenfeld, Hasbro's chief executive, on the power of synergy. It was the raison d'être of the merger. AOL and Time Warner, in combination, would be more valuable than the sum of their parts, so the thinking went. AOL Time Warner, as the new company would be named, would use its vast array of media assets—from movies to magazines to music to the Internet—to create a new way to promote its own products and services, cut costs, and generate new forms of revenue. AOL Time Warner, however, wouldn't be the only beneficiary. Hasbro, Davis explained, could also take advantage of such synergy. Imagine, for example, a Looney Tunes cartoon movie, produced by AOL Time Warner's Warner Bros. film studio, which spawned Hasbro action figures for children—toys that could speak through preprogrammed phrases downloaded from the AOL Web site. AOL could even promote the film and the toys through on-line games linked to the movie, and Hasbro, in turn, could promote toys stemming from the movie through ads placed on AOL's on-line service.

Everybody would win!

Except, of course, Mattel Inc., Hasbro's chief nemesis, which Davis was quick to point out. Hasbro was the nation's No. 2 toymaker, behind Mattel, but here, in the form of a nine-figure ad and licensing deal with AOL Time Warner, was an opportunity for Hasbro to leapfrog Mattel, which was already financially hobbled by bad acquisitions. There was no better time for Hasbro to strike.

"Alan," Davis appealed to the Hasbro chief, "you have two choices." The toymaker could do nothing and, in the process, give Mattel the opening it needed to revive itself.

"Or," Davis said, raising his steak knife menacingly, "what we like to do to a competitor that is damaged is drive the knife in their heart." And with a violent lunge, Davis plunged the steak knife into the dinner table, leaving it there to quiver like an exclamation point.

The three Time Warner executives looked on in disbelief. Hassenfeld, the Hasbro CEO, smiled and said, "I agree."

End of meeting.

The next day, Berlow summoned Davis to his office. When he arrived, Berlow explained that he had gotten a call last night at home from Bob Pittman. *Pittman.* As in the president of AOL. The three Time Warner executives, though quiet the night before, were incensed by Davis's knife-jabbing antics, not to mention that he had commandeered the meeting despite Berlow's express warnings to the contrary. As soon as dinner had ended, the Time Warner executives had complained to Pittman, who called Berlow, which was the reason that Davis was standing in his office now.

Smirking.

"What were you thinking?" Berlow demanded to know.

Davis appealed to him with an AOL–versus–Time Warner theme. "They needed to understand we wouldn't be bumped from the lot," he said of his three Time Warner colleagues. "They needed to understand we weren't going to take a backseat in the negotiations."

Berlow appeared mildly troubled. "That sounds like something I would do," he told Davis. "When you do something I would do, we have a huge problem. One of us has to be in control."

Then Berlow smiled.

In the end, Davis's steak-knife histrionics didn't result in a Hasbro deal. But by drawing its attention, AOL Time Warner managed to lure Mattel into a similar deal. "We got close enough to Hasbro to make Mattel be more interested," Davis said.

Apparently, the stratagem emboldened the AOL executive. Soon, Davis was trying to concoct other AOL–Time Warner synergies. Time Warner didn't seem to appreciate the thought. When Davis came up with the idea of an on-line movie studio, combining the assets of AOL's Internet business with Time Warner's film studios, he got slapped down. Warner Bros. executives said they were working on a similar project on their own. When

Davis tried to work out a deal with a manufacturer to buy ads on AOL and build television set-top boxes for Time Warner Cable, he got shot down again. Officials of the cable division said they already had a deal with another manufacturer to build their set-top boxes.

"It was like I was asking to sleep with their wife," Davis said.

The final straw, though, came in the summer of 2001, in the middle of AOL Time Warner's first year as a combined company. Davis was thinking about cross-company opportunities again. This time, he had worked out a deal for Nokia, the giant cell phone company, to spend $70 million in promotions—only to have Time Warner forces nix the deal because of artistic integrity.

Nokia wanted to have one of its cell phones used as a prop in the two sequels to the wildly popular sci-fi film *The Matrix,* under production at Warner Bros. For $70 million, it seemed like a good deal to Davis. It would have been one of the largest product-placement fees in the industry's history, and cell phones were already a prominent feature in the first *Matrix* film. The movie makers said they would go along with the deal only if Nokia created an entirely new phone to their specifications, designed for the movie, which they wanted Nokia to market to the public, with the film getting a percentage of the sales. Nokia agreed, on the condition that the movie makers use one of its existing phones as a prop in the narrative. Warner Bros. was willing to go along, but the Matrix movie makers called it a no-go. When it came to one of the most profitable movies in Warner Bros. history, the filmmakers held a considerable amount of sway. The message Davis said he got was, "You don't fuck with vision."

Thus, AOL Time Warner passed on $70 million.

Davis threw up his hands.

When Jerry Levin, AOL Time Warner's chief executive, found out what had happened, first he yelled at Davis, then he told him to come directly to him the next time he encountered resistance from a sister division. It was, perhaps, an early signal that those executives at the top of the company, like preoccupied parents, could not always control their warring children.

Davis wouldn't get the chance to report back to Levin. That summer, after finalizing a deal with Philips NV Electronics at an AOL official's rustic ranch in Sun Valley, Idaho, Pittman turned to Davis on his way out the door and said, "I'm not going to be able to give you air cover anymore."

Pittman, who by then had been named co–chief operating officer of the combined company, didn't elaborate on the military term, but Davis immediately understood. In the past, Davis had run afoul of Pittman, but it was of no consequence. Davis was used to it. Pittman had smacked him down when Davis wanted to do a big deal between AOL and a porn outfit. Pittman had ignored Davis when he wanted to launch a huge on-line gambling service on AOL. But this time, Davis had gone too far. Well intentioned as he was, Davis had ruffled a lot of feathers—Time Warner feathers, in particular—and Pittman was running out of room to defend AOL mavericks like Davis, who liked to freelance across the company, doing what they pleased despite the obvious displeasure of their Time Warner opposites.

"Pressure was on Myer [Berlow] to control me," Davis said.

But Davis couldn't imagine becoming a corporate automaton. The last thing he wanted to do, he said, was to "put deals down on paper and ask for permission" from other divisions. That's not the way he had done things at AOL before the Time Warner merger. "It would castrate what I felt was my talent," he said. "There was no way a hundreds-of-billions-of-dollars company, which it was at that time, would be able to survive with the kind of renegade guy I was in there."

In October 2001, he quit. Davis opened his own motion-picture production company, Smashing Entertainment. Among his projects: a Broadway musical of the story of *Playboy*. There was little room for him after the AOL–Time Warner merger. But, as it turns out, in the melding of two distinct corporate cultures, Davis wouldn't be the only odd man out.

Somebody at Time Warner hadn't been warned about AOL's David Colburn.

On the eve of the announcement of the AOL–Time Warner merger in January 2000, Colburn, AOL's notorious deal maker, was hunched over the conference table in the Dulles boardroom, reviewing the deal terms, when he turned to a Time Warner executive and curtly ordered him to fetch some more documents. The Time Warner official, unaccustomed to doing the biddings of another, took umbrage.

"You act like you're taking us over," he intoned.

"We are," Colburn snapped.

Though it was true—AOL shareholders would own 55 percent of the new company, while Time Warner investors kept 45 percent—the two companies were positioning the largest deal in U.S. history as a "merger of equals." The media wouldn't buy it, nor would Wall Street. Clearly, this was an AOL acquisition. But many Time Warner executives, jockeying for positions in the new company, were holding on to that notion of equality for dear life. Even if they hadn't convinced themselves, the genteel, mannerly Time Warner set from New York wasn't prepared for the upstarts from Virginia.

"You are so fucked," said one top AOL official in a face-to-face confrontation with a top Time Warner official in the early days of 2000, shortly after the merger announcement. The Time Warner executive called his AOL counterparts "gross creeps." His secretary felt the same way. Shocked by some AOL executives' phone etiquette—or lack thereof—she turned to her boss one day and asked, "Why are they so rude on the phone? Why are they so obnoxious?" The Time Warner executive shrugged.

Call it the dot-com bravado. AOL, pumped up on its bulging stock price, was infused with it. Throughout Dulles, officials boasted about AOL injecting Time Warner management with the Internet company's DNA. AOL's aggressive, warp-speed culture would shake things up at dusty, staid, blue-blooded Time Warner. The merger would be a celebration, a triumph of new media over old media, the installation of the Internet as lord of the manor.

From the moment the deal was announced on January 10, 2000, there were forebodings on both sides of the corporate aisle. Though AOL and Time Warner came from different worlds, their officials had tangoed with each other on various business deals before. Time Warner, for one, was well versed in the rough-and-tumble way of doing business in Dulles when it negotiated deals in which it paid to place its news and entertainment content on the AOL on-line service. "These guys would negotiate on a deal, then renege on it," said a Time Warner executive of AOL's deal makers. "They were infamous for it. If they negotiated for a dollar, they would demand two. There was a mentality of arrogance."

Thus, it was with sheer horror that many Time Warner officials looked on the announcement of the AOL–Time Warner merger, especially the provision that put Steve Case atop the organizational chart as chairman, and the nuance in the back story, as Case presented it to the public, that he had asked Levin to run his—Case's—company, the implication being that Case was calling the shots. The sense among some Time Warner hands was that Case was doing little more than tolerating Levin and his Stone Age media crew, dragging them into the Internet century.

"There was a slightly uneasy truce between Levin and Case," said Tryg Myhren, a former Time Warner executive and Levin friend. "There was disdain shown by the AOL side of Time Warner, which was seen as a tired old business."

Add to that, Case was bringing with him Bob Pittman as co–chief operating officer, a move that many at Time Warner viewed as the first step in evangelizing the old Time Warner forces in the new Internet way of doing business.

"We knew we were all toast," said a Time Warner official. "No one ever believed it would work the second [the merger] was announced."

Other Time Warner executives, already smarting from Levin's solo decision to trigger the AOL deal, could not fathom how their CEO had structured the deal. AOL was purchasing Time Warner using the currency of a stock that many already believed was overvalued in the euphoric market—and who were these young upstarts from the suburbs of Virginia, anyway?

"Immediately there was a feeling of, 'Good Lord, this is structured so that AOL is taking over Time Warner, but Time Warner is a bunch of grown-ups with real businesses that have been profitable,'" said a former Time Warner executive. "The feeling was, 'Jerry [Levin] is selling us to the kids in Virginia—the arrogant, snot-nosed kids from Virginia.'"

Gasps emerged far and wide throughout AOL as well. In Mountain View, California, the lush headquarters of Netscape, officials of the AOL software division greeted the Time Warner merger announcement with the skepticism born of an unpleasant experience.

AOL had acquired Netscape, a once-proud Internet firm, amid great expectations in 1999. But instead of powering AOL with new growth,

Netscape drowned in virtual obscurity, like an expensive but forgotten toy left in the attic. Hence, the buzz over Time Warner: *Look what happened to Netscape. Why do you think it will be different with Time Warner?*

"Total wariness, total wariness, that's what you heard," said a former Netscape official. "It was a common discussion in the cafeteria and the gym." For some at Dulles headquarters, the announcement of the AOL–Time Warner merger was also the heralding of another kind of change: the loss of innocence. Coupled with Time Warner, AOL was no longer bent on changing the world. Now, it would be *controlling* the world. And in the process, AOL would be transformed from revolutionary to a member of the establishment.

"I never really loved it [the merger]," said an AOL official. "The nice thing about AOL was it still felt like a mission-based place. The core group was passionate about the medium. That was kind of refreshing. It was pretty nice. Being a part of a giant corporation, a conglomerate, was not particularly appealing to me. We would just be part of a big corporation that controlled half the media in the world. And I thought from the moment the merger was announced that, ultimately, Time Warner would control much more of the company than the AOL side."

In most marriages, there is a honeymoon, but not in this one.

"I can't recall one," said a former Time Warner cable executive. "I guess if there was a honeymoon period, it was about as short as summertime in Minnesota."

Jerry Levin and his crew had seen this movie before: Two sides come together, get hitched, hate each other, live unhappily ever after. The name of that movie: the merger of Time Inc. and Warner Communications a decade before AOL's betrothal to Time Warner.

"We went through the same thing with the merger of Time and Warner," said Geoff Holmes, former chairman of Time Warner interactive.

That ill feelings arose from the Time-Warner union wasn't a surprise. It was a shotgun wedding. Time, fending off the unwanted advances of an acquisitive Paramount Communications, fled into the arms of Warner. But when they woke up in the morning, the newlyweds found themselves in debt, and what's worse, they found they didn't like each other.

"I can tell you, the merger between Warner Communications and Time Inc. had a clash of cultures," said Lawrence Buttenwieser, a Time Warner board member until 1997.

Levin, a Time Inc. guy, had inherited from Steven Ross, the dynamic Warner chief executive, a wild bunch of bucking corporate broncos, from the Warner Bros. movie studio to the Warner Music Group, each with his own fiercely independent ways of operating with his own marketing, legal, and public-relations staffs. Warner was glitz, pizzazz, all that jazz. Time Inc., by contrast, was a genteel place, a ponderous Ivy League–laden publisher where people took themselves seriously as journalists. They were the standard-bearers of the Luce legacy, where the public interest took precedent over the pecuniary preoccupations of a corporation. And then there was a third strand, the Ted Turner broadcasting operation, which Levin had folded into Time Warner in another merger in the mid-1990s. With it came another movie studio, CNN, and, under Turner's protective wing, an Atlanta-centric view of the world.

Levin, a receding man by nature who shied away from confrontations, was not about to tame all of these powerful executives. Instead, the Time Warner CEO seemed to stand back and let chaos reign. "In the '90s, Levin did a horrible job of trying to manage his division heads," said a former Time Warner executive. "He couldn't make this behemoth work. The bigger it got, the worse it got." Time Warner seemed less a fully integrated company than a feudal system, a loose collection of kingdoms defined by a stock price, which was fine by Wall Street as long as the media giant produced. And it did. It almost seemed that Levin hoped to fuel Time Warner's growth from the seeds of its own discontent, pitting division against division.

"I was watching the balance of power shifting depending on the success of the different divisions," said a former Time Warner executive. "You could feel who was consolidating their power and who was losing their power during each quarter, who was puffed up, who was beaten down. I think they thought that would breed a competitive spirit, but I'm not sure it did."

It did breed infighting.

The intramural competition got so intense that many Time Warner division heads relished the opportunity to go for each other's jugular during internal negotiations. There was, for example, no brotherly love between Michael Fuchs, the HBO chieftain, and Terry Semel and Robert Daly, then co-chairman of Warner Bros. film studio, who famously butted heads over such issues as how much HBO would pay to air Warner Bros. movies. Fuchs, naturally, wanted an in-house discount. The response from Warner Bros.: balderdash. Ted Turner tried to negotiate a similar sweetheart deal for his own cable networks, including TBS and TNT, but to no avail. Warner Bros. wasn't giving stuff away for free, not even to its own.

The movie studio, in turn, felt cheated in dealings with other parts of the company. For all of the Warner Bros. blockbusters, its executives felt they could never get a break from their counterparts at Time Inc., whose publications, including *Time, Entertainment Weekly,* and *People,* seemed so worried about the so-called separation of church and state—editorial versus business—that they erred on the side of giving less ink to Warner Bros. movies.

"We could always get a fairer shake at *Newsweek* than we could at *Time* because *Time* was always worried about the perception of being manipulated by a sister division," said a Time Warner official. "It was always a perception of fairness. It happened often. *Entertainment Weekly* and *People* would kill us in reviews of our movies, and I'm talking about movies that made a gazillion dollars."

In 1996, the blood feud got so bad between the dueling fiefdoms that they found themselves locked in a ferocious fight over a well-known company property: a cartoon character. "The infamous Road Runner example," said Mike Luftman, a former Time Warner cable senior executive. "It was the poster child of the autonomy of the divisions."

In what is now company legend, the Time Warner cable division wanted to use the name "Road Runner" for its high-speed Internet service, which would ride over its cable lines. The idea, naturally, was to play off the speed of the cartoon bird, a property of Warner Bros. The movie marketers were willing to license the cartoon icon to its corporate sibling. But they explained that they made their living, in part, on licensing trademarks. The movie marketers also explained that Steven Ross, the deceased Warner CEO, had always encouraged arm's-length transactions, and they had a fiduciary duty to shareholders to get the most that they could out of a deal; besides, they had financial targets to reach. "The Time Warner philosophy was, you need to do what benefits you because you're a business," said a Time Warner official. It was another way of saying they wanted to charge Time Warner Cable a reported fee of $1 billion. It took the two divisions a year to agree on terms.

"That was a stupid thing," said a Time Warner official.

Ultimately, the speedy bird cost the cable division less than a billion. But the bruising negotiations left an indelible impression on Levin, the Time Warner CEO. He had always given his division heads the latitude to do as they wished as long as they continued to meet their financial obligations. But throughout the late 1990s, as he encountered internal resistance to his digital efforts—an uphill climb to infuse Time Warner with an Internet makeover—he became increasingly persuaded that the decentralized atmosphere he had fostered was now becoming a hindrance to the company.

"It is," he said, "very hard to turn the ship around."

Some were convinced it would be even harder to turn around the AOL–Time Warner ship. "The differences between Time and Warner were not as lethal as the differences between Time Warner and AOL," said a Time Warner executive.

Tensions began to emerge when the companies revealed their first organizational chart about a week after announcing the merger in January 2000. The most salient fact was that Steve Case wasn't going to be a figurehead chairman. In the merged company, he would retain many of his top lieutenants, who would report directly to him. That included Ken Novack, AOL's vice chairman and Case's trusted adviser; George Vradenburg, AOL's senior vice president and a veteran of Washington politics; and chief technology officer William Raduchel.

Levin, to be sure, would control the operational side of the company, overseeing the co–chief operating officers, Bob Pittman and Dick Parsons. But Case was not going to go quietly into the executive suites, where many chairmen lost touch with the day-to-day operation of their company.

Neither Case nor Levin was going anywhere, not without a fight. Under a provision inserted as part of the merger agreement, the bylaws of the new company stipulated that neither man could be removed from his post unless 75 percent of the board voted for such a change. And with a board composed equally of eight members appointed by each company, it seemed likely that Case and Levin would be sticking around—at least until December 31, 2003, when the 75 percent provision expired. Then, it would take a simple majority to give either man the boot.

Attention focused not on this provision but on the subsequent management lineup announced in early May 2000. Bob Pittman emerged as the big winner.

Although the AOL president would share the title of co–chief operating officer with Parsons, Time Warner's president, the May "org chart" left little ambiguity about who would be running the show. Pittman, then forty-six years old, would oversee the company's most important assets, including the publishing division, Time Inc., all of the Time Warner cable networks, such as HBO and CNN, the Time Warner cable system, and the nascent WB Network. He would also run America Online, the on-line division. Pittman would be responsible for generating well over half of the merged company's revenue. But even more significantly, Pittman was positioned as the heir apparent. When Levin chose to step down as CEO, which seemed well into the future, Pittman seemed to be the likely choice to slide into the top post.

Parsons, by contrast, seemed almost an afterthought. The fifty-two-year-old Time Warner president's portfolio included the legal and human resources departments, neither very sexy. Parsons, however, did inherit the company's traditional content businesses in film, television production, music, and books. That meant he got the unenviable task of herding proverbial cats by overseeing the independent-minded Warner Bros., New Line Cinema, and Warner Music Group, among others.

Both Pittman and Parsons professed delight about their place in the mix. And yet, there were several others who quietly grumbled offstage, especially on the Time Warner side. Not only had AOL's Pittman gotten the lion's share of the company's operations, other AOL senior executives had grabbed key management roles in the new company. Vradenburg, the AOL lobbyist, had bested Time Warner's Timothy Boggs, who would take the high road and resign. AOL's general counsel, Paul Cappuccio, was named to the same job at the combined company, leaving Time Warner's general counsel, Christopher Bogart, with a consolation prize: either taking a lesser job within the company, or getting out altogether. (He opted for the former.) Ken Lerer, AOL's top PR man, was given the same duties at the new company, which put him on top of his Time Warner counterpart, Ed Adler. And Richard Bressler, whom many had viewed as Levin's closest confidant, was shunted off into a way station. Bressler was given the dubious honor of running the company's venture-capital fund, reporting to Steve Case. (Bressler would quickly rebound, taking the chief financial officer slot at rival media conglomerate Viacom.)

The management lineup was a stunner. If there had been any doubt about who was acquiring whom, there wasn't anymore. The Internet upstarts were storming the Bastille.

Executives of the Warner Bros. stronghold, however, saw a silver lining in the AOL coup: They wouldn't have Pittman lording it over them. Instead, they would get a known quantity: Time Warner's laid-back Parsons. "We got lucky because we got Dick, we didn't get Bob Pittman," said a Time Warner official. "There was a huge sigh of relief because we knew what kind of executives they were. We were used to autonomy and huge budgets. Micromanaging us was not going to be an acceptable way of living." But others from Time Warner could not understand how Levin, their leader, could let this happen, how he, the CEO of the new company, could allow the other side—AOL—to get the key jobs. Despite Parsons's rosy public statements, he wasn't happy either. In private, he protested to Levin, arguing for a larger portfolio in the new company, asserting that the management reorganization wasn't fair. "He objected to it 100 percent," said a close Parsons associate. "He was given the short end of the stick." But Levin, drawing on his philosophical leanings, responded by saying, "Change is good. Live with it." Said Parsons's associate, "He never wanted to hear a complaint." To Levin, it was not a question of loyalty. This was the way he wanted it. Pre-merger, Time Warner had been an unwieldy, intractable behemoth whose executives had been resistant to change wrought by the Internet. And Levin, if anything, was impatient for change. He, not Case, selected the senior management team.

"The ultimate allocation was done by me," Levin said.

In essence, the Time Warner chief threw in his lot with the AOL folks. But he felt he had no other choice.

"It's very hard to get the attention of people whose vested interest in business is in making movies, making music, making magazines, making television," he said. "They're going to view this as either threatening, which it was, because the Internet is a deconstructionist movement. Or it's going to be a sidebar, they're not going to give it the attention. At some point, I made it clear to Rich [Bressler] and Dick [Parsons], two people I relied on, that to use one of the old phrases, 'We're going to have to have a transforming transaction. We're going to have an injection here.' You couldn't internally make the culture do a one eighty. It was just too tough."

Among his toughest decisions: cutting out Ted Turner.

When Levin selected his senior managers, the voluble Turner was nowhere to be found in the management chart. As Time Warner's vice chairman, Turner had been overseeing all of its cable-programming divisions, including HBO and TNT. But in May 2000, at the age of sixty-one, Ted Turner, the media mogul, was excised. No longer would he oversee anything at the company. He would retain his title of vice chairman, but it was a sinecure. He would assume the oblique role of "senior adviser," although no one, including Turner, was quite sure what that meant. Suddenly, Turner, the largest individual shareholder in the new company to be, was among its biggest losers.

"I've been Nick Nicholas-ed," Turner told a close friend.

He was making a reference to how Levin had outmaneuvered Nick Nicholas, engineering Levin's ascension as CEO in a famous Time Warner palace coup in the early '90s. But Turner wasn't amused. And he wasn't done. Biding his time, he would fight another day.

Jane Fonda couldn't sleep. Tossing in bed, the famous actress had a bad feeling, even as her tempestuous husband, Ted Turner, slept peacefully. Jerry Levin, the chief executive of Time Warner, a minority owner in Turner's broadcasting empire, had vetoed Turner's latest scheme: an acquisition of NBC. Sooner or later, Fonda knew, Turner was bound to erupt. Only she could see it coming the night before Turner rose to the lectern in late 1994 at the National Press Club in Washington, D.C.

"They're holding me back!" he squawked in his inimitable Southern drawl, surveying the crowd, which wasn't quite sure where he was going with this. The face was craggy, but he still had that Rhett Butler mustache and the baby blue eyes drooping in a sleepy, mischievous gaze.

"I'll tell you one thing: We ran a story on clitorectomies," he went on. "Most people don't know about it, but millions of women have their clitorises cut off before they are ten or twelve years old, so they can't have fun in sex. Between 50 percent and 80 percent of Egyptian girls have had their clits cut off. You talk about barbaric mutilation."

Fonda cringed.

"Well, I'm angry," Turner bellowed. "I'm being clitorized by Time Warner."

The crowd roared. So, too, did a number of senior Time Warner executives, who caught Turner's act when it was replayed on television. "It was like watching a car wreck," said a former company official. "It was vintage Ted." Levin, the object of Turner's ire, shrugged it off, chalking it up to the ball of exploding contradictions that is Ted Turner. "Ted is another one of these great people, a visionary," Levin said, "but his humanity, it's uneven."

That's one way of putting it. Turner has been known as Captain Outrageous, the Mouth from the South, Terrible Ted, winner of the 1977 America's Cup, creator of CNN, *Time*'s Man of the Year in 1991, a womanizer, a visionary, an eccentric, a nut, a crackpot, a drunken sailor, a father of five, a bison rancher, a natural-born leader, a monumental risk taker, a restless idealist, a megalomaniac, a billionaire, an environmentalist who drives a forty-eight-miles-per-gallon hybrid gas-and-electric car, an internationalist, a philanthropist, a rogue, a maverick, an upstart, a swashbuckler who wants to save the world from nuclear weapons and overpopulation, a former cigar smoker who claimed he wouldn't hire a smoker, and America's largest individual landowner, with nearly two million acres, the equivalent of Delaware and Rhode Island combined, who owns twenty-two properties in nine states and Argentina. That guy.

As a child, Robert Edward Turner III dreamed of becoming a fighter pilot, or conquering the world. He's made more progress on the latter. But Ted Turner has spent his life as if pursued by the furies of avenging angels, consumed by one, single, solitary purpose: living up to his father's great, unyielding expectations.

Born on November 19, 1938, in Cincinnati, he was nine when his family moved to Savannah, Georgia, where his father, Robert "Ed" Turner Jr., ran a successful outdoor-advertising company. Ed was less successful in his personal affairs. When he got drunk, which was not infrequent, he took it out on his only son, often beating him with a wire hanger that he had stretched out as a whip. If his son cried, he doubled the beating. It got so bad that Ed's wife could stand it no longer and eventually left him. His son, a restless spirit, was sent off to military boarding school, where Ed hoped to instill discipline in his son. Everything was geared to push his son to succeed, even when Ed withheld affection, or when he charged his son room and board when he came home from college.

Ted Turner grew up lonely, yearning for his father's affection. And yet he defended his father, saying once, "He thought that people who were insecure worked harder, and I think that's probably true. I don't think I ever met a super-achiever who wasn't insecure to some degree. A super-achiever is somebody that's never satisfied."

Ted Turner was a huge disappointment to his father. The younger Turner was expected to attend Harvard. Instead, he enrolled at another Ivy League School, Brown University, where he proceeded to break his father's heart by majoring in the classics. Turner admired Alexander the Great, whose bust would one day adorn his New York office. But Ed Turner saw only a useless major leading to a failed future for his dissolute son.

"My dear son," he wrote in a letter in 1957. "I am appalled, even horrified, that you have adopted classics as a major. As a matter of fact, I almost puked on the way home today." Raging, he went on to say, "There is no question but this type of useless information will distinguish you, set you apart from the doers of the world."

His father needn't have worried. Turner never completed his major. He was expelled in his junior year for sneaking a young lady into his room, which left him to go work for his father. It turned out to be a blessing. The father needed the son. Ed, locked in a desperate bout of depression, spent the summer of 1961 in a psychiatric hospital. When, a year later, he spent $4 million buying several divisions of another billboard company, Turner's firm vaulted to the top of the market in the South. But that also plunged Ed into another depression, so he checked back into the psychiatric hospital and, in haste, sold the divisions to a friend in the business. On the morning of March 5, 1963, Ed had a fight with his son about the business. After breakfast, Ed went upstairs and shot himself in the head with a .38-caliber pistol. He was fifty-three. His son was twenty-four.

Suddenly, Ted Turner grew up. He immediately bought back the advertising divisions his father had sold. And then, like Alexander the Great, he went on a rampaging conquest of the media world. In 1968, he bought a Chattanooga radio station. Two years later, he bought a struggling television station in Atlanta. In 1976, taking a cue from Jerry Levin, who put HBO up on a satellite, Turner beamed his new cable network, Turner Broadcasting System, across the nation. That same year, he bought the Atlanta Braves baseball team, and four years later, on June 1, 1980, he unleashed a global revolution with the introduction of the Cable News Network, CNN. All of a sudden, news wasn't what had *already* happened; news was what was happening *now*. In a speech at Georgetown University in late 1981, Turner turned his gaze to the rafters, waving a copy of *Success* magazine, whose cover bore his profile, and, in a yearning plea, cried out, "Is this enough? Is this enough for you, Dad?"

Apparently not.

In the mid-1980s, Turner failed in a bid to buy CBS. He launched the Goodwill Games to bring together the U.S. and U.S.S.R. at a time when each was taking turns boycotting the Olympics. And in August 1985, bankrolled by Michael Milken's junk bonds, he bought MGM, saddling his company with $2 billion worth of debt. Turner almost gagged on it. Almost as soon as he had bought MGM, he was forced to sell back the studio and other parts of MGM, keeping only the film library. Though the stable of movies proved to be a boon for his cable-television programming, the debt also compelled him to seek a bailout, which he got from a group of cable companies to whom he sold about a third of his company. The bailout came with a hefty condition: Turner agreed to give his new partners veto power over any company expenditure of more than $2 million. When Turner tried to buy NBC in the early '90s, Jerry Levin invoked Time Warner's veto power as a minority owner in Turner's company. Hence, Turner's infamous declaration that Levin had clitorized him.

Turner got over it soon enough. In 1996, he sold his company to Time Warner and agreed to stay on as a top executive. Levin let him continue to run his Atlanta empire, tolerating Turner's unruly, outspoken ways. But the two men never warmed up to each other. Turner seemed to harbor anger toward Levin for foiling his plans to buy NBC. Turner still wanted Time Warner to buy the network, but Levin ignored him. Such was the give and take in their relationship. Turner proposed brassy corporate strategy, and Levin ignored him. After more than thirty years spent building a company, Turner was becoming increasingly irrelevant. By the late '90s, it seemed he was drifting, casting about for purpose. He decided to give $1 billion—a third of his wealth—to the United Nations. Meanwhile, his marriage to Jane Fonda was falling apart. By January 2000, eight years after they'd married, they separated. At almost the same moment, AOL was wedding Time Warner. It caught Turner off guard. Levin had arranged the deal without Turner's knowledge until very late in the process. Once again, Levin had cut Turner out of the loop.

It was almost too much to bear. Though Turner joined the others onstage at the merger announcement in New York, he knew this was Jerry Levin's and Steve Case's show. Shortly after the merger announcement, Case tried to make nice, calling Turner one of his heroes and vowing they would be "joined at the hip" in planning for the combined company.

Then Levin fired Turner—that's the way Turner understood it when Levin called him in the spring of 2000. Levin explained that as part of the new management lineup, Turner would no longer oversee Turner Broadcasting; that would fall to Bob Pittman, the new company's co–chief operating officer. Appealing to Turner's pride, Levin was quick to point out that Turner was too big a fish to report to Pittman. Levin tried to put the best face on it when he said that Turner would keep his title as vice chairman, which he had held at Time Warner, but that he would also be "senior adviser." Turner, desperate to keep his operational control over his beloved empire, including CNN and his television network, offered to relinquish his vice chairmanship if he could just keep running his division. Levin was unmoved. So was Steve Case, when Turner placed a series of calls to both men, pleading his case. The final insult arrived by way of a fax in early May, when Turner's plane touched down on his 580,000-acre ranch in New Mexico. The five-page fax was an AOL Time Warner press release announcing the new management lineup, sans Turner.

Combined with his divorce, he was despondent over the loss of his job. He felt, he told friends, suicidal.

For Levin, it wasn't personal. Seeing the need for change at Time Warner,

Levin viewed Turner as a vestige of the company's feudal system. No one was more protective of his turf than Turner. "TBS and Atlanta never really meshed because Ted was sitting on top of them," said Vradenburg, the AOL senior vice president.

Levin put it more bluntly. "Ted should not be managing anything," he said.

Levin had come to feel that Turner was a liability, that he was injecting his own personal views into his creation, CNN. Turner had become a titanic public figure whose liberal political views were well known, which Levin believed was a detriment to a news-gathering operation. And Turner had shown clear animosity toward other Time Warner divisions, including the WB Network, which competed against his own.cable networks.

Levin admired Turner as a media pioneer but felt that his time had come and gone. "He's probably the most amazing person I've ever met in my life, no question about that," Levin said, "but most people who start things eventually need to step back at some point." That's why Levin decided it would be better to remove Turner from an operational role in the new company. "I thought it was much healthier, although psychologically difficult, to take him out of that role. Everyone agreed at the time, by the way."

Not Turner. But for all of his business brilliance in creating CNN and a multitude of other ventures, he had been naive enough to sit idly by, not thinking to use the leverage of being the company's largest individual shareholder to bargain for a post while Levin was putting together his new management lineup at AOL Time Warner.

By October 2001, relations between Levin and Turner had become so strained that it looked as though Turner wouldn't renew his employment contract, which was to expire by year's end. Marginalized as he was, Turner was grousing in private about maybe resigning. He could remain on the board and continue making noise. But there seemed little chance of doing more than that. Then again, when did Turner ever give up?

Al Haig was uneasy, but he didn't say it.

It was July 2000, and the directors of AOL and Time Warner were meeting together in their first combined board meeting. The merger was still pending before the U.S. government, but both sides, gathering at CNN headquarters in Atlanta, were proceeding as if it would be approved. For Haig, an AOL board member, this would be his last meeting. The merger with Time Warner had created a conflict of interest. He was already a board member of a rival entertainment giant, MGM. Haig had been with AOL from the early days, in the late 1980s, when it was still Quantum Computer Services. He had seen it grow, against all odds, into an Internet giant, and now a media giant. But as he planned to step down, he felt uneasy. He had survived Vietnam and globe-trotted as Nixon's chief of staff and Reagan's secretary of state. But he wasn't sure about this merger business. All he could think was, *Jesus, let's hope they can make something out of this zoo.* "What I was worried about was the upfront, clearly discernible culture differences," he said.

AOL was a tightly centralized operation; Time Warner, he thought, "was a fiefdom of some complexity." To his way of thinking, AOL was a technology company, while Time Warner was about journalism and entertainment. He believed that "these are a special kind of people. Believe me, you have to have a keen sense of that. It isn't enough to be a good manager."

Haig, however, held his tongue. He had already made a stink, raising questions about the merger when the board voted to approve the deal. Haig didn't want to be a troublemaker this last time. Board meetings, as a general rule, are well-orchestrated affairs, and that was never more true than on this occasion. Jerry Levin, who had put together the Atlanta meeting, wanted to make sure of that. It was his first opportunity to present a five-year plan for the new company. Each business unit of the two companies furnished its own financial projections, numbers it could meet and beat. The idea was to show what an integrated AOL Time Warner would look like on paper. And the numbers looked good. AOL's numbers, courtesy of Steve Case, looked especially good. Even the Time Warner CEO was impressed. "The AOL numbers were terrific," Levin said, "and you would've come away from the meeting saying, 'Wow, we hope the Time Warner businesses can keep up."

Levin, however, had other concerns. Like a party host, he wanted everyone to have a good time. He also wanted to cultivate a different way of thinking among AOL and Time Warner officials. The meeting's purpose, he said, "was less to validate the numbers, but more to get people to start thinking about AOL Time Warner as a company, get directors focused on that, get management focused on that, throw them all together."

Levin also wanted to take them to a ball game. The Time Warner chief executive had chosen Atlanta as the site of the meeting because his company was hosting Major League Baseball's All-Star Game at nearby Turner Field. Levin had named the ballpark in deference to the cantankerous media mogul after Time Warner bought Turner's company, including his Atlanta Braves. Levin had even switched loyalties, abandoning his beloved New York Mets to root for the Braves. He was a company man first. And, just maybe, choosing Atlanta as the meeting place for the combined boards was a small gesture by Levin to placate Turner, who, without a company portfolio, was once again feeling cut off by Time Warner in general and Levin in particular.

Perhaps it worked. Turner participated in the board meeting without incident. He didn't seem upset. He wasn't even his usual rambunctious self. It was hard to read Turner, whether he was angry or just holding his counsel. "Sometimes, he's bright as hell, sometimes he's stupid as a wall," Haig said. But he assumed Turner "had to be a little bit disconcerted. TV was his world. To have that snatched out from his bosom couldn't make him happy."

Haig, though, didn't mention anything about that at the meeting, either. As a lame-duck director, he was already feeling far removed from the proceedings. The merger, despite his protestations, was essentially a "done deal," he thought, and now, the two companies were moving full-steam ahead. Climbing on a leased jet that night, however, Haig couldn't shake a nagging question about the AOL–Time Warner merger and how it would all end up. "I didn't know whether to be euphoric or to be sad," he said. "I suspect 'euphoric' wasn't the right word."

Haig's qualms were not unfounded. In the initial months after the merger announcement, there were some signs of a cultural rift between AOL and Time Warner. It even had a name: Gnutella.

In March 2000, a band of merry AOL programmers, working out of a trendy loft in San Francisco's Potrero Hill neighborhood, did what a lot of smart, iconoclastic Web masters were doing at the time: freelancing. With a little ingenuity, they posted a software program on the AOL site that made it easy for consumers to illegally copy and swap music. As it was, countless teenagers were illegally copying music from the Web using the popular MP3 format. So the AOL programmers were having a little fun of their own. What was the big deal?

The big deal, of course, was that Time Warner happened to be one of the largest music companies in the world, boasting a gargantuan stable of artists, such as Madonna and Jewel. Time Warner was none too happy that AOL, its merger partner, was actually encouraging the pirating of its tunes. Alerted to the problem, Jerry Levin lodged a complaint with AOL. Other Time Warner executives put in calls to AOL's president, Bob Pittman. Parsons, Time Warner's president, got in on the act, too, firing off an e-mail to Steve Case, explaining in no uncertain terms that Time Warner believed in protecting intellectual property (as well as its bottom line). "This," said the diplomatic Parsons, "seems to be moving in the wrong direction." Case agreed immediately, and AOL moved with dispatch to remove the illicit software program.

When the incident bubbled to the surface in press reports, AOL insisted it was an "unauthorized freelance project." And Rich Bressler, Time Warner's digital media chairman, dismissed the notion that, perhaps, Gnutella signaled a potential culture clash between AOL and Time Warner.

Others weren't convinced. Differences between the two parties were quickly becoming pronounced. AOL was new money, the Internet set. Time Warner was old money, the established class. Part of it was a matter of demographics. "Most of the AOL people were very young versus the Time Warner culture that tended to skew older," said Dave Sickert, who worked at HBO and then its on-line initiative before jumping to AOL, where he ran the on-line shopping group.

With the differences in age came a difference in outlook. At Time Warner, Sickert said, people tended to work for the long haul. They called it the "golden rubber band" effect. When people thought about leaving Time Warner, they would be *snapped* back because they realized it was a stable company with a good retirement plan. AOL operated under a different work ethos. The glue was the stock option. It was, by definition, a short-term mentality. "If you could last to each vesting period, you got a little more golden each year because the stock was doing better," Sickert said. Where AOL lived for the quick payday, Time Warner saved for retirement. "There was such a belief in the corporation that an inordinate number of people held way too much [company stock] and violated every investing principle," said a former Time Warner executive.

Many at Time Warner didn't understand AOL. They "looked down on us," said an AOL executive. "They felt that we were focused on money, and we thought being focused on money is what it's about—making more money for the company, making more money for shareholders." Early on, a Time Warner executive turned to this AOL executive and derisively said, "All you're trying to do by doing these deals is push up the stock." To which, the AOL executive snapped back, "Yeah—as opposed to what?"

There was a feeling among many AOLers that their counterparts at Time Warner were a bunch of country clubbers who resented rich AOLers and considered them lower-class Internet guys. AOLers had taken lower salaries, betting on the success of the company's stock, and it was rocketing up, which meant that, through the merger, Time Warner was now latching on to a rising star. What's more, on the day the merger was announced, Time Warner executives' stock options immediately vested; by contrast, AOLers had to wait for a year after the merger was official.

Ill feelings only grew in the latter part of 2000. Although the merger was still being held up by federal regulators, some AOL officials were already making themselves at home at Time Warner's Rockefeller Plaza headquarters. Chief among them was Bob Pittman, the AOL president, who had already set up shop on the thirty-second floor of 75 Rock. Looking to get a head start on potential synergies, he was holding court with a combination of AOL and Time Warner officials. Talk revolved around such issues as integrating their software programs and cross-promoting their products and services. The two companies had already signed about two hundred commercial agreements to help each other out. Warner Music, for example, was helping to sell AOL subscriptions by including AOL software on a compact disk from the music group matchbox twenty. AOL, in turn, had used its on-line promotions to net five hundred thousand new subscribers for Time Inc.'s stable of magazines.

Not everyone was feeling the love. Some at Time Warner were taken aback by AOL's aggressive manner. They didn't ask, they just took, some Time Warner employees felt. "I certainly didn't want to work for AOL," said a horrified Time Warner employee. She and her colleagues, feeling a bit put upon, came up with a not-so-private nickname for their new overseers:

Assholes Online.

The nickname was inspired in part by AOL's plans to move some of its top people into Time Warner's executive suites on the twenty-eighth floor even before the merger was approved. First, AOL took a large boardroom on the floor, a magnificent, dark, wood-paneled affair. The room wasn't being used anymore. It was filled with memorabilia that Jerry Levin, akin to a head of state, had received as gifts over the years, such as candlesticks from the Chinese embassy. But several Time Warner employees were appalled by AOL's presumption to commandeer the room for its own use. That alone, to some, was bad enough. But then, AOL took it a step further, hiring about ten Irish joiners and carpenters to divide the boardroom into three separate rooms, which would be turned into offices for its own executives. Now, *that* was desecration. Over about six weeks, the carpenters drilled away with power tools, while several Time Warner employees, living amid the construction, frowned in dismay. It upset the tranquility to which they had become accustomed. The executive suites were a genteel place, the kind of habitat where two maids, dressed in such civilian garb as cardigans and slacks, would be dispatched to the corporate kitchen on the floor to fetch cookies or a turkey sandwich for an executive working late. This was where Steven Ross, the famed Warner CEO, used to have his Scotch poured. Now, here were these brash AOLers, thinking they could tear up the joint! "That," said one who worked on the floor, "was easily a hundred-thousand-dollar job."

Fears of an AOL invasion prompted Time Warner officials to go to great lengths to preserve their own heritage, including stashing away a series of old Warner Bros. movie posters, including framed pictures of such classics as *The Big Sleep* and *Dial M for Murder,* that hung in the executive suites. A Time Warner executive called the widow of a deceased former executive who owned the posters and negotiated to buy them for the company. That way, Time Warner would properly own them, and no one else could take them. Time Warner didn't want such family heirlooms to fall in the hands of the wrong people, namely, the AOL people. The cost of such insurance? About $50,000, according to one former resident of the executive suites familiar with the transaction.

"It was like getting rid of the posters," she said, "because the barbarians were coming."

Not long after the merger was approved in January 2001, Myer Berlow, the AOL ad executive, stormed out of a meeting with his new Time Warner compatriots and, fuming, marched up to Bob Pittman's office, now formally situated on the twenty-ninth floor at Rockefeller Plaza. Berlow had been named president of global marketing solutions for AOL Time Warner, which was a glorified way of saying that he was still doing big ad deals, only now for the combined company, focusing in large part on synergy. And the synergy guru himself, Bob Pittman, was the new company's co–chief operating officer, which was an understated way of saying that he was really the man in charge. And yet, the impromptu meeting had the feeling of a child running up to his father, tattling on his uncooperative playmates.

In a huff, Berlow explained what had happened: He was poised to strike a $100 million ad deal with Burger King—no small feat—and yet his Time Warner colleagues were threatening to scuttle it. What Berlow had structured was a multifaceted deal in which Burger King would be promoted on various AOL and Time Warner properties. But the Time Warner folks thought they could get more money if they cut their own individual ad deals with Burger King.

Go downstairs and get along with them, Pittman ordered Berlow.

Berlow couldn't believe it. He wanted to tell Pittman, *Are you out of your fucking mind? We want this deal!* But he thought better of it. The last time Berlow tried that, it didn't go over well. "The first time one of these [Time Warner] guys gets in the way of a deal, fire the motherfucker!" Berlow had suggested to his boss. Pittman, ever the Southern gentleman, scolded Berlow then, saying, "If you behave like that, Myer, I don't want you on the team."

So Berlow said nothing this time. Pittman, though, must have sensed his resistance. The Mississippi preacher's son sang the new AOL gospel: *We can be successful,* he told Berlow, *but we must not be pushy. We must not let our aggressive culture hurt this company.* Then he added for good measure: *Just suck it up.*

Later in 2001, Pittman began to sense resistance from Warner Bros. The Burbank movie studio seemed to tolerate him, but then it ignored his calls for synergy and went about its merry business. Pittman tried to write it off as an isolated example. "He thought that Warner Bros. people were grin-fucking him," said a close associate.

Pittman came to believe it was perhaps just a West Coast thing. Warner Bros., he knew, had a long heritage of fierce independence. He did not believe Time Warner was moving toward outright rebellion. But Berlow cautioned Pittman, "It's closer than you think—it's right across the street." Pointing, Berlow was referring to the Time-Life Building, site of the publishing empire, just a short walk from Pittman's office.

Pittman seemed to appreciate Berlow's loyalty, gruff as it was. But he preached patience, that it would take time for AOL and Time Warner to come together as one, to make synergy work. *I understand,* Pittman told him. *What you want to do may take five years.*

Berlow replied, "You don't have five years."

Pittman was moving as fast as he could. As early as June 2000, he had convened a meeting at the Four Seasons hotel in New York, assembling Time Warner executives who were expected to report to him after the merger closed. By way of introduction, Pittman assured them that he had no intention of running roughshod over their operations; he understood the Time Warner heritage of autonomy, had worked in it himself, was one of them, in fact. But he also put a challenge to them: What, he asked, could each of them do to help forge synergies? What could they do to create cross-promotional opportunities over the next five years between AOL and Time Warner? Although nothing was conclusive, it was a start.

Pittman liked meetings. Or he was a glutton for punishment, because he had a lot of them in the ensuing months, working out of the Time Warner building. For all of his talk about autonomy and understanding the Time Warner heritage, Pittman was imposing his way, which was the AOL way. They called it the "Matrix." What it meant in Dulles was collaboration between various units. It encouraged overlapping duties among different divisions. Time Warner took it differently. To them, it meant there was a new sheriff in town; Pittman was shaking things up. Executive compensation, he told Time Warner executives, would no longer be based on how well their individual units performed. In the new world of AOL Time Warner, their compensation would depend in large part on how well the overall company fared. As if that wasn't motivation enough, Pittman also told Time Warner executives that he would be evaluating them weekly; before, they had been assessed monthly. They weren't used to Pittman's impatient, brusque style. At one meeting in December 2000, shortly before the merger was approved, a Time Warner executive was rambling on about abstract economic issues and the difficulty of making a go of it in a tough marketplace when suddenly Pittman short-circuited the conversation and asked, "Are you going to make your numbers?"

Pittman kept pressing the same theme: How could Time Warner cross-pollinate its media assets with AOL's Internet business to create new products and services, to grow revenue and cut costs? Time Warner executives drew back, appalled: *What happened to the old Time Warner way of doing things? Jerry Levin hated meetings like this! And what about the old Time Warner battle cry? Each division was to become the best in its class, kick the competition's ass and win market share!* "Our job wasn't to help AOL's bottom line," said a Time Warner official. "We had a fiduciary duty to make our own properties as successful as we can." But suddenly, Time Warner executives who hadn't held a meaningful meeting together in years were being summoned to New York to a table headed by Pittman. He began ordering meetings of top executives every few weeks.

Meetings were compounded by more meetings. Not satisfied with the executive meetings, Pittman formed another group called "the advertising council." Made up of about twenty top advertising and marketing executives from each division, it met every couple of weeks. And every other week, a smaller group within the council met to hash out what had already been discussed. All these meetings were intended to foster synergy. But they also created bad blood. It wasn't just the meetings themselves. It was the *travel* to the meetings, especially for those who were forced to crisscross the country at Pittman's whim. "It was physically exhausting," said one.

Meetings were taking place at such a pace that, at times, they got in the way of doing business. When Ted Waitt, the chief executive officer of

Gateway Inc., the giant computer maker on the West Coast, came to visit AOL Time Warner in New York, he found himself cooling his heels for forty-five minutes for his appointment with Barry Schuler, the Internet division head. Myer Berlow, the ad executive, kept Waitt company, trying to humor the important business partner. When Schuler finally arrived, he apologized, then explained his delay: "I had a meeting with Bob," he said, referring to Pittman.

Berlow shot up out of his chair and, speaking on behalf of Waitt, asked Schuler a pointed question: "What the fuck are you doing?"

In January 2001, Venus went overboard.

Shortly after the merger's approval, Bob Shaye, the founder of New Line Cinema, a Time Warner division, chartered a yacht and invited an assortment of friends aboard, as he often did. Among his guests was a starlet named Venus. She was Shaye's Jack Russell terrier.

The dog, who traveled everywhere with the studio executive, was the offspring of Milo, a celebrity of sorts who was featured in the comedy hit movie *The Mask*. Hence, the derivation of her name: Venus, as in Venus de Milo. Shaye loved this dog. He even threw company bashes at New Line celebrating her birthday. So it was no surprise that the studio executive cried when Venus disappeared off the yacht deck into rough waters, never to be seen again. "Bob was distraught about the dog," said a colleague. Whether it was an accident or foul play was never determined.

When Shaye returned to New Line's offices in Los Angeles, things only got worse. AOL Time Warner, in one of its first official acts as a combined company, had just laid off about 125 New Line employees, about 20 percent of its staff. A colleague approached Shaye, one of the survivors of the mass firings, and tried to console him.

"It's terrible," the colleague said.

"I know," Shaye said. "I'll miss Venus."

No one ever doubted that Shaye cared about the human toll involved in the layoffs. But the mixup left an impression on some. "It was one of those weird defining moments," said a Shaye colleague.

To many at New Line, the layoffs, triggered on January 23, didn't make business sense. The movie studio had been profitable for all but a few years in the past two decades. The past year had been difficult, to be sure. Many on Wall Street were blaming New Line's costly flameout, *Little Nicky*, an Adam Sandler feature, as the cause of many of Time Warner's financial ills. But that, to many at New Line, was too simplistic an assessment. The merger was less than a month old, and there was no way that the corporate bigwigs in New York could have done a full-fledged assessment of the movie studio. Instead, the layoffs seemed to some at New Line as a way to demonstrate to Wall Street that the company was moving quickly to cut costs to underscore the value of the merger.

"They served up New Line as a sacrificial lamb," said a New Line loyalist. "It was a target number that they were trying to hit rather than a real examination of where you could cut back efficiently. They didn't have time to really look at what the operation was and where they were cutting back. They needed to shed numbers."

The New Line layoffs were part of a broader company cutback. Less than two weeks after AOL won final regulatory approval from the government to acquire Time Warner, it shed about two thousand employees—about 3 percent of its eighty-five thousand employees worldwide. A week later, Pittman demonstrated just how quickly the new company was moving, touting the benefits of synergy. The company said it was working on more than four hundred cross-company arrangements to integrate AOL with its movie, publishing, television, cable, and music enterprises. AOL software disks were being distributed in Time Inc. magazines. Meanwhile, AOL, the on-line service, had already sold eight hundred thousand subscriptions from the stable of magazines under the Time Inc. umbrella. AOL's Internet service was also using pop-up ads on users' computer screens to sell Time Warner's basic cable-television service. And AOL had promoted HBO fights, *People* magazine's "Most Beautiful People" feature, and Madonna's latest CD, *Music*.

"We're only just beginning," Jerry Levin said then.

What Levin didn't say was that synergy wasn't quite as easy as it looked, especially when it came to Madonna. Neil Davis, the renegade AOL ad executive, knew well enough. In early 2001, he learned from his industry sources that Microsoft was close to striking a deal to sponsor Madonna's coming tour. Madonna was a Warner Music artist. How could she align with AOL's arch-enemy? "It was like the wolf in the henhouse," Davis said.

He couldn't believe it, but then he could: It was about money. He alerted people within AOL Time Warner. Pittman concurred—Microsoft needed to be stopped. Scrambling behind the scenes, Davis hopped on a plane, flew out to Beverly Hills, and barged in on the hip, sparse offices of Maverick, Madonna's record label. Davis wasted no time. "You're not going to do the Microsoft deal," he announced. "You can't do that. They're the devil." The Madonna people explained that the devil was in the details. Microsoft was prepared to pay $5 million to sponsor her concert. AOL would have to come up with a bigger package. Davis persisted. "Let's figure out," he said, "what it will take for you not to do a Microsoft deal." What it would take was a bit of creative cross-company cooperation. As the concert sponsor, AOL would sell tickets to its Internet subscribers first. It would also distribute AOL disks at the concert and release songs on-line to AOL subscribers. Finally, the AOL software would be loaded on the Madonna CD. In two weeks, AOL clinched the deal. Synergy had saved the day.

Other stabs at cooperation were proving tougher.

In the spring of 2001, tempers flared on the Mountain View campus of AOL's Netscape division. During a meeting, a Time Warner executive said he would allow *Fortune*, a magazine in his stable, to provide articles to Netbusiness, an AOL Web site. The Time Warner executive, however, politely asked to be paid. An AOL executive respectfully declined.

Why, said the AOL executive, *would I pay for something produced in-house?*

Because, responded the Time Warner official, *it costs money to write articles.*

The decibel level rose. Faces turned flush. Finally, the Time Warner executive abruptly moved to leave and sputtered, "Fuck this."

The squabble over *Fortune* and Netbusiness involved less than $1 million, a pittance for a giant conglomerate like AOL Time Warner. But the dispute was never fully resolved. *Fortune* pulled much of its content from the Web site, and AOL dramatically scaled back its operations, leaving Netbusiness stirring quietly.

While Pittman was proselytizing the AOL Time Warner masses on the benefits of synergy, many of his Time Warner operating executives were becoming even more convinced that it was a fairy-tale idea. Sure, it would be nice if one part of the company cooperated with another so that they could generate new revenue. But how about taking care of business first? The reality was, some executives said, they weren't persuaded that synergy always worked, that, for example, an advertiser would want a multimedia package, buying promotions both on the Internet through AOL and off-line through Time Warner magazines and its traditional media properties.

"Something like that sounds good in theory, but for managers inside of those businesses, it was never desirable," said a former Time Warner executive. "So many of the businesses wanted to control their own revenue streams. The idea that somebody on the buying side wanted media placements everywhere wasn't right. It doesn't work that way. It's a theoretical vision."

Don Logan, the Time Inc. chairman, was among the few to say so publicly in the early days of the merger. He opposed a move to have the on-line division and his magazine unit sell each other's advertising, explaining that each magazine required a dedicated team that understood its individual features. Others began to feel that synergy was a hollow promise. Some cross-promotional ad deals included some AOL Time Warner suppliers, which sold equipment to AOL. How much AOL Time Warner netted from the arrangement was never clear in public filings. AOL Time Warner also struck cross-promotional ad deals with companies in which it had an equity stake. Again, it was unclear how much fell to AOL Time Warner's bottom line. Others at Time Warner were dubious because the cross-promotional deals required the company to give advertisers substantial discounts. Was it worth the price?

Meanwhile, confusion began to seep into Pittman's ad council meetings, which were fraught with densely written memos that many Time Warner officials didn't bother reading. Advertisers were sometimes unsure with whom in AOL Time Warner's ad council they were supposed to deal. Each had veto power over potential ad deals. Amid the confusion, some at Time Warner were surprised that Pittman pushed so hard on synergy; after all, he was a former Time Warner guy himself. Didn't he remember his history? "Synergy was one of the buzzwords of the original Time Warner merger," said an old company hand. "The word was expunged from the Time Warner lexicon. It was déjà vu all over again. With the AOL–Time Warner merger, the word was resurrected."

Increasingly, Pittman's call for synergy fell on deaf Time Warner ears.

"He was preaching it, but a lot of it was smoke and mirrors," said Bob Grassi, a longtime HBO official who retired in March 2002. "I'm not sure how many people bought into that." Synergy, he said, became "the dreaded word" again.

AOL executives, including Myer Berlow, didn't realize how things were souring. When he flew out to meet with Warner Bros. executives in Burbank in 2001, he asked them why they were spending a smaller percentage of the movie studio's promotional budget on AOL Time Warner properties than was their competitor Paramount. Berlow, who was leading a companywide effort to boost advertising sales, was proffering a question, but the Warner Bros. executives felt bullied. "AOL's attitude was, we're all chattel," said a Time Warner official. "To them, we're all bits and bytes."

AOL officials felt slighted, too. When they brought AOL T-shirts as a gift for some Warner Bros. executives, one seemed less than enthralled. "I get my shirts done on Savile Row," he said, referring to his London tailor.

AOL executives felt ignored by Time Warner. Time Warner executives felt AOL was lording it over them. "It was an absolutely disingenuous line of reasoning for them to say they came in and just wanted to make things work," said a Time Warner executive. "They used language which was literal and symbolic that made it very clear to every senior person at the division that they were in charge." AOL executives, he said, talked about "the 'myopic' and 'antiquated old media guys.' This was not just an aside. This was endemic to their presentation and to their tone."

This Time Warner executive said he got a taste of that tone in 2001 during a meeting in New York when an AOL executive "eviscerated" a Time Warner marketing executive over a failure of synergy between the two companies. A Time Warner executive, shocked by the treatment, turned to the AOL executive and said, "We don't speak like that here."

"There was hubris in every meeting they had," said a Time Warner official. "It was all about 'what can you do for me,' not 'what can we do for each other.'" Many at Time Warner were stunned by what they considered the audacity of AOL officials to demand things that they should have known were not appropriate. On one occasion, an AOL official called a Warner Bros. official, requesting that the studio fetch movie star Mel Gibson to do a promotional voiceover welcoming AOL users when they opened their e-mail to the famous cheery tag line, "You've got mail."

"We tried to explain to them that Mel Gibson doesn't work for us," said one familiar with the incident. "Their naïveté, their level of not knowing our business, was way beyond their years. You could forgive it in a twenty-year-old, but it's hard to forgive those people who should know better."

Even when they tried in earnest, AOL and Time Warner couldn't always find a way to work together. That happened when executives from AOLTV, the on-line firm's interactive television unit, tried to come up with deals with Time Warner's television and movie studios in 2001. Both sides were excited by the prospects. Imagine, as they did, running current-event quizzes on-line that would run simultaneously on CNN. The two sides, however, were stymied at first. It wasn't a matter of egos, but of nuts and bolts.

"There was a lot of confusion between how the editorial groups were supposed to work with each other," said a former AOLTV official.

There was nothing nefarious about it. Both sides were hamstrung by minimal staffing. Neither side really understood the other's medium. And, perhaps most important, everybody was doing other things, like running their core businesses.

Who had time for synergy?

"We were two hundred and seventy-five miles away from each other," the former official said. "One was sitting in Dulles, one was in New York, and you both have other jobs to do. It was simple human things that could make it hard."

AOLTV, once considered a key element of the combined company's future, a melding of AOL's vast Internet assets with Time Warner's enormous content resources, became all but a shell of an operation. Eventually, the company stopped actively marketing it.

By May 2001, even something as basic as e-mail became a point of contention. When AOL Time Warner began switching all employees to AOL's e-mail program, protests began to emerge from various quarters of Time Warner, the loudest coming from those who worked at the magazine division, Time Inc.

It wasn't an issue of snobbery, the magazine people insisted. It was just that AOL's e-mail system was designed for computer users at home—not for corporate dwellers like themselves, who often attached big files to their e-mails. AOL e-mail, they insisted, wasn't robust enough. But AOL took it as an insult: Many at Time Warner wanted to use an e-mail system built by AOL rival Microsoft. AOL Time Warner handed down a decree: All employees would use AOL's e-mail system. Time Warner employees reluctantly went along. Did they have a choice?

But an even more pressing question lingered: How in the world were AOL and Time Warner going to work together, if they couldn't even agree on e-mail?

CHAPTER EIGHT

The Collapse

Jerry Levin gazed out of the tinted window as his driver navigated the Lincoln Town Car down the familiar streets in lower Manhattan, near Wall Street, gliding past snapshots of a time long gone, memories of local haunts scrolling in his mind.

Except for his security detail, Levin, the AOL Time Warner chief executive, was hermetically sealed from the onrushing world that December day in 2001. From his perch, the noise and furor of New York sidewalks played out like a silent pantomime.

And yet, this time was different.

Levin wasn't on his cell phone. He wasn't punching in a text note on his BlackBerry pager. There weren't a million urgent thoughts about the company racing through his head all at once.

"Stop the car," he ordered. "Let me out. I'm going to walk around for a half an hour."

His security guard, who had become something of a companion to the reclusive CEO, was stunned. The boss had never done anything like this. Levin always went straight back to AOL Time Warner's offices in midtown Manhattan following a meeting at the New York Stock Exchange, where he was a director. He never stopped for a walk. The chief of the world's largest media company never had time for a trifling thirty-minute stroll. *What was he thinking?*

"Now I know you're going to make a transition," the security guard said. He had no idea.

When Levin emerged from the Lincoln, facing an uncertain personal future, all he could think about was the past. His emotions were still raw from the September 11 terrorist attacks on the World Trade Center, in ruins nearby. But he plunged on, moving introspectively from one block to the next, burrowing deeper in time. "I just walked around downtown, visiting some of the places. I mean, I hadn't been there in twenty-five years," he said.

Jerry Levin loved downtown. "I started my life down there," he said. *There.* On Broadway. That was the first building he had ever worked in, back when he was a reed of a young man working as an attorney in the mid 1960s, before he knew what he really wanted to do with his life. Levin walked into the lobby. Breathed it in. Then moved on.

His next stop: As an idealistic young man, he had worked for David Lilienthal, the famed head of the Tennessee Valley Authority. Lilienthal had dispatched Levin on romantic adventures overseas, including Bogota, Colombia, where Levin had taught Indians to grow carnations as a means to undercut the drug trade. Levin, then twenty-nine, had traveled to Iran, leading a massive effort to build a dam to provide irrigation and electrification to a desert region. Along the way, Levin, the budding executive, had learned an important lesson: Don't be afraid of technology. "What people don't understand is, the distribution of water systems or power or electrons is the same," he said. "So when I joined Time Inc. and we had to build microwave systems [for HBO], it wasn't particularly alien to me." The overseas experience taught him another enduring lesson, one that was reinforced when he joined the media company of Henry Luce in 1972: You could make money and do good at the same time.

So much had changed since those sunny, simple days of youth. Levin had never imagined this was the direction his life would take. It was almost as if he were an accidental CEO who had actually meant to become someone else. The biblical literature major at Haverford College who had burned all his school papers out of humility had somehow lost his sense of direction and veered right when he meant to go left, and here he was, at the age of sixty-two, weathered, scowling, a solitary figure. Levin was like Ebenezer Scrooge, getting a glimpse of Christmas past, wondering where he had gone wrong, clinging to the notion that he could still rediscover the young man he once was.

"I'm the person I was at Haverford College," Levin said. "And you assume after forty-two years you've changed a lot, with new experiences, but I am that person [with] the same idealism, the same views, and the same aesthetic interest."

It is as if he willed the idea to become fact. "I want," he said, "to be that person."

Not everything was the same, not on that December day, as Levin continued his walk. All the old shops had been torn down. But he took comfort in this: He knew the area's history. That much hadn't changed. As a young lawyer, he used to give walking tours of downtown Manhattan whenever the New York State Bar Association had a meeting. The tours had held a special meaning for Levin, providing a kind of unspoken connection to his father, the merchant. Though he was a grocer by trade, Levin's father was a stock picker by avocation. He liked to invest. Wall Street was Mecca. And Levin had become one of its giants. The thought of his father made Levin think of one of his own sons, Lee. Like his father, Lee had pursued spiritual longings—only Lee was still pursuing them. Levin never became a rabbi, as his mother had wished for him long ago, but Lee was well on his way, in his fifth year at Jewish Theological Seminary. Levin was proud of his son. Lee had asked his dad to give a talk during a three-day seminar. The title: "Profits and Prophets."

In another day, Levin might not have had the time. Running a $40 billion company was a consuming affair. But suddenly, it wasn't relevant. Levin agreed to give the talk. From now on, he was going to have all the time in the world to become that person at Haverford again.

Back in early 2001, nearly a year before Levin's unusual stroll downtown, all had seemed well at AOL Time Warner—as far as the public knew.

Its debut quarter as a newly combined company seemed to prove the wisdom of the merger. In January, its market cap was an astounding $240 billion. Synergy was still largely a thing of the future, but officials trotted out a sexy example of how cross promotions were already taking hold: The creation of Eden's Crush, an all-girl band, was chronicled on *Popstars,* a show on AOL Time Warner's WB television network, and promoted on the AOL service. The band's first single, "Get Over Yourself," was a hit.

"The first quarter really indicates that the company is quick and nimble," crowed Bob Pittman, the co–chief operating officer.

A promising sign was the company's revenue, which grew at a strong rate across AOL's on-line service and Time Warner's cable network despite persistent sluggishness in advertising spending throughout the media industry. Executives demonstrated just how confident they were of the merger's power, standing by their ambitious annual company goals, which included a 12 to 15 percent increase in revenue, to more than $40 billion. Levin, Pittman, and others reckoned they had a couple of aces in the hole to help drive growth later in the year: the release of two upcoming blockbusters, *Harry Potter* and *The Lord of the Rings.*

Investors, relieved to hear the company wasn't being dragged down with other struggling media firms, cheered the first-quarter results and the prospects of good tidings to come, sending shares in the new company up 12 percent to $49 on April 18, the day the company's financial results were announced.

"We're off to a good start," Levin declared.

So, too, was Steve Case. No sooner had the merger become official than the former AOL chief and new AOL Time Warner chairman segued into his new role: industry statesman.

As he receded into the background of the company's day-to-day operations, leaving the nitty-gritty work to Levin and Pittman, Case increasingly forged a new image, that of big strategic thinker, much like his longtime rival, Bill Gates of Microsoft, who, at about the same time, had also moved upstairs to become chairman of his own company.

Case's trademark khakis and denim shirts were a thing of the past. In their place, he substituted the standard boardroom look: gray suit, blue button-down shirt, and red power tie. That was the look he presented in early May 2001 at the U.S. State Department when he offered his vision of a wired western hemisphere, calling on Latin America to lower consumer costs and trade barriers to get people on-line.

Case was by then a polished speaker, using the right inflections and appropriate pauses, even if he still relied on a written script. The speech, though, put Case in the right kind of company. His fifteen-minute talk followed appearances by President Bush and former AOL board member Colin Powell, the secretary of state. Suddenly, Steve Case was acting like a global leader. Flanked by burly security guards with Secret Service–like earpieces, Case was ferried out of the gleaming halls of the State Department through a secure side door, leaving a coterie of reporters behind, wanting more, their questions unanswered.

If Case was thinking of himself in a global role, so, too, was AOL Time Warner. Boosted by the merger, officials began to look at the next opportunity to expand overseas. For the on-line division of the new company, vanquishing new lands was a matter of necessity. While the U.S. on-line market was continuing to grow, the pace was already slowing. When Case gave his speech, about half the nation had Internet access, but the rate of growth was only half that of the previous year. Meanwhile, Internet users were growing rapidly overseas. That included Latin America, where AOL had kicked off its service inauspiciously in 1999. When some customers loaded the AOL software on their computers, they were greeted by a Brazilian samba—a factory glitch. AOL, however, recovered quickly, and by early 2001, the company already had five hundred thousand customers, ranking it fourth in the region. AOL was the closest thing to a global Internet provider, with more than thirty-two million subscribers. Since launching its international operations in 1994, AOL had planted its flag in sixteen foreign countries in eight languages, serving more than one thousand cities across the globe.

And the company wanted more.

"Where there's growth, we ought to be," Pittman said. "We're going to be in the moron hall of fame if we don't take advantage of the brand."

Brash words. But this was supposed to be the dawn of a new corporate era, or was it?

In the waning days of March 2001, Charles "Junior" Johnson, Purchase-Pro's chief executive, paid a visit to Kent Wakeford in AOL's offices in downtown New York. The business affairs deal maker was all too happy to see the CEO. Both officials were feeling desperate.

Wakeford was in a mad dash to clinch some last remaining deals before the fiscal quarter closed on March 31, AOL Time Warner's first as a combined company. Even after AOL had finalized its Time Warner merger, AOL deal makers were still at it, constructing exotic deals to boost revenue. The notorious BA specials had helped enhance AOL's financial results in the months leading up to its Time Warner takeover. Now, deal makers were devising BA specials to serve another purpose: to show that the merger was getting off on the right foot.

The drill went like this, according to an AOL official: "It's the end of the quarter, we're short of revenue [targets], how much money do we need to close the quarter?" PurchasePro was on "the list of 'in-the-family' deals, companies that are friends that help us out of jams."

Johnson had his own problems. His search for revenue had become increasingly difficult as the market worsened, and PurchasePro's stock price was dwindling. Here, both sides hoped, was a situation where each company could help the other.

Johnson was officially checked in at the Trump International Hotel & Tower on Central Park West, but he camped in an AOL conference room, hauled in a computer, and spent twelve to sixteen hours a day hashing out terms of deals with Wakeford and other AOL officials in the closing days of March. Johnson became so entrenched that he had his dry cleaning picked up and delivered to the AOL offices, while his driver sat below at curbside, awaiting his emergence.

As the days wore on, the marathon meetings quickly disintegrated into a cacophony of expletives. Things got so intense that Johnson at one point began to rail, for all to hear throughout AOL's New York offices, "AOL fucked me! AOL fucked me!"

AOL, as it turned out, was holding up on signing an agreement to pay PurchasePro to cover the promotional cost of giving customers a free month's subscription to their co-branded on-line business service. Johnson retaliated by holding up checks that PurchasePro owed AOL for commissions that it had earned from selling PurchasePro's business software.

The situation got sticky enough that it required the attention of a higher-up at AOL: Eric Keller, a senior vice president in AOL's business affairs. In the end, AOL told Johnson that it would sign the agreement to cover his promotional costs. PurchasePro faxed the paperwork to AOL so it could then confirm its payment to PurchasePro before the end of the March quarter. Johnson thought the matter was resolved when, in the first few days of April, PurchasePro received AOL's signed agreement, dated in March. But months later, AOL told PurchasePro's auditors that the agreement had not been signed until April 5, days after the quarter ended. According to AOL officials involved in the transaction, AOL wanted to enhance its first-quarter results by delaying its payment to PurchasePro until AOL's second quarter. But that forced PurchasePro to revise its financial statements. Its auditors recommended that about $9 million in revenue from AOL, which PurchasePro had booked in its March quarter, be moved to the June quarter.

"I was absolutely dumbfounded that this occurred," Johnson said. He explained that he was in AOL's New York offices when the PurchasePro agreement was faxed to AOL personnel in Dulles. "The document was signed by PurchasePro," he said. "PurchasePro sent its signed copy. I was told they [AOL] had executed it and not to wait around because they would bring the original to me the following week in New York."

Despite their differences, the two companies continued to find ways to capitalize on their relationship. AOL, for one, targeted the companies most dependent on it—vendors and firms in which AOL held a stake—and pushed them to buy PurchasePro's software as a way to boost AOL's sales commission, internal company documents show. The strategy was for AOL to threaten to take its business elsewhere unless the vendor agreed to buy the PurchasePro software.

"They were strong-arming everybody," said a dot-com executive who did business with AOL. "They targeted vendors they had the most leverage over."

AOL was keenly aware that it ran the risk of alienating its vendors. A February 8, 2001, company memo stated: "A forced [software] license purchase could engender resentment on the part of vendors."

But AOL didn't always have to rely on its muscle. In an internal company document dated March 21, 2001—nearing the end of the same fiscal quarter—AOL devised a barter deal in which PurchasePro would receive $1.8 million worth of advertising on the AOL on-line service. In return, AOL would receive an equivalent $1.8 million worth of promotions that mentioned its Netscape brand when PurchasePro ran television ads on AOL Time Warner's properties, including CNN and Headline News.

PurchasePro, however, was getting little value from the ads it ran on the AOL services, according to AOL documents. The "carriage plan" showed that many PurchasePro ads ran on AOL's ICQ service for instant messaging. The ICQ service targeted a largely teenage and foreign audience that would have little use for PurchasePro's business-to-business software. The ads appearing on ICQ's software also had "almost no 'click-through,'" an AOL official said. That meant few users actually clicked their mouse on the on-line ads to find out more about the product being touted. PurchasePro's ads also were to run on Winamp, AOL's music software player, another service that did not target PurchasePro's business clientele. AOL approved the transaction anyway, as did PurchasePro. As long as AOL helped boost its numbers, the dot-com wasn't interested in the ads. "Hell," said one involved in PurchasePro's thinking, "I didn't care where they ran."

PurchasePro alone could not save AOL Time Warner from itself. The combined company had become beholden to its own promises. To sell the merger to investors, the media, and Wall Street, AOL and Time Warner officials had vowed to reach ambitious growth targets, including double-digit revenue growth in their first year together. But they hadn't counted on a withering advertising market that showed no signs of picking up in the spring and summer of 2001. Abandoning their targets now, they thought, would be taken as a sign that the merger wasn't living up to expectations. So AOL Time Warner executives stuck to their targets. How, though, would they get there?

The answer, in part, came in a phone call in June 2001 from an official at the AOL on-line unit to the company's Time Warner Cable unit. The AOL official wanted to make a deal with his corporate brethren.

Time Warner Cable, the company's strongest-performing division then, had just completed a big transaction. The Golf Channel, a majority-owned unit of cable giant Comcast Corp., agreed to pay $200 million over five years to have its sports programming carried on Time Warner Cable. The on-line unit, suffering a slowdown in subscriber growth as well as in ad revenue, asked Time Warner Cable for help. The on-line unit wanted a piece of the Golf Channel transaction.

Can we recognize some of those carriage fees? the AOL official asked. It was a polite way of asking if Time Warner Cable would divert some of the $200 million to AOL in the form of ad revenue.

Let me think about it, the Time Warner Cable official responded.

Although both worked for the same parent company, they still viewed each other as representing two separate businesses with financial interests that did not necessarily coincide. "It's an internal negotiation over the balance sheet," an AOL official said.

The negotiation worked its way up the company chain of command, and, in the end, the two sides found a mutually agreeable solution. AOL agreed to promote Time Warner Cable on-line and through telemarketing to help drive new cable subscribers. In return, Time Warner told the Golf Channel to spend about $15 million of the total transaction cost to purchase advertising from AOL's on-line unit. The Golf Channel had few options if it wanted to be carried on Time Warner Cable. The sports channel confirmed that it agreed to buy the on-line ads because it wanted the cable deal. "We told them where and when" the ads ran, said an AOL official familiar with the deal. "They didn't have a choice."

AOL took a different approach with eBay. In the summer of 2001, AOL deal makers boarded the company jet for the San Jose, California, headquarters of the giant on-line auctioneer and returned a day later with a transaction that would help AOL meet its financial targets. AOL revised a deal in which it agreed to serve as an ad broker, selling eBay's on-line ad space, according to AOL's confidential executive summary of the deal. But AOL did not simply take the customary ad rep's commission. Instead, AOL counted all of the eBay advertising revenue as if it were AOL's own. "AOL recognizes all revenue generated from eBay inventory sales on a topline basis," AOL said in its internal documents. In this way, AOL booked $80 million in revenue in 2000 and 2001, the gross amounts from selling eBay's ads. The gross sales didn't change AOL's net income, because AOL counted the payments it forwarded to eBay—minus its broker's fee—as an expense elsewhere on its books. But with this accounting, AOL was able to report a larger amount of ad and commerce revenue.

It was, however, only a short-term solution.

In June 2001, Keller and Wakeford were quietly placed on administrative leave, pending an internal investigation of AOL's relationship with PurchasePro. AOL didn't announce the personnel moves, but when *The Washington Post* found out about them, officials took pains to say that AOL's end of the business relationship had been handled properly. "All revenues related to PurchasePro have been accounted for properly and accurately by AOL," a company spokesman said then.

But by July 2001, AOL Time Warner's situation was becoming untenable. Even with unconventional deals, the newly merged company could not reach the lofty financial goals it had set for itself in its first full year. The ad market was that bad. Rumblings first began to emerge from within the ranks of the Time Warner company divisions most sensitive to the advertising downturn—the magazine and television units. Then the chorus began to mount, becoming more hostile: *Why is corporate sticking to these ridiculously high targets? Why is Levin working so hard to justify the merger to Wall Street?*

"I think Jerry [Levin] started to run the business for the first time to kowtow to the Street," said Geoff Holmes, former chairman of Time Warner interactive. "Jerry was one of those guys who had great strategic business sense, but running a day-to-day business, personally, I think he thought he was better than he was. Jerry became his own worst enemy."

Then an internal caution came from AOL Time Warner's top financial man, J. Michael Kelly. As he was preparing the public release of the company's second-quarter financial numbers that July, the chief financial officer could not ignore how the anemic ad market was threatening to scuttle AOL Time Warner's promises to Wall Street, including achieving a revenue increase of 12 to 15 percent in the merger's first year.

It was time, Kelly argued to his bosses, for the company to go hat in hand to Wall Street and publicly lower its financial goals. This was a matter of maintaining AOL Time Warner's credibility with investors. They deserved to know. It was a compelling argument. But Kelly was overruled.

Both Levin and Pittman wanted more time. They thought, hoped—maybe even believed—there was still enough time in the year to catch up to their own targets, if they could cut enough costs and find enough synergy in the form of companywide advertising deals.

"There was a fair amount of discussion about it, whether we could do it or not," said a former company executive. "There was a strong sense from Bob [Pittman] reflecting the operating side, what I took to mean, 'We can do this.' Remember, we had pretty consistently done it. We had financial discipline. It was a matter of managing the company rather than letting the company manage you, setting the tone as the company went forward."

Levin was equally convinced that now was not the time to abandon the aggressive targets. He was not only encouraged by the drive to cut costs, but he figured the ad recession couldn't last much longer. By the fourth quarter, surely things would turn around.

"I mean, who knew?" he said.

What's more, Levin was convinced that if he let up, if he lowered the financial targets, he would be falling into a trap. That would be the perfect excuse for those within the company who were resisting change, who never liked this merger, who wanted to see it fail. He didn't want a rerun of the Time-Warner merger of a decade ago, when neither side wanted to cooperate. He had been unable to get Time Warner to work as one, to forge a digital future. That, he determined, wouldn't happen this time.

"You're trying to manage a company and keep the pressure on," Levin said. "If you take the pressure off, you'll take the pressure off of the integration and the cost reduction, so that was my thinking."

Kelly went along. He signed off on the financial statements. When AOL Time Warner announced its second-quarter financial results on July 18, 2001, Kelly told Wall Street analysts and the media that the company was confident it would reach its annual financial targets, with a big second half of the year, bolstered by *Harry Potter*. But, in a nod to the weight of the deteriorating market, he made a subtle adjustment. Where before the company said annual revenue would increase 12 to 15 percent to *more* than $40 billion, Kelly now said $40 billion would be at the top end of the range. "He also said something else which was very important, that unless advertising picks up in the fourth quarter, we won't make our numbers," Levin said. "It's in the transcript. That was the signal to the Street."

The Street got the message: That day, AOL Time Warner's stock plunged nearly 10 percent to $44.65.

Other dominoes quickly began to fall. On August 21, the company axed seventeen hundred workers, primarily targeting the on-line division. A month later, on September 24, executives finally abandoned their aggressive financial growth goals, blaming the economic damage done by the September 11 terrorist attacks and the weakening ad market. When the company announced third-quarter results on October 17, financial conditions looked no better. By November 1, Kelly became a casualty of the failed financial promises of the merger. Though the company positioned it as a lateral move, Kelly was effectively demoted—he stepped down as chief financial officer of AOL Time Warner, the parent company, to become chief operating officer of AOL, the on-line division.

Then, in early December 2001, an unlikely figure reemerged: the irascible Ted Turner.

In a talk at a cable-television convention, Turner said that selling Turner Broadcasting to Time Warner was "the biggest mistake I ever made." If only he had bought Time Warner instead of the other way around. That way, Turner said, "I could have fired Jerry Levin before he fired me."

Ted Turner had reason to be grouchy: His personal fortune, once more than $9 billion, mostly in company stock, was hemorrhaging millions by the day as AOL Time Warner's share price continued to sink. The stock had plunged from a high of about $55 in January 2001 to $35 that December, hacking off nearly $100 billion of its market cap, which now stood at about $148 billion. Turner was feeling the pain.

"His less than passionate devotion to Jerry [Levin] coincided with the decline of the stock," said Lawrence Buttenwieser, a former Time Warner director.

The loss of a couple billion dollars hurt Turner, who had committed millions to philanthropic activities, in addition to his billion-dollar giveaway to the United Nations.

"He's pissed, he's pained, he feels like he's poor," said a Turner friend. "He was furious at Jerry. He places the blame principally on Jerry."

Some Levin associates said his big mistake was not finishing the job when he marginalized Turner. It was like leaving a wounded man to die, only to see him recover and seek revenge. If Levin wanted a clear path, they said, he should have taken Turner out completely, removed him as a senior executive, taken him off the board—in effect, laid him off. But instead, Turner lived on. "He was still on the board, he still had the mouth," said a colleague. "The way he [Levin] handled Turner was part of his downfall."

Living up to his rowdy reputation, Turner wasn't shy about letting people know how he felt. When Jim Kimsey, AOL's founding CEO, fellow billionaire, and kindred maverick spirit, took Turner to an exclusive club in Washington, D.C., Turner raged about the injustices Levin had inflicted on him until he burst out, "I'm in a fighting mood!" Practically everyone in the club heard Turner. Kimsey, a rabble-rouser himself, counseled Turner to tone it down. It would behoove Turner to refrain from a public squabble with Levin, Kimsey told him, as much fun as Turner might have in such a scrum.

Others were growing disaffected, too.

"It wasn't just Ted Turner," said a Levin associate. "There was a very, very real recognition, like Saint Paul on the road to Damascus, like the clouds opening up, that this AOL [Time Warner] thing was a mess."

Among those recognizing the mess was Steve Case.

From the beginning, once the merger was approved, Levin had made it clear that he was the man in charge, and Case was a "nonexecutive" chairman. Even though Case had ceded the CEO's title to Levin, Case couldn't resist his alpha impulse to hold the reins. It wasn't a good combination. Case took offense when Levin fired off company e-mails about corporate strategy without Case's input. That included a state-of the-company dispatch that Levin sent on the cusp of Thanksgiving, in which he outlined numerous "guiding principles," such as his intent to invest in the public trust.

"It was clear he [Levin] never respected Steve," said an AOL Time Warner official. "He would ignore him."

As chairman, Case was, in title, a notch above Levin, the CEO, on the organizational chart. And yet, Case felt that Levin treated him not only as a nonexecutive but as a nonentity. As with so many things in corporate life, it came down not to money nor to power, but to pride.

"No one likes to hear that the guy who's supposed to be working for you is better than you," said a former company official. "Jerry had violated his relationship with Case. It becomes a little bit of an ego thing."

Case and Turner had something in common: Both men wanted Levin out.

Somebody had to be blamed for AOL Time Warner's disappointing financial performance, and it wasn't going to be Case. "Case, as much as anything, is scapegoating," said a former official. "It's either Case or Levin. At that point, Case does a number on Jerry."

Behind the scenes, current and former officials said, Case let it be known to his inner circle, including other board members, that he was disappointed in how Levin had failed to lower company guidance on its financial targets until it was too late. Now the company's credibility with Wall Street had been damaged. "He sort of dumped that on Jerry," said a company official. "They just got off onto different tracks, the company was going through tough times, so he said, 'Fuck it, let's get rid of him.'"

Levin, the master of previous boardroom intrigues, had boxed himself into a corner. He had infuriated Turner, the company's largest individual shareholder and a loud voice on the Time Warner side of the board. Levin had now also alienated Case, the chairman and most influential voice on the AOL side of the board. And Levin had never been close to other board members, whom he regularly left out of major company decisions.

How Levin had gotten to this point was a mystery even to him. Somewhere along the way, he had grown accustomed to his isolationist practices, becoming a prickly executive who, it seemed, was uneasy in the company of others. He believed it was the pressures of the job, the weight of taking the company helm after the death of Steven Ross of Warner Communications. It was an endeavor that consumed him, and he felt, at first, "I wasn't particularly prepared to be a CEO." More than a decade ago, he said, "I lost my sense of humor. Life was just too tough." It got much tougher in 1997 when his son Jonathan was killed.

"There is no closure," he said, on the brink of tears.

There was, however, a way out. After his son's death, Levin quietly inserted into his employment contract an early exit—a provision that allowed him to depart if he gave six months' notice. Following the destruction of the Twin Towers on September 11, a flood of emotions overwhelmed Levin. The senseless death of thousands of people reopened for Levin the wound of the senseless death of his own son. He said he began to think about getting out of the business.

As it was, Levin was not feeling well. "I was not actually in the greatest of health," he said. "Just the pressure, 24-7, the emotional impact [of being CEO], it's a tough job. So you have people like Sumner Redstone and Rupert [Murdoch], who will die in office [running rival media companies], and they love it and everything. So that's what people think, being a mogul is great. But it's a very tough job, and if you're kind of a humanist, which I am, you're not necessarily cut out for it."

After September 11, Levin's health worsened. His cholesterol level was going up, along with his blood pressure. "If anyone saw me at that time, I was a wreck, emotionally and physically," he said. "As a matter of fact, it was starting to effect my [cardiac] numbers." Levin seemed to loosen from his own personal moors. It was as if he didn't really care about coming to work anymore. "I was having trouble with the conduct of business, I was too emotional about it, I didn't have the patience for it, and I'm sure that rubbed some people the wrong way," he said. Levin noted he was "under the care of a doctor" who warned him, "Either you're going to have to change your lifestyle, or you're going to have a problem." He seemed to have some of the telltale signs of a breakdown—not just the high blood pressure, but the emotional haze that came with it. Still, he tried to brush it off. "I'm one of these macho people," Levin said. "I wasn't having a breakdown."

There was, however, a breakdown in his relationship with Steve Case. Levin said it came down to a simple thing: After the terrorist attacks, Levin wanted to cancel the upcoming board meeting; Case insisted on having it. Levin couldn't understand why. "I'm saying, 'How can we go ahead with the board meeting? The city is in flames.' So we had to make a compromise. We had a telephonic board meeting. From that point on, I just turned off. It just bothered me. My emotions were raw at the time, and there was nothing I could do about that."

Levin also seemed to turn off investors. Shortly after a tour of Ground Zero, a devastated Levin fired off an e-mail to employees, telling them, "Our commitment not just to build our business but to make a difference" was one of the company's "unique resources." Then he told a small group of investors that he intended to devote much of the company's financial resources to the "public trust," in having CNN and other company outlets report the news, and to heck with profits. In retrospect, Levin said, "The role of running the company at times wasn't as important to me as what was going on in the world." But that didn't sit well with investors.

As word spread of Levin's stance on corporate spending, some company officials became alarmed. *Sacrifice profit? Was Levin in his right mind?*

"A lot of people think he cracked, but I think he cracked when he made the [AOL] deal," said a company official.

Levin seemed just as detached from board members. He didn't consult them. He didn't ask their advice. He just went about on his own, as he had with the AOL merger, and pursued a bid to buy AT&T's cable network in the final months of 2001. "He wanted to do whatever he wanted," a company official said. "He did AT&T in secret. He kept [Vice Chairman Ken] Novack and Case out of the loop."

When board members were finally briefed on Levin's cable plans, some let him know they had reservations. The concerns, not surprisingly, were coming from the AOL side of the board, which hadn't been inculcated in the Levin way of doing business, which was to let him run things as he saw fit. The AOL board members also weren't versed in the virtues of the cable business. Why should AOL Time Warner spend tens of billions of dollars on AT&T's cable system when AOL Time Warner already had a major cable network of its own? Case, in particular, wasn't so sure this was the way the company should go, and he let Levin know that during a board meeting in late 2001. Levin immediately cut off Case, dismissing his concerns in what some took to be a bizarre, if not nasty, confrontation. Levin didn't want to school Case and his AOL board peers on the benefits of a cable acquisition, that with AT&T making it the No. 1 cable provider, AOL Time Warner would hold sway over about a third of the market, giving it an unparalleled advantage over competitors in cable-television programming and high-speed Internet service.

"The AOL board members didn't have an appreciation for cable at the time," Levin said. And he admitted, "I wasn't getting along particularly well with some of the AOL folks."

Levin was frustrated by their inability to get it. His people had tried to explain the entertainment and cable businesses. But he felt AOL board members couldn't understand because their experience had been shaped in the technology realm, "honed by a totally AOL-Microsoft world," he said.

The problem was that Levin couldn't just run roughshod over the board and forge ahead, as he had done in the old days when he controlled a Time

Warner—only board. This new AOL Time Warner board was split evenly, fifty-fifty, between AOL and Time Warner board members. A logjam was inevitable. And Levin, already wearing his emotions on his sleeve in the wake of September 11, was running out of patience. "Let's say I wasn't receptive to contrary ideas," he said, "and so there was a fair amount of tension at the time, and then I'm looking at myself and saying, I've got this provision. I'll give six months' notice, and my wife is saying, 'You look like shit.' But one thing I'll tell you clearly, Ted had nothing, had zero impact on me."

A myth has grown up that Ted Turner pounded the boardroom table, complained about Levin, and with the fist slamming set in motion the CEO's ouster. Although Turner did get upset, "Steve was actually the driver" behind Levin's ouster, said a company official close to Case.

Case made a compelling argument to his board peers that Levin's idea of a cable acquisition didn't make good business sense. For one, even if AOL Time Warner won the bidding war to buy AT&T's cable network, Case pointed out, it wasn't clear at all that it would pass muster with U.S. regulators, who had already looked askance at the AOL–Time Warner marriage. Was the company prepared to spend another year in virtual hibernation, awaiting government approval? And even if it was prepared to do so, what about the question of capital? Was the company prepared, Case asked, to expend tens of billions of dollars on this one acquisition, to the exclusion of other acquisitions? Case had been enamored of other potential acquisition targets for some time, including eBay and Amazon. "I had to logically acknowledge that's true," Levin said, "but, of course, I'm an old cable guy, and you were always taught when these systems come around, go for it, no matter what the circumstances are, because if it makes a lot of sense, it's gold."

AOL board members didn't think it made sense. Case and Turner, in particular, presented a formidable duo. But "they did not have the votes to oust" Levin, said one who was close to the boardroom struggle. Under the merger agreement, it would take a vote of at least 75 percent of the board to remove Levin. He still had his Time Warner allies—most of them. But did he want to go on this way? "If the CEO has 60 percent, is that enough to continue?" said a company official. As the cable bid attested, it would be tough going. AOL Time Warner eventually lost out to Comcast for the

AT&T assets. And a friend on the board approached Levin and offered some advice. Although the votes weren't there to give him the boot, it was fairly possible that the board would not renew his contract when it expired at the end of 2003. Levin could fight to restore his support. Or he could script his own departure.

On December 5, 2001, Levin announced his retirement.

In an e-mail to employees, he wrote, "I felt that once my work was completed and I was satisfied with the company's direction and progress, I'd invoke that [six months' notice] provision and turn my full energies to the moral and social issues I feel so passionate about. That time has arrived." He said later, "I'm not just a suit. I want the poetry back in my life."

Off Levin went, in his Lincoln Town Car, for a tour of his old stomping grounds in lower Manhattan.

"I was a little surprised by the timing, that he didn't stay another year," said Vradenburg, AOL Time Warner's former top policy maker. "This guy had constructed what he thought was a company of destiny."

Levin didn't leave without a last parting shot. "Case was the last person he'd step aside for," said a Levin colleague. "He viewed himself, not Case, as the heir of the company. He, not Case, was entrusted to run it." If Levin was stepping down, he was going to make sure the Time Warner legacy, not AOL's, ruled supreme. Like a dying man firing off one final bullet before expiring, Levin helped usher in the man who would succeed him atop AOL Time Warner: Dick Parsons.

Dick *who?*

Richard D. Parsons was born in the shadow of post–World War II America, in Brooklyn's hardscrabble Bedford-Stuyvesant neighborhood. His father Lorenzo was a technician. Isabel, his mother, was a homemaker. Parsons was nurtured in a stable, working-class household. Around the dinner table, the family waged spirited debates, unintentionally honing young Parsons's skill as a verbal jouster. This much, though, was by design: His father pushed him to succeed and his mother made him feel that it was possible. Being black in America was not an insurmountable hurdle, not for Parsons.

Parsons was a gifted child. After skipping two grades in high school, where he was a team debater, he graduated at the age of sixteen. For all of his promise, however, Parsons was a typical teenager. He had no direction. On a whim, he applied to the University of Hawaii—it seemed exotic and fun—and was accepted. There, he joined the debate team, became an average student, and had a rollicking good time, which was the point—until he met a young lady, Laura, who urged him to think about law school. She brought order to his life. Fun, he decided, was no longer a priority. Dick Parsons decided to get serious. In 1968, he and Laura married. Three years later, he graduated as the class valedictorian at Union University's Albany Law School. When he took his bar exam in New York, he didn't just pass. He earned the highest score in the state.

Anything seemed possible for the Brooklyn native. He was considering a career in finance, but someone had other plans for him: Nelson A. Rockefeller. While working as a legislative aide in Albany, young Parsons had caught the attention of the New York governor. Parsons idolized the Republican leader. Rockefeller was fiscally conservative but socially liberal, as Parsons had come to see himself. Rockefeller, he felt, was there to serve the people. So Parsons seized the opportunity to work for him in 1971, serving as assistant counsel. From then on, Parsons's star was latched firmly to Rockefeller's. When Rockefeller became vice president in 1975, Parsons went along as deputy counsel. Then Parsons was appointed general counsel and associate director of President Ford's Domestic Council, spearheading the national policy and coordinating arm of the White House.

It seemed that Parsons was destined for his own run for public office. He ultimately decided it wasn't for him, not if he intended to have any kind of family life. Instead, in 1977, he became a partner in the New York law firm of Patterson, Belknap, Webb & Tyler. The career path proved fruitful. It would set Parsons on a road less traveled, ultimately taking him to a position where he would become one of the most powerful—if not *the* most powerful—black executives in the United States.

It began with the Dime Savings Bank of New York. Parsons served as outside counsel to the thrift, building a close relationship with Harry W. Albright Jr., its chairman and chief executive officer. By 1988, Albright was convinced it was time to bring Parsons in-house. In a landmark appointment, Parsons was named president of the financially troubled bank, becoming the first black to head the 129-year-old institution. This would be the first of many firsts for the trailblazing Parsons, then forty. He didn't expect to become a banker. In fact, he said then, "I didn't think I would be this successful, because I never distinguished myself as a college student." It was a flash of the humility that would mark his career in its steady ascent. But he could not deny, even then, that there was historical magnitude to the moment.

"There is some significance to being a black American in this role in a financial service institution," he said at the time. "There is more riding on how you perform than if it was not a breakthrough." Yet he claimed he did not feel any added responsibility. "I don't feel any more pressure because I am black," he said. "Nobody wants to embarrass themselves." Besides, he added, "I never set out planning or even expecting to fail."

Parsons built on his successes. In 1991, as a corporate chieftain in demand, he was named an outside director on the Time Warner board. Three years later, he was lauded as the savior of the thrift as it merged with another savings and loan, making Dime one of the largest banks in New York. And in 1995, with little else to prove at the thrift, he became a full-time employee of Time Warner, taking the title of president under CEO Jerry Levin. Officially, Parsons was responsible for the media giant's corporate financial activities, legal affairs, corporate communications, and administration. But his real role was to be a loyal aide to Levin, taking a backseat, submerging his own ego, which was not difficult for Parsons, the seasoned politician. He understood his role. He was to be Levin's deal maker, his peacemaker among the warring divisions in the unwieldy, sprawling Time Warner empire. In August 1999, Levin rewarded Parsons by expanding his responsibilities to include oversight of the company's movie studio and music group. It was taken as an unmistakable sign. On the eve of the AOL–Time Warner merger announcement, Dick Parsons was the presumed heir apparent to Levin's throne.

That is, until Bob Pittman arrived.

When AOL Time Warner's executive lineup was announced in early 2000, Parsons was given the title of co–chief operating officer, a post shared with AOL's Pittman. But it was immediately clear that Parsons was to play second fiddle, overseeing a portfolio encompassing less than half of

AOL Time Warner's revenue. With Pittman's PR machine working over-time, vaulting him to the cover of *Business Week* days after the merger was approved in January 2001, Parsons quietly segued into his new role: the forgotten man.

"It did seem for a while that Dick was checked out," said a former company official.

At fifty-two, Parsons had apparently peaked.

He played the part of diminishing executive well. At six-foot-four, Parsons would seem to cut an imposing figure, yet he had always turned mass to mush, presenting himself as a big old teddy bear who readily moved past the handshake to the hug. There was nothing threatening about the man: His salt-and-pepper beard looked professorial and his silky-smooth baritone voice inspired confidence. Topping it off was a self-deprecating manner, which seemed to grow the higher up the corporate ladder he rose. The father of three once said, "One of my kids gave me a T-shirt that said, 'I MAY NOT BE BRIGHT, BUT I CAN LIFT HEAVY THINGS.'" A jazz aficionado, Parsons served on the Apollo Theater Foundation and used some of his $4.75 million bonus in 1999 to buy a "small" vineyard in Italy's Tuscany region. But he described himself as a "lunch-pail guy."

The lunch-pail guy played his cards right.

While Pittman was getting all the press, Parsons was working behind the scenes, where it really counted. Levin had always liked Parsons. For several years, he had considered Parsons CEO material. Levin, however, never thought of Pittman that way. He respected Pittman as a masterful day-to-day operator, which is why he gave him so much operational responsibility over the company, but Levin didn't view Pittman as a leader or a consensus builder. "I never thought that Bob would ever be the CEO," Levin said. "I had been working on succession at Time Warner for three years, and Dick was emerging as the lead candidate." Others noticed Levin's chilliness toward Pittman. "I never got the feeling that he liked Bob," said a former company official. "He always referred to him as 'Pittman,'" not by his first name. Pittman hurt his own cause when his handlers, headed by PR maestro Kenny Lerer, continued to position their man as the guy really pulling the levers of the new company—not Levin, not Case, and certainly not Parsons. Levin wasn't pleased. Add to that the new company began to falter financially in the spring of 2001, as

Pittman's call for companywide synergy seemed to generate more flash than substance.

Into this roiling mix, Parsons stepped.

His timing couldn't have been better. In the spring, Parsons notified his boss that he was being recruited to be the CEO of Philip Morris, the food and tobacco giant. It was a bombshell. It also forced Levin's hand. He didn't want to lose Parsons, not at this critical time in AOL Time Warner's young history. Levin pleaded with Parsons to stay. As an inducement, he took Parsons aside and confided that he, Levin, had inserted a provision in his employment contract that gave him an early out. With Levin facing his own problems in the corporate suites, a pincer movement from the combined forces of Steve Case and Ted Turner, Levin saw an elegant way out: elevate Parsons to CEO. It wouldn't take much convincing of the board. He could get the members' buy-in. Parsons was a popular guy. He was a consensus builder, the kind of executive who could help bridge the cultural divide between AOL and Time Warner, already a concern of the board. Pittman, for all of his success, only seemed to inspire jealousy. And Pittman's star was already beginning to fade under the failed promises of the merger, including those aggressive financial targets he had pushed so hard.

Some board members sensed a move afoot. But now Levin had to move quickly or he might lose the advantage of time, as he faced his own imminent departure. In the final weeks of 2001, Levin wandered across the executive suites, popped his head into Parsons's office, and announced, "Dick, you're ready, and I'm ready."

On his way down the hallway, where the board of directors was about to vote to make him chief executive officer, Parsons was greeted by a heckler from the AOL side of the house: David Colburn. As Parsons was passing, Colburn, the brash deal maker, yelled out an expletive. "It was hateful but it was funny," said one familiar with the exchange. "He was making fun of him right before he walked into the boardroom."

In keeping with character, Parsons just ambled along.

Parsons was never considered a media visionary like Ted Turner. He didn't sell himself as some kind of corporate innovator, as Steve Case did. He never offered himself up as an industry savant, as Jerry Levin had come to be known. "I don't think he's a dynamic person who makes things move," said a former company official. "But he's good at nudging in a direction. He's not a revolutionary kind of guy. But people love talking to him." And, unlike many of his peers, he was still standing, a rarity of sorts in AOL Time Warner's dagger-filled corporate suites.

Dick Parsons was named CEO, effective May 2002. With his wife, the lunch-pail guy toasted his promotion with a Cohiba Esplendido cigar and a $400 bottle of 1963 Taylor port.

Ted Turner celebrated, too. The media mogul, who seemed all set to leave, suddenly had a change of heart. With Levin on the way out, the diplomatic Parsons offered a chance for Turner to renew his contract in December 2001. He took it.

Turner was back in the game.

Steve Case opened the new year with a new mission: to show he was still engaged.

In January 2002, company handlers decided it was time to trot out the largely invisible chairman for a round of media interviews. It was always a difficult negotiation for reporters to get Case on the phone, let alone in person. The PR people dispensed Case in small doses and only when necessary. Now, it was necessary. A lot had been going on. In its first year as a new company, the great experiment that was AOL Time Warner had undergone major upheavals with Levin's departure, a plummeting stock, and an economic downturn that forced the company to abandon its aggressive growth targets. Now, in the midst of this mess, everyone was asking: Where is Case?

To answer that question, Case held court from his office in AOL Time Warner's headquarters, under the watchful gaze of Time Inc. founder Henry Luce, whose portrait hung on Case's wall.

"I am intellectually engaged," said the forty-three-year-old executive, who had discarded his more recent boardroom suits for a vintage AOL look. He was wearing pressed khakis, an open-neck blue dress shirt, and a navy blazer. *When in trouble, think nostalgic.* During an interview, Case worked hard to seem at ease, talking about his role as the company's diplomat in Europe and China. And, in a barely veiled slap at Levin and Pittman, who had been the most vocal about the company's aggressive financial targets, Case expressed dismay. "It's obviously a disappointment to everybody that we were not able to meet our financial targets in this first year," he said. "Maybe we shouldn't have set it that high."

Case, however, was less at ease when it came to a personal subject dear to him: the grave illness of his best friend and big brother, Dan. That's when Case would reflexively twiddle a bottled-water cap. "He got a bad diagnosis, but he's a fighter," Case said.

Dan Case, a renowned investment banker at San Francisco's Hambrecht & Quist, had resigned to undergo brain surgery in early 2001. Since then, AOL Time Warner watchers wondered whether Steve Case was distracted from the business at hand. He tried to squelch that theory, saying it was "overstated." He did say, however, that he visited Dan about once a month while he was undergoing chemotherapy in San Francisco. Case also took a vacation that summer with his older brother and bought a house a few doors down from him so that he could be closer. He quipped that the place had turned into "sort of like a commune" packed with family and friends. It wasn't funny, though. Case didn't enjoy the spotlight, even though he had become accustomed to it. He still didn't like public speaking. And he certainly didn't like being interviewed by the media. It was bad enough to have to talk about the struggles of the company he helped build, but discussing his dying brother was even more onerous. At the end of the seventy-minute interview, he lifted his arms in a stretch, displaying armpits drenched in sweat.

Case could be forgiven for betraying his nerves. Things were about to get much worse.

On January 7, in a reversal from the brash predictions of Levin, the company offered an anemic preview of its financial performance in the just-ended fourth quarter, for all of 2002 and possibly beyond, blaming a stalled economy that it didn't expect to recover anytime soon.

Parsons disclosed a whopper that day: AOL Time Warner would take a one-time noncash charge in the first quarter of 2002 of $40 billion to $60 billion, the largest ever taken by a corporation. The charge arose from new accounting rules about goodwill, a term for how much a deal's purchase price exceeds the book value of the acquired company's assets. Under old accounting rules, companies wrote down goodwill over several decades. But under new accounting rules, companies were required to discontinue the amortization of goodwill.

Parsons was quick to point out that it was a paper figure that had no bearing on the company's cash flow or day-to-day operations. But the big charge held a significant symbolic value: At the height of the Internet frenzy, AOL had used its inflated stock price to pay dearly for Time Warner.

A few weeks later, in late January, more bad news arrived, and it wasn't just on paper. The fourth quarter had been another stinker. When AOL Time Warner reported a tepid 4 percent revenue gain, investors reacted with alarm, pushing the stock down to $26.40, AOL's lowest level in more than three years. The best that Parsons could offer about the results was this: He had warned of bad financial results, and here they were, as expected.

There were no surprises when the company disclosed in March the specific amount of the noncash charge it would take: $54 billion. Wall Street shrugged it off. Parsons managed to raise more eyebrows with a seemingly minor directive. He rescinded a Pittman order forbidding employees to use rival e-mail software. Cheers erupted from certain quarters of the Time Warner side of the house. They would no longer be forced to use AOL's balky e-mail program.

Parsons was in command. This was his company, not Pittman's. If there were any doubts, Parsons put them to rest in early April when he removed Barry Schuler as chairman and chief executive of AOL, the now-struggling on-line unit, and replaced him, temporarily, with Pittman. The company tried to pass off the management change as a way to play to both men's strengths, but the facts suggested something else. Schuler was going from running a division with about eighteen thousand employees to a new group, with no staff, focused on technology products for the future.

"When you don't need to work, you don't get demoted," Schuler said then, referring to the freedom afforded by his personal wealth amassed at AOL.

Although Pittman retained his title as co–chief operating officer of AOL Time Warner, there was no mistaking what was going on: He was being dispatched from New York to Dulles to fix a brewing problem. On-line subscription growth was leveling off, advertising sales were dropping, and the vaunted synergies he had been praising weren't materializing. Pittman, the erstwhile media darling, was strangely silent about his new assignment. What went unsaid was this: Parsons had ordered Pittman down to Dulles. And Pittman didn't want to go.

Though he claimed he never wanted to be CEO, Pittman's ego had been bruised when he was passed over in favor of Parsons. Pittman, however, was a realist, and he understood that his support had been eroding since the spring. Executives from the Time Warner side were fed up with him. They were tired of his meetings. They didn't want to hear about synergy anymore. They started to ignore his directives, undermining his authority.

"It wasn't a coup," said a company official. "I would call it a psychological coup, or a subconscious coup, where all these guys were on the same side and said, 'Gee, if we all ignore him, there won't be any punishment.' The gang of dissonance became bigger and bigger."

On top of that, Pittman began to squabble with Case over strategy that spring. Pittman continued to emphasize ramping up advertising deals that AOL cut directly with chief executives of other firms. Case argued that the division was veering off course by allowing itself to be driven by profitable but ill-conceived deals, including intrusive pop-up ads, instead of focusing on subscribers. Case had never liked on-line advertising. It despoiled the medium.

Before long, Case subtly began to withdraw his support of Pittman, using his backchannel of supporters to suggest that Case wasn't happy. Part of Case's assessment was a practical consideration: Don't be associated with a sinking ship. "Steve saw that Bob was vulnerable, he was pushed to the brink," a company official said. But there was another factor at play: They had never liked each other. "There was no love lost there," said a company official who knew both men well. "There was always tension in that relationship."

The tension went back years. From the moment Pittman arrived at AOL in 1996, Case resented the media adulation heaped on his number two for helping to save AOL from an overstrained network that couldn't handle all of its customer traffic on-line. Case, said some of his colleagues, felt as though he was being overshadowed all over again by a big brother who was more dashing and less nerdy. "Steve wants to be that guy [Pittman]," said a company official.

Kenny Lerer, the PR hand brought in by Pittman, always cautioned his people not to upstage Case. *We don't want to give the impression that Bob is rescuing what Steve ruined,* he would tell people in AOL's PR shop. Many at the company were aware of Case's sensitivity. If Pittman appeared on television, Case often pouted about it. Some said Case was goaded on by his wife, Jean, the company's former PR executive, who wanted to ensure the preservation of her husband's image. "She was not necessarily in the building, but she always had a role, or say, in what he did," said a former company official. "Steve was sensitive to the media coverage that Bob got. He was sensitive to the concept that Bob saved the company." Pittman, aware of this, often imposed a moratorium on profiles about himself, although apparently not often enough. "He always believed it was Steve's company, but Steve didn't believe that," said the former official. "Steve's nutty that way. He takes things personally. He always sees a conspiracy, even when there is none."

Pittman, for his part, tried to hide his distaste for Case. Sometimes, Pittman found that difficult. In 1996, just as AOL was beginning to sell on-line ads, Case taunted Myer Berlow, his top ad man, about how Internet rival Yahoo! was producing better ad results. "Yahoo! kicked your ass," Case poked. Berlow flew in a rage up to Pittman's office, ranting about what Case had just said. Pittman turned to Berlow and said, with a flash in his one good eye, "Don't listen to him. He's an asshole."

"What?" responded Berlow, stunned by Pittman's rare candor.

"Never mind," Pittman said.

And he slipped back into his inscrutable mask, Brand Bob.

Around that time, Pittman also confronted Case, telling him to stop meddling in the day-to-day operations of the on-line service. He felt that Case was undermining his authority when, for example, Case would call a software programmer and say he didn't like a particular Web page on the on-line service. Pittman wanted Case to follow the chain of command, not dive several levels down into the company and make a unilateral change. "Stop fucking doing this," Pittman said. "If I leave, your company is dead."

Case backed off. He was smart enough to know that in Pittman he had a strong operating executive. "As much as Steve might have chafed, he had to leave Bob alone," said a former official. "It was working."

Until the spring of 2002.

With the on-line division hobbling, Wall Street analysts began to suggest that AOL Time Warner's stock—then trading at about $20—would be higher if the Internet division were subtracted from the equation. Its market capitalization had shrunk to about $100 billion, down nearly $50 billion since Levin had announced his resignation. Translation: Was AOL, what Levin had called the "crown jewel," now dragging down the whole company? That's when Parsons, the CEO-designate, intervened, ordering Pittman to Dulles. Parsons's view was that Pittman had fixed AOL before in the 1990s; he could fix it again. Case, however, had a different view. Case *himself* wanted to be the one to save the day. He wanted to fix the ailing division. "He thought he should be the guy sent down," said a former official. Case's greatest fear was that if Pittman fixed AOL again, "he'll get the credit all over again," said the former official.

By going down to Dulles, Pittman was infuriating Case. But he had no choice. Parsons, the new boss, had spoken.

"Are you okay with it?" a colleague asked Pittman just after the announcement was made.

"I didn't want to do it," he said, "but now that it's announced, I'm excited about it."

Whether he was regurgitating another Brand Bob aphorism, this much he knew: It was the penultimate moment for him at AOL Time Warner. If he didn't fix the on-line division, he knew that he shouldn't bother coming back to New York.

Dick Parsons had been reluctant to push hard on his own agenda until he was officially crowned CEO at the May 2002 annual shareholder meeting. But as that day approached, he began to put his stamp on AOL Time Warner. Among his first acts: a repudiation of the basic raison d'être of the merger itself.

In the opening days of May, Parsons made it clear to his direct reports that "convergence" was out and "best in class" was in. In other words, Parsons didn't want his division heads focusing on synergy anymore. He didn't want them laboring over how to meld AOL's digital technology with Time Warner's hard entertainment assets. Instead, he wanted his divisions to burrow ahead and become the best in their own market. For Time Warner Music, that meant beating its rivals in the music business. Warner Bros. was supposed to romp in the movie business. Same for the television people. It was more than a rebuff of AOL's Case and Pittman; it was a return to the old Time Warner way. As if to underscore who was calling the shots, at an investment conference Parsons explained that although he appreciated Case's input, the chairman was more engaged in strategy having to do with the "five- to ten-year horizon." Parsons was focused on the present.

On May 16, 2002, Parsons kicked off his reign as CEO with a more relaxed and polished style than that of Levin, his prickly predecessor. Wearing his Sunday best charcoal gray suit and gold tie, Parsons glad-handed investors as they entered the front hallway of Harlem's famed Apollo Theater for AOL Time Warner's annual shareholder meeting. Those he knew, he called out by name. He offered others a broad smile. There was, in the moment, more of the feel of a politician currying votes than a CEO taking over the world's largest media company. But it made sense. The company's stock was in full retreat, down about 40 percent since the beginning of the year, hovering at an anemic $18 and change.

Parsons tried to win over the crowd. Taking a playful turn on the Apollo's gilded stage, he rubbed his rump against the "Tree of Hope," a tree stump touched for good luck by past entertainers at the landmark theater such as Ella Fitzgerald and Sammy Davis, Jr.

"So we're good to go, right?" he quipped.

Many investors, several hundred of whom turned out at the Apollo to get a close-up of the new man in charge, didn't seem amused. One railed against the year-and-a-half-old merger, saying, "We were conned into this," calling the deal "pure hot air." Another demanded to know what executives were doing to prevent the stock from dropping even further. A repentant Steve Case told investors, "This past year has been difficult, and things didn't quite go the way we expected." He assured them, however, "This company—your company—is getting its house in order." Parsons tried to explain that the stock had been walloped by the national recession, which had weakened the advertising market, a key growth driver for AOL Time Warner. The new CEO, however, offered several short-term priorities to get the company back on track. These included revitalizing the on-line division and guarding "the integrity of our balance sheet," a reference to a rash of accounting scandals plaguing other companies.

After the meeting, shareholders and reporters rushed up to the lip of the stage, demanding more answers of Parsons. When asked whether he was aware of any concerns or questions about AOL's accounting, he said no. Pressed for a fuller answer, Parsons snapped, "I said, 'No.'"

The teddy bear sounded more like a grizzly.

Within a week, Parsons consolidated his power. In a staff memo, he announced his new team. Robert M. Kimmitt, executive vice president of global and strategic policy, and William Raduchel, the chief technology officer, would now report to him. Case was shorn of even more responsibilities; before, Kimmitt and Raduchel had reported to him. Parsons also removed Kenny Lerer as head of the company's PR operation; Lerer, a Pittman loyalist, otherwise known as a "Friend of Bob," was replaced by one of his direct reports: Ed Adler, a longtime Time Warner official. Adler had run Time Warner's PR shop before the merged company was assembled. Now, Adler was back in charge and Lerer was given the amorphous role of running the newly created Office of the CEO. Lerer tried to put the best face on it, saying that this was a role he had sought out. But there was little mistaking that Time Warner forces were retaking the proverbial hill from AOL.

For Case, things only got worse.

On June 24, his brother passed away. Dan Case was forty-four. He finally succumbed to brain cancer. At the funeral at San Francisco's Grace Cathedral, the younger Case said that, one day, he would meet Dan in heaven, where they could resume their boyhood business, Case Enterprises.

Reminiscing, Case talked about how he had always played the role of entrepreneur, while Dan was the financier. Steve would invariably be broke. Dan would give him financial assistance. Steve would use that aid to buy out his older brother, at a premium. Then the younger brother would lose interest in the make-believe venture, and Dan, seizing the opportunity, would buy back the business at a discount.

For years, Steve Case had depended on Dan. It was the elder brother who had given the younger the job at the company that became AOL. Dan had introduced Steve to Ted Leonsis, the executive who played a crucial role in AOL's successful fight against Microsoft in the early days. Dan, by all accounts, was a brilliant business mind and investment banker who had helped to fund the growth of Silicon Valley, playing a key role in the creation of such Internet stalwarts as Netscape and Amazon. He would be missed—but by none more than his little brother. Dan had always been there for him. But now, Steve Case was on his own.

On June 14, 2002, this reporter became a part of the story. On that day, I hand-delivered a letter to the company describing my yearlong investigation into a series of unconventional business practices at AOL, which *The Washington Post* was preparing to publish.

In the letter were details about a variety of unorthodox business transactions that had inflated AOL's revenue before and after its takeover of Time Warner. Company officials were quoted as saying that some of the transactions were designed to prop up AOL's finances as a means to preserve its merger with Time Warner. The deals, corroborated by hundreds of confidential company documents, involved Sun Microsystems, Wembley, Telefónica, Homestore, PurchasePro, the Golf Channel, and eBay, among others. All the transactions were approved by David Colburn, AOL's top deal maker, who reported directly to Bob Pittman.

Already, things were looking grim for Pittman. After Parsons's ascension to CEO, Pittman had become the sole chief operating officer. But he was losing ground. Parsons had dispatched him to Dulles to fix the AOL mess, and the task was looking more intractable than Pittman had expected. Ad revenue showed no signs of improving. The company's stock was in free fall. That June, its market cap had fallen under $90 billion from $240 billion in January 2001. What's more, the resistance to Pittman's call for companywide synergy had coalesced into outright revolt. The Time Warner division heads simply decided to tune him out.

"No one would follow him," said a company executive. "Below him, they didn't listen."

For many Time Warner employees, whose retirement savings had evaporated along with the company's plunging stock, their anger was focused in one direction: at Pittman.

"Bob was a lightning rod," said a company official.

The *Washington Post* letter, which began to circulate among executives at AOL Time Warner, inspired another visceral reaction: Some on the Time Warner side of the company took it as proof that Pittman and his AOL cohorts had hidden their financial weakness and bamboozled Time

Warner into the biggest merger in U.S. history, and now the whole thing was turning into a disaster.

"They knew their ship was a piece of shit, it was so fucking amazing it makes me sick," said a Time Warner official. "They're hiding behind what they know is a hairline fracture. It's beyond unconscionable. They did that to manipulate the deal. But when we pulled the hood up, it was too late."

The reaction of another influential Time Warner official was to get rid of all the key AOL executives: "Throw them out," he said.

Such talk turned into a groundswell among Time Warner forces that Parsons couldn't ignore. "Dick would hear it every day from his [division] CEOs," said a colleague. " 'Get rid of Pittman.' "

Parsons counseled patience. Always the politician, he was looking for the most elegant solution that would ruffle the fewest feathers. He didn't want to force the issue. "Let them leave of their own accord," he told a friend. "They'll all go." But Parsons quickly came to another conclusion. "He knew then he needed a new [management] team," said a company official.

Parsons always got along with Pittman, but now Parsons didn't feel he needed him anymore. It was a practical calculation: Several executives wanted Pittman's head. "There was a huge outcry," said a company official. "Time Warner people would've gone on the equivalent of a work strike, and they never would've rallied around Dick, if he had kept Bob on."

There was, however, a key consideration: Where did Steve Case stand?

The chairman let it be known he would offer no resistance to Pittman's departure. "Steve wouldn't object to it," said an associate.

Pittman thought there was time to salvage the situation. Over the July Fourth weekend, he considered his options. Friends outlined what should have been evident to him, but wasn't—he had lost. That Parsons, when he was named CEO, had won. That alone would have been reason enough for Pittman to check out. But he was all too familiar with a rash of other problems enveloping him: Case's receding support, the revolt from the division heads, and now the *Washington Post* letter. Still, Pittman thought he might be able to hang on. Not all was lost—or was it?

On July 7, a *New York Times* headline blared, "A Media Giant Needs a Script." It read, in part, "executives and shareholders are united in more or less open revolt, with much of the anger internally focused on Robert W. Pittman, the chief operating officer."

Pittman, keenly sensitive to his media image, was devastated by the public undressing. It was, however, only the first of a one-two punch. The second withering article appeared in *The Wall Street Journal* five days later. Speculating on Pittman's future at the company, the article said, "people close to Mr. Pittman say the 48-year-old executive is growing tired of the pressures at AOL Time Warner, leaving open the possibility that he will choose to leave the company altogether rather than return to the New York headquarters."

Pittman was miserable. "He hated coming to work every morning," said a colleague. Shortly after the *Journal* piece ran, he dropped his guard for a moment, confiding to a colleague, "It's not so much fun."

Then, he was Bob Pitchman again. At an industry trade conference, he gave a rousing speech about—of all things—synergy, talking off the cuff for about an hour about the incredible promise of combining the forces of old media and new media. Maybe he was inspired by a sense of freedom. The end, he knew, was near.

Kenny Lerer, until recently his PR man, advised Pittman as much. Lerer, a veteran of corporate crises, understood how this drama would unfold. "Kenny was telling Bob, 'You're not going to survive this, not now,'" said an associate of both men.

Pittman figured there was one last resort: Parsons. If he still had the CEO's support, then all could be saved. So he decided to feel him out.

"You know, maybe I've had enough," Pittman told Parsons.

Parsons, as if expecting this moment, readily agreed. "That's fine."

"There was no resistance," said a company official familiar with the conversation.

It wasn't the reaction Pittman had hoped for. He had hoped for reassurance, that it was okay, that it would blow over, that Parsons wanted him to stick around. Instead, Parsons agreed that it was time for Pittman to go.

Pittman was left to preserve whatever remained of his reputation. He authorized Lerer to help negotiate an artful exit for him, including how Pittman's resignation was phrased in a press release. Pittman wasn't in a fighting mood anymore.

"It was very unpleasant for him," said a colleague. "He was concerned about his image. He had had enough. He was tired of the bad press."

Once Pittman effectively gave himself up to Parsons, the new CEO moved quickly to reorganize his management team. One of his first calls was to Jeff Bewkes, the outspoken HBO chief who had challenged Case during that executives' meeting in the spring. Bewkes had never believed in the merger. In the mid-1990s, he had turned down the opportunity to become president of AOL before Pittman took the job. Instead, he had played his hand at Time Warner, and it turned out to be a good move. A graduate of Yale University, where he earned his undergraduate degree, and Stanford Graduate School of Business, where he got his MBA, Bewkes had run a vineyard, then worked at Citibank before he joined HBO in 1979 as a marketing manager. Since then, he had climbed up the corporate ladder, becoming the pay-channel's no-nonsense CEO in 1995, building it into a huge moneymaking and Emmy-winning machine. Now, Parsons wanted the witty, lanky executive to help salvage the company. He told Bewkes that he planned to reorganize AOL Time Warner. It would be swift and dramatic, and he wanted the fifty-year-old HBO honcho to play a key role.

About five days before AOL Time Warner's scheduled meeting of the board of directors on July 18 in Dulles, Parsons began to piece together his team, consulting with key figures, including Don Logan, the Time Inc. CEO since 1994, who had also been a voice of skepticism about AOL. Logan, circumspect but decisive, was still remembered for calling Time Warner's digital efforts in the mid-1990s a financial "black hole." The burly fifty-eight-year-old Alabama native was renowned for his cost cutting and making Time Inc. an incredibly consistent earner for the parent company.

"Dick had in his mind a rough idea of what he wanted in the structure [of the company's management] and how he wanted to do it," said a colleague. "It came about in a hurry."

Parsons also took pains to garner the support of Steve Case. On the Tuesday before the Thursday board meeting, Parsons took Case out for dinner with Bewkes and Logan. Together, they attempted to win the chairman's support. Though Case wouldn't stand in the way of Pittman's departure, he was concerned that Parsons was assembling a top team composed solely of Time Warner people, effectively shutting out AOL, except for Case himself. He didn't like it, but he didn't have a choice. When all else failed, Parsons's persuasion was left to this: As CEO, he held the power to shuffle management as he saw fit. Such a move did not require board action.

"Case reluctantly went along," said a company official.

By the time the AOL Time Warner board convened in Dulles, it was a done deal. There would be no debate. The meeting, carefully choreographed, would go forward without a hitch. Pittman's departure would be a formality. In the end, said an official, "Bob put his hand up." That afternoon, Parsons scrambled to figure out the specific titles of newly appointed executives. But the rest, said an official, "was preordained."

On July 18, 2002, the day of the AOL Time Warner board meeting, all hell broke loose.

That Thursday morning, the first article of my two-part series ran in *The Washington Post:* "Unconventional Transactions Boosted Sales," the headline read. "Amid Big Merger, Company Resisted Dot-Com Collapse." That afternoon, Robert W. Pittman, forty-eight, announced his resignation.

At the same time, the company announced a major reorganization: AOL Time Warner was being restructured into two new groups, the heads of which would report directly to Parsons. Don Logan would lead a new Media & Communications Group, which included AOL, Time Inc., Time Warner Cable, the AOL Time Warner Book Group, and Interactive Video unit. Jeff Bewkes, the HBO chairman, would become chairman of the Entertainment & Networks Group, comprising HBO, New Line Cinema, the WB television network, Turner Networks, Warner Bros. pictures, and Warner Music.

The three top corporate officers of AOL Time Warner—Case's dinner partners a few nights earlier—were Time Warner men. Case alone remained as the top AOL brass, but as chairman, his was a nonexecutive role. Even more startling, AOL, the on-line division, Case's baby, the Internet firm that had acquired Time Warner in the nation's largest takeover, was suddenly no longer even its *own* unit. AOL was subsumed, gobbled up in the Time Warner vortex, nothing more than a unit of a *division* of the company.

"It was like the Mongolian invasion of China," said a major player in the merger. "It was a takeover from within."

A day after the announcement, Pittman seemed at peace. "I'm glad to be out of there," he told a friend. "I can't take one more day of Steve [Case]."

With the loss of much of their retirement savings in the company's downward spiraling stock price, Time Warner people continued to rage. To many, Pittman's departure left only one other AOL executive in need of retirement: Steve Case.

Influential money manager Gordon Crawford wasn't happy with Case. Crawford's firm, Los Angeles–based Capital Research & Management, had lost hundreds of million of dollars by investing in the troubled media giant, much of the loss coming after the merger. For Crawford, the last straw came when he read in *The Washington Post* about how AOL had inflated its revenue before and after its merger with Time Warner.

In August, the powerful money manager boarded an airplane and headed east, prepared to take matters into his own hands. When he landed in New York, the senior vice president of Capital Research let his feelings be known in person in Case's office at Rockefeller Plaza. Without mincing words, Crawford sat down and told Case he no longer had the support of many shareholders, or of his own employees, according to those familiar with the conversation. Case, Crawford told him bluntly, should resign.

Case seemed momentarily thrown by the request, maybe even shocked. But he recovered quickly and stood his ground.

"I'm sticking around," he told Crawford.

Then, Case became defensive, telling Crawford he was not responsible for the company's problems. How could he, Case, be blamed for a national drop in advertising that was affecting all media businesses? He seemed to suggest that it was the problem of other executives who were on watch—people like Jerry Levin, Bob Pittman, and David Colburn, the notorious deal maker.

A day later, Case the conciliator called Crawford. This was not the defensive Case. He thanked Crawford for visiting, for being forthright, for not going behind his back. Case was going to be out on the West Coast in a couple of weeks, and he suggested they get together and figure out how to fix this mess.

"It was," said one familiar with the conversation, "the beginning of Steve's campaigning."

If so, it was a long-shot candidacy. In the days after the accounting scandal broke, AOL's stock plunged even lower, falling into the single digits for the first time since the fall of 1998. Shares were down about 70 percent since the merger had been completed. Investors were stampeding for the exit door. The company's market cap had plummeted to about $42 billion—about $200 billion less than its market value in January 2001, when the merger became official. Meanwhile, a blizzard of class-action lawsuits was filed on behalf of investors against AOL Time Warner and its top executives, citing the alleged accounting improprieties. By late July, there was speculation the company would effectively dump the AOL division, making it a separately traded unit, so that it would no longer be a millstone around the neck of Time Warner and its plummeting stock price.

The company insisted it had no such plans. Nonetheless, many on the Time Warner side were beginning to think it was high time to dump the AOL name, if not the division itself, and restore the company name to Time Warner. Overlooking AOL, though, was becoming difficult to do. On July 24, AOL Time Warner disclosed that the SEC had launched a civil investigation into its accounting practices. "After the [*Washington Post*] articles came out, the SEC informed us that they are conducting a fact-finding inquiry," Parsons said in a conference call with Wall Street analysts and the media. Parsons remained confident that its accounting was proper, saying that all of the deals examined by *The Washington Post* had been reviewed and confirmed by AOL Time Warner's outside auditor, Ernst & Young. Parsons, however, vowed to give investors a better understanding of the business, beginning with more detailed disclosures about its on-line division, including its advertising and commerce revenue. "Investor trust," he said, is "fundamental to our future."

Less than a week later, the company confirmed that the Justice Department had opened a criminal investigation of AOL's accounting practices. Meanwhile, the company launched its own internal probe of AOL's accounting, hiring outside attorneys from Cravath, Swaine & Moore, Time Warner's old law firm, to lead the way. Things were beginning to fall apart. Myer Berlow, the AOL ad executive, retained counsel in connection with SEC investigations of companies that did business with AOL. So did David Colburn, AOL's top deal maker. By early August, the SEC expanded its probe, investigating AOL's former business relationship with PurchasePro, the Las Vegas firm. Before long, PurchasePro would fall into bankruptcy. Then on August 13, Colburn, the AOL deal maker who had approved all of the unconventional ad deals, was locked out of his office at Dulles headquarters and fired. Berlow would eventually be squeezed out of an operational role, negotiating a job as a company consultant that left him with little to do. And business affairs—Colburn's infamous band of aggressive deal makers, the people who had orchestrated all of those unorthodox deals—was quickly dismantled, with its one hundred or so employees dispersed to different departments across the company.

There would be no more BA.

A day later, the company disclosed that at least $49 million in deals at the troubled on-line division had been "inappropriately recognized as advertising and commerce revenues." The disclosure coincided with a new deadline for chief executives to certify the accuracy of their company's accounting. (The SEC had advocated this new law in response to a series of corporate accounting scandals.) That day, Parsons issued an e-mail to employees, saying, "And, of course, there is no room at this company for any unethical behavior. We must hold ourselves to a higher standard." Although the company didn't disclose the specific deals that accounted for the $49 million in improper revenue, one of those deals involved World-Com, the troubled telecommunications company that the SEC had already charged with defrauding investors.

The bad news heaped on top of bad news begged a question: Would Steve Case resign?

Many at Time Warner already blamed Case for being the architect of what was quickly shaping up as a catastrophic merger. Some had lost small fortunes when AOL Time Warner's stock price wiped out the value of their options. The fury over Case, though, peaked with the disclosures of improper dealings at AOL. Some shareholders felt duped by Case, who had made tens of millions of dollars in the sale of company stock while they had held on to their rapidly diminishing investment. At the very least, many at Time Warner felt that Case should take responsibility for the aggressive culture at the on-line division that resulted in the improper ad deals. In private, Case continued to insist that he had not known anything about those deals, that he had been preoccupied with other pressing matters, like getting the merger approved and then focusing on big-picture strategy.

Not everyone was convinced.

The skeptics included Ted Turner. He never disliked Case; the two men had invested together in a health food business. But after reading about AOL's unorthodox deals in *The Washington Post* while traveling in Paris, Turner flew into a rage. He felt that AOL may have misled Time Warner into the merger, and he thought that Case should have known what was going on.

"If he [Case] didn't, Ted felt that's even worse," said a company official.

A longtime associate offered Case some advice: apologize. "Say sorry to Time Warner," the associate urged the chairman.

Case simply changed the subject.

By mid-September, Ted Turner appeared to be emerging from a deep depression following his divorce from Jane Fonda and the loss of his day job at AOL Time Warner. He was hard of hearing and approaching senior citizen status, but suddenly, the old maverick was showing more pep in his step. He wasn't taking anti-depressants anymore. He was showing up in the company's New York offices more frequently. He wasn't as big a billionaire as he used to be, but he was still worth an estimated $2 billion. Even more important, Ted Turner had a purpose now: Case's removal.

Case needed only three allies on the fourteen-member board to retain his chairmanship, and, for the moment, he had at least that many votes in his pocket. The September 19 board meeting in New York came and went, and Steve Case's future at the company did not come up at the meeting. But the fight over Case's future—a struggle over the heart and soul of the company—was just beginning.

When Case showed up at the Emmy Awards in September, eyebrows were raised—Time Warner eyebrows, that is.

What, some wondered, *was he doing seating himself in a row near the front with Dick Parsons and other Time Warner executives?* Never mind that he was still chairman of their company, AOL Time Warner. This, they felt, was their territory. This was a Time Warner event, not an AOL function. *How could Case have the audacity to count himself among us?*

If Case realized he was an unwelcome guest, he didn't let on. After the awards ceremony, he attended—*crashed,* if you asked some Time Warner people—an HBO party at a swank Beverly Hills restaurant. An immediate whisper buzzed through the room.

"This guy is shameless," said a company official. "I can't even look at him."

Case, however, wasn't done.

The following morning, at 8:30 A.M., he arranged a breakfast meeting in the executive dining room of Warner Bros., the company's high-powered movie studio, in Burbank. The meeting had all the accoutrements of a Hollywood power breakfast—about a dozen studio executives ate eggs, bagels, and fresh juice served on white linen by waiters wearing ties bearing the studio imprimatur: Looney Tunes cartoon characters.

But the gathering had little of the studio glamour, if only because of the somber mood. Case, back in his preppy mode, sat, midtable, humble but unapologetic. He did, however, admit that he was remiss in not keeping a closer eye on AOL during the lengthy period when he was focused on consummating the merger in 2000. He also said he was preoccupied with personal matters, including the illness of his older brother. But now, he wanted to put that behind him. "I am the chairman of the company," he reminded them. And he promised that he was fully engaged and eager to fix whatever was broken at the on-line division.

The response? Tepid.

Nobody wanted to challenge Case. It wasn't polite. "I don't think anyone was necessarily convinced he was our great leader and necessarily turning things around," said a company official familiar with the meeting. "But no one threw any barbs."

One executive, however, asked Case to look around the room as a way to make a point: Many of the attendees were over the age of fifty. They didn't have a lot of time to turn things around, not if they hoped to salvage their retirement savings, which had been disappearing with the company's plunging stock price. This, here, wasn't the Internet. Then someone respectfully explained they had to leave, saying, "We have to get back to work, sir."

Case continued his one-man road show, defending himself and the merger in meetings in New York in early October. There, at an industry conference, he drew inspiration from a great British leader who faced his own dark days. "Some of you may have seen *The Gathering Storm,* a recent HBO film about Winston Churchill—a man who knew a little something about the relationship between risk and opportunity," Case said. "Churchill once said, 'The pessimist sees difficulty in every opportunity. The optimist sees opportunity in every difficulty.' Needless to say, I am in full agreement with Mr. Churchill." Case went on to draw the connection: "The idea of AOL Time Warner is the right idea—and in my view, we're now taking the right steps to capitalize on the promise of this great company."

Privately, he was feeling less rosy. At the age of forty-four, Steve Case was fighting for his corporate life. He was tense. He was jumpy. "He looks terrible," said one of his associates who bumped into a fatigued Case and his wife that fall. Others said the chairman was raging in private, vowing to get back at those who had turned against him. In his seething, he told friends that he had been called an idiot before—and a genius, too—depending on the fashions of the day, and that he shrugged off both mantles. He reminded them that he had been mistakenly counted out before, as when AOL's on-line service was overwhelmed by busy signals in the mid-1990s. At times that fall, he groused in private about how he would relish the opportunity to spin off the AOL on-line division in Dulles and run it again on his own. "It was like he was saying, 'I'll take my toys and go away,'" said a former executive.

But Case's stance seemed more bluster than actual threat. He was not in a position to make that call—not on his own. Parsons, the chief executive, repeatedly said he had no plans to lop off the Internet division. AOL watchers buttressed Parsons's position, saying that it made little sense to spin off the division while it remained under two federal investigations. The company rebuffed several Wall Street buyout firms, including Kohlberg Kravis Roberts & Co.

AOL reckoned it wouldn't fetch a premium price. Not after October 23. On that day, AOL Time Warner said it would revise its financial results for a two-year period occurring before and after its merger in January 2001 to account for on-line ad sales and other deals that improperly inflated revenue by $190 million. It was a stunning about-face. The company had gone from denying any impropriety to admitting $49 million in improper deals to disclosing $190 million in bad transactions. Parsons left open the possibility that there could be further revisions to the company books.

By November, the AOL exodus continued. Kenny Lerer decided to leave to pursue a career in teaching. Other AOLers were asked, in no uncertain terms, to find employment elsewhere. Meanwhile, trouble continued to plague the Internet division. That month, the California State Teachers' Retirement System, the nation's third-largest public pension fund, filed suit in Los Angeles against Homestore.com, alleging financial fraud in connection with deals it had struck with AOL Time Warner. Things didn't look any better in December. The company warned that AOL's financial recovery would have to wait until at least 2004.

For Case, the bad tidings were a prelude to an abrupt personal ending.

In the first week of January 2003, he called board member Franklin D. Raines, chairman and chief executive of Fannie Mae. Case was thinking about the future—about the Internet and AOL's strategy to leverage Time Warner's content to turn things around at the on-line division. Practically convivial, Case also asked about Raines's daughter, a high school junior who was just beginning to visit prospective colleges. True to form, Case didn't mention his alma mater, Williams. He just listened.

"There was nothing about him that said, 'I'm about to change my status,'" Raines said.

A week later, on Saturday, January 11, Case called Raines again. This time, he got straight to the point: Case was resigning as chairman. He would remain a board director. Raines was stunned. So was Parsons, the CEO. Case called him, too. Case told Parsons that he had made up his mind the day before, on Friday. Case's status as chairman had never been raised at a board meeting, Parsons and Raines said. What's more, they said, Case still had more than enough support on the board to remain chairman. But Case knew that his time was running out. "The pressure was building" for his removal, said an official close to the board. Even Raines understood where this was heading. "This is a world in which everyone has to be held accountable," Raines said. "He and everybody in management, in putting the merger together and executing, have to take responsibility that it hasn't happened the way we wanted it to." Case's presence had become a huge distraction at the company. Powerful investors, led by Ted Turner and Gordon Crawford, were preparing a shareholder revolt in an attempt to vote him out of office at the May shareholder meeting. It was a longshot, given the logistics of amassing shareholder support, but such a move would, at a minimum, embarrass Case. His resignation was a "preemptory strike," Parsons said.

On Sunday, January 12, it was over. Two years and a day after the biggest merger in U.S. history, Case disclosed that he would step down as chairman, effective at the May annual shareholder meeting. "As you might expect, this decision was personally very difficult for me, as I would love to serve as chairman of this great company for many years to come, and as an architect of the merger I have felt it was important that I stay the course as chairman and help get things on track," he said in a prepared statement. Now, he said, that was not possible, as "some shareholders continue to focus their disappointment with the company's post-merger performance on me personally."

Levin was gone. Pittman was gone. Now Case, the last of the merger's architects, was gone, too. In less than a week, the board unanimously selected Parsons as the company's next chairman. By late January, Ted Turner said good-bye, too. The old maverick had helped push Levin and Case out the door. What was there left to do? Turner, at sixty-four, said he wanted to spend more time on his philanthropic activities. "I have not come to this decision lightly," he said in a statement. "As you know, this company has been a significant part of my life for over fifty years." The truth was, he wanted to be named chairman of AOL Time Warner, and it hadn't happened. His colleagues weren't prepared for that much unscripted fun. So now, Turner was resigning as vice chairman.

On the same day, the company said it was taking another big charge— $45 billion—in its fourth quarter, mostly to write down the value of its struggling Internet unit, AOL. Coming on top of the $54 billion goodwill charge it took in the first quarter, AOL Time Warner had finished 2002 with a historic bang: a loss of nearly $100 billion, the largest annual loss in U.S. corporate history. And yet it almost seemed anticlimactic.

Over twenty years, AOL had withstood a withering array of challenges, surviving as a cash-strapped on-line video firm, beating back mighty Microsoft, and overcoming the threat of the Web. Finally, AOL had succumbed to its own ambition.

The Aftermath

Jerry Levin, the scowling dark prince of AOL Time Warner, no longer stalks the executive suites on the twenty-ninth floor of 75 Rockefeller Plaza. Instead, Levin greets a visitor, holding court from his new office in a less lofty perch in the building: the second floor.

This, apparently, is where CEOs go to retire.

Levin doesn't feel the weight of juggling this far-flung empire anymore. Now he likes to look out his second-floor office windows. It's his favorite perch. Levin stops at the middle window and gazes below. New Yorkers, bundled and bustling on a crisp fall day, zigzag through a small farmers' market sandwiched between AOL Time Warner's headquarters and the Rockefeller Center ice-skating rink. He likes to watch the people. They go about their business, oblivious to him, the distant observer, a solitary figure at the window. He takes in the majestic spire of the Empire State Building in the distance, in a canyon among other major leviathans of Manhattan's skyline.

"I'm on my own journey now," he says.

Unlike Steve Case, Levin never cashed in his stock or options, which meant he missed out on potentially hundreds of millions. Not that Levin is a pauper. Over the years, he made millions in salary and bonuses, and he still draws $1 million a year as a company consultant until 2005. But real estate purchases and other outlays have left him millions in debt, which forced him to put several properties on the market, including his spacious Manhattan apartment on the East River.

That embarrassment, though, is practically nothing compared to the unceasing vitriol Levin continues to face from Time Warner employees who blame him for selling out cheap to AOL and leaving their retirement savings in tatters. Levin was reduced to a "mild hamster-ish figure" in a column by media maven Tina Brown in *The Times* of London. Levin insists he is immune from such attacks. "I'm really not interested in legacy," he says.

But he defends it. Levin still believes in the promise of AOL Time Warner. Recalling the merger announcement, he says, "I'm the one who got up and said—and there are people who play this back all the time, when we announced the deal—'I believe in the Internet and, therefore, I believe in these values.' Well, that was a terrible thing. Well, at that time, it made sense, and over time, I still think it will."

He counsels patience.

"What I assumed, and it is still an assumption, is that if you blend the two [companies] over time, you'll get something that's neither AOL nor Time Warner, but something else, which is exactly what happened with Time Warner," he says. "Time Warner was no longer the Time Inc. culture or the Warner culture. But it took a long time."

Levin tried to explain as much in his last meal with the AOL Time Warner board. Shortly after his December 2001 resignation, the group met at the Rockefeller Center Club, dining in a room full of transistor radios from the olden days. They used to hold a lot of old Time Inc. events here. It was always Levin's favorite place, even though he abhorred the principle of private clubs, a vestige of his youth as a Jew who felt excluded.

"I said, 'Instead of the normal bullshit, I'll speak for two hours, you can't interrupt me,'" Levin recalls. " 'I'm going to give you the history of Time Inc. through AOL Time Warner' because no one in the room had really been there, and it's pretty interesting."

Overlaid in his story was a lesson: In the AOL–Time Warner merger, they must understand, there was a risk, but a risk worth taking.

"There was an objective, which was, A, to understand just factually what the development was, but, B, to see where in most cases, there was always some aggressive action that may have been too early, but subsequently worked, and to know it's a whole kind of tutorial on risk assessment," Levin says. "When do you start a new magazine? When do you close a magazine? When do you start HBO? When do you decide, 'Hey, it's not working'? It was kind of a theme going through. When do you acquire rather than build internally? What about the culture? I just felt I wanted to get it off my chest."

All sixteen members of the board attended Levin's going-away dinner. That included the man who helped bring Levin to this conclusive point: Steve Case. The AOL Time Warner chairman even offered a toast. Levin can't recall what Case said.

"Something very nice," Levin is sure.

Case has come to understand how Levin feels. Case is reviled as much as Levin in many corners of the company, where officials feel they were hoodwinked into the AOL–Time Warner merger. He can't go around town, it seems, without the bubble of AOL's executive protection services, whose men keep a steady gaze on him even when he merely sits to eat at a New York restaurant.

His old buddy Bob Pittman, the third of the merger's high-profile triumvirate, has been more at ease. Or so he tells friends. After his unceremonious boot, he took a vacation with his family, traveling throughout Asia, stopping in Shanghai, Burma, and Vietnam, among other locales. "I'm retired," he insisted when friends asked what his next career move would be. "I'm retired."

In the absence of the disgraced troika, a lasting reminder looms over New York's Central Park, a colossal monument to the merger.

At Columbus Circle rises the new AOL Time Warner Center, at $1.8 billion the most expensive building in U.S. history. The twin-tower, fifty-three-story complex is big and brash and star-crossed, like the era in which it was conceived. After years of local opposition, lawsuits, and aborted plans, the site has been plagued by periodic accidents. In September 2002, a construction worker was smashed in the head by a piece of wood sent flying in howling winds.

The ambitious project also recalls a time when the accumulation of money didn't matter as much as how quickly it was spent. The complex is home not only to AOL Time Warner's headquarters and its CNN studio in New York, but also the tony Mandarin Oriental Hotel, the new Jazz at Lincoln Center, and about two hundred luxury condos ranging in price from $2 million to $40 million. Latin singer Ricky Martin and Hollywood producer Arnold Kopelson each bought a place here. It was designed for ultimate comfort. Retail fare includes Hugo Boss, Armani A/X, and Cole Haan. The way it was envisioned, those who can afford to live here can turn on their heat or air-conditioning from their cell phones. They can request nightly turndown of their bedsheets. And they can order room service from a posh steakhouse by pressing commands on a computerized touch screen in their apartments.

One day, AOL Time Warner, like the soaring building it conceived, may serve as a symbol of the Internet's ultimate triumph, or a hulking reminder of the excesses of the tumultuous dot-com era. Either way, this much seems certain: Bill von Meister, the father of AOL, a lover of excess and all things expensive, probably would have loved the new digs.

Afterword: The Name Change

"To paraphrase Winston Churchill's famous statement, this isn't the end, or even the beginning of the end. It is merely the end of the beginning."

And with that statement and little else, embattled Steve Case exited through a side door of the ballroom of the Lansdowne Resort's conference center in the sylvan suburbs of Northern Virginia.

It was May 16, 2003, and Case, the billionaire, was suddenly out of a job.

On that day, Case formally relinquished his title as chairman of AOL Time Warner. It was the price he had to pay to cling to his other title: a member of the company's board of directors. Had Case refused to step down as chairman, powerful institutional investors—angry people who had lost hundreds of millions of dollars in the dwindling stock of the failed merger—would have embarrassed Case by trying to derail his reelection to the board.

As it was, he didn't exactly win by a landslide at the annual shareholder meeting, which was held in AOL country, in the shadow of the Internet giant's Dulles campus. Case received only 78 percent of votes cast, compared with the 96 percent that most of the other directors garnered. Dick Parsons, the chief executive who formally assumed the dual role of chairman that day, got more than 90 percent, as did the irascible director Ted Turner.

The percentages, however, only told part of the story. So much had happened so quickly since Case had announced his resignation in January, just four months before the shareholder meeting.

Almost all of it was bad.

AOL, the subject of investigations by the U.S. attorney's office for the Eastern District of Virginia, the FBI and the SEC, now was facing a broader probe. In March, sources said the federal investigation into AOL's accounting was expanded to include alleged "aiding and abetting" of schemes by other companies to artificially inflate their revenue.

AOL had already restated its books by $190 million in advertising revenue from 2000 to 2002. But later in March 2003, AOL disclosed that it might have to restate up to $400 million more in advertising revenue. The SEC was questioning another complex transaction woven by AOL's clever dealmakers.

Things didn't get any better a month later when the giant University of California filed suit in state court, accusing Case and other top AOL executives of reaping nearly $1 billion in insider-trading windfalls through "tricks, contrivances and bogus transactions" before and after its merger with Time Warner.

By July, federal investigators riveted their attention to another questionable practice. It turned out AOL had not only been inflating its advertising revenue in recent years; the Internet firm had also been pumping up its other main source of revenue: subscriber numbers. AOL had been selling on-line accounts in bulk at deep discounts to some of its business partners.

Suddenly, AOL looked like a mirage.

There was little else to do—except this: In August, Jonathan Miller, the head of the on-line division, requested that "AOL" be stricken from "AOL Time Warner," the corporate parent's name. The two remaining words—Time Warner—would serve as a deafening punctuation point to the victors of this internecine corporate battle. Months before, AOL had been demoted to a unit of a division of the parent company. Now, other remnants of the on-line division, the former conqueror that had acquired Time Warner, were being eradicated. Their name wouldn't even grace the corporate letterhead anymore.

The symbolism was all too obvious: By removing "AOL" from the corporate name, Time Warner was repudiating the merger itself. It spoke volumes to the abiding belief among many from the old-line media firm that AOL had failed as the Internet engine of this great media giant. What Jerry Levin, the former CEO, had often called the "crown jewel" was now only colored glass.

The name change appeared to be an act of hara-kiri. But Miller insisted that it was his idea. He claimed that removing "AOL" from the corporate parent's name was necessary to protect the on-line division.

"I believe it's time for us to get our brand back," Miller wrote in an e-mail to employees then. "I recognize fully that it would seem to many that AOL is diminished if our corporate parent reverts to the Time Warner name. Some will think that this is a fate being forced upon us. And there is no question this will provide the media yet another opportunity to write negatively about the merger of AOL and Time Warner. But I want to emphasize that I initiated the dialogue with Dick Parsons about the name change—no one has asked me to do this—because it would be the right thing for our business."

Not quite. Disgruntled Time Warner-ites had been clamoring for months about getting rid of the AOL name, but Parsons had been reluctant to do so until the time was right and it could be done in the least inelegant way. It wasn't unlike the way Parsons had bided his time until Bob Pittman raised his hand, saying he was ready to resign as chief operating officer. Parsons didn't want it to look like Time Warner had foisted the name change on AOL; it looked better for AOL to raise its own hand.

"We had to say that," said a well-placed source.

The rest was a formality.

On October 16, "AOL" was officially lopped off the corporate name. There was no ceremony.

For many at the on-line division, the change sank in when they arrived at the Dulles campus that day, logged on to their computers and tried to check the company's stock ticker. The three letters—AOL—had once stood for a bulging stock price, the promises of personal wealth, early retirement . . .

Not anymore.

The "AOL" stock symbol had been erased. In its stead was the old Time Warner ticker: TWX.

In the end, the corporate name change was estimated to cost about

$500,000, including a new sign to be erected on the edifice of Time Warner's headquarters in New York. But for a company that had lost nearly $100 billion dollars a year before, half a million dollars was pocket change.

Parsons understood the cost of change. It had weighed on him from the moment he had become chairman of the most powerful media company on the planet, stepping into Case's shoes at the May annual meeting.

While Case invoked Churchill that day, Parsons found a more apt phrase from Shakespeare. Asked how he felt about being named chairman, Parsons quipped, "Heavy hangs the head that wears the crown."

NOTES

CHAPTER ONE: A FOOTNOTE IN HISTORY

Interviews with the following people conducted by the author: Gary Arlen, a tech industry newsletter publisher; Earl Crabb, former head of E/Soft; Bob Cross, turnaround specialist hired by Control Video Corp.; Brad Johnson, former head of manufacturing at Control Video; John Kerr, former sales executive at Control Video; James V. Kimsey, founding chief executive officer of America Online Inc.; Nora Macdonald, William von Meister's sister; George M. Middlemas, original investor in Control Video; Ed O'Brien, former executive of LaBarge Inc., manufacturer of modems for Control Video; Alan Peyser, a business associate of von Meister; Michael Schrage, former *Washington Post* reporter who covered Control Video; Dick Stone, a business associate of von Meister; Peter von Meister, William von Meister's brother; Taylor Walsh, former manager of documentation of Source Telecomputing Corp., a unit of *Reader's Digest*, which bought an on-line service developed by William von Meister.

The author also conducted interviews with several former and current AOL officials who declined to be identified, as well as sources who worked at other companies that did business with AOL.

The following research materials were also used: America Online employee handbook, mid-1990s; Paul B. Brown, "Starting Over," *Inc.*, May 1, 1987; Tom Carhart, *West Point Warriors*, Warner Books, 2002; Daniel H. Case, e-mail to John Kerr, May 9, 2001; Stephen M. Case, written report, The Marketing Group, January 1983; Stephen M. Case, letter and proposal, The Marketing Group, February 5, 1983; Stephen M. Case, strategic marketing plan, The Marketing Group, February 26, 1983; Stephen M. Case, letter and invoice, The Marketing Group, March 9, 1983; Stephen M. Case, marketing plan, The Marketing Group, April 16, 1983; Stephen M. Case, letter and expenses, The Marketing Group, April 22, 1983; Stephen M. Case, letter and report, The Marketing Group, April 25, 1983; Don Hayden, "Music Company Plans Tulsa

Test of Cable TV Recording Channel," *The Sunday Oklahoman,* December 13, 1981; GameLine pamplet, early 1980s; *Gameliner* magazine, September 1983, October 1983; The Home Music Store pamphlet, early 1980s; The Home Music Guide, early 1980s; John Kerr, letter to author, September 17, 2002; John Kerr, notes for memorial tribute to William von Meister, May 20, 1995; James V. Kimsey, sixtieth birthday video; Mark Leibovich, "From Suburban Roots to a Global Ambition," *Washington Post,* June 4, 2000; *The Red Herring,* "A succession of big cheeses has saved AOL," June 1, 2000; Michael Schrage, "Von Meister's Not-So-Trivial Pursuit," *Washington Post,* September 23, 1985; Marc Seriff, "Daddy, Where Do I Come From?" AOL company video from brown-bag seminar, April 11, 1996; Victoria Shannon, "What's Around the Corner?" *Washington Post,* February 26, 1996; Kara Swisher, *aol.com,* Times Business, 1998; Teleservices Report, February 1983, June 1983, May 1984, March 1985; Videotex Teletext News, mid-June 1983, November 1983, April 15, 1984, October 1984, January 1985, March 1985, June 24, 1985, November 1985; Julia L. Wilkinson, *My Life at AOL,* 1st Books Library, 2000.

CHAPTER TWO: A CASE OF AMBITION

Interviews with the following people conducted by the author: Cathy Anderson, former vice president, on-line services, Quantum Computer Services Inc.; Jan Brandt, former marketing executive and vice chairwoman and now part-time consultant, AOL; Bob Cross, turnaround specialist hired by Control Video; Randy Dean, former content producer, business development and advertising executive, AOL; Alexander M. Haig, former director, Quantum and AOL; Brad Johnson, former head of manufacturing, Control Video; James V. Kimsey, founding chief executive officer, AOL; Matt Korn, head of operations, AOL; Ted Leonsis, vice chairman, AOL; Alan J. Patricof, former investor in Quantum; Bill Pytlovany, former software developer at Quantum; Russell Siegelman, former head of on-line services, Microsoft Corp.; Julia L. Wilkinson, former content producer for Quantum and AOL.

The author also conducted interviews with several former and current AOL officials who declined to be identified as well as sources who worked at other companies that did business with AOL.

The following research materials were also used: *America Online Magazine,* June 1990; America Online Welcome Edition reference guide, 1989; AOL employee handbook, mid-1990s; author's visit to Quantum Computer Services' former headquarters in Vienna, Virginia; Amy Cortese and Amy Barrett, "The Online World of Steve Case," *Business Week,* April 15, 1996; James V. Kimsey, sixtieth birthday video; Alec Klein, "A 'Quantum' Leap of Humor in '89 Borne

Out by AOL," *Washington Post,* August 30, 2001; Timothy Leary, transcript of Quantum on-line chat, late 1980s; *The Quantum Quirk,* Vol. I, no. 197, 198, 199, 200, 201, 203, 204, 205, 206, 207; *The Quantum Quirk,* Vol. II, no. 101; *The Quantum Quirk,* Christmas 1990; *The Quantum Quirk,* March 26, 1992; Alan J. Patricof, internal memo assessing investment potential of Quantum; *Q-Link Update,* April 1988, October 1988, June Supplement 1989, July 1989, August 1989, September 1990; *PC-Link Update,* May/June 1989; Kara Swisher, *aol.com,* Times Business, 1998; Julia L. Wilkinson, *My Life at AOL,* 1st Books, 2000.

CHAPTER THREE: THE MERGER AND CALIGULA

Interviews with the following people conducted by the author: Steve Baldwin, former technology producer at Time Warner's Pathfinder; Timothy Boggs, former senior vice president, global public policy, Time Warner; Michael Bromley, former business development director, AOL; Bill Burrington, former senior vice president, AOL International; Lawrence Buttenwieser, former board member, Time Warner; Michael Fuchs, former HBO chairman and chief executive officer, Time Warner; Alexander M. Haig, former board member, AOL; Geoff Holmes, former chairman, Time Warner interactive; Walter Isaacson, former chairman and chief executive of CNN News Group; Bill Lessard, former Pathfinder producer, Time Warner; Gerald M. Levin, former chief executive officer, AOL Time Warner; Robert O'Connor, former AOL vice president; Dave Sickert, former Time Warner director and former head of AOL on-line shopping group; Curt Viebranz, former president of Time Inc. multimedia; George Vradenburg III, former senior vice president, global public policy, AOL Time Warner.

The author also conducted interviews with several former and current AOL, Time Warner and AOL Time Warner officials who declined to be identified as well as sources who worked at other entities or companies that interacted with AOL.

The following research materials were also used: AOL Time Warner Form S-4 registration statement, Securities and Exchange Commission, February 11, 2000; AOL Time Warner biography of Gerald M. Levin (www.aoltimewarner.com), 2002; AOL Time Warner time line (www.aoltimewarner.com), 2002; "AOL–Time Warner: Dawn of a Golden Age, or a Blow to Media Diversity?" Fairness & Accuracy in Reporting, (www.fair.org), January 13, 2000; Connie Bruck, *Master of the Game,* Simon & Schuster, 1994; Andrew Buncombe, "AOL Chief: Son's Murder Behind Decision to Resign," *The Independent,* December 7, 2001; Doreen Carvajal, "Time Inc.'s Levin Has Had Career of Many Colors," *New York Times,* January 12, 2000 (via *Portland Oregonian*); Alan Citron, and

John Lippman, "Time for Vision, New Time Warner President Gerald Levin Is a Strategist," *Los Angeles Times,* February 22, 1992; Richard M. Clurman, *To the End of Time,* Simon & Schuster, 1992; James Cox, "Levin Transformed Career with Merger Idea," *USA Today,* February 24, 1992; Julie Deardorff, "Time Warner Chairman Breaks Corporate Mold," *Chicago Tribune,* January 11, 2000; Ianthe Jeanne Dugan and Ariana Eunjung Cha, "AOL to Acquire Time Warner in Record $183 Billion Merger," *Washington Post,* January 11, 2000; Steve Ellwanger and Ann Marie Kerwin, "MPA Mantra: Beware the Black Holes," *Inside Media,* November 15, 1995; "Henry Luce, May You Lie More Peacefully in Your Grave," The Digital Journalist (www.digitaljournalist.org), 2002; Peter J. Howe, "Boston Lawyer Plays Key Role in America Online–Time Warner Deal," *Boston Globe,* January 12, 2000; "It May Be a 'Black Hole,' But More Publishers Leap into Cyberspace," *MIN Media Industry Newsletter,* November 13, 1995; Keith J. Kelly, "Tina Takes Media Titans to Task in New Column," *New York Post,* October 3, 2002; David D. Kirkpatrick, "Former Chief of Time Warner Defends Sale to America Online," *New York Times,* September 24, 2002; Mark Leibovich, *The New Imperialists,* Prentice Hall Press, 2002; Nina Munk, "Power Failure," *Vanity Fair,* July 2002; Daniel Okrent, "AOL–Time Warner Merger: Happily Ever After?" *Time,* January 24, 2000; Pathfinder, (www.pathfinder.com), Time Inc. portal, 2002; Martin Peers, "AOL Time Warner; The Day After," *Wall Street Journal,* January 12, 2000; Martin Peers, Nick Wingfield, and Laura Landro, "Media Blitz: AOL, Time Warner Leap Borders to Plan a Mammoth Merger," *Wall Street Journal,* January 11, 2000; Rihga Royal Web site, (http://rihgaroy-alny), 2002; Matthew Rose, and Martin Peers, "AOL Time Warner Transition Won't Damp Colossal Cable Ambitions," *Wall Street Journal,* December 6, 2001; Liz Smith, "You've Got Hate Mail," *Newsday,* December 7, 2002; Deborah Solomon, "Real Dealmakers Weren't CEOs," *USA Today,* January 17, 2000; Norman Solomon, "Time Magazine's Skewed Tribute to Henry Luce," Creators Syndicate (www.fair.org), 1998; David Streitfeld, "AOL Rode a Wave, Time Missed the Boat," *Washington Post,* January 16, 2000; "Unhappy Media Marriage," *New York Times,* February 26, 1992 (via *Australian Financial Review*); Thomas E. Weber, Martin Peers, and Nick Wingfield, "You've Got Time Warner!" *Wall Street Journal,* January 11, 2000; Nick Wingfield, "AOL Negotiator Helped Keep Deal on Track," *Wall Street Journal,* January 12, 2000.

CHAPTER FOUR: AOL VERSUS THE WORLD

Interviews with the following people conducted by the author: Art Amolsch, editor and publisher, *FTC Watch* newsletter; Michael E. Antalics, former deputy director, competition bureau, FTC; Ross Bagully, former chief executive officer,

Tribal Voice, a unit of CMGI Inc.; Timothy Boggs, former senior vice president, global public policy, Time Warner Inc.; Jeff Chester, executive director, Center for Digital Democracy; Stephen Heins, former marketing director, NorthNet LLC; William E. Kennard, former chairman, FTC; Gene Kimmelman, co-director, Consumers Union; Blair Levin, former consultant, CMGI; Eric London, former chief spokesman, FTC; Richard G. Parker, former director of the competition bureau, FTC; Pia Pialorsi, Republican press secretary, U.S. Senate Commerce Committee; Robert Pitofsky, former chairman, FTC; Avner Ronen, co-founder, Odigo Inc.; Andrew Jay Schwartzman, president, Media Access Project; George Vradenburg III, former senior vice president, global public policy, AOL Time Warner.

The author also conducted interviews with several former and current AOL and Time Warner officials who declined to be identified as well as sources who worked at government agencies in Washington and Europe and other companies and groups that did business, or had relationships, with AOL and Time Warner.

The following research materials were also used: AOL, "America Online's Support for Interoperability" and "Quick Facts on Instant Messaging," submissions to U.S. Senate Judiciary Committee staff, August 2, 1999; AOL and Time Warner, "Reply of America Online Inc. and Time Warner Inc.," submission to FCC, May 11, 2000; Ross Bagully, Tribal Voice chief executive officer, written testimony, FCC hearing, July 27, 2000; Harry Berkowitz, "Fade to Black," *Newsday*, May 2, 2000; Stephen M. Case, testimony, U.S. Senate Commerce, Science and Transportation Committee hearing, March 2, 2000; Ariana Eunjung Cha, "AOL's Merger Worry: Shareholders," *Washington Post*, June 16, 2000; Ariana Eunjung Cha, "Case, Levin Again Face Senators' Skepticism," *Washington Post*, March 3, 2000; Ariana Eunjung Cha, "Foes of AOL Merger Take to Capitol Hill," *Washington Post*, March 24, 2000; Ariana Eunjung Cha, "Groups Oppose AOL Merger," *Washington Post*, April 26, 2000; Ariana Eunjung Cha, "Shareholders Back AOL Pact," *Washington Post*, June 24, 2000; Ariana Eunjung Cha, and Peter S. Goodman, "AOL, Time Warner Try to Allay Fears," *Washington Post*, March 1, 2000; Kathy Chen and Joe Flint, "The Streetfighting Disney Lobbyist in a Goofy Tie," *Wall Street Journal*, May 4, 2000; Disney video, *Consumer Choice in the Broadband Marketplace of Tomorrow*, July 25, 2000; William Drozdiak, "EU Approves Merger of AOL, Time Warner," *Washington Post*, October 12, 2000; Edelman Public Relations, "IM Community to AOL: Tear Down This Wall, Mr. Case," July 27, 2000; Edelman Public Relations, "Leading Technology Companies Join Forces to Call for Open Instant Messaging Communications," June 6, 2000; FTC, commissioner biographies (www.ftc.gov); FTC, landmark (www.ftc.gov); FTC, regulations (www.ftc.gov); Free IM advertisement, "Tear Down That Wall!" 2000, Free IM stickers, Free IM buttons (www.freeim.org);

Peter S. Goodman and Ariana Eunjung Cha, "EU Plans Detailed Probe of AOL Deal," *Washington Post,* June 20, 2000; Peter S. Goodman and Alec Klein, "FCC Staff Proposes AOL Terms," *Washington Post,* September 21, 2000; James V. Grimaldi and Alec Klein, "FTC Seeks Assurances in AOL Deal," *Washington Post,* September 4, 2000; Margaret Heffernan, president and chief executive officer, iCast, written testimony, House Subcommittee on Telecommunications, Trade and Consumer Protection hearing, October 6, 2000; Sallie Hofmeister, "ABC Back on Cable TV as Dispute Is Set Aside," *Los Angeles Times,* May 3, 2000; The Holmes Report, "The 100 Best PR Programs of 2000," 2001; Julia Hood, "Edelman Salvages Instant Messaging for AOL deal," *PR Week,* 2001; IETF instant messaging working group, e-mail logs, July 1999–July 2000; IETF instant messaging working group, minutes of meeting of October 7, 1999; Alec Klein, "A Hard Look at Media Mergers," *Washington Post,* November 29, 2000; Alec Klein, "Access Issue Isn't Open-and-Shut Case," *Washington Post,* September 20, 2000; Alec Klein, "AOL Defends Time Warner Merger at EU Hearing," *Washington Post,* September 8, 2000; Alec Klein, "AOL Fires Back at Disney over Opposition to Deal," *Washington Post,* October 4, 2000; Alec Klein, "AOL Merger Clears Last Big Hurdle," *Washington Post,* December 15, 2000; Alec Klein, "AOL Restrictions Alleged," *Washington Post,* October 10, 2000; Alec Klein, "AOL Tells Wall Street It's Ready for Merger," *Washington Post,* October 19, 2000; Alec Klein, "AOL Time Warner Says It Won't Forsake Virginia," *Washington Post,* January 13, 2000; Alec Klein, "Before Approval, a Tug of War," *Washington Post,* December 24, 2000; Alec Klein, "Drop in AOL Stock Fuels Speculation About Merger," *Washington Post,* October 18, 2000; Alec Klein, "EU Wants Access Guarantees in AOL Merger," *Washington Post,* September 9, 2000; Alec Klein, "Europe Watches Warily as AOL Flexes Muscles," *Washington Post,* September 18, 2000; Alec Klein, "FCC Clears Way for AOL Time Warner Inc.," *Washington Post,* January 12, 2001; Alec Klein, "FTC, AOL Extend Talks on Merger," *Washington Post,* November 10, 2000; Alec Klein, "FTC, AOL Remain Apart as Merger Deadline Nears," *Washington Post,* October 14, 2000; Alec Klein, "FTC Nears Approval of AOL Merger," *Washington Post,* December 11, 2000; Alec Klein, "House Opens AOL Hearing," *Washington Post,* September 28, 2000; Alec Klein, "Merger Puts AOL's Methods on Trial," *Washington Post,* November 3, 2000; Alec Klein, "Time Warner Access Pledge Questioned," *Washington Post,* September 30, 2000; Alec Klein, "Time Warner, EarthLink Reach Deal," *Washington Post,* November 21, 2000; Alec Klein, "Time Warner Terms for Cable Criticized," *Washington Post,* October 7, 2000; Andrew K. Long, letter on behalf of AOL to FCC, December 14, 2000; John Markoff, "Microsoft, AOL Playing Internet Cloak and Dagger," *New York Times,* August 14, 1999; Carolyn Duffy Marsan, "AOL Out of Instant Messaging Standard Bake-Off," *Network*

World Fusion, August 7, 2000; John Mintz and John Schwartz, "Expecting a Fight, AOL and Time Flex Lobbying Muscle," *Washington Post,* January 22, 2000; Vijay Saraswat, e-mail to IETF instant-messaging working group, July 29, 1999; Robert Schmidt, "From Arrogance to Approval," *Cable World* (adapted from *Brill's Content*), March 26, 2001; Barry Schuler, president, America Online interactive services, letter to the editor, *USA Today,* June 1, 2000; Barry Schuler, president, America Online interactive services, letter to Vijay Saraswat, co chairman, IETF instant-messaging working group, July 29, 1999; Steven Teplitz, vice president and associate general counsel, AOL Time Warner, letter to Marlene H. Dortch, secretary, FCC, July 16, 2002; "Time Warner Counsel Gets Huge Fee if Merger Occurs," *Wall Street Journal,* January 21, 2000; John R. Wilke, "Coming to Terms: Both Sides Get Tough as Crunch Time Nears on AOL–Time Warner," *Wall Street Journal,* September 25, 2000.

CHAPTER FIVE: SKIN GAME

Interviews with the following people conducted by the author: Chris Benyo, former senior vice president, PurchasePro.com Inc.; Myer Berlow, former president, global marketing solutions, AOL Time Warner; Timothy Boggs, former senior vice president, global public policy, Time Warner; Michael Bromley, former business development director, AOL; Neil Davis, former senior vice president, and head of strategy development, AOL; Randy Dean, former vice president Western regional sales, AOL; James V. Kimsey, former chief executive and chairman, AOL; Tracey Lakatos, former administrative assistant, business affairs, AOL; Robert O'Connor, former vice president of finance and operations, interactive services, AOL; Bill O'Luanaigh, former senior project manager, AOL; Ted Rogers, former manager, business affairs, AOL; Jonathan Salkoff, former manager, business affairs, AOL; Dave Sickert, former director of merchant relations, Time Warner, and former director of on-line shopping, AOL; Steve Stern, former vice president of communications, PurchasePro; Mark Walsh, former senior vice president and general manager of branded Internet services, AOL.

The author also conducted interviews with several former and current AOL, Time Warner, and AOL Time Warner officials who declined to be identified as well as sources who worked at other companies and groups that did business, or had relationships, with AOL, Time Warner, and AOL Time Warner.

The following research materials were also used: "America Online Announces Strategic Three-Year Distribution and Co-Marketing Deal with N2K," September 18, 1997 (press release); Julia Angwin and Rebecca Blumenstein, "AOL Deal Maker Was Renowned For Tough Style," *Wall Street Journal,* Aug. 23, 2002; "AOL Time Warner Creates Global Marketing Solutions Group to Drive Growth of Cross-Brand Advertising and Marketing Initiatives," Business Wire, August 17, 2001; "Digits," *Wall Street Journal,* September 9, 1999; "Early AOL Ad Sales Efforts Corral Consumer Market Biz," *Interactive Marketing News,* October 4, 1996; Tobi Elkin, "Cross-Media Deals," *Advertising Age,* April 29, 2002; Lloyd Grove, "The Reliable Source," *Washington Post,* June 7, 2000, and March 19, 2002; David D. Kirkpatrick, "Ouster at AOL, but Where Does Trail End" *New York Times,* September 1, 2002; Alec Klein, "Creative Transactions Earned Team Rewards," *Washington Post,* July 19, 2002; Alec Klein, *Washington Post* letter submitted to AOL Time Warner, enumerating questions regarding AOL accounting and business affairs, June 14, 2002; Alec Klein, "Unconventional Transactions Boosted Sales," *Washington Post,* July 18, 2002; Alec Klein, "Unorthodox Partnership Produced Financial Gains," *Washington Post,* July 19, 2002; "Manhattan Transfers," *New York Observer,* April 16, 2001; Maryland Department of Assessments and Taxation search of David M. Colburn records; Maryland Voter Registration search of David M. Colburn records; National Comprehensive Report Plus Associates, database search of public records of David M. Colburn; "Overset: Interactive–America Online," *Media Daily,* May 27, 1997; Gary Rivlin, "AOL's Rough Riders," *The Industry Standard,* October 30, 2000; "Tel-Save Announces Innovative Agreement with America Online to Provide Telecommunications Services to AOL Members," PR Newswire, February 25, 1997.

CHAPTER SIX: WHO LET THE DOGS OUT?

Interviews with the following people conducted by the author: Chris Benyo, former senior vice president, PurchasePro.com; Myer Berlow, former president, global marketing solutions, AOL Time Warner; Michael Bromley, former business development director, AOL; Neil Davis, former senior vice president and head of strategy development, AOL; Randy Dean, former vice president, Western regional sales, AOL; Stephen Heins, former marketing director, NorthNet LLC; William E. Kennard, former chairman, FCC; Tracey Lakatos, former administrative assistant, business affairs, AOL; Blair Levin, former consultant to CMGI; Robert O'Connor, former vice president of finance and operations, interactive services, AOL; Bill O'Luanaigh, former senior project manager, AOL; Ted Rogers, former manager, business affairs, AOL; Jonathan Salkoff, former manager, business affairs, AOL; Dave Sickert, former director of merchant relations, Time Warner, and former director of on-line shopping, AOL; Steve Stern, former vice president of communications, PurchasePro; George Vradenburg III, former senior vice president, global public policy, AOL Time Warner; Mark Walsh, former senior vice president and general manager of branded Internet services, AOL.

The author also conducted interviews with several former and current AOL, Time Warner, and AOL Time Warner officials who declined to be identified as well as sources who worked at other companies and groups that did business, or had relationships, with AOL, Time Warner, and AOL Time Warner.

The following research materials were also used: "America Online and PurchasePro.com Join Forces in Strategic Alliance to Create Universal B2B Exchange," Business Wire, March 20, 2000; "AOL and PurchasePro Accelerate New B2B and e-commerce effort," Business Wire, March 28, 2001; AOL confidential document, "AOL Advertising Insertion Order," PurchasePro deal, March 14, 2001; AOL confidential document, "AOL Advertising Insertion Order," Wembley deal, September 25, 2000; AOL confidential document, "AOL/PurchasePro Vendor Marketplace Analysis," February 8, 2001; AOL confidential document, "AOL Vendor Descriptions," undated; AOL confidential document, "Business Development Deal Process and Status Evaluation," undated; AOL confidential document, "Forecasted Restructurings/Termination Revenue Impact," October 5, 2000; AOL confidential document, "Interactive Marketing AdOps," February 15, 2002; AOL confidential document, "Interactive Marketing Deal Restructurings," August 18, 2000; AOL confidential document, "Interactive Marketing Deal Restructurings," August 24, 2000; AOL confidential document, "Interactive Marketing FY01 Q2 Budget Analysis—Ad Forecast," September 26, 2000; AOL confidential document, "Interactive Marketing Key Dates," August 24, 2000; AOL confidential document, "Interactive Marketing Key Deals Summary," November 4, 1999; AOL confidential document, "Interactive Marketing Key Deals Summary," November 10, 1999; AOL confidential document, "Interactive Marketing Key Deals Summary," January 14, 2000; AOL confidential document, "Interactive Marketing Key Deals Summary," March 21, 2000; AOL confidential document, "Interactive Marketing Key Deals Summary," August 18, 2000; AOL confidential document, "Interactive Marketing Key Deals Summary," August 24, 2000; AOL confidential document, "Interactive Marketing Key Deals Summary," November 6, 2000; AOL confidential document, "Interactive Marketing Key Deals Summary," November 16, 2000; AOL confidential document, "Interactive Marketing Key Deals Summary," January 4, 2001; AOL confidential document, "Interactive Marketing Q2 Deals At Risk Potential Exposure," December 2000; AOL confidential document, "Marketing Ops Top Vendors," undated; AOL confidential document, "MarketPlace Pipeline Report," PurchasePro deal, March 26, 2001; AOL confidential document, "Multi-Brand Commerce Dependencies," January 11, 2001; AOL confidential document, "PurchasePro Deal Summary," March 21, 2000; AOL confidential document, "PurchasePro—Executive Summary," March 21, 2001; AOL confidential document, "PurchasePro MarketPlace Pipeline," undated;

AOL confidential document, "PurchasePro Warrant Summary," December 20, 2000; AOL confidential document, "Sales and Revenue Productivity Summary by Group," August 1, 2001; AOL confidential document, "Settlement Agreement and Mutual Releases," Wembley deal, September 26, 2000; AOL confidential document, "Sun Microsystems—Executive Summary," June 28, 2000; AOL confidential document, "Telefónica EIOs—Executive Summary," December 15, 2000; AOL confidential document, Ticketmaster deal, September 5, 2000; AOL confidential document, "Value of Ad Served Impressions," January 2002; AOL confidential document, "Vendor Pipeline," PurchasePro deal, undated; AOL internal e-mail, subject line: "Last Time," from Myer Berlow, then AOL Time Warner president of global marketing solutions, to Barry Schuler, then chairman and chief executive of America Online, March 8, 2002; AOL internal presentation to senior AOL executives, presentation outline, regarding ad revenue problems, February 2002; "AOL, PurchasePro.com Form Three-Year Business-to-Business Alliance," *Dow Jones Business News,* March 20, 2000; "Arch Coal Renews Software License Pact with PurchasePro," Dow Jones News Service, September 20, 2001; "Buhrmann Unit Buys PurchasePro E-Market Software License," Dow Jones News Service, October 31, 2001; Paul T. Cappuccio, AOL Time Warner executive vice president, general counsel, and secretary, letter to *Washington Post,* June 17, 2002; Steve Case, chairman and chief executive, AOL, written testimony, House Subcommittee on Telecommunications, Trade and Consumer Protection, September 27, 2000; Bob Driehaus, "Dot.com plunge," *Cincinnati Post,* June 9, 2001; Aaron Elstein, "Investors Want CEO to Buy More Shares in PurchasePro," *Dow Jones Business News,* November 29, 2001; Raymond Hennessey, "PurchasePro.com Opens," Dow Jones News Service, September 14, 1999; Charles E. Johnson, database search, National Comprehensive Report Plus Associates; Alec Klein, "AOL Opens Probe, Puts 2 on Leave," *Washington Post,* June 19, 2001; Alec Klein, "Creative Transactions Earned Team Rewards," *Washington Post,* July 19, 2002; Alec Klein, *Washington Post* letter to AOL Time Warner, June 14, 2002; Alec Klein, *Washington Post* letters to AOL Time Warner outside attorneys, June 24, 2002, June 25, 2002, June 26, 2002, June 27, 2002, June 28, 2002, July 16, 2002; Alec Klein, "Unconventional Transactions Boosted Sales," *Washington Post,* July 18, 2002; Alec Klein, "Unorthodox Partnership Produced Financial Gains," *Washington Post,* July 19, 2002; Moviefone Inc. 10-Q, May 17, 1999; "Netscape Netbusiness Expands with Improved News Services, Features and New Streamlined Interface," press release, December 1, 2000; *Pacer/Cats/CCS* vs. *Moviefone Inc, Promofone Inc. and the Teleticketing Co., LP,* Supreme Court of the state of New York, County of New York, complaint, July 7, 1995; Promofone Inc.–Pacer Cats Corp. agreement, February 14, 1992; "PurchasePro Announces Contract with Bayer Corp.," Dow Jones News Service, February 5, 2002; "PurchasePro Completes $6M Financing," Dow Jones News Service, February 14, 2002; "PurchasePro Engages Grant Thornton as Independent Auditors," Dow Jones News Service, December 17, 2001; Dow Jones News Service, February 11, 2002; "PurchasePro Restructures Pact with AOL, Eliminating Future Payments," Dow Jones Business News, September 17, 2001; "Purchase-Pro's Auditor, Arthur Andersen, Resigns Over a Dispute," *Wall Street Journal,* November 30, 2001; "PurchasePro.com Inc.: Pact with AOL Revamped," *Wall Street Journal,* September 18, 2001; "PurchasePro.com Inc.: Software to be Licensed to Honeywell International," *Wall Street Journal,* January 15, 2002; Ross Snel, "AOL Pact Seen Expanding PurchasePro's B2B Markets," Dow Jones News Service, March 20, 2000; "Strategic Alliances," Purchasepro.com Web site; Sandra Ward, "Worth the Price?" *Barron's,* February 5, 2001; Wembley PLC, annual report and accounts, 2000; Wembley, "Settlement of US arbitration award," press release, October 5, 2000; Tish Williams, "A CEO's True Faith," *Upside Today,* November 3, 1999; Thomas D. Yannucci, outside attorney representing AOL Time Warner, letters to *The Washington Post,* June 21, 2002, June 25, 2002, June 26, 2002, July 1, 2002, July 10, 2002, July 17, 2002; Eric Young, "PurchasePro's Flashy CEO Resigns," The Standard.com, May 21, 2001.

The chapter also relied on extensive research of AOL's public filings with the SEC over the past several years. In addition, the author reviewed company announcements regarding its financial statements over several years as well as scores of news accounts of AOL's financial condition, including its quarterly earnings and its interactions with the SEC.

CHAPTER SEVEN: THE SHORT-LIVED HONEYMOON

Interviews with the following people conducted by the author: Myer Berlow, former president, global marketing solutions, AOL Time Warner.; Timothy Boggs, former senior vice president, global public policy, Time Warner; Bill Burrington, former senior vice president, AOL International; Lawrence Buttenwieser, former board member, Time Warner; Neil Davis, former senior vice president and head of strategy development, AOL; Michael Fuchs, former HBO chairman and chief executive officer, Time Warner; Bob Grassi, former HBO executive vice president, affiliate relations, Time Warner; Alexander M. Haig, former board member, AOL; Geoff Holmes, former chairman, Time Warner interactive; Ted Leonsis, vice chairman, AOL; Gerald M. Levin, former chief executive officer, AOL Time Warner; Mike Luftman, former Time Warner Cable spokesman; Tryg Myhren, former ATC chief executive officer, chairman, and president, Time Warner; Robert O'Connor, former vice president of finance and operations, interactive services, AOL; Richard D. Parsons, chairman and chief executive, AOL Time

Warner; Franklin D. Raines, AOL Time Warner board member; Dave Sickert, former director of merchant relations, Time Warner, and former director of on-line shopping, AOL; George Vradenburg III, former senior vice president, global public policy, AOL Time Warner; Mark Walsh, former senior vice president and general manager of branded Internet services, AOL.

The author also conducted interviews with several former and current AOL, Time Warner, and AOL Time Warner officials who declined to be identified as well as sources who worked at other companies and groups that did business, or had relationships, with AOL, Time Warner, and AOL Time Warner.

The following research materials were also used: Frank Ahrens, "No. 2 Officer Quits at AOL Time Warner," *Washington Post,* July 19, 2002; Susan Antilla, "Drexel's PR Work Faces Ultimate Test," *USA Today,* November 28, 1988; Susan Antilla, "She Shapes Images," *USA Today,* December 1, 1988; AOL Time Warner corporate Web site, Kenneth B. Lerer profile (www.aoltimewarner.com), undated; AOL Time Warner corporate Web site, Ted Turner profile (www.aoltimewarner.com), undated; Jonathan Auerbach "Six Flags CEO, Pittman, to Join Realty Firm," *Wall Street Journal,* August 2, 1995; Ken Auletta, "The Lost Tycoon," *New Yorker,* April 23–30, 2001; Porter Bibb, *Ted Turner: It Ain't As Easy As It Looks,* Johnson Books, 1993; Bryan Burrough and John Helyar, *Barbarians at the Gate,* HarperCollins, 1990; Maurice Carroll, *New York Times,* February 6, 1977; Raad Cawthon, "Ted Turner's high-flying mind," *Atlanta Journal and Constitution,* June 29, 1986; Raad Cawthon, "Turner chases American dream at full speed," *Atlanta Journal and Constitution,* June 30, 1986; Ariana Eunjung Cha, "Case's Spot: No. 2 With A Bullet," *Washington Post,* May 5, 2000; Rajiv Chandrasekaran, "AOL's Man With a Mission," *Washington Post,* February 15, 1998; James Coates and Tim Jones, "America Online Embraces the Internet," *Chicago Tribune,* October 30, 1996; Daniel Eisenberg, "And Then There Were Two," *Time,* July 29, 2002; Paul Farhi, "Nothing Left but Billions," *Washington Post,* April 4, 2001; Peter Finch, "Can MTV's Wunderkind Turn Multimedia Mogul?" *Business Week,* June 27, 1988; Jon Fine, "Crunchtime: Bob Pittman is promising the world," *Advertising Age,* May 7, 2001; Joe Flint, "AOL's Pittman is Tapped to Control Much of Combined AOL-Time Warner," *Wall Street Journal,* May 5, 2000; "Former MTV Developer Named to Head Time Warner Enterprises Unit," Associated Press, March 22, 1990; Robert Goldberg and Gerald Jay, "Citizen Turner," *Playboy,* June 1995; Joe Hagan, "Pittman's Last Stand," *New York Observer,* July 29, 2002; Kathleen Hays, "Ted Turner Re-Ups with AOL Time Warner," CNNfn, December 21, 2001; David S. Hilzenrath, "Turnaround Task at AOL," *Washington Post,* October 31, 1996; "James Lake Steps Down at Robinson Lake," *PR News,* October 30, 1995; Joanne Kaufman, "Socialite Scales Highest Peaks," *Wall Street Journal,* March 21, 1996; Paul Keegan, "Making AOL

Rock," *Upside Magazine*, November 1, 1998; Matt Kempner, "Turner's influence re-emerges at AOL," *Atlanta Journal and Constitution*, October 27, 2002; David D. Kirkpatrick, "A Media Giant Needs a Script," *New York Times*, July 7, 2002; David D. Kirkpatrick, "AOL Chairman's No. 1 Ally Turns Into His Biggest Foe," *New York Times*, October 1, 2002; Alec Klein, "A Merger Taken AOL-Ill," *Washington Post*, October 21, 2002; Alec Klein, "AOL Continues Reshuffling at the Top," *Washington Post*, April 10, 2002; Alec Klein, "AOL Time Warner Prepares Ad Blitz," *Washington Post*, February 1, 2001; Alec Klein, "AOL to Cut 300 Jobs in Area," *Washington Post*, January 24, 2001; Alec Klein, "New Firm to Follow 3 Leaders," *Washington Post*, December 15, 2000; Dan Koeppel, "PR's Failed Promise," *BrandWeek*, October 21, 1991; Kathryn Kranhold, "Growing Young & Rubicam Buys Robinson, Lerer & Montgomery," *Wall Street Journal*, March 1, 2000; Laura Landro, "A Whiz Kid Goes on Without His MTV," *Wall Street Journal*, June 22, 1987; Laura Landro, "MTV President Robert Pittman Is Said Near Pact to Form His Own Company," *Wall Street Journal*, August 7, 1986; Laura Landro, "Pittman May Sever Ties With MCA, Return to Warner," *Wall Street Journal*, March 1, 1989; Robert Lenzer and Maria Matzer, "Late Bloomer," *Forbes*, October 17, 1994; Terry Maxon, "Cable Panel to Draft New Service Standards," *Dallas Morning News;* John M. McGuire, "Video Visionary Robert Pittman, who thought up MTV, is now putting his spin on Six Flags," *St. Louis Post-Dispatch*, June 3, 1992; Nancy Millman, "Bozell, Jacobs buys Robinson, Lake & Lerer," *Chicago Sun-Times*, September 4, 1986; Daniel Okrent, "Happily Ever After?" *Time*, January 24, 2000; Martin Peers, "AOL Reorganizes Who Reports to Whom Inside Company," Dow Jones News Service, May 24, 2002; Martin Peers, "Turner Isn't Expected to Renew Contract with AOL Time Warner," *Wall Street Journal*, October 5, 2001; Martin Peers and Julia Angwin, "At AOL, Three More Executives Close to Pittman Head for Exit," *Wall Street Journal*, November 5, 2002; Martin Peers and Julia Angwin, "Internet Time: AOL, Time Warner Are Already Putting Operations Together," *Wall Street Journal*, November 10, 2000; Martin Peers and Joann S. Lublin, "In Sorry Shape, America Online Seeks New CEO," *Wall Street Journal*, July 12, 2002; Martin Peers and Nick Wingfield, "Seeking Harmony, AOL and Warner Music Hit Some Dissonant Notes," *Wall Street Journal*, April 18, 2000; Roberta Plutzik, "Adventure Capitalist Bob Pittman's Fun for the Nineties," *The Record*, April 12, 1992; Donnie Radcliffe, "Washington Ways," *Washington Post*, July 8, 1986; Abigail Rayner, "Merger hit trouble from day one," *The Times* (London), July 20, 2002; John Riley, "Pro-Milken Propaganda," *Newsday*, May 15, 1989; Matthew Rose, Julia Angwin, and Martin Peers, "Bad Connection: Failed Effort to Coordinate Ads Signals Deeper Woes at AOL," *Wall Street Journal*, July 18, 2002; Tom Shales, "Ted Turner, On Top of the World," *Washington Post*, April 13, 1989;

Eben Shapiro, "Exiting Six Flags CEO Wanted Stake, But $20 Million Payout isn't Peanuts," *Wall Street Journal*, May 8, 1995; Sally Bedell Smith, "MTV Mastermind Creates New, More Mellow Channel," *New York Times*, January 2, 1985; Susan Stellin, "Cultures Clash as AOL Switches to its e-mail," *New York Times*, May 16, 2001; James B. Stewart, *Den of Thieves*, Simon & Schuster, 1991; "Talk Show Host Agrees to $125,000 Settlement in Car Accident," Associated Press, October 22, 1993; Jeffrey A. Trachtenberg, "Quantum Leaps," *Forbes*, June 1, 1987; "Warner Acquiring Lorimar in Stock Deal," Associated Press, May 11, 1988; Nick Wingfield, "Lerer's Dual Posts at AOL and PR Firm May Raise a Conflict-of-Interest Issue," *Wall Street Journal*, February 2, 2000; Catherine Yang, Ronald Grover, and Ann Therese Palmer, "Show Time for AOL Time Warner," *Business Week*, January 15, 2001.

CHAPTER EIGHT: THE COLLAPSE

Interviews with the following people conducted by the author: Myer Berlow, former president, global marketing solutions, AOL Time Warner; Timothy Boggs, former senior vice president, global public policy, Time Warner; Bill Burrington, former senior vice president, AOL International; Lawrence Buttenwieser, former board member, Time Warner; Neil Davis, former senior vice president and head of strategy development, AOL; Michael Fuchs, former HBO chairman and chief executive officer, Time Warner; Bob Grassi, former HBO executive vice president, affiliate relations, Time Warner; Alexander M. Haig, former board member, AOL; Geoff Holmes, former chairman, Time Warner interactive; James V. Kimsey, founding chief executive officer of America Online Inc.; Ted Leonsis, vice chairman, AOL; Gerald M. Levin, former chief executive officer, AOL Time Warner; Mike Luftman, former Time Warner Cable spokesman; Tryg Myhren, former ATC chief executive officer, chairman, and president, Time Warner; Robert O'Connor, former vice president of finance and operations, interactive services, AOL; Dave Sickert, former director of merchant relations, Time Warner, and former director of on-line shopping, AOL; George Vradenburg III, former senior vice president, global public policy, AOL Time Warner; Mark Walsh, former senior vice president and general manager of branded Internet services, AOL.

The author also conducted interviews with several former and current AOL, Time Warner, and AOL Time Warner officials who declined to be identified as well as sources who worked at other companies and groups that did business, or had relationships, with AOL, Time Warner, and AOL Time Warner.

The following research materials were also used: Frank Ahrens, "A Conciliator as CEO," *Washington Post*, December 6, 2001; Frank Ahrens, "AOL Discloses

Revenue Errors," *Washington Post,* August 15, 2002; Frank Ahrens, "No. 2 Officer Quits at AOL Time Warner," *Washington Post,* July 19, 2002; Frank Ahrens and Alec Klein, "Energized Steve Case Emerges From the Shadows," *Washington Post,* January 17, 2002; Frank Ahrens and Alec Klein, "Former Head of Key Unit at AOL Leaves," *Washington Post,* August 14, 2002; Julia Angwin and Martin Peers, "Spinoff of AOL Unit Not Likely," *Wall Street Journal,* July 22, 2002; Julia Angwin and Martin Peers, "The Re-Emergence of Steve Case," *Wall Street Journal,* January 17, 2002; AOL stock price, historical, Dow Jones Interactive; "AOL Time Warner Announces New Operating Structure and Senior Leadership Appointments," Business Wire, July 18, 2002; "AOL Time Warner chief pushes cancer research," *Deseret News,* June 5, 2002; AOL Time Warner corporate Web page, Jeffrey L. Bewkes profile (www.aoltimewarner.com), undated; AOL Time Warner corporate Web page, Don Logan profile (www.aoltimewarner.com), undated; AOL Time Warner corporate Web page, Richard D. Parsons profile (www.aoltimewarner.com), undated; "AOL to let employees use rival e-mail," Bloomberg, March 23, 2002; David Bauder, "HBO, the U.S. pay cable service, thrives because it offers creative freedom," Associated Press, March 6, 2002; Sally Beatty, "Pay TV: Unconventional HBO Finds Its Own Success is a Hard Act to Follow," *Wall Street Journal,* September 29, 2000; Valerie Block, "No Time to Pause," *Crain's New York Business,* April 5, 1999; Lisa Brownlee, "His HBO Is Hot Property," *New York Post,* January 23, 2000; Steve Case, speech transcript, Communicopia Conference, October 1, 2002; Adam Cohen, "Can A Nice Guy Run This Thing?" *Time,* December 17, 2001; Frank Cucci, supervisor, executive protection services, AOL, Steve Case detail, business card; "Dan Case, investment banker," Reuters, June 28, 2002; "Don Logan Named President of Time Inc.," PR Newswire, June 9, 1992; Scott Donaton, "Shake-up Stirs Hopes of Calm at Time Inc.," *Advertising Age,* June 15, 1992; Elaine Dutka, "Shake-up at Time Warner," *Los Angeles Times,* November 17, 1995; Daniel Eisenberg, "And Then There Were Two," *Time,* July 29, 2002; "Jeff Bewkes Named President of Home Box Office," PR Newswire, September 11, 1991; Lisa Granatstein, "Logan's Run," *Brandweek,* March 5, 2001; Christopher Grimes, "New media skeptic is quick on the drawl," *Financial Times,* July 19, 2002; Christopher Grimes and Peter Thal Larsen, "Logan's late run for AOL Time Warner," *Financial Times,* July 21, 2002; Joe Hagan, "Pittman's Last Stand," *New York Observer,* July 29, 2002; Kathleen Hays, "Ted Turner Re-Ups with AOL Time Warner," CNNfn, December 21, 2001; Neil Hickey, "Will Time Inc. Get Back on Top?" *Columbia Journalism Review,* November/December 2002; David S. Hilzenrath, "Emergency Overhaul for AOL," *Washington Post,* October 30, 1996; Sallie Hofmeister, "Shake-up at AOL," *Los Angeles Times,* July 19, 2002; "JPMorgan H&Q CEO Daniel Case resigns," Associated Press Newswires, May 1, 2001;

Jeremy Kahn and Bill Powell, "Can These Guys Fix AOL?" *Fortune*, September 2, 2002; Keith J. Kelly, "Time Inc. Chief Outflanked on 'Net," *New York Post*, June 20, 1999; Matt Kempner, "Turner's influence re-emerges at AOL," *Atlanta Journal and Constitution*, October 27, 2002; David D. Kirkpatrick, "A Search for Harmony Within a Feuding AOL," *New York Times*, July 21, 2002; David D. Kirkpatrick, "AOL Chairman Fights Back As Problems Surround Him," *New York Times*, December 2, 2002; David D. Kirkpatrick, "AOL Chairman's No. 1 Ally Turns Into His Biggest Foe," *New York Times*, October 1, 2002; David D. Kirkpatrick, "Former Chief of Time Warner Defends Sale to America Online," *New York Times*, September 24, 2002; David D. Kirkpatrick, "New Charges Against AOL Made in Suit on Homestore," *New York Times*, November 16, 2002; David D. Kirkpatrick, "Some Directors Said to Seek Ouster at AOL," *New York Times*, September 17, 2002; David D. Kirkpatrick, "The Outer Limits of Optimism," *New York Times*, October 14, 2002; David D. Kirkpatrick and David Carr, "A Media Giant Needs a Script," *New York Times*, July 7, 2002; Alec Klein, "A Merger Taken AO-Ill," *Washington Post*, October 21, 2002; Alec Klein, "Ad Falloff Bites into AOL Revenue," July 19, 2001; Alec Klein, "AOL Continues Reshuffling at the Top," *Washington Post*, April 10, 2002; Alec Klein, "AOL Opens Probe, Puts 2 on Leave," *Washington Post*, June 19, 2001; Alec Klein, "AOL Time Warner CFO Shifted," *Washington Post*, November 2, 2001; Alec Klein, "AOL Time Warner Cuts Its Earnings Forecast," *Washington Post*, September 25, 2001; Alec Klein, "AOL Time Warner Discloses SEC Probe," *Washington Post*, July 25, 2002; Alec Klein, "AOL Time Warner Has Charge of $54 Billion," *Washington Post*, March 26, 2002; Alec Klein, "AOL Time Warner Lost $1.82 Billion," *Washington Post*, January 31, 2002; Alec Klein, "AOL Time Warner Lowers Expectations," *Washington Post*, January 1, 2002; Alec Klein, "AOL Time Warner Posts Huge Loss," *Washington Post*, April 25, 2002; Alec Klein, "AOL Time Warner Upbeat," *Washington Post*, April 19, 2001; Alec Klein, "Case Seeks A More Wired Latin America," *Washington Post*, May 8, 2001; Alec Klein, "Creative Transactions Earned Team Rewards," *Washington Post*, July 19, 2002; "For AOL, the World is Next," *Washington Post*, May 30, 2001; Alec Klein, *Washington Post* e-mail to AOL Time Warner outside attorney, June 25, 2002; Alec Klein, *Washington Post* letter to AOL Time Warner, June 14, 2002; Alec Klein, *Washington Post* letters to AOL Time Warner outside attorneys, June 24, 2002, June 26, 2002, June 27, 2002, June 28, 2002, July 16, 2002; Alec Klein, "Levin To Leave AOL Time Warner," *Washington Post*, December 6, 2001; Alec Klein, "More Cuts Planned at AOL Time Warner," *Washington Post*, October 18, 2001; Alec Klein, "Parsons Reassures Shareholders, Hopes to 'Revitalize' AOL," *Washington Post*, May 17, 2002; Alec Klein, "SEC Expands Probe of AOL," *Washington Post*, August 2, 2002; Alec Klein, "Unconventional Transactions Boosted

Sales," *Washington Post,* July 18, 2002; Alec Klein, "Unorthodox Partnership Produced Financial Gains," *Washington Post,* July 19, 2002; Alec Klein, "U.S. Opens Criminal AOL Probe," *Washington Post,* August 1, 2002; Alec Klein, "World-Com Deal With AOL Under Scrutiny," *Washington Post,* August 22, 2002; Alec Klein and Amy Joyce, "AOL to Lay Off 1,700 More Workers," *Washington Post,* August 22, 2001; Bruce G. Knecht, "Parsons Did a 'Number of Things Right' To Turn Around Ailing Dime Bancorp," *Wall Street Journal,* July 8, 1994; Laura, Landro, "Time Warner Names Bewkes to Posts of President, Operating Officer at HBO," *Wall Street Journal,* September 12, 1991; David Lieberman and Paul Davidson, "AOL reshuffles its management deck," *USA Today,* July 19, 2002; John Lippman, "In the Wings: Time Warner's Next Generation," *Wall Street Journal,* July 22, 1999; "Logan's run," *The Economist,* August 31, 2002; Tom Lowry, "The Man Who Made Levin Look Good," *Business Week,* January 15, 2001; Tom Lowry, Catherine Yang, and Ronald Grover, "What Jerry Levin's Shocker Means," *Business Week Online,* December 4, 2001; Robert McNatt, "Nelson's Protégé Stacking His Dimes," *Crain's New York Business,* May 21, 1990; Rob Morse, "Farewell to a genuinely good man," *San Francisco Chronicle,* July 5, 2002; Martin Peers, "AOL CEO Parsons Reorganizes Executive Ranks," *Dow Jones Business News,* May 24, 2002; Martin Peers, "AOL's Case Goes on Offensive, Defends Time Warner Merger," *Wall Street Journal,* October 2, 2002; Martin Peers, "In Shift, AOL Time Warner to De-Emphasize 'Convergence,'" *Wall Street Journal,* May 13, 2002; Martin Peers, "Will Steve Case Leave AOL?" *Wall Street Journal,* September 12, 2002; Martin Peers and Julia Angwin, "At AOL, Three More Executives Close to Pittman Head for Exit," *Wall Street Journal,* November 5, 2002; Martin Peers and Julia Angwin, "Case Muses About Spinning Off AOL Unit From Time Warner," *Wall Street Journal,* October 29, 2002; Martin Peers and John Lippman, "Time Warner's President Will Broaden Duties to Movie Studio, Music Group," *Wall Street Journal Europe,* August 3, 1999; Martin Peers and Joann S. Lublin, "In Sorry Shape, America Online Seeks New CEO," *Wall Street Journal,* July 12, 2002; Ken Parish Perkins, "Viewers Lust After Erotica," *Fort Worth Star-Telegram,"* September 3, 1998; Fred Pfaff, "Where the buck stops at Time Inc.," *Inside Media,* September 23, 1992; Abigail Rayner, "Merger hit trouble from day one," *The Times* (London), July 20, 2002; Patrick M. Reilly "A Maverick Gets the CEO Post at Time Inc.," *Wall Street Journal,* August 4, 1994; Johnnie L. Roberts, "Big Business," *Newsweek,* July 29, 2002; Johnnie L. Roberts, "How It All Fell Apart," *Newsweek,* December 9, 2002; Johnnie L. Roberts, "Make Way for the CEO," *Newsweek,* December 17, 2001; Johnnie L. Roberts, "Playing for Time," *Newsweek,* May 6, 1996; Christine Romans, Pat Kiernan, and Greg Clarkin, Don Logan television interview, CNNfn, December 3, 2002; Matthew Rose, Julia Angwin, and Martin Peers,

"Bad Connection: Failed Effort to Coordinate Ads Signal Deeper Woes at AOL," *Wall Street Journal,* July 18, 2002; Geanne Rosenberg, "Tom Yannucci: On the attack," *Columbia Journalism Review,* September 1, 2000; Jared Sandberg, "America Online Plans $385 million charge," *Wall Street Journal,* October 30, 1996; David Shook, "An Ink-Stained Exec's AOL Challenge," *BusinessWeek Online,* August 5, 2002; Franklin Smith, "Dime's Parsons Unfazed by Role as Trailblazer," *American Banker,* March 1, 1989; Andrew Ross Sorkin, "Offers for AOL Online Unit Were Rejected," *New York Times,* December 2, 2002; Kara Swisher, "Illness Forces Tech Stalwart to Slow Down," *Wall Street Journal,* April 30, 2001; Curtis L. Taylor, "Dime Savings Gets First Black President," *Newsday,* July 1, 1988; "The New Establishment 2002," *Vanity Fair,* October 2002; "The Top 25 Managers," *Business Week,* January 14, 2002; "Time Inc. Names Don Logan President, Operating Chief," June 9, 1992; "Time Warner Names New President," *Washington Post,* November 1, 1994; David A. Vise, "AOL Officials' Role in Homestore Deals Scrutinized," *Washington Post,* November 27, 2002; David A. Vise, "AOL Says It Won't Rebound Before '04," *Washington Post,* December 4, 2002; David A. Vise and Alec Klein, "AOL To Revise Financial Results," *Washington Post,* October 24, 2002; David A. Vise and Alec Klein, "Case Plays to Win AOL's 'Survivor,'" *Washington Post,* December 6, 2002; "Who's afraid of AOL Time Warner?" *The Economist,* January 26, 2002; Thomas D. Yannucci, outside attorney representing AOL Time Warner, letters to *Washington Post,* June 21, 2002, June 25, 2002, June 26, 2002; July 1, 2002; July 10, 2002, July 17, 2002.

Acknowledgments

Where do I start?

In a book informed by more than two years of reporting, there are so many to thank, so many people who shed light on the amazing roller-coaster ride that is AOL Time Warner. Let me begin with special thanks to Art Amolsch, Cathy Anderson, Michael E. Antalics, Gary Arlen, Ross Bagully, Steve Baldwin, Chris Benyo, Myer Berlow, Nancy Shuba Bloomer, Timothy Boggs, Jan Brandt, Michael Bromley, John Buckley, Bill Burrington, Lawrence Buttenwieser, Jeff Chester, Earl Crabb, Bob Cross, Alana Davis, Neil Davis, Randy Dean, Michael Fuchs, Bob Grassi, General Alexander M. Haig, Stephen Heins, Geoff Holmes, Walter Isaacson, Brad Johnson, William E. Kennard, John Kerr, Gene Kimmelman, James V. Kimsey, Peter Kirsch, Matt Korn, Tracey Lakatos, Ted Leonsis, Bill Lessard, Blair Levin, Gerald M. Levin, Mike Luftman, Nora Macdonald, George M. Middlemas, Tryg Myhren, Ed O'Brien, Robert O'Connor, Bill O'Luanaigh, Richard G. Parker, Richard D. Parsons, Alan J. Patricof, James Patti, Alan Peyser, Robert Pitofsky, Bill Pytlovany, Franklin D. Raines, Avner Ronen, Jonathan Salkoff, Michael Schrage, Andrew Jay Schwartzman, Dave Sickert, Russell Siegelman, Steve Stern, Dick Stone, Curt Viebranz, Peter von Meister, George Vradenburg III, Mark Walsh, and Julia Wilkinson.

Acknowledgments

Thanks also to family and friends, including Billy, Ricky, and Scott Breakstone, James Cury, Bob, Emiko, and Kathy Goodnough, Eileen Graziano, J. P. Graziano, Frida and James Graziano, Paul and Julie Graziano, Joel and Orly Grosberg, Cynthia Hanson and Aaron Degodny, Ann-Marie and Joe Hayes, Sorin Iarovici, Hidetsune and Chie Iwata, Karen, Dolores, and Edward Klein, Emily Lemole, and Norma and Arnold Rosenberg. I would also like to thank some of my past editors, including Kevin Armstrong, Jim Asher, John Carroll, Bill Grueskin, Dennis Hartig, Dan Hertzberg, Bill Marimow, Gerry Merrell, Gary Putka, and Greg Schneider.

Special thanks to Heidi Poccia and Simon & Schuster's Johanna Li, Elisa Rivlin, Elizabeth Hayes, and Bob Bender, my terrific editor, and Esther Newberg, my super agent at ICM. I also owe a special debt of gratitude to my colleagues at *The Washington Post*, including Mary Ann Werner, Eric Lieberman, Joe Elbert, Dan Beyers, Larry Roberts, Jill Dutt, Steve Coll, Len Downie, Bo Jones, and Don Graham.

Most of all, I thank Julie-Ann, who makes it all worthwhile.

INDEX